AUTOMATE THE BORING STUFF
WITH PYTHON

AUTOMATE THE BORING STUFF WITH PYTHON

Practical Programming for Total Beginners

by Al Sweigart

no starch press

San Francisco

AUTOMATE THE BORING STUFF WITH PYTHON. Copyright © 2015 by Al Sweigart.

Printed in USA

Thirteenth printing

22 21 20 19   13 14 15 16

ISBN-10: 1-59327-599-4
ISBN-13: 978-1-59327-599-0

Publisher: William Pollock
Production Editor: Laurel Chun
Cover Illustration: Josh Ellingson
Interior Design: Octopod Studios
Developmental Editors: Jennifer Griffith-Delgado, Greg Poulos, and Leslie Shen
Technical Reviewer: Ari Lacenski
Copyeditor: Kim Wimpsett
Compositor: Susan Glinert Stevens
Proofreader: Lisa Devoto Farrell
Indexer: BIM Indexing and Proofreading Services

For information on distribution, translations, or bulk sales, please contact No Starch Press, Inc. directly:

No Starch Press, Inc.
245 8th Street, San Francisco, CA 94103
phone: 1.415.863.9900; info@nostarch.com
www.nostarch.com

Library of Congress Control Number: 2014953114

For my nephew Jack

About the Author

Al Sweigart is a software developer and tech book author living in San Francisco. Python is his favorite programming language, and he is the developer of several open source modules for it. His other books are freely available under a Creative Commons license on his website *http://www .inventwithpython.com/*. His cat weighs 14 pounds.

About the Tech Reviewer

Ari Lacenski is a developer of Android applications and Python software. She lives in San Leandro, where she writes about Android programming at *http://gradlewhy.ghost.io/* and mentors with Women Who Code. She's also a folk guitarist.

BRIEF CONTENTS

CONTENTS IN DETAIL

3
FUNCTIONS 61

4
LISTS 79

5
DICTIONARIES AND STRUCTURING DATA   105

6
MANIPULATING STRINGS   123

PART II: AUTOMATING TASKS

145

7
PATTERN MATCHING WITH REGULAR EXPRESSIONS

147

8
READING AND WRITING FILES

173

9
ORGANIZING FILES

197

10
DEBUGGING

215

11
WEB SCRAPING

12
WORKING WITH EXCEL SPREADSHEETS   265

15
KEEPING TIME, SCHEDULING TASKS, AND LAUNCHING PROGRAMS
335

16
SENDING EMAIL AND TEXT MESSAGES
361

17
MANIPULATING IMAGES

387

18
CONTROLLING THE KEYBOARD AND MOUSE
WITH GUI AUTOMATION   **413**

A
INSTALLING THIRD-PARTY MODULES 441

B
RUNNING PROGRAMS 443

C
ANSWERS TO THE PRACTICE QUESTIONS 447

INDEX 461

ACKNOWLEDGMENTS

I couldn't have written a book like this without the help of a lot of people. I'd like to thank Bill Pollock; my editors, Laurel Chun, Leslie Shen, Greg Poulos, and Jennifer Griffith-Delgado; and the rest of the staff at No Starch Press for their invaluable help. Thanks to my tech reviewer, Ari Lacenski, for great suggestions, edits, and support.

Many thanks to our Benevolent Dictator For Life, Guido van Rossum, and everyone at the Python Software Foundation for their great work. The Python community is the best one I've found in the tech industry.

Finally, I would like to thank my family, friends, and the gang at Shotwell's for not minding the busy life I've had while writing this book. Cheers!

INTRODUCTION

"You've just done in two hours what it takes the three of us two days to do." My college roommate was working at a retail electronics store in the early 2000s. Occasionally, the store would receive a spreadsheet of thousands of product prices from its competitor. A team of three employees would print the spreadsheet onto a thick stack of paper and split it among themselves. For each product price, they would look up their store's price and note all the products that their competitors sold for less. It usually took a couple of days.

"You know, I could write a program to do that if you have the original file for the printouts," my roommate told them, when he saw them sitting on the floor with papers scattered and stacked around them.

After a couple of hours, he had a short program that read a competitor's price from a file, found the product in the store's database, and noted whether the competitor was cheaper. He was still new to programming, and he spent most of his time looking up documentation in a programming book. The actual program took only a few seconds to run. My roommate and his co-workers took an extra-long lunch that day.

This is the power of computer programming. A computer is like a Swiss Army knife that you can configure for countless tasks. Many people spend hours clicking and typing to perform repetitive tasks, unaware that the machine they're using could do their job in seconds if they gave it the right instructions.

Whom Is This Book For?

Software is at the core of so many of the tools we use today: Nearly everyone uses social networks to communicate, many people have Internet-connected computers in their phones, and most office jobs involve interacting with a computer to get work done. As a result, the demand for people who can code has skyrocketed. Countless books, interactive web tutorials, and developer boot camps promise to turn ambitious beginners into software engineers with six-figure salaries.

This book is not for those people. It's for everyone else.

On its own, this book won't turn you into a professional software developer any more than a few guitar lessons will turn you into a rock star. But if you're an office worker, administrator, academic, or anyone else who uses a computer for work or fun, you will learn the basics of programming so that you can automate simple tasks such as the following:

- Moving and renaming thousands of files and sorting them into folders
- Filling out online forms, no typing required
- Downloading files or copy text from a website whenever it updates
- Having your computer text you custom notifications
- Updating or formatting Excel spreadsheets
- Checking your email and sending out prewritten responses

These tasks are simple but time-consuming for humans, and they're often so trivial or specific that there's no ready-made software to perform them. Armed with a little bit of programming knowledge, you can have your computer do these tasks for you.

Conventions

This book is not designed as a reference manual; it's a guide for beginners. The coding style sometimes goes against best practices (for example, some programs use global variables), but that's a trade-off to make the code simpler to learn. This book is made for people to write throwaway code, so there's not much time spent on style and elegance. Sophisticated programming concepts—like object-oriented programming, list comprehensions, and generators—aren't covered because of the complexity they add. Veteran programmers may point out ways the code in this book could be changed to improve efficiency, but this book is mostly concerned with getting programs to work with the least amount of effort.

What Is Programming?

Television shows and films often show programmers furiously typing cryptic streams of 1s and 0s on glowing screens, but modern programming isn't that mysterious. *Programming* is simply the act of entering instructions for the computer to perform. These instructions might crunch some numbers, modify text, look up information in files, or communicate with other computers over the Internet.

All programs use basic instructions as building blocks. Here are a few of the most common ones, in English:

"Do this; then do that."

"If this condition is true, perform this action; otherwise, do that action."

"Do this action that number of times."

"Keep doing that until this condition is true."

You can combine these building blocks to implement more intricate decisions, too. For example, here are the programming instructions, called the *source code*, for a simple program written in the Python programming language. Starting at the top, the Python software runs each line of code (some lines are run only *if* a certain condition is true or *else* Python runs some other line) until it reaches the bottom.

```
❶ passwordFile = open('SecretPasswordFile.txt')
❷ secretPassword = passwordFile.read()
❸ print('Enter your password.')
   typedPassword = input()
❹ if typedPassword == secretPassword:
❺     print('Access granted')
❻     if typedPassword == '12345':
❼         print('That password is one that an idiot puts on their luggage.')
   else:
❽     print('Access denied')
```

You might not know anything about programming, but you could probably make a reasonable guess at what the previous code does just by reading it. First, the file *SecretPasswordFile.txt* is opened ❶, and the secret password in it is read ❷. Then, the user is prompted to input a password (from the keyboard) ❸. These two passwords are compared ❹, and if they're the same, the program prints *Access granted* to the screen ❺. Next, the program checks to see whether the password is *12345* ❻ and hints that this choice might not be the best for a password ❼. If the passwords are not the same, the program prints *Access denied* to the screen ❽.

What Is Python?

Python refers to the Python programming language (with syntax rules for writing what is considered valid Python code) and the Python interpreter software that reads source code (written in the Python language) and performs its instructions. The Python interpreter is free to download from *http://python.org/*, and there are versions for Linux, OS X, and Windows.

The name Python comes from the surreal British comedy group Monty Python, not from the snake. Python programmers are affectionately called Pythonistas, and both Monty Python and serpentine references usually pepper Python tutorials and documentation.

Programmers Don't Need to Know Much Math

The most common anxiety I hear about learning to program is that people think it requires a lot of math. Actually, most programming doesn't require math beyond basic arithmetic. In fact, being good at programming isn't that different from being good at solving Sudoku puzzles.

To solve a Sudoku puzzle, the numbers 1 through 9 must be filled in for each row, each column, and each 3×3 interior square of the full 9×9 board. You find a solution by applying deduction and logic from the starting numbers. For example, since 5 appears in the top left of the Sudoku puzzle shown in Figure 0-1, it cannot appear elsewhere in the top row, in the leftmost column, or in the top-left 3×3 square. Solving one row, column, or square at a time will provide more number clues for the rest of the puzzle.

5	3			7				
6			1	9	5			
	9	8					6	
8				6				3
4			8		3			1
7				2				6
	6					2	8	
			4	1	9			5
				8			7	9

5	3	4	6	7	8	9	1	2
6	7	2	1	9	5	3	4	8
1	9	8	3	4	2	5	6	7
8	5	9	7	6	1	4	2	3
4	2	6	8	5	3	7	9	1
7	1	3	9	2	4	8	5	6
9	6	1	5	3	7	2	8	4
2	8	7	4	1	9	6	3	5
3	4	5	2	8	6	1	7	9

Figure 0-1: A new Sudoku puzzle (left) and its solution (right). Despite using numbers, Sudoku doesn't involve much math. (Images © Wikimedia Commons)

Just because Sudoku involves numbers doesn't mean you have to be good at math to figure out the solution. The same is true of programming. Like solving a Sudoku puzzle, writing programs involves breaking down a problem into individual, detailed steps. Similarly, when *debugging* programs (that is, finding and fixing errors), you'll patiently observe what the program is doing and find the cause of the bugs. And like all skills, the more you program, the better you'll become.

Programming Is a Creative Activity

Programming is a creative task, somewhat like constructing a castle out of LEGO bricks. You start with a basic idea of what you want your castle to look like and inventory your available blocks. Then you start building. Once you've finished building your program, you can pretty up your code just like you would your castle.

The difference between programming and other creative activities is that when programming, you have all the raw materials you need in your computer; you don't need to buy any additional canvas, paint, film, yarn, LEGO bricks, or electronic components. When your program is written, it can easily be shared online with the entire world. And though you'll make mistakes when programming, the activity is still a lot of fun.

About This Book

The first part of this book covers basic Python programming concepts, and the second part covers various tasks you can have your computer automate. Each chapter in the second part has project programs for you to study. Here's a brief rundown of what you'll find in each chapter:

Part I: Python Programming Basics

Chapter 1: Python Basics   Covers expressions, the most basic type of Python instruction, and how to use the Python interactive shell software to experiment with code.

Chapter 2: Flow Control   Explains how to make programs decide which instructions to execute so your code can intelligently respond to different conditions.

Chapter 3: Functions   Instructs you on how to define your own functions so that you can organize your code into more manageable chunks.

Chapter 4: Lists   Introduces the list data type and explains how to organize data.

Chapter 5: Dictionaries and Structuring Data   Introduces the dictionary data type and shows you more powerful ways to organize data.

Chapter 6: Manipulating Strings   Covers working with text data (called *strings* in Python).

Part II: Automating Tasks

Chapter 7: Pattern Matching with Regular Expressions   Covers how Python can manipulate strings and search for text patterns with regular expressions.

Chapter 8: Reading and Writing Files   Explains how your programs can read the contents of text files and save information to files on your hard drive.

Chapter 9: Organizing Files   Shows how Python can copy, move, rename, and delete large numbers of files much faster than a human user can. It also explains compressing and decompressing files.

Chapter 10: Debugging   Shows how to use Python's various bug-finding and bug-fixing tools.

Chapter 11: Web Scraping   Shows how to write programs that can automatically download web pages and parse them for information. This is called *web scraping.*

Chapter 12: Working with Excel Spreadsheets   Covers programmatically manipulating Excel spreadsheets so that you don't have to read them. This is helpful when the number of documents you have to analyze is in the hundreds or thousands.

Chapter 13: Working with PDF and Word Documents   Covers programmatically reading Word and PDF documents.

Chapter 14: Working with CSV Files and JSON Data   Continues to explain how to programmatically manipulate documents with CSV and JSON files.

Chapter 15: Keeping Time, Scheduling Tasks, and Launching Programs   Explains how time and dates are handled by Python programs and how to schedule your computer to perform tasks at certain times. This chapter also shows how your Python programs can launch non-Python programs.

Chapter 16: Sending Email and Text Messages   Explains how to write programs that can send emails and text messages on your behalf.

Chapter 17: Manipulating Images   Explains how to programmatically manipulate images such as JPEG or PNG files.

Chapter 18: Controlling the Keyboard and Mouse with GUI Automation Explains how to programmatically control the mouse and keyboard to automate clicks and keypresses.

Downloading and Installing Python

You can download Python for Windows, OS X, and Ubuntu for free from *http://python.org/downloads/*. If you download the latest version from the website's download page, all of the programs in this book should work.

WARNING   *Be sure to download a version of Python 3 (such as 3.4.0). The programs in this book are written to run on Python 3 and may not run correctly, if at all, on Python 2.*

You'll find Python installers for 64-bit and 32-bit computers for each operating system on the download page, so first figure out which installer you need. If you bought your computer in 2007 or later, it is most likely a 64-bit system. Otherwise, you have a 32-bit version, but here's how to find out for sure:

- On Windows, select **Start ▶ Control Panel ▶ System** and check whether System Type says 64-bit or 32-bit.

- On OS X, go the Apple menu, select **About This Mac ▸ More Info ▸ System Report ▸ Hardware**, and then look at the Processor Name field. If it says Intel Core Solo or Intel Core Duo, you have a 32-bit machine. If it says anything else (including Intel Core 2 Duo), you have a 64-bit machine.

- On Ubuntu Linux, open a Terminal and run the command `uname -m`. A response of `i686` means 32-bit, and `x86_64` means 64-bit.

On Windows, download the Python installer (the filename will end with *.msi*) and double-click it. Follow the instructions the installer displays on the screen to install Python, as listed here:

1. Select **Install for All Users** and then click **Next**.
2. Install to the *C:\Python34* folder by clicking **Next**.
3. Click **Next** again to skip the Customize Python section.

On Mac OS X, download the *.dmg* file that's right for your version of OS X and double-click it. Follow the instructions the installer displays on the screen to install Python, as listed here:

1. When the DMG package opens in a new window, double-click the *Python.mpkg* file. You may have to enter the administrator password.
2. Click **Continue** through the Welcome section and click **Agree** to accept the license.
3. Select **HD Macintosh** (or whatever name your hard drive has) and click **Install**.

If you're running Ubuntu, you can install Python from the Terminal by following these steps:

1. Open the Terminal window.
2. Enter `sudo apt-get install python3`.
3. Enter `sudo apt-get install idle3`.
4. Enter `sudo apt-get install python3-pip`.

Starting IDLE

While the *Python interpreter* is the software that runs your Python programs, the *interactive development environment (IDLE)* software is where you'll enter your programs, much like a word processor. Let's start IDLE now.

- On Windows 7 or newer, click the Start icon in the lower-left corner of your screen, enter `IDLE` in the search box, and select **IDLE (Python GUI)**.

- On Windows XP, click the **Start** button and then select **Programs ▸ Python 3.4 ▸ IDLE (Python GUI)**.

- On Mac OS X, open the Finder window, click **Applications**, click **Python 3.4**, and then click the IDLE icon.
- On Ubuntu, select **Applications ▸ Accessories ▸ Terminal** and then enter `idle3`. (You may also be able to click **Applications** at the top of the screen, select **Programming**, and then click **IDLE 3**.)

The Interactive Shell

No matter which operating system you're running, the IDLE window that first appears should be mostly blank except for text that looks something like this:

```
Python 3.4.0 (v3.4.0:04f714765c13, Mar 16 2014, 19:25:23) [MSC v.1600 64
bit (AMD64)] on win32Type "copyright", "credits" or "license()" for more
information.
>>>
```

This window is called the *interactive shell*. A shell is a program that lets you type instructions into the computer, much like the Terminal or Command Prompt on OS X and Windows, respectively. Python's interactive shell lets you enter instructions for the Python interpreter software to run. The computer reads the instructions you enter and runs them immediately.

For example, enter the following into the interactive shell next to the `>>>` prompt:

```
>>> print('Hello world!')
```

After you type that line and press ENTER, the interactive shell should display this in response:

```
>>> print('Hello world!')
Hello world!
```

How to Find Help

Solving programming problems on your own is easier than you might think. If you're not convinced, then let's cause an error on purpose: Enter `'42' + 3` into the interactive shell. You don't need to know what this instruction means right now, but the result should look like this:

```
>>> '42' + 3
❶ Traceback (most recent call last):
    File "<pyshell#0>", line 1, in <module>
      '42' + 3
❷ TypeError: Can't convert 'int' object to str implicitly
>>>
```

The error message ❷ appeared here because Python couldn't understand your instruction. The traceback part ❶ of the error message shows the specific instruction and line number that Python had trouble with. If you're not sure what to make of a particular error message, search online for the exact error message. Enter **"TypeError: Can't convert 'int' object to str implicitly"** (including the quotes) into your favorite search engine, and you should see tons of links explaining what the error message means and what causes it, as shown in Figure 0-2.

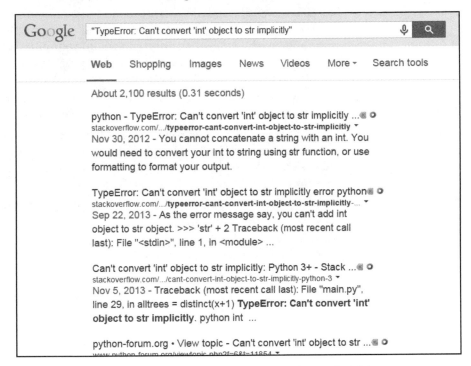

Figure 0-2: The Google results for an error message can be very helpful.

You'll often find that someone else had the same question as you and that some other helpful person has already answered it. No one person can know everything about programming, so an everyday part of any software developer's job is looking up answers to technical questions.

Asking Smart Programming Questions

If you can't find the answer by searching online, try asking people in a web forum such as Stack Overflow (*http://stackoverflow.com/*) or the "learn programming" subreddit at *http://reddit.com/r/learnprogramming/*. But keep in mind there are smart ways to ask programming questions that help others help you. Be sure to read the Frequently Asked Questions sections these websites have about the proper way to post questions.

When asking programming questions, remember to do the following:

- Explain what you are trying to do, not just what you did. This lets your helper know if you are on the wrong track.

- Specify the point at which the error happens. Does it occur at the very start of the program or only after you do a certain action?

- Copy and paste the *entire* error message and your code to *http://pastebin.com/* or *http://gist.github.com/*.

    These websites make it easy to share large amounts of code with people over the Web, without the risk of losing any text formatting. You can then put the URL of the posted code in your email or forum post. For example, here some pieces of code I've posted: *http://pastebin.com/SzP2DbFx/* and *https://gist.github.com/asweigart/6912168/*.

- Explain what you've already tried to do to solve your problem. This tells people you've already put in some work to figure things out on your own.

- List the version of Python you're using. (There are some key differences between version 2 Python interpreters and version 3 Python interpreters.) Also, say which operating system and version you're running.

- If the error came up after you made a change to your code, explain exactly what you changed.

- Say whether you're able to reproduce the error every time you run the program or whether it happens only after you perform certain actions. Explain what those actions are, if so.

Always follow good online etiquette as well. For example, don't post your questions in all caps or make unreasonable demands of the people trying to help you.

Summary

For most people, their computer is just an appliance instead of a tool. But by learning how to program, you'll gain access to one of the most powerful tools of the modern world, and you'll have fun along the way. Programming isn't brain surgery—it's fine for amateurs to experiment and make mistakes.

I love helping people discover Python. I write programming tutorials on my blog at *http://inventwithpython.com/blog/*, and you can contact me with questions at *al@inventwithpython.com*.

This book will start you off from zero programming knowledge, but you may have questions beyond its scope. Remember that asking effective questions and knowing how to find answers are invaluable tools on your programming journey.

Let's begin!

PART I

PYTHON PROGRAMMING BASICS

1

PYTHON BASICS

The Python programming language has a wide range of syntactical constructions, standard library functions, and interactive development environment features. Fortunately, you can ignore most of that; you just need to learn enough to write some handy little programs.

You will, however, have to learn some basic programming concepts before you can do anything. Like a wizard-in-training, you might think these concepts seem arcane and tedious, but with some knowledge and practice, you'll be able to command your computer like a magic wand to perform incredible feats.

This chapter has a few examples that encourage you to type into the interactive shell, which lets you execute Python instructions one at a time and shows you the results instantly. Using the interactive shell is great for learning what basic Python instructions do, so give it a try as you follow along. You'll remember the things you do much better than the things you only read.

Entering Expressions into the Interactive Shell

You run the interactive shell by launching IDLE, which you installed with Python in the introduction. On Windows, open the Start menu, select **All Programs** ▸ **Python 3.3**, and then select **IDLE (Python GUI)**. On OS X, select **Applications** ▸ **MacPython 3.3** ▸ **IDLE**. On Ubuntu, open a new Terminal window and enter `idle3`.

A window with the >>> prompt should appear; that's the interactive shell. Enter **2 + 2** at the prompt to have Python do some simple math.

```
>>> 2 + 2
4
```

The IDLE window should now show some text like this:

```
Python 3.3.2 (v3.3.2:d047928ae3f6, May 16 2013, 00:06:53) [MSC v.1600 64 bit
(AMD64)] on win32
Type "copyright", "credits" or "license()" for more information.
>>> 2 + 2
4
>>>
```

In Python, 2 + 2 is called an *expression*, which is the most basic kind of programming instruction in the language. Expressions consist of *values* (such as 2) and *operators* (such as +), and they can always *evaluate* (that is, reduce) down to a single value. That means you can use expressions anywhere in Python code that you could also use a value.

In the previous example, 2 + 2 is evaluated down to a single value, 4. A single value with no operators is also considered an expression, though it evaluates only to itself, as shown here:

```
>>> 2
2
```

ERRORS ARE OKAY!

Programs will crash if they contain code the computer can't understand, which will cause Python to show an error message. An error message won't break your computer, though, so don't be afraid to make mistakes. A *crash* just means the program stopped running unexpectedly.

If you want to know more about an error message, you can search for the exact message text online to find out more about that specific error. You can also check out the resources at *http://nostarch.com/automatestuff/* to see a list of common Python error messages and their meanings.

There are plenty of other operators you can use in Python expressions, too. For example, Table 1-1 lists all the math operators in Python.

Table 1-1: Math Operators from Highest to Lowest Precedence

Operator	Operation	Example	Evaluates to...
**	Exponent	2 ** 3	8
%	Modulus/remainder	22 % 8	6
//	Integer division/floored quotient	22 // 8	2
/	Division	22 / 8	2.75
*	Multiplication	3 * 5	15
-	Subtraction	5 - 2	3
+	Addition	2 + 2	4

The order of operations (also called *precedence*) of Python math operators is similar to that of mathematics. The ** operator is evaluated first; the *, /, //, and % operators are evaluated next, from left to right; and the + and - operators are evaluated last (also from left to right). You can use parentheses to override the usual precedence if you need to. Enter the following expressions into the interactive shell:

```
>>> 2 + 3 * 6
20
>>> (2 + 3) * 6
30
>>> 48565878 * 578453
28093077826734
>>> 2 ** 8
256
>>> 23 / 7
3.2857142857142856
>>> 23 // 7
3
>>> 23 % 7
2
>>> 2      +           2
4
>>> (5 - 1) * ((7 + 1) / (3 - 1))
16.0
```

In each case, you as the programmer must enter the expression, but Python does the hard part of evaluating it down to a single value. Python will keep evaluating parts of the expression until it becomes a single value, as shown in Figure 1-1.

```
(5 - 1) * ((7 + 1) / (3 - 1))
        ↓
    4 * ((7 + 1) / (3 - 1))
        ↓
    4 * (  8  ) / (3 - 1))
        ↓
    4 * (  8  ) / (  2  )
        ↓
    4 * 4.0
        ↓
    16.0
```

Figure 1-1: Evaluating an expression reduces it to a single value.

These rules for putting operators and values together to form expressions are a fundamental part of Python as a programming language, just like the grammar rules that help us communicate. Here's an example:

This is a grammatically correct English sentence.

This grammatically is sentence not English correct a.

The second line is difficult to parse because it doesn't follow the rules of English. Similarly, if you type in a bad Python instruction, Python won't be able to understand it and will display a SyntaxError error message, as shown here:

```
>>> 5 +
  File "<stdin>", line 1
    5 +
      ^
SyntaxError: invalid syntax
>>> 42 + 5 + * 2
  File "<stdin>", line 1
    42 + 5 + * 2
            ^
SyntaxError: invalid syntax
```

You can always test to see whether an instruction works by typing it into the interactive shell. Don't worry about breaking the computer: The worst thing that could happen is that Python responds with an error message. Professional software developers get error messages while writing code all the time.

The Integer, Floating-Point, and String Data Types

Remember that expressions are just values combined with operators, and they always evaluate down to a single value. A *data type* is a category for values, and every value belongs to exactly one data type. The most common data types in Python are listed in Table 1-2. The values -2 and 30, for example, are said to be *integer* values. The integer (or *int*) data type indicates values that are whole numbers. Numbers with a decimal point, such as 3.14, are called *floating-point numbers* (or *floats*). Note that even though the value 42 is an integer, the value 42.0 would be a floating-point number.

Table 1-2: Common Data Types

Data type	Examples
Integers	-2, -1, 0, 1, 2, 3, 4, 5
Floating-point numbers	-1.25, -1.0, --0.5, 0.0, 0.5, 1.0, 1.25
Strings	'a', 'aa', 'aaa', 'Hello!', '11 cats'

Python programs can also have text values called *strings*, or *strs* (pronounced "stirs"). Always surround your string in single quote (') characters (as in 'Hello' or 'Goodbye cruel world!') so Python knows where the string begins and ends. You can even have a string with no characters in it, '', called a *blank string*. Strings are explained in greater detail in Chapter 4.

If you ever see the error message SyntaxError: EOL while scanning string literal, you probably forgot the final single quote character at the end of the string, such as in this example:

```
>>> 'Hello world!
SyntaxError: EOL while scanning string literal
```

String Concatenation and Replication

The meaning of an operator may change based on the data types of the values next to it. For example, + is the addition operator when it operates on two integers or floating-point values. However, when + is used on two string values, it joins the strings as the *string concatenation* operator. Enter the following into the interactive shell:

```
>>> 'Alice' + 'Bob'
'AliceBob'
```

The expression evaluates down to a single, new string value that combines the text of the two strings. However, if you try to use the + operator on a string and an integer value, Python will not know how to handle this, and it will display an error message.

```
>>> 'Alice' + 42
Traceback (most recent call last):
  File "<pyshell#26>", line 1, in <module>
    'Alice' + 42
TypeError: Can't convert 'int' object to str implicitly
```

The error message `Can't convert 'int' object to str implicitly` means that Python thought you were trying to concatenate an integer to the string `'Alice'`. Your code will have to explicitly convert the integer to a string, because Python cannot do this automatically. (Converting data types will be explained in "Dissecting Your Program" on page 22 when talking about the `str()`, `int()`, and `float()` functions.)

The * operator is used for multiplication when it operates on two integer or floating-point values. But when the * operator is used on one string value and one integer value, it becomes the *string replication* operator. Enter a string multiplied by a number into the interactive shell to see this in action.

```
>>> 'Alice' * 5
'AliceAliceAliceAliceAlice'
```

The expression evaluates down to a single string value that repeats the original a number of times equal to the integer value. String replication is a useful trick, but it's not used as often as string concatenation.

The * operator can be used with only two numeric values (for multiplication) or one string value and one integer value (for string replication). Otherwise, Python will just display an error message.

```
>>> 'Alice' * 'Bob'
Traceback (most recent call last):
  File "<pyshell#32>", line 1, in <module>
    'Alice' * 'Bob'
TypeError: can't multiply sequence by non-int of type 'str'
>>> 'Alice' * 5.0
Traceback (most recent call last):
  File "<pyshell#33>", line 1, in <module>
    'Alice' * 5.0
TypeError: can't multiply sequence by non-int of type 'float'
```

It makes sense that Python wouldn't understand these expressions: You can't multiply two words, and it's hard to replicate an arbitrary string a fractional number of times.

Storing Values in Variables

A *variable* is like a box in the computer's memory where you can store a single value. If you want to use the result of an evaluated expression later in your program, you can save it inside a variable.

Assignment Statements

You'll store values in variables with an *assignment statement*. An assignment statement consists of a variable name, an equal sign (called the *assignment operator*), and the value to be stored. If you enter the assignment statement `spam = 42`, then a variable named spam will have the integer value 42 stored in it.

Think of a variable as a labeled box that a value is placed in, as in Figure 1-2.

Figure 1-2: spam = 42 is like telling the program, "The variable spam now has the integer value 42 in it."

For example, enter the following into the interactive shell:

```
❶ >>> spam = 40
   >>> spam
   40
   >>> eggs = 2
❷ >>> spam + eggs
   42
   >>> spam + eggs + spam
   82
❸ >>> spam = spam + 2
   >>> spam
   42
```

A variable is *initialized* (or created) the first time a value is stored in it ❶. After that, you can use it in expressions with other variables and values ❷. When a variable is assigned a new value ❸, the old value is forgotten, which is why spam evaluated to 42 instead of 40 at the end of the example. This is called *overwriting* the variable. Enter the following code into the interactive shell to try overwriting a string:

```
>>> spam = 'Hello'
>>> spam
'Hello'
>>> spam = 'Goodbye'
>>> spam
'Goodbye'
```

Just like the box in Figure 1-3, the spam variable in this example stores 'Hello' until you replace it with 'Goodbye'.

Figure 1-3: When a new value is assigned to a variable, the old one is forgotten.

Variable Names

Table 1-3 has examples of legal variable names. You can name a variable anything as long as it obeys the following three rules:

1. It can be only one word.
2. It can use only letters, numbers, and the underscore (_) character.
3. It can't begin with a number.

Table 1-3: Valid and Invalid Variable Names

Valid variable names	Invalid variable names
balance	current-balance (hyphens are not allowed)
currentBalance	current balance (spaces are not allowed)
current_balance	4account (can't begin with a number)
_spam	42 (can't begin with a number)
SPAM	total_$um (special characters like $ are not allowed)
account4	'hello' (special characters like ' are not allowed)

Variable names are case-sensitive, meaning that spam, SPAM, Spam, and sPaM are four different variables. It is a Python convention to start your variables with a lowercase letter.

This book uses camelcase for variable names instead of underscores; that is, variables lookLikeThis instead of looking_like_this. Some experienced programmers may point out that the official Python code style, PEP 8, says that underscores should be used. I unapologetically prefer camelcase and point to "A Foolish Consistency Is the Hobgoblin of Little Minds" in PEP 8 itself:

> "Consistency with the style guide is important. But most importantly: know when to be inconsistent—sometimes the style guide just doesn't apply. When in doubt, use your best judgment."

A good variable name describes the data it contains. Imagine that you moved to a new house and labeled all of your moving boxes as *Stuff*. You'd never find anything! The variable names spam, eggs, and bacon are used as generic names for the examples in this book and in much of Python's documentation (inspired by the Monty Python "Spam" sketch), but in your programs, a descriptive name will help make your code more readable.

Your First Program

While the interactive shell is good for running Python instructions one at a time, to write entire Python programs, you'll type the instructions into the file editor. The *file editor* is similar to text editors such as Notepad or TextMate, but it has some specific features for typing in source code. To open the file editor in IDLE, select **File ▸ New File**.

The window that appears should contain a cursor awaiting your input, but it's different from the interactive shell, which runs Python instructions as soon as you press ENTER. The file editor lets you type in many instructions, save the file, and run the program. Here's how you can tell the difference between the two:

- The interactive shell window will always be the one with the >>> prompt.
- The file editor window will not have the >>> prompt.

Now it's time to create your first program! When the file editor window opens, type the following into it:

```
❶ # This program says hello and asks for my name.

❷ print('Hello world!')
  print('What is your name?')    # ask for their name
❸ myName = input()
❹ print('It is good to meet you, ' + myName)
❺ print('The length of your name is:')
  print(len(myName))
```

```
❻ print('What is your age?')     # ask for their age
  myAge = input()
  print('You will be ' + str(int(myAge) + 1) + ' in a year.')
```

Once you've entered your source code, save it so that you won't have to retype it each time you start IDLE. From the menu at the top of the file editor window, select **File ▸ Save As**. In the Save As window, enter `hello.py` in the File Name field and then click **Save**.

You should save your programs every once in a while as you type them. That way, if the computer crashes or you accidentally exit from IDLE, you won't lose the code. As a shortcut, you can press CTRL-S on Windows and Linux or ⌘-S on OS X to save your file.

Once you've saved, let's run our program. Select **Run ▸ Run Module** or just press the **F5** key. Your program should run in the interactive shell window that appeared when you first started IDLE. Remember, you have to press F5 from the file editor window, not the interactive shell window. Enter your name when your program asks for it. The program's output in the interactive shell should look something like this:

```
Python 3.3.2 (v3.3.2:d047928ae3f6, May 16 2013, 00:06:53) [MSC v.1600 64 bit
(AMD64)] on win32
Type "copyright", "credits" or "license()" for more information.
>>> ============================ RESTART ============================
>>>
Hello world!
What is your name?
Al
It is good to meet you, Al
The length of your name is:
2
What is your age?
4
You will be 5 in a year.
>>>
```

When there are no more lines of code to execute, the Python program *terminates*; that is, it stops running. (You can also say that the Python program *exits*.)

You can close the file editor by clicking the X at the top of the window. To reload a saved program, select **File ▸ Open** from the menu. Do that now, and in the window that appears, choose *hello.py*, and click the **Open** button. Your previously saved *hello.py* program should open in the file editor window.

Dissecting Your Program

With your new program open in the file editor, let's take a quick tour of the Python instructions it uses by looking at what each line of code does.

Comments

The following line is called a *comment*.

---

❶ `# This program says hello and asks for my name.`

Python ignores comments, and you can use them to write notes or remind yourself what the code is trying to do. Any text for the rest of the line following a hash mark (#) is part of a comment.

Sometimes, programmers will put a # in front of a line of code to temporarily remove it while testing a program. This is called *commenting out* code, and it can be useful when you're trying to figure out why a program doesn't work. You can remove the # later when you are ready to put the line back in.

Python also ignores the blank line after the comment. You can add as many blank lines to your program as you want. This can make your code easier to read, like paragraphs in a book.

The print() Function

The `print()` function displays the string value inside the parentheses on the screen.

---

❷ `print('Hello world!')`
`print('What is your name?') # ask for their name`

The line `print('Hello world!')` means "Print out the text in the string `'Hello world!'`." When Python executes this line, you say that Python is *calling* the `print()` function and the string value is being *passed* to the function. A value that is passed to a function call is an *argument*. Notice that the quotes are not printed to the screen. They just mark where the string begins and ends; they are not part of the string value.

NOTE *You can also use this function to put a blank line on the screen; just call* `print()` *with nothing in between the parentheses.*

When writing a function name, the opening and closing parentheses at the end identify it as the name of a function. This is why in this book you'll see `print()` rather than `print`. Chapter 2 describes functions in more detail.

The input() Function

The `input()` function waits for the user to type some text on the keyboard and press ENTER.

---

❸ `myName = input()`

This function call evaluates to a string equal to the user's text, and the previous line of code assigns the `myName` variable to this string value.

You can think of the input() function call as an expression that evaluates to whatever string the user typed in. If the user entered 'Al', then the expression would evaluate to myName = 'Al'.

Printing the User's Name

The following call to print() actually contains the expression 'It is good to meet you, ' + myName between the parentheses.

---

❹ print('It is good to meet you, ' + myName)

Remember that expressions can always evaluate to a single value. If 'Al' is the value stored in myName on the previous line, then this expression evaluates to 'It is good to meet you, Al'. This single string value is then passed to print(), which prints it on the screen.

The len() Function

You can pass the len() function a string value (or a variable containing a string), and the function evaluates to the integer value of the number of characters in that string.

---

❺ print('The length of your name is:')
print(len(myName))

Enter the following into the interactive shell to try this:

```
>>> len('hello')
5
>>> len('My very energetic monster just scarfed nachos.')
46
>>> len('')
0
```

Just like those examples, len(myName) evaluates to an integer. It is then passed to print() to be displayed on the screen. Notice that print() allows you to pass it either integer values or string values. But notice the error that shows up when you type the following into the interactive shell:

```
>>> print('I am ' + 29 + ' years old.')
Traceback (most recent call last):
  File "<pyshell#6>", line 1, in <module>
    print('I am ' + 29 + ' years old.')
TypeError: Can't convert 'int' object to str implicitly
```

The print() function isn't causing that error, but rather it's the expression you tried to pass to print(). You get the same error message if you type the expression into the interactive shell on its own.

```
>>> 'I am ' + 29 + ' years old.'
Traceback (most recent call last):
  File "<pyshell#7>", line 1, in <module>
    'I am ' + 29 + ' years old.'
TypeError: Can't convert 'int' object to str implicitly
```

Python gives an error because you can use the + operator only to add two integers together or concatenate two strings. You can't add an integer to a string because this is ungrammatical in Python. You can fix this by using a string version of the integer instead, as explained in the next section.

The str(), int(), and float() Functions

If you want to concatenate an integer such as 29 with a string to pass to print(), you'll need to get the value '29', which is the string form of 29. The str() function can be passed an integer value and will evaluate to a string value version of it, as follows:

```
>>> str(29)
'29'
>>> print('I am ' + str(29) + ' years old.')
I am 29 years old.
```

Because str(29) evaluates to '29', the expression 'I am ' + str(29) + ' years old.' evaluates to 'I am ' + '29' + ' years old.', which in turn evaluates to 'I am 29 years old.'. This is the value that is passed to the print() function.

The str(), int(), and float() functions will evaluate to the string, integer, and floating-point forms of the value you pass, respectively. Try converting some values in the interactive shell with these functions, and watch what happens.

```
>>> str(0)
'0'
>>> str(-3.14)
'-3.14'
>>> int('42')
42
>>> int('-99')
-99
>>> int(1.25)
1
>>> int(1.99)
1
>>> float('3.14')
3.14
>>> float(10)
10.0
```

The previous examples call the str(), int(), and float() functions and pass them values of the other data types to obtain a string, integer, or floating-point form of those values.

The str() function is handy when you have an integer or float that you want to concatenate to a string. The int() function is also helpful if you have a number as a string value that you want to use in some mathematics. For example, the input() function always returns a string, even if the user enters a number. Enter **spam = input()** into the interactive shell and enter **101** when it waits for your text.

```
>>> spam = input()
101
>>> spam
'101'
```

The value stored inside spam isn't the integer 101 but the string '101'. If you want to do math using the value in spam, use the int() function to get the integer form of spam and then store this as the new value in spam.

```
>>> spam = int(spam)
>>> spam
101
```

Now you should be able to treat the spam variable as an integer instead of a string.

```
>>> spam * 10 / 5
202.0
```

Note that if you pass a value to int() that it cannot evaluate as an integer, Python will display an error message.

```
>>> int('99.99')
Traceback (most recent call last):
  File "<pyshell#18>", line 1, in <module>
    int('99.99')
ValueError: invalid literal for int() with base 10: '99.99'
>>> int('twelve')
Traceback (most recent call last):
  File "<pyshell#19>", line 1, in <module>
    int('twelve')
ValueError: invalid literal for int() with base 10: 'twelve'
```

The int() function is also useful if you need to round a floating-point number down.

```
>>> int(7.7)
7
>>> int(7.7) + 1
8
```

In your program, you used the int() and str() functions in the last three lines to get a value of the appropriate data type for the code.

❻
```
print('What is your age?') # ask for their age
myAge = input()
print('You will be ' + str(int(myAge) + 1) + ' in a year.')
```

The myAge variable contains the value returned from input(). Because the input() function always returns a string (even if the user typed in a number), you can use the int(myAge) code to return an integer value of the string in myAge. This integer value is then added to 1 in the expression int(myAge) + 1.

The result of this addition is passed to the str() function: str(int(myAge) + 1). The string value returned is then concatenated with the strings 'You will be ' and ' in a year.' to evaluate to one large string value. This large string is finally passed to print() to be displayed on the screen.

Let's say the user enters the string '4' for myAge. The string '4' is converted to an integer, so you can add one to it. The result is 5. The str() function converts the result back to a string, so you can concatenate it with the second string, 'in a year.', to create the final message. These evaluation steps would look something like Figure 1-4.

TEXT AND NUMBER EQUIVALENCE

Although the string value of a number is considered a completely different value from the integer or floating-point version, an integer can be equal to a floating point.

```
>>> 42 == '42'
False
>>> 42 == 42.0
True
>>> 42.0 == 0042.000
True
```

Python makes this distinction because strings are text, while integers and floats are both numbers.

```
  print('You will be ' + str(int(myAge) + 1) + ' in a year.')

  print('You will be ' + str(int( '4' ) + 1) + ' in a year.')

  print('You will be ' + str(   4 + 1   ) + ' in a year.')

  print('You will be ' + str(   5      ) + ' in a year.')

  print('You will be ' +           '5'        + ' in a year.')

  print('You will be 5'                       + ' in a year.')

  print('You will be 5 in a year.')
```

Figure 1-4: The evaluation steps, if 4 was stored in myAge

Summary

You can compute expressions with a calculator or type string concatenations with a word processor. You can even do string replication easily by copying and pasting text. But expressions, and their component values—operators, variables, and function calls—are the basic building blocks that make programs. Once you know how to handle these elements, you will be able to instruct Python to operate on large amounts of data for you.

It is good to remember the different types of operators (+, -, *, /, //, %, and ** for math operations, and + and * for string operations) and the three data types (integers, floating-point numbers, and strings) introduced in this chapter.

A few different functions were introduced as well. The print() and input() functions handle simple text output (to the screen) and input (from the keyboard). The len() function takes a string and evaluates to an int of the number of characters in the string. The str(), int(), and float() functions will evaluate to the string, integer, or floating-point number form of the value they are passed.

In the next chapter, you will learn how to tell Python to make intelligent decisions about what code to run, what code to skip, and what code to repeat based on the values it has. This is known as *flow control*, and it allows you to write programs that make intelligent decisions.

Practice Questions

1. Which of the following are operators, and which are values?

```
*
'hello'
-88.8
-
/
+
5
```

2. Which of the following is a variable, and which is a string?

```
spam
'spam'
```

3. Name three data types.
4. What is an expression made up of? What do all expressions do?
5. This chapter introduced assignment statements, like spam = 10. What is the difference between an expression and a statement?
6. What does the variable bacon contain after the following code runs?

```
bacon = 20
bacon + 1
```

7. What should the following two expressions evaluate to?

```
'spam' + 'spamspam'
'spam' * 3
```

8. Why is eggs a valid variable name while 100 is invalid?
9. What three functions can be used to get the integer, floating-point number, or string version of a value?
10. Why does this expression cause an error? How can you fix it?

```
'I have eaten ' + 99 + ' burritos.'
```

Extra credit: Search online for the Python documentation for the len() function. It will be on a web page titled "Built-in Functions." Skim the list of other functions Python has, look up what the round() function does, and experiment with it in the interactive shell.

2

FLOW CONTROL

So you know the basics of individual instructions and that a program is just a series of instructions. But the real strength of programming isn't just running (or *executing*) one instruction after another like a weekend errand list. Based on how the expressions evaluate, the program can decide to skip instructions, repeat them, or choose one of several instructions to run. In fact, you almost never want your programs to start from the first line of code and simply execute every line, straight to the end. *Flow control statements* can decide which Python instructions to execute under which conditions.

These flow control statements directly correspond to the symbols in a flowchart, so I'll provide flowchart versions of the code discussed in this chapter. Figure 2-1 shows a flowchart for what to do if it's raining. Follow the path made by the arrows from Start to End.

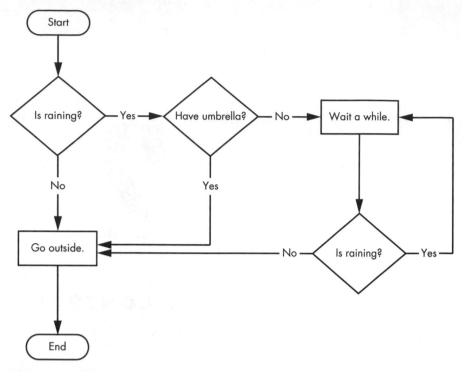

Figure 2-1: A flowchart to tell you what to do if it is raining

In a flowchart, there is usually more than one way to go from the start to the end. The same is true for lines of code in a computer program. Flowcharts represent these branching points with diamonds, while the other steps are represented with rectangles. The starting and ending steps are represented with rounded rectangles.

But before you learn about flow control statements, you first need to learn how to represent those *yes* and *no* options, and you need to understand how to write those branching points as Python code. To that end, let's explore Boolean values, comparison operators, and Boolean operators.

Boolean Values

While the integer, floating-point, and string data types have an unlimited number of possible values, the *Boolean* data type has only two values: True and False. (Boolean is capitalized because the data type is named after mathematician George Boole.) When typed as Python code, the Boolean values True and False lack the quotes you place around strings, and they always start with a capital *T* or *F*, with the rest of the word in lowercase. Enter the following into the interactive shell. (Some of these instructions are intentionally incorrect, and they'll cause error messages to appear.)

```
❶ >>> spam = True
   >>> spam
   True
❷ >>> true
   Traceback (most recent call last):
     File "<pyshell#2>", line 1, in <module>
       true
   NameError: name 'true' is not defined
❸ >>> True = 2 + 2
   SyntaxError: assignment to keyword
```

Like any other value, Boolean values are used in expressions and can be stored in variables ❶. If you don't use the proper case ❷ or you try to use True and False for variable names ❸, Python will give you an error message.

Comparison Operators

Comparison operators compare two values and evaluate down to a single Boolean value. Table 2-1 lists the comparison operators.

Table 2-1: Comparison Operators

Operator	Meaning
==	Equal to
!=	Not equal to
<	Less than
>	Greater than
<=	Less than or equal to
>=	Greater than or equal to

These operators evaluate to True or False depending on the values you give them. Let's try some operators now, starting with == and !=.

```
>>> 42 == 42
True
>>> 42 == 99
False
>>> 2 != 3
True
>>> 2 != 2
False
```

As you might expect, == (equal to) evaluates to True when the values on both sides are the same, and != (not equal to) evaluates to True when the two values are different. The == and != operators can actually work with values of any data type.

```
>>> 'hello' == 'hello'
True
>>> 'hello' == 'Hello'
False
>>> 'dog' != 'cat'
True
>>> True == True
True
>>> True != False
True
>>> 42 == 42.0
True
❶ >>> 42 == '42'
False
```

Note that an integer or floating-point value will always be unequal to a string value. The expression 42 == '42' ❶ evaluates to False because Python considers the integer 42 to be different from the string '42'.

The <, >, <=, and >= operators, on the other hand, work properly only with integer and floating-point values.

```
>>> 42 < 100
True
>>> 42 > 100
False
>>> 42 < 42
False
>>> eggCount = 42
❶ >>> eggCount <= 42
True
>>> myAge = 29
❷ >>> myAge >= 10
True
```

THE DIFFERENCE BETWEEN THE == AND = OPERATORS

You might have noticed that the == operator (equal to) has two equal signs, while the = operator (assignment) has just one equal sign. It's easy to confuse these two operators with each other. Just remember these points:

- The == operator (equal to) asks whether two values are the same as each other.

- The = operator (assignment) puts the value on the right into the variable on the left.

To help remember which is which, notice that the == operator (equal to) consists of two characters, just like the != operator (not equal to) consists of two characters.

You'll often use comparison operators to compare a variable's value to some other value, like in the eggCount <= 42 ❶ and myAge >= 10 ❷ examples. (After all, instead of typing 'dog' != 'cat' in your code, you could have just typed True.) You'll see more examples of this later when you learn about flow control statements.

Boolean Operators

The three Boolean operators (and, or, and not) are used to compare Boolean values. Like comparison operators, they evaluate these expressions down to a Boolean value. Let's explore these operators in detail, starting with the and operator.

Binary Boolean Operators

The and and or operators always take two Boolean values (or expressions), so they're considered *binary* operators. The and operator evaluates an expression to True if *both* Boolean values are True; otherwise, it evaluates to False. Enter some expressions using and into the interactive shell to see it in action.

```
>>> True and True
True
>>> True and False
False
```

A *truth table* shows every possible result of a Boolean operator. Table 2-2 is the truth table for the and operator.

Table 2-2: The and Operator's Truth Table

Expression	Evaluates to...
True and True	True
True and False	False
False and True	False
False and False	False

On the other hand, the or operator evaluates an expression to True if *either* of the two Boolean values is True. If both are False, it evaluates to False.

```
>>> False or True
True
>>> False or False
False
```

You can see every possible outcome of the or operator in its truth table, shown in Table 2-3.

Table 2-3: The or Operator's Truth Table

Expression	Evaluates to...
True or True	True
True or False	True
False or True	True
False or False	False

The not Operator

Unlike and and or, the not operator operates on only one Boolean value (or expression). The not operator simply evaluates to the opposite Boolean value.

```
>>> not True
False
❶ >>> not not not not True
True
```

Much like using double negatives in speech and writing, you can nest not operators ❶, though there's never not no reason to do this in real programs. Table 2-4 shows the truth table for not.

Table 2-4: The not Operator's Truth Table

Expression	Evaluates to...
not True	False
not False	True

Mixing Boolean and Comparison Operators

Since the comparison operators evaluate to Boolean values, you can use them in expressions with the Boolean operators.

Recall that the and, or, and not operators are called Boolean operators because they always operate on the Boolean values True and False. While expressions like 4 < 5 aren't Boolean values, they are expressions that evaluate down to Boolean values. Try entering some Boolean expressions that use comparison operators into the interactive shell.

```
>>> (4 < 5) and (5 < 6)
True
>>> (4 < 5) and (9 < 6)
False
>>> (1 == 2) or (2 == 2)
True
```

The computer will evaluate the left expression first, and then it will evaluate the right expression. When it knows the Boolean value for each, it will then evaluate the whole expression down to one Boolean value. You can think of the computer's evaluation process for (4 < 5) and (5 < 6) as shown in Figure 2-2.

You can also use multiple Boolean operators in an expression, along with the comparison operators.

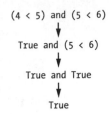

Figure 2-2: The process of evaluating (4 < 5) and (5 < 6) to True.

```
>>> 2 + 2 == 4 and not 2 + 2 == 5 and 2 * 2 == 2 + 2
True
```

The Boolean operators have an order of operations just like the math operators do. After any math and comparison operators evaluate, Python evaluates the not operators first, then the and operators, and then the or operators.

Elements of Flow Control

Flow control statements often start with a part called the *condition*, and all are followed by a block of code called the *clause*. Before you learn about Python's specific flow control statements, I'll cover what a condition and a block are.

Conditions

The Boolean expressions you've seen so far could all be considered conditions, which are the same thing as expressions; *condition* is just a more specific name in the context of flow control statements. Conditions always evaluate down to a Boolean value, True or False. A flow control statement decides what to do based on whether its condition is True or False, and almost every flow control statement uses a condition.

Blocks of Code

Lines of Python code can be grouped together in *blocks*. You can tell when a block begins and ends from the indentation of the lines of code. There are three rules for blocks.

1. Blocks begin when the indentation increases.
2. Blocks can contain other blocks.
3. Blocks end when the indentation decreases to zero or to a containing block's indentation.

Blocks are easier to understand by looking at some indented code, so let's find the blocks in part of a small game program, shown here:

```
if name == 'Mary':
❶    print('Hello Mary')
     if password == 'swordfish':
❷        print('Access granted.')
     else:
❸        print('Wrong password.')
```

The first block of code ❶ starts at the line print('Hello Mary') and contains all the lines after it. Inside this block is another block ❷, which has only a single line in it: print('Access Granted.'). The third block ❸ is also one line long: print('Wrong password.').

Program Execution

In the previous chapter's *hello.py* program, Python started executing instructions at the top of the program going down, one after another. The *program execution* (or simply, *execution*) is a term for the current instruction being executed. If you print the source code on paper and put your finger on each line as it is executed, you can think of your finger as the program execution.

Not all programs execute by simply going straight down, however. If you use your finger to trace through a program with flow control statements, you'll likely find yourself jumping around the source code based on conditions, and you'll probably skip entire clauses.

Flow Control Statements

Now, let's explore the most important piece of flow control: the statements themselves. The statements represent the diamonds you saw in the flowchart in Figure 2-1, and they are the actual decisions your programs will make.

if Statements

The most common type of flow control statement is the if statement. An if statement's clause (that is, the block following the if statement) will execute if the statement's condition is True. The clause is skipped if the condition is False.

In plain English, an if statement could be read as, "If this condition is true, execute the code in the clause." In Python, an if statement consists of the following:

- The if keyword
- A condition (that is, an expression that evaluates to True or False)
- A colon
- Starting on the next line, an indented block of code (called the if clause)

For example, let's say you have some code that checks to see whether someone's name is Alice. (Pretend name was assigned some value earlier.)

```
if name == 'Alice':
    print('Hi, Alice.')
```

All flow control statements end with a colon and are followed by a new block of code (the clause). This if statement's clause is the block with print('Hi, Alice.'). Figure 2-3 shows what a flowchart of this code would look like.

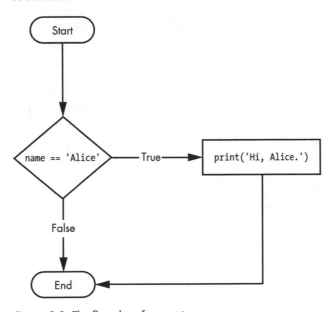

Figure 2-3: The flowchart for an if statement

else Statements

An if clause can optionally be followed by an else statement. The else clause is executed only when the if statement's condition is False. In plain English, an else statement could be read as, "If this condition is true, execute this code. Or else, execute that code." An else statement doesn't have a condition, and in code, an else statement always consists of the following:

- The else keyword
- A colon
- Starting on the next line, an indented block of code (called the else clause)

Returning to the Alice example, let's look at some code that uses an else statement to offer a different greeting if the person's name isn't Alice.

```
if name == 'Alice':
    print('Hi, Alice.')
```

```
else:
    print('Hello, stranger.')
```

Figure 2-4 shows what a flowchart of this code would look like.

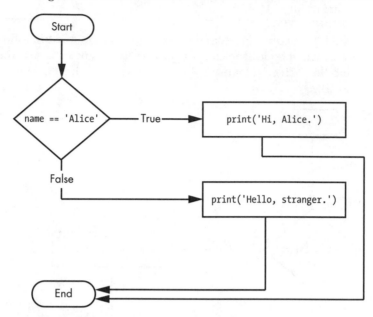

Figure 2-4: The flowchart for an else statement

elif Statements

While only one of the if or else clauses will execute, you may have a case where you want one of *many* possible clauses to execute. The elif statement is an "else if" statement that always follows an if or another elif statement. It provides another condition that is checked only if all of the previous conditions were False. In code, an elif statement always consists of the following:

- The elif keyword
- A condition (that is, an expression that evaluates to True or False)
- A colon
- Starting on the next line, an indented block of code (called the elif clause)

Let's add an elif to the name checker to see this statement in action.

```
if name == 'Alice':
    print('Hi, Alice.')
elif age < 12:
    print('You are not Alice, kiddo.')
```

This time, you check the person's age, and the program will tell them something different if they're younger than 12. You can see the flowchart for this in Figure 2-5.

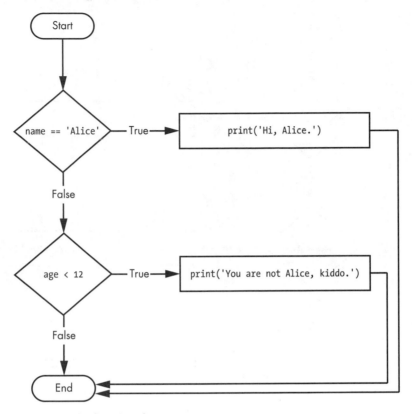

Figure 2-5: The flowchart for an elif statement

The elif clause executes if age < 12 is True and name == 'Alice' is False. However, if both of the conditions are False, then both of the clauses are skipped. It is *not* guaranteed that at least one of the clauses will be executed. When there is a chain of elif statements, only one or none of the clauses will be executed. Once one of the statements' conditions is found to be True, the rest of the elif clauses are automatically skipped. For example, open a new file editor window and enter the following code, saving it as *vampire.py*:

```
if name == 'Alice':
    print('Hi, Alice.')
elif age < 12:
    print('You are not Alice, kiddo.')
elif age > 2000:
    print('Unlike you, Alice is not an undead, immortal vampire.')
elif age > 100:
    print('You are not Alice, grannie.')
```

Here I've added two more elif statements to make the name checker greet a person with different answers based on age. Figure 2-6 shows the flowchart for this.

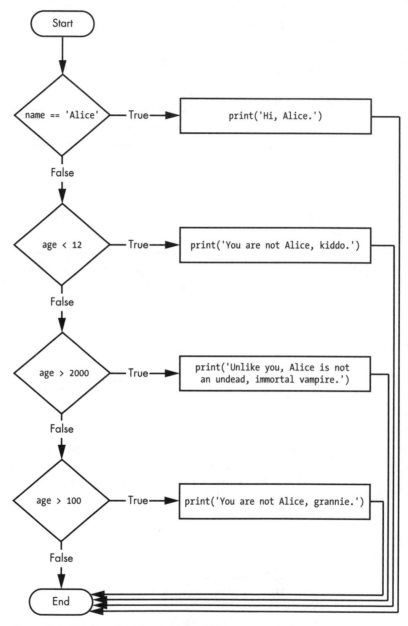

Figure 2-6: The flowchart for multiple elif statements in the vampire.py program

The order of the elif statements does matter, however. Let's rearrange them to introduce a bug. Remember that the rest of the elif clauses are automatically skipped once a True condition has been found, so if you swap around some of the clauses in *vampire.py*, you run into a problem. Change the code to look like the following, and save it as *vampire2.py*:

```
if name == 'Alice':
    print('Hi, Alice.')
elif age < 12:
    print('You are not Alice, kiddo.')
❶ elif age > 100:
    print('You are not Alice, grannie.')
elif age > 2000:
    print('Unlike you, Alice is not an undead, immortal vampire.')
```

Say the age variable contains the value 3000 before this code is executed. You might expect the code to print the string 'Unlike you, Alice is not an undead, immortal vampire.'. However, because the age > 100 condition is True (after all, 3000 *is* greater than 100) ❶, the string 'You are not Alice, grannie.' is printed, and the rest of the elif statements are automatically skipped. Remember, at most only one of the clauses will be executed, and for elif statements, the order matters!

Figure 2-7 shows the flowchart for the previous code. Notice how the diamonds for age > 100 and age > 2000 are swapped.

Optionally, you can have an else statement after the last elif statement. In that case, it *is* guaranteed that at least one (and only one) of the clauses will be executed. If the conditions in every if and elif statement are False, then the else clause is executed. For example, let's re-create the Alice program to use if, elif, and else clauses.

```
if name == 'Alice':
    print('Hi, Alice.')
elif age < 12:
    print('You are not Alice, kiddo.')
else:
    print('You are neither Alice nor a little kid.')
```

Figure 2-8 shows the flowchart for this new code, which we'll save as *littleKid.py*.

In plain English, this type of flow control structure would be, "If the first condition is true, do this. Else, if the second condition is true, do that. Otherwise, do something else." When you use all three of these statements together, remember these rules about how to order them to avoid bugs like the one in Figure 2-7. First, there is always exactly one if statement. Any elif statements you need should follow the if statement. Second, if you want to be sure that at least one clause is executed, close the structure with an else statement.

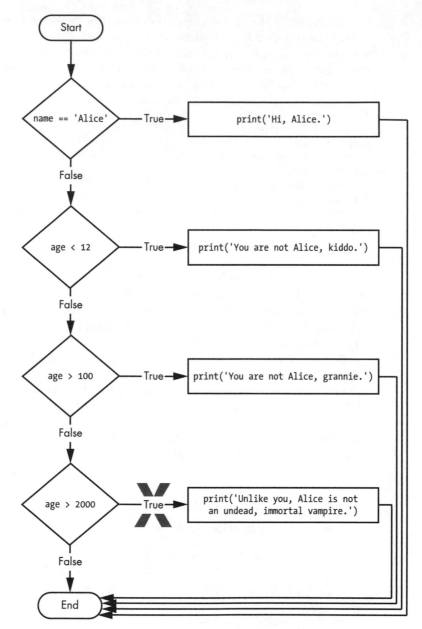

Figure 2-7: The flowchart for the vampire2.py program. The crossed-out path will logically never happen, because if age were greater than 2000, it would have already been greater than 100.

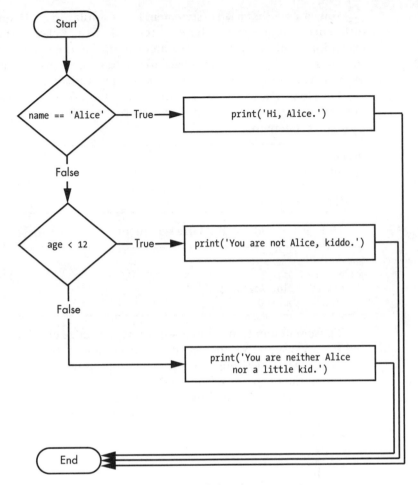

Figure 2-8: Flowchart for the previous littleKid.py *program*

while Loop Statements

You can make a block of code execute over and over again with a while statement. The code in a while clause will be executed as long as the while statement's condition is True. In code, a while statement always consists of the following:

- The while keyword
- A condition (that is, an expression that evaluates to True or False)
- A colon
- Starting on the next line, an indented block of code (called the while clause)

You can see that a while statement looks similar to an if statement. The difference is in how they behave. At the end of an if clause, the program execution continues after the if statement. But at the end of a while clause, the program execution jumps back to the start of the while statement. The while clause is often called the *while loop* or just the *loop*.

Let's look at an if statement and a while loop that use the same condition and take the same actions based on that condition. Here is the code with an if statement:

```
spam = 0
if spam < 5:
    print('Hello, world.')
    spam = spam + 1
```

Here is the code with a while statement:

```
spam = 0
while spam < 5:
    print('Hello, world.')
    spam = spam + 1
```

These statements are similar—both if and while check the value of spam, and if it's less than five, they print a message. But when you run these two code snippets, something very different happens for each one. For the if statement, the output is simply "Hello, world.". But for the while statement, it's "Hello, world." repeated five times! Take a look at the flowcharts for these two pieces of code, Figures 2-9 and 2-10, to see why this happens.

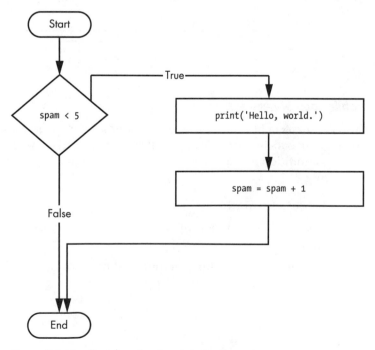

Figure 2-9: The flowchart for the if statement code

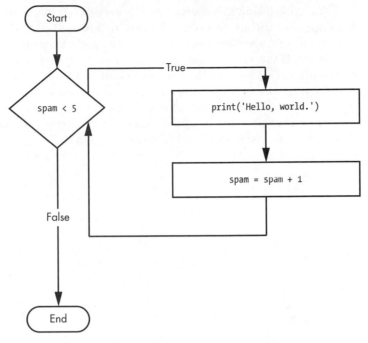

Figure 2-10: The flowchart for the while statement code

The code with the if statement checks the condition, and it prints Hello, world. only once if that condition is true. The code with the while loop, on the other hand, will print it five times. It stops after five prints because the integer in spam is incremented by one at the end of each loop iteration, which means that the loop will execute five times before spam < 5 is False.

In the while loop, the condition is always checked at the start of each *iteration* (that is, each time the loop is executed). If the condition is True, then the clause is executed, and afterward, the condition is checked again. The first time the condition is found to be False, the while clause is skipped.

An Annoying while Loop

Here's a small example program that will keep asking you to type, literally, your name. Select **File ▶ New Window** to open a new file editor window, enter the following code, and save the file as *yourName.py*:

```
❶ name = ''
❷ while name != 'your name':
      print('Please type your name.')
❸     name = input()
❹ print('Thank you!')
```

First, the program sets the name variable ❶ to an empty string. This is so that the name != 'your name' condition will evaluate to True and the program execution will enter the while loop's clause ❷.

The code inside this clause asks the user to type their name, which is assigned to the name variable ❸. Since this is the last line of the block, the execution moves back to the start of the while loop and reevaluates the condition. If the value in name is *not equal* to the string 'your name', then the condition is True, and the execution enters the while clause again.

But once the user types **your name**, the condition of the while loop will be 'your name' != 'your name', which evaluates to False. The condition is now False, and instead of the program execution reentering the while loop's clause, it skips past it and continues running the rest of the program ❹. Figure 2-11 shows a flowchart for the *yourName.py* program.

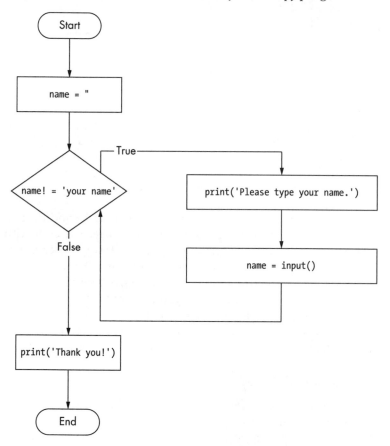

Figure 2-11: A flowchart of the yourName.py program

Now, let's see *yourName.py* in action. Press **F5** to run it, and enter something other than **your name** a few times before you give the program what it wants.

```
Please type your name.
Al
Please type your name.
Albert
```

```
Please type your name.
%#@#%*(^&!!!
Please type your name.
your name
Thank you!
```

If you never enter **your name**, then the while loop's condition will never be False, and the program will just keep asking forever. Here, the input() call lets the user enter the right string to make the program move on. In other programs, the condition might never actually change, and that can be a problem. Let's look at how you can break out of a while loop.

break Statements

There is a shortcut to getting the program execution to break out of a while loop's clause early. If the execution reaches a break statement, it immediately exits the while loop's clause. In code, a break statement simply contains the break keyword.

Pretty simple, right? Here's a program that does the same thing as the previous program, but it uses a break statement to escape the loop. Enter the following code, and save the file as *yourName2.py*:

```
❶ while True:
      print('Please type your name.')
❷     name = input()
❸     if name == 'your name':
❹         break
❺ print('Thank you!')
```

The first line ❶ creates an *infinite loop*; it is a while loop whose condition is always True. (The expression True, after all, always evaluates down to the value True.) The program execution will always enter the loop and will exit it only when a break statement is executed. (An infinite loop that *never* exits is a common programming bug.)

Just like before, this program asks the user to type **your name** ❷. Now, however, while the execution is still inside the while loop, an if statement gets executed ❸ to check whether name is equal to your name. If this condition is True, the break statement is run ❹, and the execution moves out of the loop to print('Thank you!') ❺. Otherwise, the if statement's clause with the break statement is skipped, which puts the execution at the end of the while loop. At this point, the program execution jumps back to the start of the while statement ❶ to recheck the condition. Since this condition is merely the True Boolean value, the execution enters the loop to ask the user to type **your name** again. See Figure 2-12 for the flowchart of this program.

Run *yourName2.py*, and enter the same text you entered for *yourName.py*. The rewritten program should respond in the same way as the original.

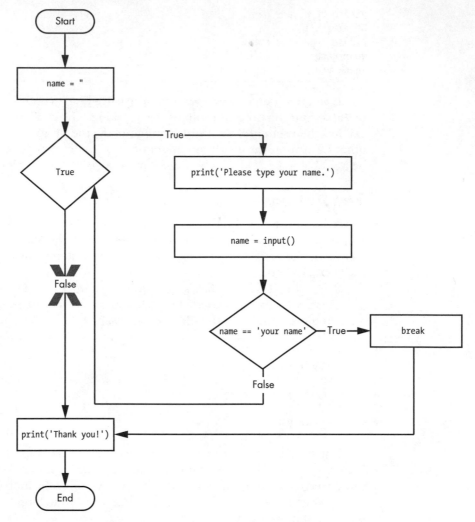

Figure 2-12: The flowchart for the yourName2.py program with an infinite loop. Note that the X path will logically never happen because the loop condition is always True.

continue Statements

Like break statements, continue statements are used inside loops. When the program execution reaches a continue statement, the program execution immediately jumps back to the start of the loop and reevaluates the loop's condition. (This is also what happens when the execution reaches the end of the loop.)

Let's use continue to write a program that asks for a name and password. Enter the following code into a new file editor window and save the program as *swordfish.py*.

```
  while True:
      print('Who are you?')
      name = input()
❶     if name != 'Joe':
❷         continue
      print('Hello, Joe. What is the password? (It is a fish.)')
❸     password = input()
      if password == 'swordfish':
❹         break
❺ print('Access granted.')
```

If the user enters any name besides Joe ❶, the continue statement ❷ causes the program execution to jump back to the start of the loop. When it reevaluates the condition, the execution will always enter the loop, since the condition is simply the value True. Once they make it past that if statement, the user is asked for a password ❸. If the password entered is swordfish, then the break statement ❹ is run, and the execution jumps out of the while loop to print Access granted ❺. Otherwise, the execution continues to the end of the while loop, where it then jumps back to the start of the loop. See Figure 2-13 for this program's flowchart.

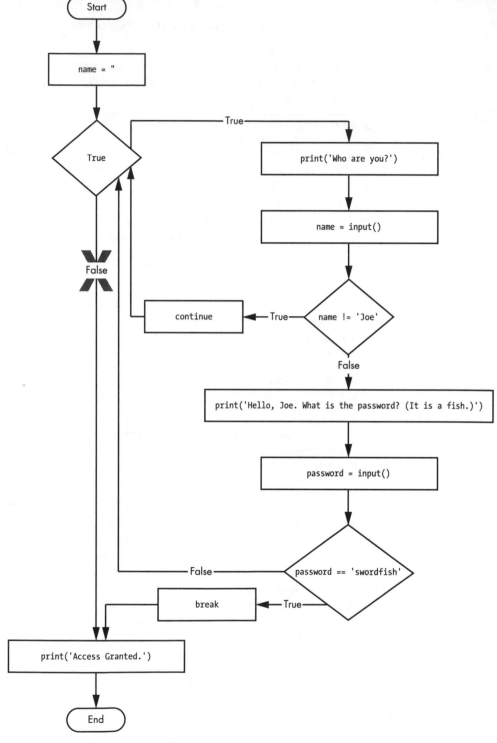

Figure 2-13: A flowchart for swordfish.py. *The X path will logically never happen because the loop condition is always True.*

"TRUTHY" AND "FALSEY" VALUES

There are some values in other data types that conditions will consider equivalent to True and False. When used in conditions, 0, 0.0, and '' (the empty string) are considered False, while all other values are considered True. For example, look at the following program:

```
name = ''
while not name:❶
    print('Enter your name:')
    name = input()
print('How many guests will you have?')
numOfGuests = int(input())
if numOfGuests:❷
    print('Be sure to have enough room for all your guests.')❸
print('Done')
```

If the user enters a blank string for name, then the while statement's condition will be True ❶, and the program continues to ask for a name. If the value for numOfGuests is not 0 ❷, then the condition is considered to be True, and the program will print a reminder for the user ❸.

You could have typed not name != '' instead of not name, and numOfGuests != 0 instead of numOfGuests, but using the truthy and falsey values can make your code easier to read.

Run this program and give it some input. Until you claim to be Joe, it shouldn't ask for a password, and once you enter the correct password, it should exit.

```
Who are you?
I'm fine, thanks. Who are you?
Who are you?
Joe
Hello, Joe. What is the password? (It is a fish.)
Mary
Who are you?
Joe
Hello, Joe. What is the password? (It is a fish.)
swordfish
Access granted.
```

for Loops and the range() Function

The while loop keeps looping while its condition is True (which is the reason for its name), but what if you want to execute a block of code only a certain number of times? You can do this with a for loop statement and the range() function.

In code, a for statement looks something like for i in range(5): and always includes the following:

- The for keyword
- A variable name
- The in keyword
- A call to the range() method with up to three integers passed to it
- A colon
- Starting on the next line, an indented block of code (called the for clause)

Let's create a new program called *fiveTimes.py* to help you see a for loop in action.

```python
print('My name is')
for i in range(5):
    print('Jimmy Five Times (' + str(i) + ')')
```

The code in the for loop's clause is run five times. The first time it is run, the variable i is set to 0. The print() call in the clause will print Jimmy Five Times (0). After Python finishes an iteration through all the code inside the for loop's clause, the execution goes back to the top of the loop, and the for statement increments i by one. This is why range(5) results in five iterations through the clause, with i being set to 0, then 1, then 2, then 3, and then 4. The variable i will go up to, but will not include, the integer passed to range(). Figure 2-14 shows a flowchart for the *fiveTimes.py* program.

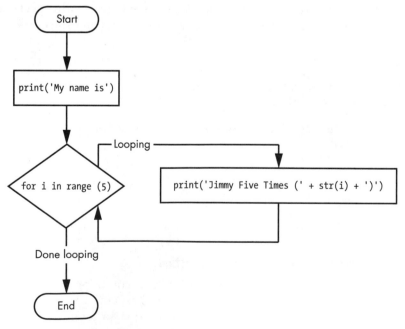

Figure 2-14: The flowchart for fiveTimes.py

When you run this program, it should print `Jimmy Five Times` followed by the value of i five times before leaving the for loop.

```
My name is
Jimmy Five Times (0)
Jimmy Five Times (1)
Jimmy Five Times (2)
Jimmy Five Times (3)
Jimmy Five Times (4)
```

NOTE *You can use break and continue statements inside for loops as well. The continue statement will continue to the next value of the for loop's counter, as if the program execution had reached the end of the loop and returned to the start. In fact, you can use continue and break statements only inside while and for loops. If you try to use these statements elsewhere, Python will give you an error.*

As another for loop example, consider this story about the mathematician Karl Friedrich Gauss. When Gauss was a boy, a teacher wanted to give the class some busywork. The teacher told them to add up all the numbers from 0 to 100. Young Gauss came up with a clever trick to figure out the answer in a few seconds, but you can write a Python program with a for loop to do this calculation for you.

```
❶ total = 0
❷ for num in range(101):
❸     total = total + num
❹ print(total)
```

The result should be 5,050. When the program first starts, the total variable is set to 0 ❶. The for loop ❷ then executes total = total + num ❸ 100 times. By the time the loop has finished all of its 100 iterations, every integer from 0 to 100 will have been added to total. At this point, total is printed to the screen ❹. Even on the slowest computers, this program takes less than a second to complete.

(Young Gauss figured out that there were 50 pairs of numbers that added up to 101: 1 + 100, 2 + 99, 3 + 98, and so on, until 50 + 51. Since 50 × 101 is 5,050, the sum of all the numbers from 0 to 100 is 5,050. Clever kid!)

An Equivalent while Loop

You can actually use a while loop to do the same thing as a for loop; for loops are just more concise. Let's rewrite *fiveTimes.py* to use a while loop equivalent of a for loop.

```
print('My name is')
i = 0
while i < 5:
    print('Jimmy Five Times (' + str(i) + ')')
    i = i + 1
```

If you run this program, the output should look the same as the *fiveTimes.py* program, which uses a for loop.

The Starting, Stopping, and Stepping Arguments to range()

Some functions can be called with multiple arguments separated by a comma, and range() is one of them. This lets you change the integer passed to range() to follow any sequence of integers, including starting at a number other than zero.

```
for i in range(12, 16):
    print(i)
```

The first argument will be where the for loop's variable starts, and the second argument will be up to, but not including, the number to stop at.

```
12
13
14
15
```

The range() function can also be called with three arguments. The first two arguments will be the start and stop values, and the third will be the *step argument*. The step is the amount that the variable is increased by after each iteration.

```
for i in range(0, 10, 2):
    print(i)
```

So calling range(0, 10, 2) will count from zero to eight by intervals of two.

```
0
2
4
6
8
```

The range() function is flexible in the sequence of numbers it produces for for loops. *For* example (I never apologize for my puns), you can even use a negative number for the step argument to make the for loop count down instead of up.

```
for i in range(5, -1, -1):
    print(i)
```

Running a for loop to print i with range(5, -1, -1) should print from five down to zero.

```
5
4
```

```
3
2
1
0
```

Importing Modules

All Python programs can call a basic set of functions called *built-in functions*, including the print(), input(), and len() functions you've seen before. Python also comes with a set of modules called the *standard library*. Each module is a Python program that contains a related group of functions that can be embedded in your programs. For example, the math module has mathematics-related functions, the random module has random number–related functions, and so on.

Before you can use the functions in a module, you must import the module with an import statement. In code, an import statement consists of the following:

- The import keyword
- The name of the module
- Optionally, more module names, as long as they are separated by commas

Once you import a module, you can use all the cool functions of that module. Let's give it a try with the random module, which will give us access to the random.randint() function.

Enter this code into the file editor, and save it as *printRandom.py*:

```python
import random
for i in range(5):
    print(random.randint(1, 10))
```

When you run this program, the output will look something like this:

```
4
1
8
4
1
```

The random.randint() function call evaluates to a random integer value between the two integers that you pass it. Since randint() is in the random module, you must first type **random.** in front of the function name to tell Python to look for this function inside the random module.

Here's an example of an import statement that imports four different modules:

```python
import random, sys, os, math
```

Now we can use any of the functions in these four modules. We'll learn more about them later in the book.

from import Statements

An alternative form of the import statement is composed of the from keyword, followed by the module name, the import keyword, and a star; for example, from random import *.

With this form of import statement, calls to functions in random will not need the random. prefix. However, using the full name makes for more readable code, so it is better to use the normal form of the import statement.

Ending a Program Early with sys.exit()

The last flow control concept to cover is how to terminate the program. This always happens if the program execution reaches the bottom of the instructions. However, you can cause the program to terminate, or exit, by calling the sys.exit() function. Since this function is in the sys module, you have to import sys before your program can use it.

Open a new file editor window and enter the following code, saving it as *exitExample.py*:

```
import sys

while True:
    print('Type exit to exit.')
    response = input()
    if response == 'exit':
        sys.exit()
    print('You typed ' + response + '.')
```

Run this program in IDLE. This program has an infinite loop with no break statement inside. The only way this program will end is if the user enters exit, causing sys.exit() to be called. When response is equal to exit, the program ends. Since the response variable is set by the input() function, the user must enter exit in order to stop the program.

Summary

By using expressions that evaluate to True or False (also called *conditions*), you can write programs that make decisions on what code to execute and what code to skip. You can also execute code over and over again in a loop while a certain condition evaluates to True. The break and continue statements are useful if you need to exit a loop or jump back to the start.

These flow control statements will let you write much more intelligent programs. There's another type of flow control that you can achieve by writing your own functions, which is the topic of the next chapter.

Practice Questions

1. What are the two values of the Boolean data type? How do you write them?

2. What are the three Boolean operators?

3. Write out the truth tables of each Boolean operator (that is, every possible combination of Boolean values for the operator and what they evaluate to).

4. What do the following expressions evaluate to?

```
(5 > 4) and (3 == 5)
not (5 > 4)
(5 > 4) or (3 == 5)
not ((5 > 4) or (3 == 5))
(True and True) and (True == False)
(not False) or (not True)
```

5. What are the six comparison operators?

6. What is the difference between the equal to operator and the assignment operator?

7. Explain what a condition is and where you would use one.

8. Identify the three blocks in this code:

```
spam = 0
if spam == 10:
    print('eggs')
    if spam > 5:
        print('bacon')
    else:
        print('ham')
    print('spam')
print('spam')
```

9. Write code that prints Hello if 1 is stored in spam, prints Howdy if 2 is stored in spam, and prints Greetings! if anything else is stored in spam.

10. What can you press if your program is stuck in an infinite loop?

11. What is the difference between break and continue?

12. What is the difference between range(10), range(0, 10), and range(0, 10, 1) in a for loop?

13. Write a short program that prints the numbers 1 to 10 using a for loop. Then write an equivalent program that prints the numbers 1 to 10 using a while loop.

14. If you had a function named bacon() inside a module named spam, how would you call it after importing spam?

    Extra credit: Look up the round() and abs() functions on the Internet, and find out what they do. Experiment with them in the interactive shell.

3

FUNCTIONS

You're already familiar with the print(),
input(), and len() functions from the previous chapters. Python provides several built-
in functions like these, but you can also write
your own functions. A *function* is like a mini-program
within a program.

To better understand how functions work, let's create one. Type this
program into the file editor and save it as *helloFunc.py*:

```
❶ def hello():
❷     print('Howdy!')
      print('Howdy!!!')
      print('Hello there.')

❸ hello()
  hello()
  hello()
```

The first line is a def statement ❶, which defines a function named hello(). The code in the block that follows the def statement ❷ is the body of the function. This code is executed when the function is called, not when the function is first defined.

The hello() lines after the function ❸ are function calls. In code, a function call is just the function's name followed by parentheses, possibly with some number of arguments in between the parentheses. When the program execution reaches these calls, it will jump to the top line in the function and begin executing the code there. When it reaches the end of the function, the execution returns to the line that called the function and continues moving through the code as before.

Since this program calls hello() three times, the code in the hello() function is executed three times. When you run this program, the output looks like this:

```
Howdy!
Howdy!!!
Hello there.
Howdy!
Howdy!!!
Hello there.
Howdy!
Howdy!!!
Hello there.
```

A major purpose of functions is to group code that gets executed multiple times. Without a function defined, you would have to copy and paste this code each time, and the program would look like this:

```
print('Howdy!')
print('Howdy!!!')
print('Hello there.')
print('Howdy!')
print('Howdy!!!')
print('Hello there.')
print('Howdy!')
print('Howdy!!!')
print('Hello there.')
```

In general, you always want to avoid duplicating code, because if you ever decide to update the code—if, for example, you find a bug you need to fix—you'll have to remember to change the code everywhere you copied it.

As you get more programming experience, you'll often find yourself *deduplicating* code, which means getting rid of duplicated or copy-and-pasted code. Deduplication makes your programs shorter, easier to read, and easier to update.

def Statements with Parameters

When you call the print() or len() function, you pass in values, called *arguments* in this context, by typing them between the parentheses. You can also define your own functions that accept arguments. Type this example into the file editor and save it as *helloFunc2.py*:

```
❶ def hello(name):
❷     print('Hello ' + name)

❸ hello('Alice')
   hello('Bob')
```

When you run this program, the output looks like this:

```
Hello Alice
Hello Bob
```

The definition of the hello() function in this program has a parameter called name ❶. A *parameter* is a variable that an argument is stored in when a function is called. The first time the hello() function is called, it's with the argument 'Alice' ❸. The program execution enters the function, and the variable name is automatically set to 'Alice', which is what gets printed by the print() statement ❷.

One special thing to note about parameters is that the value stored in a parameter is forgotten when the function returns. For example, if you added print(name) after hello('Bob') in the previous program, the program would give you a NameError because there is no variable named name. This variable was destroyed after the function call hello('Bob') had returned, so print(name) would refer to a name variable that does not exist.

This is similar to how a program's variables are forgotten when the program terminates. I'll talk more about why that happens later in the chapter, when I discuss what a function's local scope is.

Return Values and return Statements

When you call the len() function and pass it an argument such as 'Hello', the function call evaluates to the integer value 5, which is the length of the string you passed it. In general, the value that a function call evaluates to is called the *return value* of the function.

When creating a function using the def statement, you can specify what the return value should be with a return statement. A return statement consists of the following:

- The return keyword
- The value or expression that the function should return

When an expression is used with a return statement, the return value is what this expression evaluates to. For example, the following program defines a function that returns a different string depending on what number it is passed as an argument. Type this code into the file editor and save it as *magic8Ball.py*:

```
❶ import random

❷ def getAnswer(answerNumber):
❸     if answerNumber == 1:
          return 'It is certain'
      elif answerNumber == 2:
          return 'It is decidedly so'
      elif answerNumber == 3:
          return 'Yes'
      elif answerNumber == 4:
          return 'Reply hazy try again'
      elif answerNumber == 5:
          return 'Ask again later'
      elif answerNumber == 6:
          return 'Concentrate and ask again'
      elif answerNumber == 7:
          return 'My reply is no'
      elif answerNumber == 8:
          return 'Outlook not so good'
      elif answerNumber == 9:
          return 'Very doubtful'

❹ r = random.randint(1, 9)
❺ fortune = getAnswer(r)
❻ print(fortune)
```

When this program starts, Python first imports the random module ❶. Then the getAnswer() function is defined ❷. Because the function is being defined (and not called), the execution skips over the code in it. Next, the random.randint() function is called with two arguments, 1 and 9 ❹. It evaluates to a random integer between 1 and 9 (including 1 and 9 themselves), and this value is stored in a variable named r.

The getAnswer() function is called with r as the argument ❺. The program execution moves to the top of the getAnswer() function ❸, and the value r is stored in a parameter named answerNumber. Then, depending on this value in answerNumber, the function returns one of many possible string values. The program execution returns to the line at the bottom of the program that originally called getAnswer() ❺. The returned string is assigned to a variable named fortune, which then gets passed to a print() call ❻ and is printed to the screen.

Note that since you can pass return values as an argument to another function call, you could shorten these three lines:

```
r = random.randint(1, 9)
fortune = getAnswer(r)
print(fortune)
```

to this single equivalent line:

```
print(getAnswer(random.randint(1, 9)))
```

Remember, expressions are composed of values and operators. A function call can be used in an expression because it evaluates to its return value.

The None Value

In Python there is a value called None, which represents the absence of a value. None is the only value of the NoneType data type. (Other programming languages might call this value null, nil, or undefined.) Just like the Boolean True and False values, None must be typed with a capital *N*.

This value-without-a-value can be helpful when you need to store something that won't be confused for a real value in a variable. One place where None is used is as the return value of print(). The print() function displays text on the screen, but it doesn't need to return anything in the same way len() or input() does. But since all function calls need to evaluate to a return value, print() returns None. To see this in action, enter the following into the interactive shell:

```
>>> spam = print('Hello!')
Hello!
>>> None == spam
True
```

Behind the scenes, Python adds return None to the end of any function definition with no return statement. This is similar to how a while or for loop implicitly ends with a continue statement. Also, if you use a return statement without a value (that is, just the return keyword by itself), then None is returned.

Keyword Arguments and print()

Most arguments are identified by their position in the function call. For example, random.randint(1, 10) is different from random.randint(10, 1). The function call random.randint(1, 10) will return a random integer between 1 and 10, because the first argument is the low end of the range and the second argument is the high end (while random.randint(10, 1) causes an error).

However, *keyword arguments* are identified by the keyword put before them in the function call. Keyword arguments are often used for optional parameters. For example, the print() function has the optional parameters end and sep to specify what should be printed at the end of its arguments and between its arguments (separating them), respectively.

If you ran the following program:

```
print('Hello')
print('World')
```

the output would look like this:

```
Hello
World
```

The two strings appear on separate lines because the print() function automatically adds a newline character to the end of the string it is passed. However, you can set the end keyword argument to change this to a different string. For example, if the program were this:

```
print('Hello', end='')
print('World')
```

the output would look like this:

```
HelloWorld
```

The output is printed on a single line because there is no longer a new-line printed after 'Hello'. Instead, the blank string is printed. This is useful if you need to disable the newline that gets added to the end of every print() function call.

Similarly, when you pass multiple string values to print(), the function will automatically separate them with a single space. Enter the following into the interactive shell:

```
>>> print('cats', 'dogs', 'mice')
cats dogs mice
```

But you could replace the default separating string by passing the sep keyword argument. Enter the following into the interactive shell:

```
>>> print('cats', 'dogs', 'mice', sep=',')
cats,dogs,mice
```

You can add keyword arguments to the functions you write as well, but first you'll have to learn about the list and dictionary data types in the next two chapters. For now, just know that some functions have optional keyword arguments that can be specified when the function is called.

Local and Global Scope

Parameters and variables that are assigned in a called function are said to exist in that function's *local scope*. Variables that are assigned outside all functions are said to exist in the *global scope*. A variable that exists in a local scope is called a *local variable*, while a variable that exists in the global scope is called a *global variable*. A variable must be one or the other; it cannot be both local and global.

Think of a *scope* as a container for variables. When a scope is destroyed, all the values stored in the scope's variables are forgotten. There is only one global scope, and it is created when your program begins. When your program terminates, the global scope is destroyed, and all its variables are forgotten. Otherwise, the next time you ran your program, the variables would remember their values from the last time you ran it.

A local scope is created whenever a function is called. Any variables assigned in this function exist within the local scope. When the function returns, the local scope is destroyed, and these variables are forgotten. The next time you call this function, the local variables will not remember the values stored in them from the last time the function was called.

Scopes matter for several reasons:

- Code in the global scope cannot use any local variables.
- However, a local scope can access global variables.
- Code in a function's local scope cannot use variables in any other local scope.
- You can use the same name for different variables if they are in different scopes. That is, there can be a local variable named spam and a global variable also named spam.

The reason Python has different scopes instead of just making everything a global variable is so that when variables are modified by the code in a particular call to a function, the function interacts with the rest of the program only through its parameters and the return value. This narrows down the list code lines that may be causing a bug. If your program contained nothing but global variables and had a bug because of a variable being set to a bad value, then it would be hard to track down where this bad value was set. It could have been set from anywhere in the program—and your program could be hundreds or thousands of lines long! But if the bug is because of a local variable with a bad value, you know that only the code in that one function could have set it incorrectly.

While using global variables in small programs is fine, it is a bad habit to rely on global variables as your programs get larger and larger.

Local Variables Cannot Be Used in the Global Scope

Consider this program, which will cause an error when you run it:

```
def spam():
    eggs = 31337
```

```
spam()
print(eggs)
```

If you run this program, the output will look like this:

```
Traceback (most recent call last):
  File "C:/test3784.py", line 4, in <module>
    print(eggs)
NameError: name 'eggs' is not defined
```

The error happens because the eggs variable exists only in the local scope created when spam() is called. Once the program execution returns from spam, that local scope is destroyed, and there is no longer a variable named eggs. So when your program tries to run print(eggs), Python gives you an error saying that eggs is not defined. This makes sense if you think about it; when the program execution is in the global scope, no local scopes exist, so there can't be any local variables. This is why only global variables can be used in the global scope.

Local Scopes Cannot Use Variables in Other Local Scopes

A new local scope is created whenever a function is called, including when a function is called from another function. Consider this program:

```
  def spam():
❶     eggs = 99
❷     bacon()
❸     print(eggs)

  def bacon():
      ham = 101
❹     eggs = 0

❺ spam()
```

When the program starts, the spam() function is called ❺, and a local scope is created. The local variable eggs ❶ is set to 99. Then the bacon() function is called ❷, and a second local scope is created. Multiple local scopes can exist at the same time. In this new local scope, the local variable ham is set to 101, and a local variable eggs—which is different from the one in spam()'s local scope—is also created ❹ and set to 0.

When bacon() returns, the local scope for that call is destroyed. The program execution continues in the spam() function to print the value of eggs ❸, and since the local scope for the call to spam() still exists here, the eggs variable is set to 99. This is what the program prints.

The upshot is that local variables in one function are completely separate from the local variables in another function.

Global Variables Can Be Read from a Local Scope

Consider the following program:

```python
def spam():
    print(eggs)
eggs = 42
spam()
print(eggs)
```

Since there is no parameter named eggs or any code that assigns eggs a value in the spam() function, when eggs is used in spam(), Python considers it a reference to the global variable eggs. This is why 42 is printed when the previous program is run.

Local and Global Variables with the Same Name

To simplify your life, avoid using local variables that have the same name as a global variable or another local variable. But technically, it's perfectly legal to do so in Python. To see what happens, type the following code into the file editor and save it as *sameName.py*:

```python
  def spam():
❶     eggs = 'spam local'
      print(eggs)    # prints 'spam local'

  def bacon():
❷     eggs = 'bacon local'
      print(eggs)    # prints 'bacon local'
      spam()
      print(eggs)    # prints 'bacon local'

❸ eggs = 'global'
  bacon()
  print(eggs)        # prints 'global'
```

When you run this program, it outputs the following:

```
bacon local
spam local
bacon local
global
```

There are actually three different variables in this program, but confusingly they are all named eggs. The variables are as follows:

❶ A variable named eggs that exists in a local scope when spam() is called.

❷ A variable named eggs that exists in a local scope when bacon() is called.

❸ A variable named eggs that exists in the global scope.

Since these three separate variables all have the same name, it can be confusing to keep track of which one is being used at any given time. This is why you should avoid using the same variable name in different scopes.

The global Statement

If you need to modify a global variable from within a function, use the global statement. If you have a line such as global eggs at the top of a function, it tells Python, "In this function, eggs refers to the global variable, so don't create a local variable with this name." For example, type the following code into the file editor and save it as *sameName2.py*:

```
def spam():
❶     global eggs
❷     eggs = 'spam'

eggs = 'global'
spam()
print(eggs)
```

When you run this program, the final print() call will output this:

```
spam
```

Because eggs is declared global at the top of spam() ❶, when eggs is set to 'spam' ❷, this assignment is done to the globally scoped eggs. No local eggs variable is created.

There are four rules to tell whether a variable is in a local scope or global scope:

1. If a variable is being used in the global scope (that is, outside of all functions), then it is always a global variable.

2. If there is a global statement for that variable in a function, it is a global variable.

3. Otherwise, if the variable is used in an assignment statement in the function, it is a local variable.

4. But if the variable is not used in an assignment statement, it is a global variable.

To get a better feel for these rules, here's an example program. Type the following code into the file editor and save it as *sameName3.py*:

```
def spam():
❶     global eggs
       eggs = 'spam' # this is the global

def bacon():
❷     eggs = 'bacon' # this is a local
```

```
    def ham():
❸    print(eggs) # this is the global

    eggs = 42 # this is the global
    spam()
    print(eggs)
```

In the spam() function, eggs is the global eggs variable, because there's a global statement for eggs at the beginning of the function ❶. In bacon(), eggs is a local variable, because there's an assignment statement for it in that function ❷. In ham() ❸, eggs is the global variable, because there is no assignment statement or global statement for it in that function. If you run *sameName3.py*, the output will look like this:

```
spam
```

In a function, a variable will either always be global or always be local. There's no way that the code in a function can use a local variable named eggs and then later in that same function use the global eggs variable.

NOTE *If you ever want to modify the value stored in a global variable from in a function, you must use a global statement on that variable.*

If you try to use a local variable in a function before you assign a value to it, as in the following program, Python will give you an error. To see this, type the following into the file editor and save it as *sameName4.py*:

```
def spam():
    print(eggs) # ERROR!
❶    eggs = 'spam local'

❷ eggs = 'global'
    spam()
```

If you run the previous program, it produces an error message.

```
Traceback (most recent call last):
  File "C:/test3784.py", line 6, in <module>
    spam()
  File "C:/test3784.py", line 2, in spam
    print(eggs) # ERROR!
UnboundLocalError: local variable 'eggs' referenced before assignment
```

This error happens because Python sees that there is an assignment statement for eggs in the spam() function ❶ and therefore considers eggs to be local. But because print(eggs) is executed before eggs is assigned anything, the local variable eggs doesn't exist. Python will *not* fall back to using the global eggs variable ❷.

Exception Handling

Right now, getting an error, or *exception*, in your Python program means the entire program will crash. You don't want this to happen in real-world programs. Instead, you want the program to detect errors, handle them, and then continue to run.

For example, consider the following program, which has a "divide-by-zero" error. Open a new file editor window and enter the following code, saving it as *zeroDivide.py*:

```python
def spam(divideBy):
    return 42 / divideBy

print(spam(2))
print(spam(12))
print(spam(0))
print(spam(1))
```

We've defined a function called spam, given it a parameter, and then printed the value of that function with various parameters to see what happens. This is the output you get when you run the previous code:

```
21.0
3.5
Traceback (most recent call last):
  File "C:/zeroDivide.py", line 6, in <module>
    print(spam(0))
  File "C:/zeroDivide.py", line 2, in spam
    return 42 / divideBy
ZeroDivisionError: division by zero
```

A ZeroDivisionError happens whenever you try to divide a number by zero. From the line number given in the error message, you know that the return statement in spam() is causing an error.

Errors can be handled with try and except statements. The code that could potentially have an error is put in a try clause. The program execution moves to the start of a following except clause if an error happens.

You can put the previous divide-by-zero code in a try clause and have an except clause contain code to handle what happens when this error occurs.

```
def spam(divideBy):
    try:
        return 42 / divideBy
    except ZeroDivisionError:
        print('Error: Invalid argument.')

print(spam(2))
print(spam(12))
print(spam(0))
print(spam(1))
```

When code in a try clause causes an error, the program execution immediately moves to the code in the except clause. After running that code, the execution continues as normal. The output of the previous program is as follows:

```
21.0
3.5
Error: Invalid argument.
None
42.0
```

Note that any errors that occur in function calls in a try block will also be caught. Consider the following program, which instead has the spam() calls in the try block:

```
def spam(divideBy):
    return 42 / divideBy

try:
    print(spam(2))
    print(spam(12))
    print(spam(0))
    print(spam(1))
except ZeroDivisionError:
    print('Error: Invalid argument.')
```

When this program is run, the output looks like this:

```
21.0
3.5
Error: Invalid argument.
```

The reason print(spam(1)) is never executed is because once the execution jumps to the code in the except clause, it does not return to the try clause. Instead, it just continues moving down as normal.

A Short Program: Guess the Number

The toy examples I've show you so far are useful for introducing basic concepts, but now let's see how everything you've learned comes together in a more complete program. In this section, I'll show you a simple "guess the number" game. When you run this program, the output will look something like this:

```
I am thinking of a number between 1 and 20.
Take a guess.
10
Your guess is too low.
Take a guess.
15
Your guess is too low.
Take a guess.
17
Your guess is too high.
Take a guess.
16
Good job! You guessed my number in 4 guesses!
```

Type the following source code into the file editor, and save the file as *guessTheNumber.py*:

```python
# This is a guess the number game.
import random
secretNumber = random.randint(1, 20)
print('I am thinking of a number between 1 and 20.')

# Ask the player to guess 6 times.
for guessesTaken in range(1, 7):
    print('Take a guess.')
    guess = int(input())

    if guess < secretNumber:
        print('Your guess is too low.')
    elif guess > secretNumber:
        print('Your guess is too high.')
    else:
        break    # This condition is the correct guess!

if guess == secretNumber:
    print('Good job! You guessed my number in ' + str(guessesTaken) + ' guesses!')
else:
    print('Nope. The number I was thinking of was ' + str(secretNumber))
```

Let's look at this code line by line, starting at the top.

```
# This is a guess the number game.
import random
secretNumber = random.randint(1, 20)
```

First, a comment at the top of the code explains what the program does. Then, the program imports the random module so that it can use the random.randint() function to generate a number for the user to guess. The return value, a random integer between 1 and 20, is stored in the variable secretNumber.

```
print('I am thinking of a number between 1 and 20.')

# Ask the player to guess 6 times.
for guessesTaken in range(1, 7):
    print('Take a guess.')
    guess = int(input())
```

The program tells the player that it has come up with a secret number and will give the player six chances to guess it. The code that lets the player enter a guess and checks that guess is in a for loop that will loop at most six times. The first thing that happens in the loop is that the player types in a guess. Since input() returns a string, its return value is passed straight into int(), which translates the string into an integer value. This gets stored in a variable named guess.

```
    if guess < secretNumber:
        print('Your guess is too low.')
    elif guess > secretNumber:
        print('Your guess is too high.')
```

These few lines of code check to see whether the guess is less than or greater than the secret number. In either case, a hint is printed to the screen.

```
    else:
        break    # This condition is the correct guess!
```

If the guess is neither higher nor lower than the secret number, then it must be equal to the secret number, in which case you want the program execution to break out of the for loop.

```
if guess == secretNumber:
    print('Good job! You guessed my number in ' + str(guessesTaken) + ' guesses!')
else:
    print('Nope. The number I was thinking of was ' + str(secretNumber))
```

After the for loop, the previous if...else statement checks whether the player has correctly guessed the number and prints an appropriate message to the screen. In both cases, the program displays a variable that contains an integer value (guessesTaken and secretNumber). Since it must concatenate these integer values to strings, it passes these variables to the str() function, which returns the string value form of these integers. Now these strings can be concatenated with the + operators before finally being passed to the print() function call.

Summary

Functions are the primary way to compartmentalize your code into logical groups. Since the variables in functions exist in their own local scopes, the code in one function cannot directly affect the values of variables in other functions. This limits what code could be changing the values of your variables, which can be helpful when it comes to debugging your code.

Functions are a great tool to help you organize your code. You can think of them as black boxes: They have inputs in the form of parameters and outputs in the form of return values, and the code in them doesn't affect variables in other functions.

In previous chapters, a single error could cause your programs to crash. In this chapter, you learned about try and except statements, which can run code when an error has been detected. This can make your programs more resilient to common error cases.

Practice Questions

1. Why are functions advantageous to have in your programs?
2. When does the code in a function execute: when the function is defined or when the function is called?
3. What statement creates a function?
4. What is the difference between a function and a function call?
5. How many global scopes are there in a Python program? How many local scopes?
6. What happens to variables in a local scope when the function call returns?
7. What is a return value? Can a return value be part of an expression?
8. If a function does not have a return statement, what is the return value of a call to that function?
9. How can you force a variable in a function to refer to the global variable?
10. What is the data type of None?
11. What does the import areallyourpetsnamederic statement do?
12. If you had a function named bacon() in a module named spam, how would you call it after importing spam?
13. How can you prevent a program from crashing when it gets an error?
14. What goes in the try clause? What goes in the except clause?

Practice Projects

For practice, write programs to do the following tasks.

The Collatz Sequence

Write a function named collatz() that has one parameter named number. If number is even, then collatz() should print number // 2 and return this value. If number is odd, then collatz() should print and return 3 * number + 1.

Then write a program that lets the user type in an integer and that keeps calling collatz() on that number until the function returns the value 1. (Amazingly enough, this sequence actually works for any integer—sooner or later, using this sequence, you'll arrive at 1! Even mathematicians aren't sure why. Your program is exploring what's called the *Collatz sequence*, sometimes called "the simplest impossible math problem.")

Remember to convert the return value from input() to an integer with the int() function; otherwise, it will be a string value.

Hint: An integer number is even if number % 2 == 0, and it's odd if number % 2 == 1.

The output of this program could look something like this:

```
Enter number:
3
10
5
16
8
4
2
1
```

Input Validation

Add try and except statements to the previous project to detect whether the user types in a noninteger string. Normally, the int() function will raise a ValueError error if it is passed a noninteger string, as in int('puppy'). In the except clause, print a message to the user saying they must enter an integer.

4

LISTS

One more topic you'll need to understand before you can begin writing programs in earnest is the list data type and its cousin, the tuple. Lists and tuples can contain multiple values, which makes it easier to write programs that handle large amounts of data. And since lists themselves can contain other lists, you can use them to arrange data into hierarchical structures.

In this chapter, I'll discuss the basics of lists. I'll also teach you about methods, which are functions that are tied to values of a certain data type. Then I'll briefly cover the list-like tuple and string data types and how they compare to list values. In the next chapter, I'll introduce you to the dictionary data type.

The List Data Type

A *list* is a value that contains multiple values in an ordered sequence. The term *list value* refers to the list itself (which is a value that can be stored in a variable or passed to a function like any other value), not the values inside the list value. A list value looks like this: ['cat', 'bat', 'rat', 'elephant']. Just as string values are typed with quote characters to mark where the string begins and ends, a list begins with an opening square bracket and ends with a closing square bracket, []. Values inside the list are also called *items*. Items are separated with commas (that is, they are *comma-delimited*). For example, enter the following into the interactive shell:

```
>>> [1, 2, 3]
[1, 2, 3]
>>> ['cat', 'bat', 'rat', 'elephant']
['cat', 'bat', 'rat', 'elephant']
>>> ['hello', 3.1415, True, None, 42]
['hello', 3.1415, True, None, 42]
❶ >>> spam = ['cat', 'bat', 'rat', 'elephant']
>>> spam
['cat', 'bat', 'rat', 'elephant']
```

The spam variable ❶ is still assigned only one value: the list value. But the list value itself contains other values. The value [] is an empty list that contains no values, similar to '', the empty string.

Getting Individual Values in a List with Indexes

Say you have the list ['cat', 'bat', 'rat', 'elephant'] stored in a variable named spam. The Python code spam[0] would evaluate to 'cat', and spam[1] would evaluate to 'bat', and so on.

The integer inside the square brackets that follows the list is called an *index*. The first value in the list is at index 0, the second value is at index 1, the third value is at index 2, and so on. Figure 4-1 shows a list value assigned to spam, along with what the index expressions would evaluate to.

```
spam = ["cat", "bat", "rat", "elephant"]

spam[0]   spam[1]   spam[2]   spam[3]
```

Figure 4-1: A list value stored in the variable spam, showing which value each index refers to

For example, type the following expressions into the interactive shell. Start by assigning a list to the variable spam.

```
>>> spam = ['cat', 'bat', 'rat', 'elephant']
>>> spam[0]
'cat'
>>> spam[1]
'bat'
>>> spam[2]
'rat'
>>> spam[3]
'elephant'
```

```
>>> ['cat', 'bat', 'rat', 'elephant'][3]
'elephant'
❶ >>> 'Hello ' + spam[0]
❷ 'Hello cat'
>>> 'The ' + spam[1] + ' ate the ' + spam[0] + '.'
'The bat ate the cat.'
```

Notice that the expression 'Hello ' + spam[0] ❶ evaluates to 'Hello ' + 'cat' because spam[0] evaluates to the string 'cat'. This expression in turn evaluates to the string value 'Hello cat' ❷.

Python will give you an IndexError error message if you use an index that exceeds the number of values in your list value.

```
>>> spam = ['cat', 'bat', 'rat', 'elephant']
>>> spam[10000]
Traceback (most recent call last):
  File "<pyshell#9>", line 1, in <module>
    spam[10000]
IndexError: list index out of range
```

Indexes can be only integer values, not floats. The following example will cause a TypeError error:

```
>>> spam = ['cat', 'bat', 'rat', 'elephant']
>>> spam[1]
'bat'
>>> spam[1.0]
Traceback (most recent call last):
  File "<pyshell#13>", line 1, in <module>
    spam[1.0]
TypeError: list indices must be integers, not float
>>> spam[int(1.0)]
'bat'
```

Lists can also contain other list values. The values in these lists of lists can be accessed using multiple indexes, like so:

```
>>> spam = [['cat', 'bat'], [10, 20, 30, 40, 50]]
>>> spam[0]
['cat', 'bat']
>>> spam[0][1]
'bat'
>>> spam[1][4]
50
```

The first index dictates which list value to use, and the second indicates the value within the list value. For example, spam[0][1] prints 'bat', the second value in the first list. If you only use one index, the program will print the full list value at that index.

Negative Indexes

While indexes start at 0 and go up, you can also use negative integers for the index. The integer value -1 refers to the last index in a list, the value -2 refers to the second-to-last index in a list, and so on. Enter the following into the interactive shell:

```
>>> spam = ['cat', 'bat', 'rat', 'elephant']
>>> spam[-1]
'elephant'
>>> spam[-3]
'bat'
>>> 'The ' + spam[-1] + ' is afraid of the ' + spam[-3] + '.'
'The elephant is afraid of the bat.'
```

Getting Sublists with Slices

Just as an index can get a single value from a list, a *slice* can get several values from a list, in the form of a new list. A slice is typed between square brackets, like an index, but it has two integers separated by a colon. Notice the difference between indexes and slices.

- spam[2] is a list with an index (one integer).
- spam[1:4] is a list with a slice (two integers).

In a slice, the first integer is the index where the slice starts. The second integer is the index where the slice ends. A slice goes up to, but will not include, the value at the second index. A slice evaluates to a new list value. Enter the following into the interactive shell:

```
>>> spam = ['cat', 'bat', 'rat', 'elephant']
>>> spam[0:4]
['cat', 'bat', 'rat', 'elephant']
>>> spam[1:3]
['bat', 'rat']
>>> spam[0:-1]
['cat', 'bat', 'rat']
```

As a shortcut, you can leave out one or both of the indexes on either side of the colon in the slice. Leaving out the first index is the same as using 0, or the beginning of the list. Leaving out the second index is the same as using the length of the list, which will slice to the end of the list. Enter the following into the interactive shell:

```
>>> spam = ['cat', 'bat', 'rat', 'elephant']
>>> spam[:2]
['cat', 'bat']
>>> spam[1:]
['bat', 'rat', 'elephant']
```

```
>>> spam[:]
['cat', 'bat', 'rat', 'elephant']
```

Getting a List's Length with len()

The len() function will return the number of values that are in a list value passed to it, just like it can count the number of characters in a string value. Enter the following into the interactive shell:

```
>>> spam = ['cat', 'dog', 'moose']
>>> len(spam)
3
```

Changing Values in a List with Indexes

Normally a variable name goes on the left side of an assignment statement, like spam = 42. However, you can also use an index of a list to change the value at that index. For example, spam[1] = 'aardvark' means "Assign the value at index 1 in the list spam to the string 'aardvark'." Enter the following into the interactive shell:

```
>>> spam = ['cat', 'bat', 'rat', 'elephant']
>>> spam[1] = 'aardvark'
>>> spam
['cat', 'aardvark', 'rat', 'elephant']
>>> spam[2] = spam[1]
>>> spam
['cat', 'aardvark', 'aardvark', 'elephant']
>>> spam[-1] = 12345
>>> spam
['cat', 'aardvark', 'aardvark', 12345]
```

List Concatenation and List Replication

The + operator can combine two lists to create a new list value in the same way it combines two strings into a new string value. The * operator can also be used with a list and an integer value to replicate the list. Enter the following into the interactive shell:

```
>>> [1, 2, 3] + ['A', 'B', 'C']
[1, 2, 3, 'A', 'B', 'C']
>>> ['X', 'Y', 'Z'] * 3
['X', 'Y', 'Z', 'X', 'Y', 'Z', 'X', 'Y', 'Z']
>>> spam = [1, 2, 3]
>>> spam = spam + ['A', 'B', 'C']
>>> spam
[1, 2, 3, 'A', 'B', 'C']
```

Removing Values from Lists with del Statements

The `del` statement will delete values at an index in a list. All of the values in the list after the deleted value will be moved up one index. For example, enter the following into the interactive shell:

```
>>> spam = ['cat', 'bat', 'rat', 'elephant']
>>> del spam[2]
>>> spam
['cat', 'bat', 'elephant']
>>> del spam[2]
>>> spam
['cat', 'bat']
```

The `del` statement can also be used on a simple variable to delete it, as if it were an "unassignment" statement. If you try to use the variable after deleting it, you will get a `NameError` error because the variable no longer exists.

In practice, you almost never need to delete simple variables. The `del` statement is mostly used to delete values from lists.

Working with Lists

When you first begin writing programs, it's tempting to create many individual variables to store a group of similar values. For example, if I wanted to store the names of my cats, I might be tempted to write code like this:

```
catName1 = 'Zophie'
catName2 = 'Pooka'
catName3 = 'Simon'
catName4 = 'Lady Macbeth'
catName5 = 'Fat-tail'
catName6 = 'Miss Cleo'
```

(I don't actually own this many cats, I swear.) It turns out that this is a bad way to write code. For one thing, if the number of cats changes, your program will never be able to store more cats than you have variables. These types of programs also have a lot of duplicate or nearly identical code in them. Consider how much duplicate code is in the following program, which you should enter into the file editor and save as *allMyCats1.py*:

```
print('Enter the name of cat 1:')
catName1 = input()
print('Enter the name of cat 2:')
catName2 = input()
print('Enter the name of cat 3:')
catName3 = input()
print('Enter the name of cat 4:')
catName4 = input()
print('Enter the name of cat 5:')
catName5 = input()
```

```
print('Enter the name of cat 6:')
catName6 = input()
print('The cat names are:')
print(catName1 + ' ' + catName2 + ' ' + catName3 + ' ' + catName4 + ' ' +
catName5 + ' ' + catName6)
```

Instead of using multiple, repetitive variables, you can use a single variable that contains a list value. For example, here's a new and improved version of the *allMyCats1.py* program. This new version uses a single list and can store any number of cats that the user types in. In a new file editor window, type the following source code and save it as *allMyCats2.py*:

```
catNames = []
while True:
    print('Enter the name of cat ' + str(len(catNames) + 1) +
        ' (Or enter nothing to stop.):')
    name = input()
    if name == '':
        break
    catNames = catNames + [name]  # list concatenation
print('The cat names are:')
for name in catNames:
    print('  ' + name)
```

When you run this program, the output will look something like this:

```
Enter the name of cat 1 (Or enter nothing to stop.):
Zophie
Enter the name of cat 2 (Or enter nothing to stop.):
Pooka
Enter the name of cat 3 (Or enter nothing to stop.):
Simon
Enter the name of cat 4 (Or enter nothing to stop.):
Lady Macbeth
Enter the name of cat 5 (Or enter nothing to stop.):
Fat-tail
Enter the name of cat 6 (Or enter nothing to stop.):
Miss Cleo
Enter the name of cat 7 (Or enter nothing to stop.):

The cat names are:
  Zophie
  Pooka
  Simon
  Lady Macbeth
  Fat-tail
  Miss Cleo
```

The benefit of using a list is that your data is now in a structure, so your program is much more flexible in processing the data than it would be with several repetitive variables.

Using for Loops with Lists

In Chapter 2, you learned about using for loops to execute a block of code a certain number of times. Technically, a for loop repeats the code block once for each value in a list or list-like value. For example, if you ran this code:

```
for i in range(4):
    print(i)
```

the output of this program would be as follows:

```
0
1
2
3
```

This is because the return value from range(4) is a list-like value that Python considers similar to [0, 1, 2, 3]. The following program has the same output as the previous one:

```
for i in [0, 1, 2, 3]:
    print(i)
```

What the previous for loop actually does is loop through its clause with the variable i set to a successive value in the [0, 1, 2, 3] list in each iteration.

NOTE   *In this book, I use the term* list-like *to refer to data types that are technically named* sequences. *You don't need to know the technical definitions of this term, though.*

A common Python technique is to use range(len(someList)) with a for loop to iterate over the indexes of a list. For example, enter the following into the interactive shell:

```
>>> supplies = ['pens', 'staplers', 'flame-throwers', 'binders']
>>> for i in range(len(supplies)):
    print('Index ' + str(i) + ' in supplies is: ' + supplies[i])

Index 0 in supplies is: pens
Index 1 in supplies is: staplers
Index 2 in supplies is: flame-throwers
Index 3 in supplies is: binders
```

Using range(len(supplies)) in the previously shown for loop is handy because the code in the loop can access the index (as the variable i) and the value at that index (as supplies[i]). Best of all, range(len(supplies)) will iterate through all the indexes of supplies, no matter how many items it contains.

The in and not in Operators

You can determine whether a value is or isn't in a list with the in and not in operators. Like other operators, in and not in are used in expressions and connect two values: a value to look for in a list and the list where it may be found. These expressions will evaluate to a Boolean value. Enter the following into the interactive shell:

```
>>> 'howdy' in ['hello', 'hi', 'howdy', 'heyas']
True
>>> spam = ['hello', 'hi', 'howdy', 'heyas']
>>> 'cat' in spam
False
>>> 'howdy' not in spam
False
>>> 'cat' not in spam
True
```

For example, the following program lets the user type in a pet name and then checks to see whether the name is in a list of pets. Open a new file editor window, enter the following code, and save it as *myPets.py*:

```
myPets = ['Zophie', 'Pooka', 'Fat-tail']
print('Enter a pet name:')
name = input()
if name not in myPets:
    print('I do not have a pet named ' + name)
else:
    print(name + ' is my pet.')
```

The output may look something like this:

```
Enter a pet name:
Footfoot
I do not have a pet named Footfoot
```

The Multiple Assignment Trick

The *multiple assignment trick* is a shortcut that lets you assign multiple variables with the values in a list in one line of code. So instead of doing this:

```
>>> cat = ['fat', 'black', 'loud']
>>> size = cat[0]
>>> color = cat[1]
>>> disposition = cat[2]
```

you could type this line of code:

```
>>> cat = ['fat', 'black', 'loud']
>>> size, color, disposition = cat
```

The number of variables and the length of the list must be exactly equal, or Python will give you a ValueError:

```
>>> cat = ['fat', 'black', 'loud']
>>> size, color, disposition, name = cat
Traceback (most recent call last):
  File "<pyshell#84>", line 1, in <module>
    size, color, disposition, name = cat
ValueError: need more than 3 values to unpack
```

Augmented Assignment Operators

When assigning a value to a variable, you will frequently use the variable itself. For example, after assigning 42 to the variable spam, you would increase the value in spam by 1 with the following code:

```
>>> spam = 42
>>> spam = spam + 1
>>> spam
43
```

As a shortcut, you can use the augmented assignment operator += to do the same thing:

```
>>> spam = 42
>>> spam += 1
>>> spam
43
```

There are augmented assignment operators for the +, -, *, /, and % operators, described in Table 4-1.

Table 4-1: The Augmented Assignment Operators

Augmented assignment statement	Equivalent assignment statement
spam += 1	spam = spam + 1
spam -= 1	spam = spam - 1
spam *= 1	spam = spam * 1
spam /= 1	spam = spam / 1
spam %= 1	spam = spam % 1

The += operator can also do string and list concatenation, and the *= operator can do string and list replication. Enter the following into the interactive shell:

```
>>> spam = 'Hello'
>>> spam += ' world!'
>>> spam
'Hello world!'
```

```
>>> bacon = ['Zophie']
>>> bacon *= 3
>>> bacon
['Zophie', 'Zophie', 'Zophie']
```

Methods

A *method* is the same thing as a function, except it is "called on" a value. For example, if a list value were stored in spam, you would call the index() list method (which I'll explain next) on that list like so: spam.index('hello'). The method part comes after the value, separated by a period.

Each data type has its own set of methods. The list data type, for example, has several useful methods for finding, adding, removing, and otherwise manipulating values in a list.

Finding a Value in a List with the index() Method

List values have an index() method that can be passed a value, and if that value exists in the list, the index of the value is returned. If the value isn't in the list, then Python produces a ValueError error. Enter the following into the interactive shell:

```
>>> spam = ['hello', 'hi', 'howdy', 'heyas']
>>> spam.index('hello')
0
>>> spam.index('heyas')
3
>>> spam.index('howdy howdy howdy')
Traceback (most recent call last):
  File "<pyshell#31>", line 1, in <module>
    spam.index('howdy howdy howdy')
ValueError: 'howdy howdy howdy' is not in list
```

When there are duplicates of the value in the list, the index of its first appearance is returned. Enter the following into the interactive shell, and notice that index() returns 1, not 3:

```
>>> spam = ['Zophie', 'Pooka', 'Fat-tail', 'Pooka']
>>> spam.index('Pooka')
1
```

Adding Values to Lists with the append() and insert() Methods

To add new values to a list, use the append() and insert() methods. Enter the following into the interactive shell to call the append() method on a list value stored in the variable spam:

```
>>> spam = ['cat', 'dog', 'bat']
>>> spam.append('moose')
```

```
>>> spam
['cat', 'dog', 'bat', 'moose']
```

The previous append() method call adds the argument to the end of the list. The insert() method can insert a value at any index in the list. The first argument to insert() is the index for the new value, and the second argument is the new value to be inserted. Enter the following into the interactive shell:

```
>>> spam = ['cat', 'dog', 'bat']
>>> spam.insert(1, 'chicken')
>>> spam
['cat', 'chicken', 'dog', 'bat']
```

Notice that the code is spam.append('moose') and spam.insert(1, 'chicken'), not spam = spam.append('moose') and spam = spam.insert(1, 'chicken'). Neither append() nor insert() gives the new value of spam as its return value. (In fact, the return value of append() and insert() is None, so you definitely wouldn't want to store this as the new variable value.) Rather, the list is modified *in place*. Modifying a list in place is covered in more detail later in "Mutable and Immutable Data Types" on page 94.

Methods belong to a single data type. The append() and insert() methods are list methods and can be called only on list values, not on other values such as strings or integers. Enter the following into the interactive shell, and note the AttributeError error messages that show up:

```
>>> eggs = 'hello'
>>> eggs.append('world')
Traceback (most recent call last):
  File "<pyshell#19>", line 1, in <module>
    eggs.append('world')
AttributeError: 'str' object has no attribute 'append'
>>> bacon = 42
>>> bacon.insert(1, 'world')
Traceback (most recent call last):
  File "<pyshell#22>", line 1, in <module>
    bacon.insert(1, 'world')
AttributeError: 'int' object has no attribute 'insert'
```

Removing Values from Lists with remove()

The remove() method is passed the value to be removed from the list it is called on. Enter the following into the interactive shell:

```
>>> spam = ['cat', 'bat', 'rat', 'elephant']
>>> spam.remove('bat')
>>> spam
['cat', 'rat', 'elephant']
```

Attempting to delete a value that does not exist in the list will result in a `ValueError` error. For example, enter the following into the interactive shell and notice the error that is displayed:

```
>>> spam = ['cat', 'bat', 'rat', 'elephant']
>>> spam.remove('chicken')
Traceback (most recent call last):
  File "<pyshell#11>", line 1, in <module>
    spam.remove('chicken')
ValueError: list.remove(x): x not in list
```

If the value appears multiple times in the list, only the first instance of the value will be removed. Enter the following into the interactive shell:

```
>>> spam = ['cat', 'bat', 'rat', 'cat', 'hat', 'cat']
>>> spam.remove('cat')
>>> spam
['bat', 'rat', 'cat', 'hat', 'cat']
```

The `del` statement is good to use when you know the index of the value you want to remove from the list. The `remove()` method is good when you know the value you want to remove from the list.

Sorting the Values in a List with the sort() Method

Lists of number values or lists of strings can be sorted with the `sort()` method. For example, enter the following into the interactive shell:

```
>>> spam = [2, 5, 3.14, 1, -7]
>>> spam.sort()
>>> spam
[-7, 1, 2, 3.14, 5]
>>> spam = ['ants', 'cats', 'dogs', 'badgers', 'elephants']
>>> spam.sort()
>>> spam
['ants', 'badgers', 'cats', 'dogs', 'elephants']
```

You can also pass `True` for the reverse keyword argument to have `sort()` sort the values in reverse order. Enter the following into the interactive shell:

```
>>> spam.sort(reverse=True)
>>> spam
['elephants', 'dogs', 'cats', 'badgers', 'ants']
```

There are three things you should note about the `sort()` method. First, the `sort()` method sorts the list in place; don't try to capture the return value by writing code like `spam = spam.sort()`.

Second, you cannot sort lists that have both number values *and* string values in them, since Python doesn't know how to compare these values. Type the following into the interactive shell and notice the TypeError error:

```
>>> spam = [1, 3, 2, 4, 'Alice', 'Bob']
>>> spam.sort()
Traceback (most recent call last):
  File "<pyshell#70>", line 1, in <module>
    spam.sort()
TypeError: unorderable types: str() < int()
```

Third, sort() uses "ASCIIbetical order" rather than actual alphabetical order for sorting strings. This means uppercase letters come before lowercase letters. Therefore, the lowercase *a* is sorted so that it comes *after* the uppercase *Z*. For an example, enter the following into the interactive shell:

```
>>> spam = ['Alice', 'ants', 'Bob', 'badgers', 'Carol', 'cats']
>>> spam.sort()
>>> spam
['Alice', 'Bob', 'Carol', 'ants', 'badgers', 'cats']
```

If you need to sort the values in regular alphabetical order, pass str.lower for the key keyword argument in the sort() method call.

```
>>> spam = ['a', 'z', 'A', 'Z']
>>> spam.sort(key=str.lower)
>>> spam
['a', 'A', 'z', 'Z']
```

This causes the sort() method to treat all the items in the list as if they were lowercase without actually changing the values in the list.

Example Program: Magic 8 Ball with a List

Using lists, you can write a much more elegant version of the previous chapter's Magic 8 Ball program. Instead of several lines of nearly identical elif statements, you can create a single list that the code works with. Open a new file editor window and enter the following code. Save it as *magic8Ball2.py*.

```
import random

messages = ['It is certain',
    'It is decidedly so',
    'Yes definitely',
    'Reply hazy try again',
    'Ask again later',
    'Concentrate and ask again',
    'My reply is no',
    'Outlook not so good',
    'Very doubtful']

print(messages[random.randint(0, len(messages) - 1)])
```

When you run this program, you'll see that it works the same as the previous *magic8Ball.py* program.

Notice the expression you use as the index into messages: random .randint(0, len(messages) - 1). This produces a random number to use for the index, regardless of the size of messages. That is, you'll get a random number between 0 and the value of len(messages) - 1. The benefit of this approach is that you can easily add and remove strings to the messages list without changing other lines of code. If you later update your code, there will be fewer lines you have to change and fewer chances for you to introduce bugs.

List-like Types: Strings and Tuples

Lists aren't the only data types that represent ordered sequences of values. For example, strings and lists are actually similar, if you consider a string to be a "list" of single text characters. Many of the things you can do with lists can also be done with strings: indexing; slicing; and using them with for loops, with len(), and with the in and not in operators. To see this, enter the following into the interactive shell:

```
>>> name = 'Zophie'
>>> name[0]
'Z'
>>> name[-2]
'i'
>>> name[0:4]
'Zoph'
>>> 'Zo' in name
True
>>> 'z' in name
False
>>> 'p' not in name
False
>>> for i in name:
        print('* * * ' + i + ' * * *')


* * * Z * * *
* * * o * * *
* * * p * * *
* * * h * * *
* * * i * * *
* * * e * * *
```

Mutable and Immutable Data Types

But lists and strings are different in an important way. A list value is a *mutable* data type: It can have values added, removed, or changed. However, a string is *immutable*: It cannot be changed. Trying to reassign a single character in a string results in a TypeError error, as you can see by entering the following into the interactive shell:

```
>>> name = 'Zophie a cat'
>>> name[7] = 'the'
Traceback (most recent call last):
  File "<pyshell#50>", line 1, in <module>
    name[7] = 'the'
TypeError: 'str' object does not support item assignment
```

The proper way to "mutate" a string is to use slicing and concatenation to build a *new* string by copying from parts of the old string. Enter the following into the interactive shell:

```
>>> name = 'Zophie a cat'
>>> newName = name[0:7] + 'the' + name[8:12]
>>> name
'Zophie a cat'
```

```
>>> newName
'Zophie the cat'
```

We used [0:7] and [8:12] to refer to the characters that we don't wish to replace. Notice that the original 'Zophie a cat' string is not modified because strings are immutable.

Although a list value *is* mutable, the second line in the following code does not modify the list eggs:

```
>>> eggs = [1, 2, 3]
>>> eggs = [4, 5, 6]
>>> eggs
[4, 5, 6]
```

The list value in eggs isn't being changed here; rather, an entirely new and different list value ([4, 5, 6]) is overwriting the old list value ([1, 2, 3]). This is depicted in Figure 4-2.

If you wanted to actually modify the original list in eggs to contain [4, 5, 6], you would have to do something like this:

```
>>> eggs = [1, 2, 3]
>>> del eggs[2]
>>> del eggs[1]
>>> del eggs[0]
>>> eggs.append(4)
>>> eggs.append(5)
>>> eggs.append(6)
>>> eggs
[4, 5, 6]
```

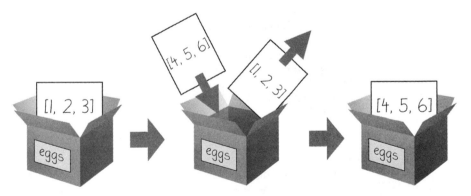

Figure 4-2: When eggs = [4, 5, 6] is executed, the contents of eggs are replaced with a new list value.

In the first example, the list value that eggs ends up with is the same list value it started with. It's just that this list has been changed, rather than overwritten. Figure 4-3 depicts the seven changes made by the first seven lines in the previous interactive shell example.

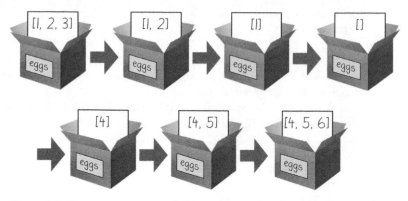

Figure 4-3: The del statement and the append() method modify the same list value in place.

Changing a value of a mutable data type (like what the del statement and append() method do in the previous example) changes the value in place, since the variable's value is not replaced with a new list value.

Mutable versus immutable types may seem like a meaningless distinction, but "Passing References" on page 100 will explain the different behavior when calling functions with mutable arguments versus immutable arguments. But first, let's find out about the tuple data type, which is an immutable form of the list data type.

The Tuple Data Type

The *tuple* data type is almost identical to the list data type, except in two ways. First, tuples are typed with parentheses, (and), instead of square brackets, [and]. For example, enter the following into the interactive shell:

```
>>> eggs = ('hello', 42, 0.5)
>>> eggs[0]
'hello'
>>> eggs[1:3]
(42, 0.5)
>>> len(eggs)
3
```

But the main way that tuples are different from lists is that tuples, like strings, are immutable. Tuples cannot have their values modified, appended, or removed. Enter the following into the interactive shell, and look at the TypeError error message:

```
>>> eggs = ('hello', 42, 0.5)
>>> eggs[1] = 99
Traceback (most recent call last):
  File "<pyshell#5>", line 1, in <module>
    eggs[1] = 99
TypeError: 'tuple' object does not support item assignment
```

If you have only one value in your tuple, you can indicate this by placing a trailing comma after the value inside the parentheses. Otherwise, Python will think you've just typed a value inside regular parentheses. The comma is what lets Python know this is a tuple value. (Unlike some other programming languages, in Python it's fine to have a trailing comma after the last item in a list or tuple.) Enter the following type() function calls into the interactive shell to see the distinction:

```
>>> type(('hello',))
<class 'tuple'>
>>> type(('hello'))
<class 'str'>
```

You can use tuples to convey to anyone reading your code that you don't intend for that sequence of values to change. If you need an ordered sequence of values that never changes, use a tuple. A second benefit of using tuples instead of lists is that, because they are immutable and their contents don't change, Python can implement some optimizations that make code using tuples slightly faster than code using lists.

Converting Types with the list() and tuple() Functions

Just like how str(42) will return '42', the string representation of the integer 42, the functions list() and tuple() will return list and tuple versions of the values passed to them. Enter the following into the interactive shell, and notice that the return value is of a different data type than the value passed:

```
>>> tuple(['cat', 'dog', 5])
('cat', 'dog', 5)
>>> list(('cat', 'dog', 5))
['cat', 'dog', 5]
>>> list('hello')
['h', 'e', 'l', 'l', 'o']
```

Converting a tuple to a list is handy if you need a mutable version of a tuple value.

References

As you've seen, variables store strings and integer values. Enter the following into the interactive shell:

```
>>> spam = 42
>>> cheese = spam
>>> spam = 100
>>> spam
100
>>> cheese
42
```

You assign 42 to the spam variable, and then you copy the value in spam and assign it to the variable cheese. When you later change the value in spam to 100, this doesn't affect the value in cheese. This is because spam and cheese are different variables that store different values.

But lists don't work this way. When you assign a list to a variable, you are actually assigning a list *reference* to the variable. A reference is a value that points to some bit of data, and a list reference is a value that points to a list. Here is some code that will make this distinction easier to understand. Enter this into the interactive shell:

```
❶ >>> spam = [0, 1, 2, 3, 4, 5]
❷ >>> cheese = spam
❸ >>> cheese[1] = 'Hello!'
   >>> spam
   [0, 'Hello!', 2, 3, 4, 5]
   >>> cheese
   [0, 'Hello!', 2, 3, 4, 5]
```

This might look odd to you. The code changed only the cheese list, but it seems that both the cheese and spam lists have changed.

When you create the list ❶, you assign a reference to it in the spam variable. But the next line ❷ copies only the list reference in spam to cheese, not the list value itself. This means the values stored in spam and cheese now both refer to the same list. There is only one underlying list because the list itself was never actually copied. So when you modify the first element of cheese ❸, you are modifying the same list that spam refers to.

Remember that variables are like boxes that contain values. The previous figures in this chapter show that lists in boxes aren't exactly accurate because list variables don't actually contain lists—they contain *references* to lists. (These references will have ID numbers that Python uses internally, but you can ignore them.) Using boxes as a metaphor for variables, Figure 4-4 shows what happens when a list is assigned to the spam variable.

Figure 4-4: spam = [0, 1, 2, 3, 4, 5] stores a reference to a list, not the actual list.

Then, in Figure 4-5, the reference in spam is copied to cheese. Only a new reference was created and stored in cheese, not a new list. Note how both references refer to the same list.

Figure 4-5: spam = cheese copies the reference, not the list.

When you alter the list that cheese refers to, the list that spam refers to is also changed, because both cheese and spam refer to the same list. You can see this in Figure 4-6.

Figure 4-6: cheese[1] = 'Hello!' modifies the list that both variables refer to.

Variables will contain references to list values rather than list values themselves. But for strings and integer values, variables simply contain the string or integer value. Python uses references whenever variables must store values of mutable data types, such as lists or dictionaries. For values of immutable data types such as strings, integers, or tuples, Python variables will store the value itself.

Although Python variables technically contain references to list or dictionary values, people often casually say that the variable contains the list or dictionary.

Passing References

References are particularly important for understanding how arguments get passed to functions. When a function is called, the values of the arguments are copied to the parameter variables. For lists (and dictionaries, which I'll describe in the next chapter), this means a copy of the reference is used for the parameter. To see the consequences of this, open a new file editor window, enter the following code, and save it as *passingReference.py*:

```
def eggs(someParameter):
    someParameter.append('Hello')

spam = [1, 2, 3]
eggs(spam)
print(spam)
```

Notice that when eggs() is called, a return value is not used to assign a new value to spam. Instead, it modifies the list in place, directly. When run, this program produces the following output:

```
[1, 2, 3, 'Hello']
```

Even though spam and someParameter contain separate references, they both refer to the same list. This is why the append('Hello') method call inside the function affects the list even after the function call has returned.

Keep this behavior in mind: Forgetting that Python handles list and dictionary variables this way can lead to confusing bugs.

The copy Module's copy() and deepcopy() Functions

Although passing around references is often the handiest way to deal with lists and dictionaries, if the function modifies the list or dictionary that is passed, you may not want these changes in the original list or dictionary value. For this, Python provides a module named copy that provides both the copy() and deepcopy() functions. The first of these, copy.copy(), can be used to make a duplicate copy of a mutable value like a list or dictionary, not just a copy of a reference. Enter the following into the interactive shell:

```
>>> import copy
>>> spam = ['A', 'B', 'C', 'D']
>>> cheese = copy.copy(spam)
>>> cheese[1] = 42
>>> spam
['A', 'B', 'C', 'D']
>>> cheese
['A', 42, 'C', 'D']
```

Now the spam and cheese variables refer to separate lists, which is why only the list in cheese is modified when you assign 42 at index 1. As you can see in Figure 4-7, the reference ID numbers are no longer the same for both variables because the variables refer to independent lists.

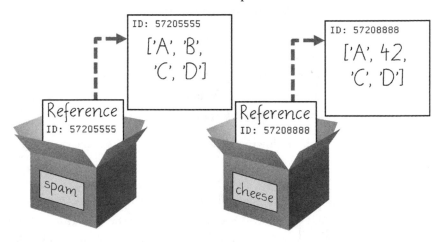

Figure 4-7: cheese = copy.copy(spam) creates a second list that can be modified independently of the first.

If the list you need to copy contains lists, then use the copy.deepcopy() function instead of copy.copy(). The deepcopy() function will copy these inner lists as well.

Summary

Lists are useful data types since they allow you to write code that works on a modifiable number of values in a single variable. Later in this book, you will see programs using lists to do things that would be difficult or impossible to do without them.

Lists are mutable, meaning that their contents can change. Tuples and strings, although list-like in some respects, are immutable and cannot be changed. A variable that contains a tuple or string value can be overwritten with a new tuple or string value, but this is not the same thing as modifying the existing value in place—like, say, the append() or remove() methods do on lists.

Variables do not store list values directly; they store *references* to lists. This is an important distinction when copying variables or passing lists as arguments in function calls. Because the value that is being copied is the list reference, be aware that any changes you make to the list might impact another variable in your program. You can use copy() or deepcopy() if you want to make changes to a list in one variable without modifying the original list.

Practice Questions

1. What is []?

2. How would you assign the value 'hello' as the third value in a list stored in a variable named spam? (Assume spam contains [2, 4, 6, 8, 10].)

For the following three questions, let's say spam contains the list ['a', 'b', 'c', 'd'].

3. What does spam[int(int('3' * 2) // 11)] evaluate to?

4. What does spam[-1] evaluate to?

5. What does spam[:2] evaluate to?

For the following three questions, let's say bacon contains the list [3.14, 'cat', 11, 'cat', True].

6. What does bacon.index('cat') evaluate to?

7. What does bacon.append(99) make the list value in bacon look like?

8. What does bacon.remove('cat') make the list value in bacon look like?

9. What are the operators for list concatenation and list replication?

10. What is the difference between the append() and insert() list methods?

11. What are two ways to remove values from a list?

12. Name a few ways that list values are similar to string values.

13. What is the difference between lists and tuples?

14. How do you type the tuple value that has just the integer value 42 in it?

15. How can you get the tuple form of a list value? How can you get the list form of a tuple value?

16. Variables that "contain" list values don't actually contain lists directly. What do they contain instead?

17. What is the difference between copy.copy() and copy.deepcopy()?

Practice Projects

For practice, write programs to do the following tasks.

Comma Code

Say you have a list value like this:

```
spam = ['apples', 'bananas', 'tofu', 'cats']
```

Write a function that takes a list value as an argument and returns a string with all the items separated by a comma and a space, with *and* inserted before the last item. For example, passing the previous spam list to the function would return 'apples, bananas, tofu, and cats'. But your function should be able to work with any list value passed to it.

Character Picture Grid

Say you have a list of lists where each value in the inner lists is a one-character string, like this:

```
grid = [['.', '.', '.', '.', '.', '.'],
        ['.', '0', '0', '.', '.', '.'],
        ['0', '0', '0', '0', '.', '.'],
        ['0', '0', '0', '0', '0', '.'],
        ['.', '0', '0', '0', '0', '0'],
        ['0', '0', '0', '0', '0', '.'],
        ['0', '0', '0', '0', '.', '.'],
        ['.', '0', '0', '.', '.', '.'],
        ['.', '.', '.', '.', '.', '.']]
```

You can think of grid[x][y] as being the character at the x- and y-coordinates of a "picture" drawn with text characters. The (0, 0) origin will be in the upper-left corner, the x-coordinates increase going right, and the y-coordinates increase going down.

Copy the previous grid value, and write code that uses it to print the image.

```
..00.00..
.0000000.
.0000000.
..00000..
...000...
....0....
```

Hint: You will need to use a loop in a loop in order to print grid[0][0], then grid[1][0], then grid[2][0], and so on, up to grid[8][0]. This will finish the first row, so then print a newline. Then your program should print grid[0][1], then grid[1][1], then grid[2][1], and so on. The last thing your program will print is grid[8][5].

Also, remember to pass the end keyword argument to print() if you don't want a newline printed automatically after each print() call.

5

DICTIONARIES AND STRUCTURING DATA

In this chapter, I will cover the dictionary data type, which provides a flexible way to access and organize data. Then, combining dictionaries with your knowledge of lists from the previous chapter, you'll learn how to create a data structure to model a tic-tac-toe board.

The Dictionary Data Type

Like a list, a *dictionary* is a collection of many values. But unlike indexes for lists, indexes for dictionaries can use many different data types, not just integers. Indexes for dictionaries are called *keys*, and a key with its associated value is called a *key-value pair*.

In code, a dictionary is typed with braces, {}. Enter the following into the interactive shell:

```
>>> myCat = {'size': 'fat', 'color': 'gray', 'disposition': 'loud'}
```

This assigns a dictionary to the myCat variable. This dictionary's keys are 'size', 'color', and 'disposition'. The values for these keys are 'fat', 'gray', and 'loud', respectively. You can access these values through their keys:

```
>>> myCat['size']
'fat'
>>> 'My cat has ' + myCat['color'] + ' fur.'
'My cat has gray fur.'
```

Dictionaries can still use integer values as keys, just like lists use integers for indexes, but they do not have to start at 0 and can be any number.

```
>>> spam = {12345: 'Luggage Combination', 42: 'The Answer'}
```

Dictionaries vs. Lists

Unlike lists, items in dictionaries are unordered. The first item in a list named spam would be spam[0]. But there is no "first" item in a dictionary. While the order of items matters for determining whether two lists are the same, it does not matter in what order the key-value pairs are typed in a dictionary. Enter the following into the interactive shell:

```
>>> spam = ['cats', 'dogs', 'moose']
>>> bacon = ['dogs', 'moose', 'cats']
>>> spam == bacon
False
>>> eggs = {'name': 'Zophie', 'species': 'cat', 'age': '8'}
>>> ham = {'species': 'cat', 'age': '8', 'name': 'Zophie'}
>>> eggs == ham
True
```

Because dictionaries are not ordered, they can't be sliced like lists.

Trying to access a key that does not exist in a dictionary will result in a KeyError error message, much like a list's "out-of-range" IndexError error message. Enter the following into the interactive shell, and notice the error message that shows up because there is no 'color' key:

```
>>> spam = {'name': 'Zophie', 'age': 7}
>>> spam['color']
Traceback (most recent call last):
  File "<pyshell#1>", line 1, in <module>
    spam['color']
KeyError: 'color'
```

Though dictionaries are not ordered, the fact that you can have arbitrary values for the keys allows you to organize your data in powerful ways. Say you wanted your program to store data about your friends' birthdays. You can use a dictionary with the names as keys and the birthdays as values. Open a new file editor window and enter the following code. Save it as *birthdays.py*.

```
❶ birthdays = {'Alice': 'Apr 1', 'Bob': 'Dec 12', 'Carol': 'Mar 4'}

  while True:
      print('Enter a name: (blank to quit)')
      name = input()
      if name == '':
          break

❷     if name in birthdays:
❸         print(birthdays[name] + ' is the birthday of ' + name)
      else:
          print('I do not have birthday information for ' + name)
          print('What is their birthday?')
          bday = input()
❹         birthdays[name] = bday
          print('Birthday database updated.')
```

You create an initial dictionary and store it in birthdays ❶. You can see if the entered name exists as a key in the dictionary with the in keyword ❷, just as you did for lists. If the name is in the dictionary, you access the associated value using square brackets ❸; if not, you can add it using the same square bracket syntax combined with the assignment operator ❹.

When you run this program, it will look like this:

```
Enter a name: (blank to quit)
Alice
Apr 1 is the birthday of Alice
Enter a name: (blank to quit)
Eve
I do not have birthday information for Eve
What is their birthday?
Dec 5
Birthday database updated.
Enter a name: (blank to quit)
Eve
Dec 5 is the birthday of Eve
Enter a name: (blank to quit)
```

Of course, all the data you enter in this program is forgotten when the program terminates. You'll learn how to save data to files on the hard drive in Chapter 8.

The keys(), values(), and items() Methods

There are three dictionary methods that will return list-like values of the dictionary's keys, values, or both keys and values: keys(), values(), and items(). The values returned by these methods are not true lists: They cannot be modified and do not have an append() method. But these data types (dict_keys, dict_values, and `dict_items`, respectively) *can* be used in for loops. To see how these methods work, enter the following into the interactive shell:

```
>>> spam = {'color': 'red', 'age': 42}
>>> for v in spam.values():
        print(v)

red
42
```

Here, a for loop iterates over each of the values in the spam dictionary. A for loop can also iterate over the keys or both keys and values:

```
>>> for k in spam.keys():
        print(k)

color
age
>>> for i in spam.items():
        print(i)

('color', 'red')
('age', 42)
```

Using the keys(), values(), and items() methods, a for loop can iterate over the keys, values, or key-value pairs in a dictionary, respectively. Notice that the values in the dict_items value returned by the items() method are tuples of the key and value.

If you want a true list from one of these methods, pass its list-like return value to the list() function. Enter the following into the interactive shell:

```
>>> spam = {'color': 'red', 'age': 42}
>>> spam.keys()
dict_keys(['color', 'age'])
>>> list(spam.keys())
['color', 'age']
```

The list(spam.keys()) line takes the dict_keys value returned from keys() and passes it to list(), which then returns a list value of ['color', 'age'].

You can also use the multiple assignment trick in a for loop to assign the key and value to separate variables. Enter the following into the interactive shell:

```
>>> spam = {'color': 'red', 'age': 42}
>>> for k, v in spam.items():
        print('Key: ' + k + ' Value: ' + str(v))

Key: age Value: 42
Key: color Value: red
```

Checking Whether a Key or Value Exists in a Dictionary

Recall from the previous chapter that the in and not in operators can check whether a value exists in a list. You can also use these operators to see whether a certain key or value exists in a dictionary. Enter the following into the interactive shell:

```
>>> spam = {'name': 'Zophie', 'age': 7}
>>> 'name' in spam.keys()
True
>>> 'Zophie' in spam.values()
True
>>> 'color' in spam.keys()
False
>>> 'color' not in spam.keys()
True
>>> 'color' in spam
False
```

In the previous example, notice that 'color' in spam is essentially a shorter version of writing 'color' in spam.keys(). This is always the case: If you ever want to check whether a value is (or isn't) a key in the dictionary, you can simply use the in (or not in) keyword with the dictionary value itself.

The get() Method

It's tedious to check whether a key exists in a dictionary before accessing that key's value. Fortunately, dictionaries have a get() method that takes two arguments: the key of the value to retrieve and a fallback value to return if that key does not exist.

Enter the following into the interactive shell:

```
>>> picnicItems = {'apples': 5, 'cups': 2}
>>> 'I am bringing ' + str(picnicItems.get('cups', 0)) + ' cups.'
'I am bringing 2 cups.'
>>> 'I am bringing ' + str(picnicItems.get('eggs', 0)) + ' eggs.'
'I am bringing 0 eggs.'
```

Because there is no 'eggs' key in the picnicItems dictionary, the default value 0 is returned by the get() method. Without using get(), the code would have caused an error message, such as in the following example:

```
>>> picnicItems = {'apples': 5, 'cups': 2}
>>> 'I am bringing ' + str(picnicItems['eggs']) + ' eggs.'
Traceback (most recent call last):
  File "<pyshell#34>", line 1, in <module>
    'I am bringing ' + str(picnicItems['eggs']) + ' eggs.'
KeyError: 'eggs'
```

The setdefault() Method

You'll often have to set a value in a dictionary for a certain key only if that key does not already have a value. The code looks something like this:

```
spam = {'name': 'Pooka', 'age': 5}
if 'color' not in spam:
    spam['color'] = 'black'
```

The setdefault() method offers a way to do this in one line of code. The first argument passed to the method is the key to check for, and the second argument is the value to set at that key if the key does not exist. If the key does exist, the setdefault() method returns the key's value. Enter the following into the interactive shell:

```
>>> spam = {'name': 'Pooka', 'age': 5}
>>> spam.setdefault('color', 'black')
'black'
>>> spam
{'color': 'black', 'age': 5, 'name': 'Pooka'}
>>> spam.setdefault('color', 'white')
'black'
>>> spam
{'color': 'black', 'age': 5, 'name': 'Pooka'}
```

The first time setdefault() is called, the dictionary in spam changes to {'color': 'black', 'age': 5, 'name': 'Pooka'}. The method returns the value 'black' because this is now the value set for the key 'color'. When spam.setdefault('color', 'white') is called next, the value for that key is *not* changed to 'white' because spam already has a key named 'color'.

The setdefault() method is a nice shortcut to ensure that a key exists. Here is a short program that counts the number of occurrences of each letter in a string. Open the file editor window and enter the following code, saving it as *characterCount.py*:

```
message = 'It was a bright cold day in April, and the clocks were striking thirteen.'
count = {}

for character in message:
    count.setdefault(character, 0)
    count[character] = count[character] + 1

print(count)
```

The program loops over each character in the message variable's string, counting how often each character appears. The setdefault() method call ensures that the key is in the count dictionary (with a default value of 0)

so the program doesn't throw a KeyError error when count[character] =
count[character] + 1 is executed. When you run this program, the output
will look like this:

```
{' ': 13, ',': 1, '.': 1, 'A': 1, 'I': 1, 'a': 4, 'c': 3, 'b': 1, 'e': 5, 'd': 3, 'g': 2, 'i':
6, 'h': 3, 'k': 2, 'l': 3, 'o': 2, 'n': 4, 'p': 1, 's': 3, 'r': 5, 't': 6, 'w': 2, 'y': 1}
```

From the output, you can see that the lowercase letter *c* appears 3 times,
the space character appears 13 times, and the uppercase letter *A* appears
1 time. This program will work no matter what string is inside the message
variable, even if the string is millions of characters long!

Pretty Printing

If you import the pprint module into your programs, you'll have access to
the pprint() and pformat() functions that will "pretty print" a dictionary's
values. This is helpful when you want a cleaner display of the items in a
dictionary than what print() provides. Modify the previous *characterCount.py*
program and save it as *prettyCharacterCount.py*.

```
import pprint
message = 'It was a bright cold day in April, and the clocks were striking
thirteen.'
count = {}

for character in message:
    count.setdefault(character, 0)
    count[character] = count[character] + 1

pprint.pprint(count)
```

This time, when the program is run, the output looks much cleaner,
with the keys sorted.

```
{' ': 13,
 ',': 1,
 '.': 1,
 'A': 1,
 'I': 1,
 'a': 4,
 'b': 1,
 'c': 3,
 'd': 3,
 'e': 5,
 'g': 2,
 'h': 3,
 'i': 6,
```

```
    'k': 2,
    'l': 3,
    'n': 4,
    'o': 2,
    'p': 1,
    'r': 5,
    's': 3,
    't': 6,
    'w': 2,
    'y': 1}
```

The pprint.pprint() function is especially helpful when the dictionary itself contains nested lists or dictionaries.

If you want to obtain the prettified text as a string value instead of displaying it on the screen, call pprint.pformat() instead. These two lines are equivalent to each other:

```
pprint.pprint(someDictionaryValue)
print(pprint.pformat(someDictionaryValue))
```

Using Data Structures to Model Real-World Things

Even before the Internet, it was possible to play a game of chess with someone on the other side of the world. Each player would set up a chessboard at their home and then take turns mailing a postcard to each other describing each move. To do this, the players needed a way to unambiguously describe the state of the board and their moves.

In *algebraic chess notation*, the spaces on the chessboard are identified by a number and letter coordinate, as in Figure 5-1.

Figure 5-1: The coordinates of a chessboard in algebraic chess notation

The chess pieces are identified by letters: *K* for king, *Q* for queen, *R* for rook, *B* for bishop, and *N* for knight. Describing a move uses the letter of the piece and the coordinates of its destination. A pair of these moves describes what happens in a single turn (with white going first); for instance, the notation *2. Nf3 Nc6* indicates that white moved a knight to f3 and black moved a knight to c6 on the second turn of the game.

There's a bit more to algebraic notation than this, but the point is that you can use it to unambiguously describe a game of chess without needing to be in front of a chessboard. Your opponent can even be on the other side of the world! In fact, you don't even need a physical chess set if you have a good memory: You can just read the mailed chess moves and update boards you have in your imagination.

Computers have good memories. A program on a modern computer can easily store billions of strings like '2. Nf3 Nc6'. This is how computers can play chess without having a physical chessboard. They model data to represent a chessboard, and you can write code to work with this model.

This is where lists and dictionaries can come in. You can use them to model real-world things, like chessboards. For the first example, you'll use a game that's a little simpler than chess: tic-tac-toe.

A Tic-Tac-Toe Board

A tic-tac-toe board looks like a large hash symbol (#) with nine slots that can each contain an *X*, an *O*, or a blank. To represent the board with a dictionary, you can assign each slot a string-value key, as shown in Figure 5-2.

You can use string values to represent what's in each slot on the board: 'X', 'O', or ' ' (a space character). Thus, you'll need to store nine strings. You can use a dictionary of values for this. The string value with the key 'top-R' can represent the top-right corner, the string value with the key 'low-L' can represent the bottom-left corner, the string value with the key 'mid-M' can represent the middle, and so on.

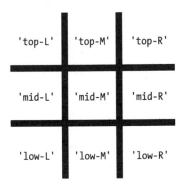

Figure 5-2: The slots of a tic-tac-toe board with their corresponding keys

This dictionary is a data structure that represents a tic-tac-toe board. Store this board-as-a-dictionary in a variable named theBoard. Open a new file editor window, and enter the following source code, saving it as *ticTacToe.py*:

```
theBoard = {'top-L': ' ', 'top-M': ' ', 'top-R': ' ',
            'mid-L': ' ', 'mid-M': ' ', 'mid-R': ' ',
            'low-L': ' ', 'low-M': ' ', 'low-R': ' '}
```

The data structure stored in the theBoard variable represents the tic-tac-toe board in Figure 5-3.

Figure 5-3: An empty tic-tac-toe board

Since the value for every key in theBoard is a single-space string, this dictionary represents a completely clear board. If player X went first and chose the middle space, you could represent that board with this dictionary:

```
theBoard = {'top-L': ' ', 'top-M': ' ', 'top-R': ' ',
            'mid-L': ' ', 'mid-M': 'X', 'mid-R': ' ',
            'low-L': ' ', 'low-M': ' ', 'low-R': ' '}
```

The data structure in theBoard now represents the tic-tac-toe board in Figure 5-4.

Figure 5-4: The first move

A board where player O has won by placing Os across the top might look like this:

```
theBoard = {'top-L': 'O', 'top-M': 'O', 'top-R': 'O',
            'mid-L': 'X', 'mid-M': 'X', 'mid-R': ' ',
            'low-L': ' ', 'low-M': ' ', 'low-R': 'X'}
```

The data structure in theBoard now represents the tic-tac-toe board in Figure 5-5.

Figure 5-5: Player O wins.

Of course, the player sees only what is printed to the screen, not the contents of variables. Let's create a function to print the board dictionary onto the screen. Make the following addition to *ticTacToe.py* (new code is in bold):

```
theBoard = {'top-L': ' ', 'top-M': ' ', 'top-R': ' ',
            'mid-L': ' ', 'mid-M': ' ', 'mid-R': ' ',
            'low-L': ' ', 'low-M': ' ', 'low-R': ' '}
def printBoard(board):
    print(board['top-L'] + '|' + board['top-M'] + '|' + board['top-R'])
    print('-+-+-')
    print(board['mid-L'] + '|' + board['mid-M'] + '|' + board['mid-R'])
    print('-+-+-')
    print(board['low-L'] + '|' + board['low-M'] + '|' + board['low-R'])
printBoard(theBoard)
```

When you run this program, `printBoard()` will print out a blank tic-tac-toe board.

```
 | |
-+-+-
 | |
-+-+-
 | |
```

The `printBoard()` function can handle any tic-tac-toe data structure you pass it. Try changing the code to the following:

```
theBoard = {'top-L': 'O', 'top-M': 'O', 'top-R': 'O', 'mid-L': 'X', 'mid-M':
'X', 'mid-R': ' ', 'low-L': ' ', 'low-M': ' ', 'low-R': 'X'}

def printBoard(board):
    print(board['top-L'] + '|' + board['top-M'] + '|' + board['top-R'])
    print('-+-+-')
    print(board['mid-L'] + '|' + board['mid-M'] + '|' + board['mid-R'])
    print('-+-+-')
    print(board['low-L'] + '|' + board['low-M'] + '|' + board['low-R'])
printBoard(theBoard)
```

Now when you run this program, the new board will be printed to the screen.

```
O|O|O
-+-+-
X|X|
-+-+-
 | |X
```

Because you created a data structure to represent a tic-tac-toe board and wrote code in printBoard() to interpret that data structure, you now have a program that "models" the tic-tac-toe board. You could have organized your data structure differently (for example, using keys like 'TOP-LEFT' instead of 'top-L'), but as long as the code works with your data structures, you will have a correctly working program.

For example, the printBoard() function expects the tic-tac-toe data structure to be a dictionary with keys for all nine slots. If the dictionary you passed was missing, say, the 'mid-L' key, your program would no longer work.

```
O|O|O
-+-+-
Traceback (most recent call last):
  File "ticTacToe.py", line 10, in <module>
    printBoard(theBoard)
  File "ticTacToe.py", line 6, in printBoard
    print(board['mid-L'] + '|' + board['mid-M'] + '|' + board['mid-R'])
KeyError: 'mid-L'
```

Now let's add code that allows the players to enter their moves. Modify the *ticTacToe.py* program to look like this:

```
theBoard = {'top-L': ' ', 'top-M': ' ', 'top-R': ' ', 'mid-L': ' ', 'mid-M': '
', 'mid-R': ' ', 'low-L': ' ', 'low-M': ' ', 'low-R': ' '}

def printBoard(board):
    print(board['top-L'] + '|' + board['top-M'] + '|' + board['top-R'])
    print('-+-+-')
    print(board['mid-L'] + '|' + board['mid-M'] + '|' + board['mid-R'])
    print('-+-+-')
    print(board['low-L'] + '|' + board['low-M'] + '|' + board['low-R'])
turn = 'X'
for i in range(9):
❶    printBoard(theBoard)
     print('Turn for ' + turn + '. Move on which space?')
❷    move = input()
❸    theBoard[move] = turn
❹    if turn == 'X':
         turn = 'O'
     else:
         turn = 'X'
printBoard(theBoard)
```

The new code prints out the board at the start of each new turn ❶, gets the active player's move ❷, updates the game board accordingly ❸, and then swaps the active player ❹ before moving on to the next turn.

When you run this program, it will look something like this:

```
 | |
-+-+-
 | |
-+-+-
 | |
Turn for X. Move on which space?
mid-M
 | |
-+-+-
 |X|
-+-+-
 | |
Turn for O. Move on which space?
low-L
 | |
-+-+-
 |X|
-+-+-
O| |

--snip--

O|O|X
-+-+-
X|X|O
-+-+-
O| |X
Turn for X. Move on which space?
low-M
O|O|X
-+-+-
X|X|O
-+-+-
O|X|X
```

This isn't a complete tic-tac-toe game—for instance, it doesn't ever check whether a player has won—but it's enough to see how data structures can be used in programs.

NOTE   *If you are curious, the source code for a complete tic-tac-toe program is described in the resources available from* http://nostarch.com/automatestuff/.

Nested Dictionaries and Lists

Modeling a tic-tac-toe board was fairly simple: The board needed only a single dictionary value with nine key-value pairs. As you model more complicated things, you may find you need dictionaries and lists that contain other dictionaries and lists. Lists are useful to contain an ordered series of values, and dictionaries are useful for associating keys with values. For example, here's a program that uses a dictionary that contains other dictionaries in order to see who is bringing what to a picnic. The totalBrought() function can read this data structure and calculate the total number of an item being brought by all the guests.

```
allGuests = {'Alice': {'apples': 5, 'pretzels': 12},
             'Bob': {'ham sandwiches': 3, 'apples': 2},
             'Carol': {'cups': 3, 'apple pies': 1}}

def totalBrought(guests, item):
    numBrought = 0
❶   for k, v in guests.items():
❷       numBrought = numBrought + v.get(item, 0)
    return numBrought

print('Number of things being brought:')
print(' - Apples         ' + str(totalBrought(allGuests, 'apples')))
print(' - Cups           ' + str(totalBrought(allGuests, 'cups')))
print(' - Cakes          ' + str(totalBrought(allGuests, 'cakes')))
print(' - Ham Sandwiches ' + str(totalBrought(allGuests, 'ham sandwiches')))
print(' - Apple Pies     ' + str(totalBrought(allGuests, 'apple pies')))
```

Inside the totalBrought() function, the for loop iterates over the key-value pairs in guests ❶. Inside the loop, the string of the guest's name is assigned to k, and the dictionary of picnic items they're bringing is assigned to v. If the item parameter exists as a key in this dictionary, it's value (the quantity) is added to numBrought ❷. If it does not exist as a key, the get() method returns 0 to be added to numBrought.

The output of this program looks like this:

```
Number of things being brought:
 - Apples 7
 - Cups 3
 - Cakes 0
 - Ham Sandwiches 3
 - Apple Pies      1
```

This may seem like such a simple thing to model that you wouldn't need to bother with writing a program to do it. But realize that this same totalBrought() function could easily handle a dictionary that contains thousands of guests, each bringing *thousands* of different picnic items. Then having this information in a data structure along with the totalBrought() function would save you a lot of time!

You can model things with data structures in whatever way you like, as long as the rest of the code in your program can work with the data model correctly. When you first begin programming, don't worry so much about the "right" way to model data. As you gain more experience, you may come up with more efficient models, but the important thing is that the data model works for your program's needs.

Summary

You learned all about dictionaries in this chapter. Lists and dictionaries are values that can contain multiple values, including other lists and dictionaries. Dictionaries are useful because you can map one item (the key) to another (the value), as opposed to lists, which simply contain a series of values in order. Values inside a dictionary are accessed using square brackets just as with lists. Instead of an integer index, dictionaries can have keys of a variety of data types: integers, floats, strings, or tuples. By organizing a program's values into data structures, you can create representations of real-world objects. You saw an example of this with a tic-tac-toe board.

Practice Questions

1. What does the code for an empty dictionary look like?
2. What does a dictionary value with a key 'foo' and a value 42 look like?
3. What is the main difference between a dictionary and a list?
4. What happens if you try to access spam['foo'] if spam is {'bar': 100}?
5. If a dictionary is stored in spam, what is the difference between the expressions 'cat' in spam and 'cat' in spam.keys()?
6. If a dictionary is stored in spam, what is the difference between the expressions 'cat' in spam and 'cat' in spam.values()?
7. What is a shortcut for the following code?

```
if 'color' not in spam:
    spam['color'] = 'black'
```

8. What module and function can be used to "pretty print" dictionary values?

Practice Projects

For practice, write programs to do the following tasks.

Fantasy Game Inventory

You are creating a fantasy video game. The data structure to model the player's inventory will be a dictionary where the keys are string values describing the item in the inventory and the value is an integer value detailing how many of that item the player has. For example, the dictionary value {'rope': 1, 'torch': 6, 'gold coin': 42, 'dagger': 1, 'arrow': 12} means the player has 1 rope, 6 torches, 42 gold coins, and so on.

Write a function named `displayInventory()` that would take any possible "inventory" and display it like the following:

```
Inventory:
12 arrow
42 gold coin
1 rope
6 torch
1 dagger
Total number of items: 62
```

Hint: You can use a for loop to loop through all the keys in a dictionary.

```python
# inventory.py
stuff = {'rope': 1, 'torch': 6, 'gold coin': 42, 'dagger': 1, 'arrow': 12}

def displayInventory(inventory):
    print("Inventory:")
    item_total = 0
    for k, v in inventory.items():
        # FILL THIS PART IN
    print("Total number of items: " + str(item_total))

displayInventory(stuff)
```

List to Dictionary Function for Fantasy Game Inventory

Imagine that a vanquished dragon's loot is represented as a list of strings like this:

```python
dragonLoot = ['gold coin', 'dagger', 'gold coin', 'gold coin', 'ruby']
```

Write a function named `addToInventory(inventory, addedItems)`, where the inventory parameter is a dictionary representing the player's inventory (like in the previous project) and the `addedItems` parameter is a list like `dragonLoot`. The `addToInventory()` function should return a dictionary that represents the updated inventory. Note that the `addedItems` list can contain multiples of the same item. Your code could look something like this:

```python
def addToInventory(inventory, addedItems):
    # your code goes here

inv = {'gold coin': 42, 'rope': 1}
dragonLoot = ['gold coin', 'dagger', 'gold coin', 'gold coin', 'ruby']
inv = addToInventory(inv, dragonLoot)
displayInventory(inv)
```

The previous program (with your `displayInventory()` function from the previous project) would output the following:

```
Inventory:
45 gold coin
1 rope
1 ruby
1 dagger

Total number of items: 48
```

6

MANIPULATING STRINGS

Text is one of the most common forms of data your programs will handle. You already know how to concatenate two string values together with the + operator, but you can do much more than that. You can extract partial strings from string values, add or remove spacing, convert letters to lowercase or uppercase, and check that strings are formatted correctly. You can even write Python code to access the clipboard for copying and pasting text.

In this chapter, you'll learn all this and more. Then you'll work through two different programming projects: a simple password manager and a program to automate the boring chore of formatting pieces of text.

Working with Strings

Let's look at some of the ways Python lets you write, print, and access strings in your code.

String Literals

Typing string values in Python code is fairly straightforward: They begin and end with a single quote. But then how can you use a quote inside a string? Typing `'That is Alice's cat.'` won't work, because Python thinks the string ends after `Alice`, and the rest (`s cat.'`) is invalid Python code. Fortunately, there are multiple ways to type strings.

Double Quotes

Strings can begin and end with double quotes, just as they do with single quotes. One benefit of using double quotes is that the string can have a single quote character in it. Enter the following into the interactive shell:

```
>>> spam = "That is Alice's cat."
```

Since the string begins with a double quote, Python knows that the single quote is part of the string and not marking the end of the string. However, if you need to use both single quotes and double quotes in the string, you'll need to use escape characters.

Escape Characters

An *escape character* lets you use characters that are otherwise impossible to put into a string. An escape character consists of a backslash (\) followed by the character you want to add to the string. (Despite consisting of two characters, it is commonly referred to as a singular escape character.) For example, the escape character for a single quote is \'. You can use this inside a string that begins and ends with single quotes. To see how escape characters work, enter the following into the interactive shell:

```
>>> spam = 'Say hi to Bob\'s mother.'
```

Python knows that since the single quote in `Bob\'s` has a backslash, it is not a single quote meant to end the string value. The escape characters \' and \" let you put single quotes and double quotes inside your strings, respectively.

Table 6-1 lists the escape characters you can use.

Table 6-1: Escape Characters

Escape character	Prints as
\'	Single quote
\"	Double quote
\t	Tab
\n	Newline (line break)
\\	Backslash

Enter the following into the interactive shell:

```
>>> print("Hello there!\nHow are you?\nI\'m doing fine.")
Hello there!
How are you?
I'm doing fine.
```

Raw Strings

You can place an r before the beginning quotation mark of a string to make it a raw string. A *raw string* completely ignores all escape characters and prints any backslash that appears in the string. For example, type the following into the interactive shell:

```
>>> print(r'That is Carol\'s cat.')
That is Carol\'s cat.
```

Because this is a raw string, Python considers the backslash as part of the string and not as the start of an escape character. Raw strings are helpful if you are typing string values that contain many backslashes, such as the strings used for regular expressions described in the next chapter.

Multiline Strings with Triple Quotes

While you can use the \n escape character to put a newline into a string, it is often easier to use multiline strings. A multiline string in Python begins and ends with either three single quotes or three double quotes. Any quotes, tabs, or newlines in between the "triple quotes" are considered part of the string. Python's indentation rules for blocks do not apply to lines inside a multiline string.

Open the file editor and write the following:

```
print('''Dear Alice,

Eve's cat has been arrested for catnapping, cat burglary, and extortion.

Sincerely,
Bob''')
```

Save this program as *catnapping.py* and run it. The output will look like this:

```
Dear Alice,

Eve's cat has been arrested for catnapping, cat burglary, and extortion.

Sincerely,
Bob
```

Notice that the single quote character in Eve's does not need to be escaped. Escaping single and double quotes is optional in multiline strings. The following print() call would print identical text but doesn't use a multiline string:

```
print('Dear Alice,\n\nEve\'s cat has been arrested for catnapping, cat
burglary, and extortion.\n\nSincerely,\nBob')
```

Multiline Comments

While the hash character (#) marks the beginning of a comment for the rest of the line, a multiline string is often used for comments that span multiple lines. The following is perfectly valid Python code:

```
"""This is a test Python program.
Written by Al Sweigart al@inventwithpython.com

This program was designed for Python 3, not Python 2.
"""

def spam():
    """This is a multiline comment to help
    explain what the spam() function does."""
    print('Hello!')
```

Indexing and Slicing Strings

Strings use indexes and slices the same way lists do. You can think of the string 'Hello world!' as a list and each character in the string as an item with a corresponding index.

```
 '   H   e   l   l   o       w   o   r   l   d   !   '
     0   1   2   3   4   5   6   7   8   9   10  11
```

The space and exclamation point are included in the character count, so 'Hello world!' is 12 characters long, from H at index 0 to ! at index 11.

Enter the following into the interactive shell:

```
>>> spam = 'Hello world!'
>>> spam[0]
'H'
>>> spam[4]
'o'
>>> spam[-1]
'!'
>>> spam[0:5]
'Hello'
```

```
>>> spam[:5]
'Hello'
>>> spam[6:]
'world!'
```

If you specify an index, you'll get the character at that position in the string. If you specify a range from one index to another, the starting index is included and the ending index is not. That's why, if spam is 'Hello world!', spam[0:5] is 'Hello'. The substring you get from spam[0:5] will include everything from spam[0] to spam[4], leaving out the space at index 5.

Note that slicing a string does not modify the original string. You can capture a slice from one variable in a separate variable. Try typing the following into the interactive shell:

```
>>> spam = 'Hello world!'
>>> fizz = spam[0:5]
>>> fizz
'Hello'
```

By slicing and storing the resulting substring in another variable, you can have both the whole string and the substring handy for quick, easy access.

The in and not in Operators with Strings

The in and not in operators can be used with strings just like with list values. An expression with two strings joined using in or not in will evaluate to a Boolean True or False. Enter the following into the interactive shell:

```
>>> 'Hello' in 'Hello World'
True
>>> 'Hello' in 'Hello'
True
>>> 'HELLO' in 'Hello World'
False
>>> '' in 'spam'
True
>>> 'cats' not in 'cats and dogs'
False
```

These expressions test whether the first string (the exact string, case sensitive) can be found within the second string.

Useful String Methods

Several string methods analyze strings or create transformed string values. This section describes the methods you'll be using most often.

The upper(), lower(), isupper(), and islower() String Methods

The upper() and lower() string methods return a new string where all the letters in the original string have been converted to uppercase or lowercase, respectively. Nonletter characters in the string remain unchanged. Enter the following into the interactive shell:

```
>>> spam = 'Hello world!'
>>> spam = spam.upper()
>>> spam
'HELLO WORLD!'
>>> spam = spam.lower()
>>> spam
'hello world!'
```

Note that these methods do not change the string itself but return new string values. If you want to change the original string, you have to call upper() or lower() on the string and then assign the new string to the variable where the original was stored. This is why you must use spam = spam.upper() to change the string in spam instead of simply spam.upper(). (This is just like if a variable eggs contains the value 10. Writing eggs + 3 does not change the value of eggs, but eggs = eggs + 3 does.)

The upper() and lower() methods are helpful if you need to make a case-insensitive comparison. The strings 'great' and 'GREat' are not equal to each other. But in the following small program, it does not matter whether the user types Great, GREAT, or grEAT, because the string is first converted to lowercase.

```
print('How are you?')
feeling = input()
if feeling.lower() == 'great':
    print('I feel great too.')
else:
    print('I hope the rest of your day is good.')
```

When you run this program, the question is displayed, and entering a variation on great, such as GREat, will still give the output I feel great too. Adding code to your program to handle variations or mistakes in user input, such as inconsistent capitalization, will make your programs easier to use and less likely to fail.

```
How are you?
GREat
I feel great too.
```

The isupper() and islower() methods will return a Boolean True value if the string has at least one letter and all the letters are uppercase or lowercase, respectively. Otherwise, the method returns False. Enter the following into the interactive shell, and notice what each method call returns:

```
>>> spam = 'Hello world!'
>>> spam.islower()
False
>>> spam.isupper()
False
>>> 'HELLO'.isupper()
True
>>> 'abc12345'.islower()
True
>>> '12345'.islower()
False
>>> '12345'.isupper()
False
```

Since the upper() and lower() string methods themselves return strings, you can call string methods on *those* returned string values as well. Expressions that do this will look like a chain of method calls. Enter the following into the interactive shell:

```
>>> 'Hello'.upper()
'HELLO'
>>> 'Hello'.upper().lower()
'hello'
>>> 'Hello'.upper().lower().upper()
'HELLO'
>>> 'HELLO'.lower()
'hello'
>>> 'HELLO'.lower().islower()
True
```

The isX String Methods

Along with islower() and isupper(), there are several string methods that have names beginning with the word *is*. These methods return a Boolean value that describes the nature of the string. Here are some common isX string methods:

- isalpha() returns True if the string consists only of letters and is not blank.
- isalnum() returns True if the string consists only of letters and numbers and is not blank.
- isdecimal() returns True if the string consists only of numeric characters and is not blank.

- isspace() returns True if the string consists only of spaces, tabs, and newlines and is not blank.

- istitle() returns True if the string consists only of words that begin with an uppercase letter followed by only lowercase letters.

Enter the following into the interactive shell:

```
>>> 'hello'.isalpha()
True
>>> 'hello123'.isalpha()
False
>>> 'hello123'.isalnum()
True
>>> 'hello'.isalnum()
True
>>> '123'.isdecimal()
True
>>> '    '.isspace()
True
>>> 'This Is Title Case'.istitle()
True
>>> 'This Is Title Case 123'.istitle()
True
>>> 'This Is not Title Case'.istitle()
False
>>> 'This Is NOT Title Case Either'.istitle()
False
```

The isX string methods are helpful when you need to validate user input. For example, the following program repeatedly asks users for their age and a password until they provide valid input. Open a new file editor window and enter this program, saving it as *validateInput.py*:

```
while True:
    print('Enter your age:')
    age = input()
    if age.isdecimal():
        break
    print('Please enter a number for your age.')

while True:
    print('Select a new password (letters and numbers only):')
    password = input()
    if password.isalnum():
        break
    print('Passwords can only have letters and numbers.')
```

In the first while loop, we ask the user for their age and store their input in age. If age is a valid (decimal) value, we break out of this first while loop and move on to the second, which asks for a password. Otherwise, we inform the user that they need to enter a number and again ask them to enter their age. In the second while loop, we ask for a password, store the user's input in password, and break out of the loop if the input was alphanumeric. If it wasn't, we're not satisfied so we tell the user the password needs to be alphanumeric and again ask them to enter a password.

When run, the program's output looks like this:

```
Enter your age:
forty two
Please enter a number for your age.
Enter your age:
42
Select a new password (letters and numbers only):
secr3t!
Passwords can only have letters and numbers.
Select a new password (letters and numbers only):
secr3t
```

Calling isdecimal() and isalnum() on variables, we're able to test whether the values stored in those variables are decimal or not, alphanumeric or not. Here, these tests help us reject the input forty two and accept 42, and reject secr3t! and accept secr3t.

The startswith() and endswith() String Methods

The startswith() and endswith() methods return True if the string value they are called on begins or ends (respectively) with the string passed to the method; otherwise, they return False. Enter the following into the interactive shell:

```
>>> 'Hello world!'.startswith('Hello')
True
>>> 'Hello world!'.endswith('world!')
True
>>> 'abc123'.startswith('abcdef')
False
>>> 'abc123'.endswith('12')
False
>>> 'Hello world!'.startswith('Hello world!')
True
>>> 'Hello world!'.endswith('Hello world!')
True
```

These methods are useful alternatives to the == equals operator if you need to check only whether the first or last part of the string, rather than the whole thing, is equal to another string.

The join() and split() String Methods

The join() method is useful when you have a list of strings that need to be joined together into a single string value. The join() method is called on a string, gets passed a list of strings, and returns a string. The returned string is the concatenation of each string in the passed-in list. For example, enter the following into the interactive shell:

```
>>> ', '.join(['cats', 'rats', 'bats'])
'cats, rats, bats'
>>> ' '.join(['My', 'name', 'is', 'Simon'])
'My name is Simon'
>>> 'ABC'.join(['My', 'name', 'is', 'Simon'])
'MyABCnameABCisABCSimon'
```

Notice that the string join() calls on is inserted between each string of the list argument. For example, when join(['cats', 'rats', 'bats']) is called on the ', ' string, the returned string is 'cats, rats, bats'.

Remember that join() is called on a string value and is passed a list value. (It's easy to accidentally call it the other way around.) The split() method does the opposite: It's called on a string value and returns a list of strings. Enter the following into the interactive shell:

```
>>> 'My name is Simon'.split()
['My', 'name', 'is', 'Simon']
```

By default, the string 'My name is Simon' is split wherever whitespace characters such as the space, tab, or newline characters are found. These whitespace characters are not included in the strings in the returned list. You can pass a delimiter string to the split() method to specify a different string to split upon. For example, enter the following into the interactive shell:

```
>>> 'MyABCnameABCisABCSimon'.split('ABC')
['My', 'name', 'is', 'Simon']
>>> 'My name is Simon'.split('m')
['My na', 'e is Si', 'on']
```

A common use of split() is to split a multiline string along the newline characters. Enter the following into the interactive shell:

```
>>> spam = '''Dear Alice,
How have you been? I am fine.
There is a container in the fridge
that is labeled "Milk Experiment".

Please do not drink it.
Sincerely,
Bob'''
>>> spam.split('\n')
['Dear Alice,', 'How have you been? I am fine.', 'There is a container in the
fridge', 'that is labeled "Milk Experiment".', '', 'Please do not drink it.',
'Sincerely,', 'Bob']
```

Passing split() the argument '\n' lets us split the multiline string stored in spam along the newlines and return a list in which each item corresponds to one line of the string.

Justifying Text with rjust(), ljust(), and center()

The rjust() and ljust() string methods return a padded version of the string they are called on, with spaces inserted to justify the text. The first argument to both methods is an integer length for the justified string. Enter the following into the interactive shell:

```
>>> 'Hello'.rjust(10)
'     Hello'
>>> 'Hello'.rjust(20)
'               Hello'
>>> 'Hello World'.rjust(20)
'         Hello World'
>>> 'Hello'.ljust(10)
'Hello     '
```

'Hello'.rjust(10) says that we want to right-justify 'Hello' in a string of total length 10. 'Hello' is five characters, so five spaces will be added to its left, giving us a string of 10 characters with 'Hello' justified right.

An optional second argument to rjust() and ljust() will specify a fill character other than a space character. Enter the following into the interactive shell:

```
>>> 'Hello'.rjust(20, '*')
'***************Hello'
>>> 'Hello'.ljust(20, '-')
'Hello---------------'
```

The center() string method works like ljust() and rjust() but centers the text rather than justifying it to the left or right. Enter the following into the interactive shell:

```
>>> 'Hello'.center(20)
'       Hello        '
>>> 'Hello'.center(20, '=')
'=======Hello========'
```

These methods are especially useful when you need to print tabular data that has the correct spacing. Open a new file editor window and enter the following code, saving it as *picnicTable.py*:

```
def printPicnic(itemsDict, leftWidth, rightWidth):
    print('PICNIC ITEMS'.center(leftWidth + rightWidth, '-'))
    for k, v in itemsDict.items():
        print(k.ljust(leftWidth, '.') + str(v).rjust(rightWidth))
```

```
picnicItems = {'sandwiches': 4, 'apples': 12, 'cups': 4, 'cookies': 8000}
printPicnic(picnicItems, 12, 5)
printPicnic(picnicItems, 20, 6)
```

In this program, we define a printPicnic() method that will take in a dictionary of information and use center(), ljust(), and rjust() to display that information in a neatly aligned table-like format.

The dictionary that we'll pass to printPicnic() is picnicItems. In picnicItems, we have 4 sandwiches, 12 apples, 4 cups, and 8000 cookies. We want to organize this information into two columns, with the name of the item on the left and the quantity on the right.

To do this, we decide how wide we want the left and right columns to be. Along with our dictionary, we'll pass these values to printPicnic().

printPicnic() takes in a dictionary, a leftWidth for the left column of a table, and a rightWidth for the right column. It prints a title, PICNIC ITEMS, centered above the table. Then, it loops through the dictionary, printing each key-value pair on a line with the key justified left and padded by periods, and the value justified right and padded by spaces.

After defining printPicnic(), we define the dictionary picnicItems and call printPicnic() twice, passing it different widths for the left and right table columns.

When you run this program, the picnic items are displayed twice. The first time the left column is 12 characters wide, and the right column is 5 characters wide. The second time they are 20 and 6 characters wide, respectively.

```
---PICNIC ITEMS--
sandwiches..    4
apples......   12
cups........    4
cookies..... 8000
-------PICNIC ITEMS-------
sandwiches..........       4
apples..............      12
cups................       4
cookies.............    8000
```

Using rjust(), ljust(), and center() lets you ensure that strings are neatly aligned, even if you aren't sure how many characters long your strings are.

Removing Whitespace with strip(), rstrip(), and lstrip()

Sometimes you may want to strip off whitespace characters (space, tab, and newline) from the left side, right side, or both sides of a string. The strip() string method will return a new string without any whitespace characters at the beginning or end. The lstrip() and rstrip() methods will remove whitespace characters from the left and right ends, respectively. Enter the following into the interactive shell:

```
>>> spam = '    Hello World    '
>>> spam.strip()
'Hello World'
>>> spam.lstrip()
'Hello World    '
>>> spam.rstrip()
'    Hello World'
```

Optionally, a string argument will specify which characters on the ends should be stripped. Enter the following into the interactive shell:

```
>>> spam = 'SpamSpamBaconSpamEggsSpamSpam'
>>> spam.strip('ampS')
'BaconSpamEggs'
```

Passing strip() the argument 'ampS' will tell it to strip occurrences of a, m, p, and capital S from the ends of the string stored in spam. The order of the characters in the string passed to strip() does not matter: strip('ampS') will do the same thing as strip('mapS') or strip('Spam').

Copying and Pasting Strings with the pyperclip Module

The pyperclip module has copy() and paste() functions that can send text to and receive text from your computer's clipboard. Sending the output of your program to the clipboard will make it easy to paste it to an email, word processor, or some other software.

Pyperclip does not come with Python. To install it, follow the directions for installing third-party modules in Appendix A. After installing the pyperclip module, enter the following into the interactive shell:

```
>>> import pyperclip
>>> pyperclip.copy('Hello world!')
>>> pyperclip.paste()
'Hello world!'
```

Of course, if something outside of your program changes the clipboard contents, the paste() function will return it. For example, if I copied this sentence to the clipboard and then called paste(), it would look like this:

```
>>> pyperclip.paste()
'For example, if I copied this sentence to the clipboard and then called
paste(), it would look like this:'
```

Project: Password Locker

You probably have accounts on many different websites. It's a bad habit to use the same password for each of them because if any of those sites has a security breach, the hackers will learn the password to all of your other accounts. It's best to use password manager software on your computer that uses one master password to unlock the password manager. Then you can copy any account password to the clipboard and paste it into the website's Password field.

The password manager program you'll create in this example isn't secure, but it offers a basic demonstration of how such programs work.

THE CHAPTER PROJECTS

This is the first "chapter project" of the book. From here on, each chapter will have projects that demonstrate the concepts covered in the chapter. The projects are written in a style that takes you from a blank file editor window to a full, working program. Just like with the interactive shell examples, don't only read the project sections—follow along on your computer!

Step 1: Program Design and Data Structures

You want to be able to run this program with a command line argument that is the account's name—for instance, *email* or *blog*. That account's password will be copied to the clipboard so that the user can paste it into a Password field. This way, the user can have long, complicated passwords without having to memorize them.

Open a new file editor window and save the program as *pw.py*. You need to start the program with a #! (*shebang*) line (see Appendix B) and should also write a comment that briefly describes the program. Since you want to associate each account's name with its password, you can store these as strings in a dictionary. The dictionary will be the data structure that organizes your account and password data. Make your program look like the following:

```
#! python3
# pw.py - An insecure password locker program.

PASSWORDS = {'email': 'F7minlBDDuvMJuxESSKHFhTxTjVB6',
             'blog': 'VmALvQyKAxiVH5G8v01if1MLZF3sdt',
             'luggage': '12345'}
```

Step 2: Handle Command Line Arguments

The command line arguments will be stored in the variable sys.argv. (See Appendix B for more information on how to use command line arguments in your programs.) The first item in the sys.argv list should always be a string containing the program's filename ('pw.py'), and the second item should be the first command line argument. For this program, this argument is the name of the account whose password you want. Since the command line argument is mandatory, you display a usage message to the user if they forget to add it (that is, if the sys.argv list has fewer than two values in it). Make your program look like the following:

```
#! python3
# pw.py - An insecure password locker program.

PASSWORDS = {'email': 'F7minlBDDuvMJuxESSKHFhTxTjVB6',
             'blog': 'VmALvQyKAxiVH5G8v01if1MLZF3sdt',
             'luggage': '12345'}

import sys
if len(sys.argv) < 2:
    print('Usage: python pw.py [account] - copy account password')
    sys.exit()

account = sys.argv[1]    # first command line arg is the account name
```

Step 3: Copy the Right Password

Now that the account name is stored as a string in the variable account, you need to see whether it exists in the PASSWORDS dictionary as a key. If so, you want to copy the key's value to the clipboard using pyperclip.copy(). (Since you're using the pyperclip module, you need to import it.) Note that you don't actually *need* the account variable; you could just use sys.argv[1] everywhere account is used in this program. But a variable named account is much more readable than something cryptic like sys.argv[1].

Make your program look like the following:

```
#! python3
# pw.py - An insecure password locker program.
```

```
PASSWORDS = {'email': 'F7minlBDDuvMJuxESSKHFhTxFtjVB6',
             'blog': 'VmALvQyKAxiVH5G8vO1if1MLZF3sdt',
             'luggage': '12345'}

import sys, pyperclip
if len(sys.argv) < 2:
    print('Usage: py pw.py [account] - copy account password')
    sys.exit()

account = sys.argv[1]    # first command line arg is the account name

if account in PASSWORDS:
    pyperclip.copy(PASSWORDS[account])
    print('Password for ' + account + ' copied to clipboard.')
else:
    print('There is no account named ' + account)
```

This new code looks in the PASSWORDS dictionary for the account name. If the account name is a key in the dictionary, we get the value corresponding to that key, copy it to the clipboard, and print a message saying that we copied the value. Otherwise, we print a message saying there's no account with that name.

That's the complete script. Using the instructions in Appendix B for launching command line programs easily, you now have a fast way to copy your account passwords to the clipboard. You will have to modify the PASSWORDS dictionary value in the source whenever you want to update the program with a new password.

Of course, you probably don't want to keep all your passwords in one place where anyone could easily copy them. But you can modify this program and use it to quickly copy regular text to the clipboard. Say you are sending out several emails that have many of the same stock paragraphs in common. You could put each paragraph as a value in the PASSWORDS dictionary (you'd probably want to rename the dictionary at this point), and then you would have a way to quickly select and copy one of many standard pieces of text to the clipboard.

On Windows, you can create a batch file to run this program with the WIN-R Run window. (For more about batch files, see Appendix B.) Type the following into the file editor and save the file as *pw.bat* in the *C:\Windows* folder:

```
@py.exe C:\Python34\pw.py %*
@pause
```

With this batch file created, running the password-safe program on Windows is just a matter of pressing WIN-R and typing pw <account name>.

Project: Adding Bullets to Wiki Markup

When editing a Wikipedia article, you can create a bulleted list by putting each list item on its own line and placing a star in front. But say you have a really large list that you want to add bullet points to. You could just type those stars at the beginning of each line, one by one. Or you could automate this task with a short Python script.

The *bulletPointAdder.py* script will get the text from the clipboard, add a star and space to the beginning of each line, and then paste this new text to the clipboard. For example, if I copied the following text (for the Wikipedia article "List of Lists of Lists") to the clipboard:

```
Lists of animals
Lists of aquarium life
Lists of biologists by author abbreviation
Lists of cultivars
```

and then ran the *bulletPointAdder.py* program, the clipboard would then contain the following:

```
* Lists of animals
* Lists of aquarium life
* Lists of biologists by author abbreviation
* Lists of cultivars
```

This star-prefixed text is ready to be pasted into a Wikipedia article as a bulleted list.

Step 1: Copy and Paste from the Clipboard

You want the *bulletPointAdder.py* program to do the following:

1. Paste text from the clipboard
2. Do something to it
3. Copy the new text to the clipboard

That second step is a little tricky, but steps 1 and 3 are pretty straightforward: They just involve the `pyperclip.copy()` and `pyperclip.paste()` functions. For now, let's just write the part of the program that covers steps 1 and 3. Enter the following, saving the program as *bulletPointAdder.py*:

```python
#! python3
# bulletPointAdder.py - Adds Wikipedia bullet points to the start
# of each line of text on the clipboard.

import pyperclip
text = pyperclip.paste()
```

```
# TODO: Separate lines and add stars.

pyperclip.copy(text)
```

The TODO comment is a reminder that you should complete this part of the program eventually. The next step is to actually implement that piece of the program.

Step 2: Separate the Lines of Text and Add the Star

The call to pyperclip.paste() returns all the text on the clipboard as one big string. If we used the "List of Lists of Lists" example, the string stored in text would look like this:

```
'Lists of animals\nLists of aquarium life\nLists of biologists by author
abbreviation\nLists of cultivars'
```

The \n newline characters in this string cause it to be displayed with multiple lines when it is printed or pasted from the clipboard. There are many "lines" in this one string value. You want to add a star to the start of each of these lines.

You could write code that searches for each \n newline character in the string and then adds the star just after that. But it would be easier to use the split() method to return a list of strings, one for each line in the original string, and then add the star to the front of each string in the list.

Make your program look like the following:

```
#! python3
# bulletPointAdder.py - Adds Wikipedia bullet points to the start
# of each line of text on the clipboard.

import pyperclip
text = pyperclip.paste()

# Separate lines and add stars.
lines = text.split('\n')
for i in range(len(lines)):    # loop through all indexes in the "lines" list
    lines[i] = '* ' + lines[i] # add star to each string in "lines" list

pyperclip.copy(text)
```

We split the text along its newlines to get a list in which each item is one line of the text. We store the list in lines and then loop through the items in lines. For each line, we add a star and a space to the start of the line. Now each string in lines begins with a star.

Step 3: Join the Modified Lines

The lines list now contains modified lines that start with stars. But pyperclip.copy() is expecting a single string value, not a list of string values. To make this single string value, pass lines into the join() method to get a single string joined from the list's strings. Make your program look like the following:

```python
#! python3
# bulletPointAdder.py - Adds Wikipedia bullet points to the start
# of each line of text on the clipboard.

import pyperclip
text = pyperclip.paste()

# Separate lines and add stars.
lines = text.split('\n')
for i in range(len(lines)):    # loop through all indexes for "lines" list
    lines[i] = '* ' + lines[i] # add star to each string in "lines" list
text = '\n'.join(lines)
pyperclip.copy(text)
```

When this program is run, it replaces the text on the clipboard with text that has stars at the start of each line. Now the program is complete, and you can try running it with text copied to the clipboard.

Even if you don't need to automate this specific task, you might want to automate some other kind of text manipulation, such as removing trailing spaces from the end of lines or converting text to uppercase or lowercase. Whatever your needs, you can use the clipboard for input and output.

Summary

Text is a common form of data, and Python comes with many helpful string methods to process the text stored in string values. You will make use of indexing, slicing, and string methods in almost every Python program you write.

The programs you are writing now don't seem too sophisticated—they don't have graphical user interfaces with images and colorful text. So far, you're displaying text with print() and letting the user enter text with input(). However, the user can quickly enter large amounts of text through the clipboard. This ability provides a useful avenue for writing programs that manipulate massive amounts of text. These text-based programs might not have flashy windows or graphics, but they can get a lot of useful work done quickly.

Another way to manipulate large amounts of text is reading and writing files directly off the hard drive. You'll learn how to do this with Python in the next chapter.

That just about covers all the basic concepts of Python programming! You'll continue to learn new concepts throughout the rest of this book, but you now know enough to start writing some useful programs that can automate tasks. You might not think you have enough Python knowledge to do things such as download web pages, update spreadsheets, or send text messages, but that's where Python modules come in! These modules, written by other programmers, provide functions that make it easy for you to do all these things. So let's learn how to write real programs to do useful automated tasks.

Practice Questions

1. What are escape characters?

2. What do the \n and \t escape characters represent?

3. How can you put a \ backslash character in a string?

4. The string value "Howl's Moving Castle" is a valid string. Why isn't it a problem that the single quote character in the word Howl's isn't escaped?

5. If you don't want to put \n in your string, how can you write a string with newlines in it?

6. What do the following expressions evaluate to?

    • 'Hello world!'[1]

    • 'Hello world!'[0:5]

    • 'Hello world!'[:5]

    • 'Hello world!'[3:]

7. What do the following expressions evaluate to?

    • 'Hello'.upper()

    • 'Hello'.upper().isupper()

    • 'Hello'.upper().lower()

8. What do the following expressions evaluate to?

    • 'Remember, remember, the fifth of November.'.split()

    • '-'.join('There can be only one.'.split())

9. What string methods can you use to right-justify, left-justify, and center a string?

10. How can you trim whitespace characters from the beginning or end of a string?

Practice Project

For practice, write a program that does the following.

Table Printer

Write a function named printTable() that takes a list of lists of strings and displays it in a well-organized table with each column right-justified. Assume that all the inner lists will contain the same number of strings. For example, the value could look like this:

```
tableData = [['apples', 'oranges', 'cherries', 'banana'],
             ['Alice', 'Bob', 'Carol', 'David'],
             ['dogs', 'cats', 'moose', 'goose']]
```

Your printTable() function would print the following:

```
  apples Alice  dogs
 oranges   Bob  cats
cherries Carol moose
  banana David goose
```

Hint: Your code will first have to find the longest string in each of the inner lists so that the whole column can be wide enough to fit all the strings. You can store the maximum width of each column as a list of integers. The printTable() function can begin with colWidths = [0] * len(tableData), which will create a list containing the same number of 0 values as the number of inner lists in tableData. That way, colWidths[0] can store the width of the longest string in tableData[0], colWidths[1] can store the width of the longest string in tableData[1], and so on. You can then find the largest value in the colWidths list to find out what integer width to pass to the rjust() string method.

PART II

AUTOMATING TASKS

7

PATTERN MATCHING WITH REGULAR EXPRESSIONS

You may be familiar with searching for text by pressing CTRL-F and typing in the words you're looking for. *Regular expressions* go one step further: They allow you to specify a *pattern* of text to search for. You may not know a business's exact phone number, but if you live in the United States or Canada, you know it will be three digits, followed by a hyphen, and then four more digits (and optionally, a three-digit area code at the start). This is how you, as a human, know a phone number when you see it: 415-555-1234 is a phone number, but 4,155,551,234 is not.

Regular expressions are helpful, but not many non-programmers know about them even though most modern text editors and word processors, such as Microsoft Word or OpenOffice, have find and find-and-replace features that can search based on regular expressions. Regular expressions are huge time-savers, not just for software users but also for programmers. In fact, tech writer Cory Doctorow argues that even before teaching programming, we should be teaching regular expressions:

> "Knowing [regular expressions] can mean the difference between solving a problem in 3 steps and solving it in 3,000 steps. When you're a nerd, you forget that the problems you solve with a couple keystrokes can take other people days of tedious, error-prone work to slog through."[1]

In this chapter, you'll start by writing a program to find text patterns *without* using regular expressions and then see how to use regular expressions to make the code much less bloated. I'll show you basic matching with regular expressions and then move on to some more powerful features, such as string substitution and creating your own character classes. Finally, at the end of the chapter, you'll write a program that can automatically extract phone numbers and email addresses from a block of text.

Finding Patterns of Text Without Regular Expressions

Say you want to find a phone number in a string. You know the pattern: three numbers, a hyphen, three numbers, a hyphen, and four numbers. Here's an example: 415-555-4242.

Let's use a function named isPhoneNumber() to check whether a string matches this pattern, returning either True or False. Open a new file editor window and enter the following code; then save the file as *isPhoneNumber.py*:

```
   def isPhoneNumber(text):
❶      if len(text) != 12:
           return False
       for i in range(0, 3):
❷          if not text[i].isdecimal():
               return False
❸      if text[3] != '-':
           return False
       for i in range(4, 7):
❹          if not text[i].isdecimal():
               return False
❺      if text[7] != '-':
           return False
       for i in range(8, 12):
❻          if not text[i].isdecimal():
               return False
❼      return True

   print('415-555-4242 is a phone number:')
   print(isPhoneNumber('415-555-4242'))
   print('Moshi moshi is a phone number:')
   print(isPhoneNumber('Moshi moshi'))
```

---

1. Cory Doctorow, "Here's what ICT should really teach kids: how to do regular expressions," *Guardian*, December 4, 2012, *http://www.theguardian.com/technology/2012/dec/04/ict-teach-kids-regular-expressions/*.

When this program is run, the output looks like this:

```
415-555-4242 is a phone number:
True
Moshi moshi is a phone number:
False
```

The isPhoneNumber() function has code that does several checks to see whether the string in text is a valid phone number. If any of these checks fail, the function returns False. First the code checks that the string is exactly 12 characters ❶. Then it checks that the area code (that is, the first three characters in text) consists of only numeric characters ❷. The rest of the function checks that the string follows the pattern of a phone number: The number must have the first hyphen after the area code ❸, three more numeric characters ❹, then another hyphen ❺, and finally four more numbers ❻. If the program execution manages to get past all the checks, it returns True ❼.

Calling isPhoneNumber() with the argument '415-555-4242' will return True. Calling isPhoneNumber() with 'Moshi moshi' will return False; the first test fails because 'Moshi moshi' is not 12 characters long.

You would have to add even more code to find this pattern of text in a larger string. Replace the last four print() function calls in *isPhoneNumber.py* with the following:

```
message = 'Call me at 415-555-1011 tomorrow. 415-555-9999 is my office.'
for i in range(len(message)):
❶    chunk = message[i:i+12]
❷    if isPhoneNumber(chunk):
        print('Phone number found: ' + chunk)
print('Done')
```

When this program is run, the output will look like this:

```
Phone number found: 415-555-1011
Phone number found: 415-555-9999
Done
```

On each iteration of the for loop, a new chunk of 12 characters from message is assigned to the variable chunk ❶. For example, on the first iteration, i is 0, and chunk is assigned message[0:12] (that is, the string 'Call me at 4'). On the next iteration, i is 1, and chunk is assigned message[1:13] (the string 'all me at 41').

You pass chunk to isPhoneNumber() to see whether it matches the phone number pattern ❷, and if so, you print the chunk.

Continue to loop through message, and eventually the 12 characters in chunk will be a phone number. The loop goes through the entire string, testing each 12-character piece and printing any chunk it finds that satisfies isPhoneNumber(). Once we're done going through message, we print Done.

While the string in message is short in this example, it could be millions of characters long and the program would still run in less than a second. A similar program that finds phone numbers using regular expressions would also run in less than a second, but regular expressions make it quicker to write these programs.

Finding Patterns of Text with Regular Expressions

The previous phone number–finding program works, but it uses a lot of code to do something limited: The isPhoneNumber() function is 17 lines but can find only one pattern of phone numbers. What about a phone number formatted like 415.555.4242 or (415) 555-4242? What if the phone number had an extension, like 415-555-4242 x99? The isPhoneNumber() function would fail to validate them. You could add yet more code for these additional patterns, but there is an easier way.

Regular expressions, called *regexes* for short, are descriptions for a pattern of text. For example, a \d in a regex stands for a digit character— that is, any single numeral 0 to 9. The regex \d\d\d-\d\d\d-\d\d\d\d is used by Python to match the same text the previous isPhoneNumber() function did: a string of three numbers, a hyphen, three more numbers, another hyphen, and four numbers. Any other string would not match the \d\d\d-\d\d\d-\d\d \d\d regex.

But regular expressions can be much more sophisticated. For example, adding a 3 in curly brackets ({3}) after a pattern is like saying, "Match this pattern three times." So the slightly shorter regex \d{3}-\d{3}-\d{4} also matches the correct phone number format.

Creating Regex Objects

All the regex functions in Python are in the re module. Enter the following into the interactive shell to import this module:

```
>>> import re
```

NOTE *Most of the examples that follow in this chapter will require the re module, so remember to import it at the beginning of any script you write or any time you restart IDLE. Otherwise, you'll get a NameError: name 're' is not defined error message.*

Passing a string value representing your regular expression to re.compile() returns a Regex pattern object (or simply, a Regex object).

To create a Regex object that matches the phone number pattern, enter the following into the interactive shell. (Remember that \d means "a digit character" and \d\d\d-\d\d\d-\d\d\d\d is the regular expression for the correct phone number pattern.)

```
>>> phoneNumRegex = re.compile(r'\d\d\d-\d\d\d-\d\d\d\d')
```

Now the phoneNumRegex variable contains a Regex object.

PASSING RAW STRINGS TO RE.COMPILE()

Remember that escape characters in Python use the backslash (\). The string value '\n' represents a single newline character, not a backslash followed by a lowercase *n*. You need to enter the escape character \\ to print a single backslash. So '\\n' is the string that represents a backslash followed by a lowercase *n*. However, by putting an r before the first quote of the string value, you can mark the string as a *raw string*, which does not escape characters.

Since regular expressions frequently use backslashes in them, it is convenient to pass raw strings to the re.compile() function instead of typing extra backslashes. Typing r'\d\d\d-\d\d\d-\d\d\d\d' is much easier than typing '\\d\\d\\d-\\d\\d\\d-\\d\\d\\d\\d'.

Matching Regex Objects

A Regex object's search() method searches the string it is passed for any matches to the regex. The search() method will return None if the regex pattern is not found in the string. If the pattern *is* found, the search() method returns a Match object. Match objects have a group() method that will return the actual matched text from the searched string. (I'll explain groups shortly.) For example, enter the following into the interactive shell:

```
>>> phoneNumRegex = re.compile(r'\d\d\d-\d\d\d-\d\d\d\d')
>>> mo = phoneNumRegex.search('My number is 415-555-4242.')
>>> print('Phone number found: ' + mo.group())
Phone number found: 415-555-4242
```

The mo variable name is just a generic name to use for Match objects. This example might seem complicated at first, but it is much shorter than the earlier *isPhoneNumber.py* program and does the same thing.

Here, we pass our desired pattern to re.compile() and store the resulting Regex object in phoneNumRegex. Then we call search() on phoneNumRegex and pass search() the string we want to search for a match. The result of the search gets stored in the variable mo. In this example, we know that our pattern will be found in the string, so we know that a Match object will be returned. Knowing that mo contains a Match object and not the null value None, we can call group() on mo to return the match. Writing mo.group() inside our print statement displays the whole match, 415-555-4242.

Review of Regular Expression Matching

While there are several steps to using regular expressions in Python, each step is fairly simple.

1. Import the regex module with import re.
2. Create a Regex object with the re.compile() function. (Remember to use a raw string.)
3. Pass the string you want to search into the Regex object's search() method. This returns a Match object.
4. Call the Match object's group() method to return a string of the actual matched text.

NOTE   *While I encourage you to enter the example code into the interactive shell, you should also make use of web-based regular expression testers, which can show you exactly how a regex matches a piece of text that you enter. I recommend the tester at* http://regexpal.com/.

More Pattern Matching with Regular Expressions

Now that you know the basic steps for creating and finding regular expression objects with Python, you're ready to try some of their more powerful pattern-matching capabilities.

Grouping with Parentheses

Say you want to separate the area code from the rest of the phone number. Adding parentheses will create *groups* in the regex: (\d\d\d)-(\d\d\d-\d\d\d\d). Then you can use the group() match object method to grab the matching text from just one group.

The first set of parentheses in a regex string will be group 1. The second set will be group 2. By passing the integer 1 or 2 to the group() match object method, you can grab different parts of the matched text. Passing 0 or nothing to the group() method will return the entire matched text. Enter the following into the interactive shell:

```
>>> phoneNumRegex = re.compile(r'(\d\d\d)-(\d\d\d-\d\d\d\d)')
>>> mo = phoneNumRegex.search('My number is 415-555-4242.')
>>> mo.group(1)
'415'
>>> mo.group(2)
'555-4242'
>>> mo.group(0)
'415-555-4242'
>>> mo.group()
'415-555-4242'
```

If you would like to retrieve all the groups at once, use the groups() method—note the plural form for the name.

```
>>> mo.groups()
('415', '555-4242')
>>> areaCode, mainNumber = mo.groups()
>>> print(areaCode)
415
>>> print(mainNumber)
555-4242
```

Since mo.groups() returns a tuple of multiple values, you can use the multiple-assignment trick to assign each value to a separate variable, as in the previous areaCode, mainNumber = mo.groups() line.

Parentheses have a special meaning in regular expressions, but what do you do if you need to match a parenthesis in your text? For instance, maybe the phone numbers you are trying to match have the area code set in parentheses. In this case, you need to escape the (and) characters with a backslash. Enter the following into the interactive shell:

```
>>> phoneNumRegex = re.compile(r'(\(\d\d\d\)) (\d\d\d-\d\d\d\d)')
>>> mo = phoneNumRegex.search('My phone number is (415) 555-4242.')
>>> mo.group(1)
'(415)'
>>> mo.group(2)
'555-4242'
```

The \(and \) escape characters in the raw string passed to re.compile() will match actual parenthesis characters.

Matching Multiple Groups with the Pipe

The | character is called a *pipe*. You can use it anywhere you want to match one of many expressions. For example, the regular expression r'Batman|Tina Fey' will match either 'Batman' or 'Tina Fey'.

When *both* Batman and Tina Fey occur in the searched string, the first occurrence of matching text will be returned as the Match object. Enter the following into the interactive shell:

```
>>> heroRegex = re.compile (r'Batman|Tina Fey')
>>> mo1 = heroRegex.search('Batman and Tina Fey.')
>>> mo1.group()
'Batman'

>>> mo2 = heroRegex.search('Tina Fey and Batman.')
>>> mo2.group()
'Tina Fey'
```

NOTE   *You can find all matching occurrences with the findall() method that's discussed in "The findall() Method" on page 157.*

You can also use the pipe to match one of several patterns as part of your regex. For example, say you wanted to match any of the strings 'Batman', 'Batmobile', 'Batcopter', and 'Batbat'. Since all these strings start with Bat, it would be nice if you could specify that prefix only once. This can be done with parentheses. Enter the following into the interactive shell:

```
>>> batRegex = re.compile(r'Bat(man|mobile|copter|bat)')
>>> mo = batRegex.search('Batmobile lost a wheel')
>>> mo.group()
'Batmobile'
>>> mo.group(1)
'mobile'
```

The method call mo.group() returns the full matched text 'Batmobile', while mo.group(1) returns just the part of the matched text inside the first parentheses group, 'mobile'. By using the pipe character and grouping parentheses, you can specify several alternative patterns you would like your regex to match.

If you need to match an actual pipe character, escape it with a backslash, like \|.

Optional Matching with the Question Mark

Sometimes there is a pattern that you want to match only optionally. That is, the regex should find a match whether or not that bit of text is there. The ? character flags the group that precedes it as an optional part of the pattern. For example, enter the following into the interactive shell:

```
>>> batRegex = re.compile(r'Bat(wo)?man')
>>> mo1 = batRegex.search('The Adventures of Batman')
>>> mo1.group()
'Batman'

>>> mo2 = batRegex.search('The Adventures of Batwoman')
>>> mo2.group()
'Batwoman'
```

The (wo)? part of the regular expression means that the pattern wo is an optional group. The regex will match text that has zero instances or one instance of *wo* in it. This is why the regex matches both 'Batwoman' and 'Batman'.

Using the earlier phone number example, you can make the regex look for phone numbers that do or do not have an area code. Enter the following into the interactive shell:

```
>>> phoneRegex = re.compile(r'(\d\d\d-)?\d\d\d-\d\d\d\d')
>>> mo1 = phoneRegex.search('My number is 415-555-4242')
>>> mo1.group()
'415-555-4242'
```

```
>>> mo2 = phoneRegex.search('My number is 555-4242')
>>> mo2.group()
'555-4242'
```

You can think of the ? as saying, "Match zero or one of the group preceding this question mark."

If you need to match an actual question mark character, escape it with \?.

Matching Zero or More with the Star

The * (called the *star* or *asterisk*) means "match zero or more"—the group that precedes the star can occur any number of times in the text. It can be completely absent or repeated over and over again. Let's look at the Batman example again.

```
>>> batRegex = re.compile(r'Bat(wo)*man')
>>> mo1 = batRegex.search('The Adventures of Batman')
>>> mo1.group()
'Batman'

>>> mo2 = batRegex.search('The Adventures of Batwoman')
>>> mo2.group()
'Batwoman'

>>> mo3 = batRegex.search('The Adventures of Batwowowowoman')
>>> mo3.group()
'Batwowowowoman'
```

For 'Batman', the (wo)* part of the regex matches zero instances of wo in the string; for 'Batwoman', the (wo)* matches one instance of wo; and for 'Batwowowowoman', (wo)* matches four instances of wo.

If you need to match an actual star character, prefix the star in the regular expression with a backslash, *.

Matching One or More with the Plus

While * means "match zero or more," the + (or *plus*) means "match one or more." Unlike the star, which does not require its group to appear in the matched string, the group preceding a plus must appear *at least once*. It is not optional. Enter the following into the interactive shell, and compare it with the star regexes in the previous section:

```
>>> batRegex = re.compile(r'Bat(wo)+man')
>>> mo1 = batRegex.search('The Adventures of Batwoman')
>>> mo1.group()
'Batwoman'

>>> mo2 = batRegex.search('The Adventures of Batwowowowoman')
>>> mo2.group()
'Batwowowowoman'
```

```
>>> mo3 = batRegex.search('The Adventures of Batman')
>>> mo3 == None
True
```

The regex Bat(wo)+man will not match the string 'The Adventures of Batman' because at least one wo is required by the plus sign.

If you need to match an actual plus sign character, prefix the plus sign with a backslash to escape it: \+.

Matching Specific Repetitions with Curly Brackets

If you have a group that you want to repeat a specific number of times, follow the group in your regex with a number in curly brackets. For example, the regex (Ha){3} will match the string 'HaHaHa', but it will not match 'HaHa', since the latter has only two repeats of the (Ha) group.

Instead of one number, you can specify a range by writing a minimum, a comma, and a maximum in between the curly brackets. For example, the regex (Ha){3,5} will match 'HaHaHa', 'HaHaHaHa', and 'HaHaHaHaHa'.

You can also leave out the first or second number in the curly brackets to leave the minimum or maximum unbounded. For example, (Ha){3,} will match three or more instances of the (Ha) group, while (Ha){,5} will match zero to five instances. Curly brackets can help make your regular expressions shorter. These two regular expressions match identical patterns:

```
(Ha){3}
(Ha)(Ha)(Ha)
```

And these two regular expressions also match identical patterns:

```
(Ha){3,5}
((Ha)(Ha)(Ha))|((Ha)(Ha)(Ha)(Ha))|((Ha)(Ha)(Ha)(Ha)(Ha))
```

Enter the following into the interactive shell:

```
>>> haRegex = re.compile(r'(Ha){3}')
>>> mo1 = haRegex.search('HaHaHa')
>>> mo1.group()
'HaHaHa'

>>> mo2 = haRegex.search('Ha')
>>> mo2 == None
True
```

Here, (Ha){3} matches 'HaHaHa' but not 'Ha'. Since it doesn't match 'Ha', search() returns None.

Greedy and Nongreedy Matching

Since (Ha){3,5} can match three, four, or five instances of Ha in the string 'HaHaHaHaHa', you may wonder why the Match object's call to group() in the previous curly bracket example returns 'HaHaHaHaHa' instead of the shorter possibilities. After all, 'HaHaHa' and 'HaHaHaHa' are also valid matches of the regular expression (Ha){3,5}.

Python's regular expressions are *greedy* by default, which means that in ambiguous situations they will match the longest string possible. The *nongreedy* version of the curly brackets, which matches the shortest string possible, has the closing curly bracket followed by a question mark.

Enter the following into the interactive shell, and notice the difference between the greedy and nongreedy forms of the curly brackets searching the same string:

```
>>> greedyHaRegex = re.compile(r'(Ha){3,5}')
>>> mo1 = greedyHaRegex.search('HaHaHaHaHa')
>>> mo1.group()
'HaHaHaHaHa'

>>> nongreedyHaRegex = re.compile(r'(Ha){3,5}?')
>>> mo2 = nongreedyHaRegex.search('HaHaHaHaHa')
>>> mo2.group()
'HaHaHa'
```

Note that the question mark can have two meanings in regular expressions: declaring a nongreedy match or flagging an optional group. These meanings are entirely unrelated.

The findall() Method

In addition to the search() method, Regex objects also have a findall() method. While search() will return a Match object of the *first* matched text in the searched string, the findall() method will return the strings of *every* match in the searched string. To see how search() returns a Match object only on the first instance of matching text, enter the following into the interactive shell:

```
>>> phoneNumRegex = re.compile(r'\d\d\d-\d\d\d-\d\d\d\d')
>>> mo = phoneNumRegex.search('Cell: 415-555-9999 Work: 212-555-0000')
>>> mo.group()
'415-555-9999'
```

On the other hand, findall() will not return a Match object but a list of strings—*as long as there are no groups in the regular expression*. Each string in the list is a piece of the searched text that matched the regular expression. Enter the following into the interactive shell:

```
>>> phoneNumRegex = re.compile(r'\d\d\d-\d\d\d-\d\d\d\d') # has no groups
>>> phoneNumRegex.findall('Cell: 415-555-9999 Work: 212-555-0000')
['415-555-9999', '212-555-0000']
```

If there *are* groups in the regular expression, then findall() will return a list of tuples. Each tuple represents a found match, and its items are the matched strings for each group in the regex. To see `findall()` in action, enter the following into the interactive shell (notice that the regular expression being compiled now has groups in parentheses):

```
>>> phoneNumRegex = re.compile(r'(\d\d\d)-(\d\d\d)-(\d\d\d\d)') # has groups
>>> phoneNumRegex.findall('Cell: 415-555-9999 Work: 212-555-0000')
[('415', '555', '9999'), ('212', '555', '0000')]
```

To summarize what the `findall()` method returns, remember the following:

1. When called on a regex with no groups, such as \d\d\d-\d\d\d-\d\d\d\d, the method `findall()` returns a list of string matches, such as ['415-555-9999', '212-555-0000'].

2. When called on a regex that has groups, such as (\d\d\d)-(\d\d\d)-(\d\d\d\d), the method `findall()` returns a list of tuples of strings (one string for each group), such as [('415', '555', '9999'), ('212', '555', '0000')].

Character Classes

In the earlier phone number regex example, you learned that \d could stand for any numeric digit. That is, \d is shorthand for the regular expression (0|1|2|3|4|5|6|7|8|9). There are many such *shorthand character classes*, as shown in Table 7-1.

Table 7-1: Shorthand Codes for Common Character Classes

Shorthand character class	Represents
\d	Any numeric digit from 0 to 9.
\D	Any character that is *not* a numeric digit from 0 to 9.
\w	Any letter, numeric digit, or the underscore character. (Think of this as matching "word" characters.)
\W	Any character that is *not* a letter, numeric digit, or the underscore character.
\s	Any space, tab, or newline character. (Think of this as matching "space" characters.)
\S	Any character that is *not* a space, tab, or newline.

Character classes are nice for shortening regular expressions. The character class [0-5] will match only the numbers 0 to 5; this is much shorter than typing (0|1|2|3|4|5).

For example, enter the following into the interactive shell:

```
>>> xmasRegex = re.compile(r'\d+\s\w+')
>>> xmasRegex.findall('12 drummers, 11 pipers, 10 lords, 9 ladies, 8 maids, 7
swans, 6 geese, 5 rings, 4 birds, 3 hens, 2 doves, 1 partridge')
['12 drummers', '11 pipers', '10 lords', '9 ladies', '8 maids', '7 swans', '6
geese', '5 rings', '4 birds', '3 hens', '2 doves', '1 partridge']
```

The regular expression \d+\s\w+ will match text that has one or more numeric digits (\d+), followed by a whitespace character (\s), followed by one or more letter/digit/underscore characters (\w+). The findall() method returns all matching strings of the regex pattern in a list.

Making Your Own Character Classes

There are times when you want to match a set of characters but the shorthand character classes (\d, \w, \s, and so on) are too broad. You can define your own character class using square brackets. For example, the character class [aeiouAEIOU] will match any vowel, both lowercase and uppercase. Enter the following into the interactive shell:

```
>>> vowelRegex = re.compile(r'[aeiouAEIOU]')
>>> vowelRegex.findall('RoboCop eats baby food. BABY FOOD.')
['o', 'o', 'o', 'e', 'a', 'a', 'o', 'o', 'A', 'O', 'O']
```

You can also include ranges of letters or numbers by using a hyphen. For example, the character class [a-zA-Z0-9] will match all lowercase letters, uppercase letters, and numbers.

Note that inside the square brackets, the normal regular expression symbols are not interpreted as such. This means you do not need to escape the ., *, ?, or () characters with a preceding backslash. For example, the character class [0-5.] will match digits 0 to 5 and a period. You do not need to write it as [0-5\.].

By placing a caret character (^) just after the character class's opening bracket, you can make a *negative character class*. A negative character class will match all the characters that are *not* in the character class. For example, enter the following into the interactive shell:

```
>>> consonantRegex = re.compile(r'[^aeiouAEIOU]')
>>> consonantRegex.findall('RoboCop eats baby food. BABY FOOD.')
['R', 'b', 'c', 'p', ' ', 't', 's', ' ', 'b', 'b', 'y', ' ', 'f', 'd', '.', '
', 'B', 'B', 'Y', ' ', 'F', 'D', '.']
```

Now, instead of matching every vowel, we're matching every character that isn't a vowel.

The Caret and Dollar Sign Characters

You can also use the caret symbol (^) at the start of a regex to indicate that a match must occur at the *beginning* of the searched text. Likewise, you can put a dollar sign ($) at the end of the regex to indicate the string must *end* with this regex pattern. And you can use the ^ and $ together to indicate that the entire string must match the regex—that is, it's not enough for a match to be made on some subset of the string.

For example, the r'^Hello' regular expression string matches strings that begin with 'Hello'. Enter the following into the interactive shell:

```
>>> beginsWithHello = re.compile(r'^Hello')
>>> beginsWithHello.search('Hello world!')
<_sre.SRE_Match object; span=(0, 5), match='Hello'>
>>> beginsWithHello.search('He said hello.') == None
True
```

The r'\d$' regular expression string matches strings that end with a numeric character from 0 to 9. Enter the following into the interactive shell:

```
>>> endsWithNumber = re.compile(r'\d$')
>>> endsWithNumber.search('Your number is 42')
<_sre.SRE_Match object; span=(16, 17), match='2'>
>>> endsWithNumber.search('Your number is forty two.') == None
True
```

The r'^\d+$' regular expression string matches strings that both begin and end with one or more numeric characters. Enter the following into the interactive shell:

```
>>> wholeStringIsNum = re.compile(r'^\d+$')
>>> wholeStringIsNum.search('1234567890')
<_sre.SRE_Match object; span=(0, 10), match='1234567890'>
>>> wholeStringIsNum.search('12345xyz67890') == None
True
>>> wholeStringIsNum.search('12  34567890') == None
True
```

The last two search() calls in the previous interactive shell example demonstrate how the entire string must match the regex if ^ and $ are used.

I always confuse the meanings of these two symbols, so I use the mnemonic "Carrots cost dollars" to remind myself that the caret comes first and the dollar sign comes last.

The Wildcard Character

The . (or *dot*) character in a regular expression is called a *wildcard* and will match any character except for a newline. For example, enter the following into the interactive shell:

```
>>> atRegex = re.compile(r'.at')
>>> atRegex.findall('The cat in the hat sat on the flat mat.')
['cat', 'hat', 'sat', 'lat', 'mat']
```

Remember that the dot character will match just one character, which is why the match for the text flat in the previous example matched only lat. To match an actual dot, escape the dot with a backslash: \..

Matching Everything with Dot-Star

Sometimes you will want to match everything and anything. For example, say you want to match the string 'First Name:', followed by any and all text, followed by 'Last Name:', and then followed by anything again. You can use the dot-star (.*) to stand in for that "anything." Remember that the dot character means "any single character except the newline," and the star character means "zero or more of the preceding character."

Enter the following into the interactive shell:

```
>>> nameRegex = re.compile(r'First Name: (.*) Last Name: (.*)')
>>> mo = nameRegex.search('First Name: Al Last Name: Sweigart')
>>> mo.group(1)
'Al'
>>> mo.group(2)
'Sweigart'
```

The dot-star uses *greedy* mode: It will always try to match as much text as possible. To match any and all text in a *nongreedy* fashion, use the dot, star, and question mark (.*?). Like with curly brackets, the question mark tells Python to match in a nongreedy way.

Enter the following into the interactive shell to see the difference between the greedy and nongreedy versions:

```
>>> nongreedyRegex = re.compile(r'<.*?>')
>>> mo = nongreedyRegex.search('<To serve man> for dinner.>')
>>> mo.group()
'<To serve man>'

>>> greedyRegex = re.compile(r'<.*>')
>>> mo = greedyRegex.search('<To serve man> for dinner.>')
>>> mo.group()
'<To serve man> for dinner.>'
```

Both regexes roughly translate to "Match an opening angle bracket, followed by anything, followed by a closing angle bracket." But the string '<To serve man> for dinner.>' has two possible matches for the closing angle bracket. In the nongreedy version of the regex, Python matches the shortest possible string: '<To serve man>'. In the greedy version, Python matches the longest possible string: '<To serve man> for dinner.>'.

Matching Newlines with the Dot Character

The dot-star will match everything except a newline. By passing re.DOTALL as the second argument to re.compile(), you can make the dot character match *all* characters, including the newline character.

Enter the following into the interactive shell:

```
>>> noNewlineRegex = re.compile('.*')
>>> noNewlineRegex.search('Serve the public trust.\nProtect the innocent.
\nUphold the law.').group()
'Serve the public trust.'

>>> newlineRegex = re.compile('.*', re.DOTALL)
>>> newlineRegex.search('Serve the public trust.\nProtect the innocent.
\nUphold the law.').group()
'Serve the public trust.\nProtect the innocent.\nUphold the law.'
```

The regex noNewlineRegex, which did not have re.DOTALL passed to the re.compile() call that created it, will match everything only up to the first newline character, whereas newlineRegex, which *did* have re.DOTALL passed to re.compile(), matches everything. This is why the newlineRegex.search() call matches the full string, including its newline characters.

Review of Regex Symbols

This chapter covered a lot of notation, so here's a quick review of what you learned:

- The ? matches zero or one of the preceding group.
- The * matches zero or more of the preceding group.
- The + matches one or more of the preceding group.
- The {n} matches exactly *n* of the preceding group.
- The {n,} matches *n* or more of the preceding group.
- The {,m} matches 0 to *m* of the preceding group.
- The {n,m} matches at least *n* and at most *m* of the preceding group.
- {n,m}? or *? or +? performs a nongreedy match of the preceding group.
- ^spam means the string must begin with *spam*.
- spam$ means the string must end with *spam*.
- The . matches any character, except newline characters.
- \d, \w, and \s match a digit, word, or space character, respectively.
- \D, \W, and \S match anything except a digit, word, or space character, respectively.
- [abc] matches any character between the brackets (such as *a*, *b*, or *c*).
- [^abc] matches any character that isn't between the brackets.

Case-Insensitive Matching

Normally, regular expressions match text with the exact casing you specify. For example, the following regexes match completely different strings:

```
>>> regex1 = re.compile('RoboCop')
>>> regex2 = re.compile('ROBOCOP')
>>> regex3 = re.compile('robOcop')
>>> regex4 = re.compile('RobocOp')
```

But sometimes you care only about matching the letters without worrying whether they're uppercase or lowercase. To make your regex case-insensitive, you can pass re.IGNORECASE or re.I as a second argument to re.compile(). Enter the following into the interactive shell:

```
>>> robocop = re.compile(r'robocop', re.I)
>>> robocop.search('RoboCop is part man, part machine, all cop.').group()
'RoboCop'

>>> robocop.search('ROBOCOP protects the innocent.').group()
'ROBOCOP'

>>> robocop.search('Al, why does your programming book talk about robocop so much?').group()
'robocop'
```

Substituting Strings with the sub() Method

Regular expressions can not only find text patterns but can also substitute new text in place of those patterns. The sub() method for Regex objects is passed two arguments. The first argument is a string to replace any matches. The second is the string for the regular expression. The sub() method returns a string with the substitutions applied.

For example, enter the following into the interactive shell:

```
>>> namesRegex = re.compile(r'Agent \w+')
>>> namesRegex.sub('CENSORED', 'Agent Alice gave the secret documents to Agent Bob.')
'CENSORED gave the secret documents to CENSORED.'
```

Sometimes you may need to use the matched text itself as part of the substitution. In the first argument to sub(), you can type \1, \2, \3, and so on, to mean "Enter the text of group 1, 2, 3, and so on, in the substitution."

For example, say you want to censor the names of the secret agents by showing just the first letters of their names. To do this, you could use the regex Agent (\w)\w* and pass r'\1****' as the first argument to sub(). The \1 in that string will be replaced by whatever text was matched by group 1—that is, the (\w) group of the regular expression.

```
>>> agentNamesRegex = re.compile(r'Agent (\w)\w*')
>>> agentNamesRegex.sub(r'\1****', 'Agent Alice told Agent Carol that Agent
Eve knew Agent Bob was a double agent.')
A**** told C**** that E**** knew B**** was a double agent.'
```

Managing Complex Regexes

Regular expressions are fine if the text pattern you need to match is simple. But matching complicated text patterns might require long, convoluted regular expressions. You can mitigate this by telling the re.compile() function to ignore whitespace and comments inside the regular expression string. This "verbose mode" can be enabled by passing the variable re.VERBOSE as the second argument to re.compile().

Now instead of a hard-to-read regular expression like this:

```
phoneRegex = re.compile(r'((\d{3}|\(\d{3}\))?(\s|-|\.)?\d{3}(\s|-|\.)\d{4}
(\s*(ext|x|ext.)\s*\d{2,5})?)')
```

you can spread the regular expression over multiple lines with comments like this:

```
phoneRegex = re.compile(r'''(
    (\d{3}|\(\d{3}\))?            # area code
    (\s|-|\.)?                   # separator
    \d{3}                        # first 3 digits
    (\s|-|\.)                    # separator
    \d{4}                        # last 4 digits
    (\s*(ext|x|ext.)\s*\d{2,5})? # extension
    )''', re.VERBOSE)
```

Note how the previous example uses the triple-quote syntax (''') to create a multiline string so that you can spread the regular expression definition over many lines, making it much more legible.

The comment rules inside the regular expression string are the same as regular Python code: The # symbol and everything after it to the end of the line are ignored. Also, the extra spaces inside the multiline string for the regular expression are not considered part of the text pattern to be matched. This lets you organize the regular expression so it's easier to read.

Combining re.IGNORECASE, re.DOTALL, and re.VERBOSE

What if you want to use re.VERBOSE to write comments in your regular expression but also want to use re.IGNORECASE to ignore capitalization? Unfortunately, the re.compile() function takes only a single value as its second argument. You can get around this limitation by combining the re.IGNORECASE, re.DOTALL, and re.VERBOSE variables using the pipe character (|), which in this context is known as the *bitwise or* operator.

So if you want a regular expression that's case-insensitive *and* includes newlines to match the dot character, you would form your re.compile() call like this:

```
>>> someRegexValue = re.compile('foo', re.IGNORECASE | re.DOTALL)
```

All three options for the second argument will look like this:

```
>>> someRegexValue = re.compile('foo', re.IGNORECASE | re.DOTALL | re.VERBOSE)
```

This syntax is a little old-fashioned and originates from early versions of Python. The details of the bitwise operators are beyond the scope of this book, but check out the resources at *http://nostarch.com/automatestuff/* for more information. You can also pass other options for the second argument; they're uncommon, but you can read more about them in the resources, too.

Project: Phone Number and Email Address Extractor

Say you have the boring task of finding every phone number and email address in a long web page or document. If you manually scroll through the page, you might end up searching for a long time. But if you had a program that could search the text in your clipboard for phone numbers and email addresses, you could simply press CTRL-A to select all the text, press CTRL-C to copy it to the clipboard, and then run your program. It could replace the text on the clipboard with just the phone numbers and email addresses it finds.

Whenever you're tackling a new project, it can be tempting to dive right into writing code. But more often than not, it's best to take a step back and consider the bigger picture. I recommend first drawing up a high-level plan for what your program needs to do. Don't think about the actual code yet—you can worry about that later. Right now, stick to broad strokes.

For example, your phone and email address extractor will need to do the following:

- Get the text off the clipboard.
- Find all phone numbers and email addresses in the text.
- Paste them onto the clipboard.

Now you can start thinking about how this might work in code. The code will need to do the following:

- Use the pyperclip module to copy and paste strings.
- Create two regexes, one for matching phone numbers and the other for matching email addresses.
- Find all matches, not just the first match, of both regexes.
- Neatly format the matched strings into a single string to paste.
- Display some kind of message if no matches were found in the text.

This list is like a road map for the project. As you write the code, you can focus on each of these steps separately. Each step is fairly manageable and expressed in terms of things you already know how to do in Python.

Step 1: Create a Regex for Phone Numbers

First, you have to create a regular expression to search for phone numbers. Create a new file, enter the following, and save it as *phoneAndEmail.py*:

```
#! python3
# phoneAndEmail.py - Finds phone numbers and email addresses on the clipboard.

import pyperclip, re

phoneRegex = re.compile(r'''(
    (\d{3}|\(\d{3}\))?            # area code
    (\s|-|\.)?                    # separator
    (\d{3})                      # first 3 digits
    (\s|-|\.)                    # separator
    (\d{4})                      # last 4 digits
    (\s*(ext|x|ext.)\s*(\d{2,5}))?  # extension
    )''', re.VERBOSE)

# TODO: Create email regex.

# TODO: Find matches in clipboard text.

# TODO: Copy results to the clipboard.
```

The TODO comments are just a skeleton for the program. They'll be replaced as you write the actual code.

The phone number begins with an *optional* area code, so the area code group is followed with a question mark. Since the area code can be just three digits (that is, \d{3}) *or* three digits within parentheses (that is, \(\d{3}\)), you should have a pipe joining those parts. You can add the regex comment # Area code to this part of the multiline string to help you remember what (\d{3}|\(\d{3}\))? is supposed to match.

The phone number separator character can be a space (\s), hyphen (-), or period (.), so these parts should also be joined by pipes. The next few parts of the regular expression are straightforward: three digits, followed by another separator, followed by four digits. The last part is an optional extension made up of any number of spaces followed by ext, x, or ext., followed by two to five digits.

Step 2: Create a Regex for Email Addresses

You will also need a regular expression that can match email addresses. Make your program look like the following:

```
#! python3
# phoneAndEmail.py - Finds phone numbers and email addresses on the clipboard.
```

```
import pyperclip, re

phoneRegex = re.compile(r'''(
--snip--

# Create email regex.
emailRegex = re.compile(r'''(
    [a-zA-Z0-9._%+-]+      # username
    @                      # @ symbol
    [a-zA-Z0-9.-]+         # domain name
    (\.[a-zA-Z]{2,4})      # dot-something
    )''', re.VERBOSE)

# TODO: Find matches in clipboard text.

# TODO: Copy results to the clipboard.
```

❶ ❷ ❸ (margin markers for the three commented regex lines above)

The username part of the email address ❶ is one or more characters that can be any of the following: lowercase and uppercase letters, numbers, a dot, an underscore, a percent sign, a plus sign, or a hyphen. You can put all of these into a character class: [a-zA-Z0-9._%+-].

The domain and username are separated by an @ symbol ❷. The domain name ❸ has a slightly less permissive character class with only letters, numbers, periods, and hyphens: [a-zA-Z0-9.-]. And last will be the "dot-com" part (technically known as the *top-level domain*), which can really be dot-anything. This is between two and four characters.

The format for email addresses has a lot of weird rules. This regular expression won't match every possible valid email address, but it'll match almost any typical email address you'll encounter.

Step 3: Find All Matches in the Clipboard Text

Now that you have specified the regular expressions for phone numbers and email addresses, you can let Python's re module do the hard work of finding all the matches on the clipboard. The pyperclip.paste() function will get a string value of the text on the clipboard, and the findall() regex method will return a list of tuples.

Make your program look like the following:

```
#! python3
# phoneAndEmail.py - Finds phone numbers and email addresses on the clipboard.

import pyperclip, re

phoneRegex = re.compile(r'''(
--snip--

# Find matches in clipboard text.
text = str(pyperclip.paste())
```

```
❶ matches = []
❷ for groups in phoneRegex.findall(text):
       phoneNum = '-'.join([groups[1], groups[3], groups[5]])
       if groups[8] != '':
           phoneNum += ' x' + groups[8]
       matches.append(phoneNum)
❸ for groups in emailRegex.findall(text):
       matches.append(groups[0])

   # TODO: Copy results to the clipboard.
```

There is one tuple for each match, and each tuple contains strings for each group in the regular expression. Remember that group 0 matches the entire regular expression, so the group at index 0 of the tuple is the one you are interested in.

As you can see at ❶, you'll store the matches in a list variable named matches. It starts off as an empty list, and a couple for loops. For the email addresses, you append group 0 of each match ❸. For the matched phone numbers, you don't want to just append group 0. While the program *detects* phone numbers in several formats, you want the phone number appended to be in a single, standard format. The phoneNum variable contains a string built from groups 1, 3, 5, and 8 of the matched text ❷. (These groups are the area code, first three digits, last four digits, and extension.)

Step 4: Join the Matches into a String for the Clipboard

Now that you have the email addresses and phone numbers as a list of strings in matches, you want to put them on the clipboard. The pyperclip.copy() function takes only a single string value, not a list of strings, so you call the join() method on matches.

To make it easier to see that the program is working, let's print any matches you find to the terminal. And if no phone numbers or email addresses were found, the program should tell the user this.

Make your program look like the following:

```
#! python3
# phoneAndEmail.py - Finds phone numbers and email addresses on the clipboard.

--snip--
for groups in emailRegex.findall(text):
    matches.append(groups[0])

# Copy results to the clipboard.
if len(matches) > 0:
    pyperclip.copy('\n'.join(matches))
    print('Copied to clipboard:')
    print('\n'.join(matches))
else:
    print('No phone numbers or email addresses found.')
```

Running the Program

For an example, open your web browser to the No Starch Press contact page at *http://www.nostarch.com/contactus.htm*, press CTRL-A to select all the text on the page, and press CTRL-C to copy it to the clipboard. When you run this program, the output will look something like this:

```
Copied to clipboard:
800-420-7240
415-863-9900
415-863-9950
info@nostarch.com
media@nostarch.com
academic@nostarch.com
help@nostarch.com
```

Ideas for Similar Programs

Identifying patterns of text (and possibly substituting them with the sub() method) has many different potential applications.

- Find website URLs that begin with *http://* or *https://*.
- Clean up dates in different date formats (such as 3/14/2015, 03-14-2015, and 2015/3/14) by replacing them with dates in a single, standard format.
- Remove sensitive information such as Social Security or credit card numbers.
- Find common typos such as multiple spaces between   words, accidentally accidentally repeated words, or multiple exclamation marks at the end of sentences. Those are annoying!!

Summary

While a computer can search for text quickly, it must be told precisely what to look for. Regular expressions allow you to specify the precise patterns of characters you are looking for. In fact, some word processing and spreadsheet applications provide find-and-replace features that allow you to search using regular expressions.

The re module that comes with Python lets you compile Regex objects. These values have several methods: search() to find a single match, findall() to find all matching instances, and sub() to do a find-and-replace substitution of text.

There's a bit more to regular expression syntax than is described in this chapter. You can find out more in the official Python documentation at *http://docs.python.org/3/library/re.html*. The tutorial website *http://www.regular-expressions.info/* is also a useful resource.

Now that you have expertise manipulating and matching strings, it's time to dive into how to read from and write to files on your computer's hard drive.

Practice Questions

1. What is the function that creates Regex objects?

2. Why are raw strings often used when creating Regex objects?

3. What does the search() method return?

4. How do you get the actual strings that match the pattern from a Match object?

5. In the regex created from r'(\d\d\d)-(\d\d\d-\d\d\d\d)', what does group 0 cover? Group 1? Group 2?

6. Parentheses and periods have specific meanings in regular expression syntax. How would you specify that you want a regex to match actual parentheses and period characters?

7. The findall() method returns a list of strings or a list of tuples of strings. What makes it return one or the other?

8. What does the | character signify in regular expressions?

9. What two things does the ? character signify in regular expressions?

10. What is the difference between the + and * characters in regular expressions?

11. What is the difference between {3} and {3,5} in regular expressions?

12. What do the \d, \w, and \s shorthand character classes signify in regular expressions?

13. What do the \D, \W, and \S shorthand character classes signify in regular expressions?

14. How do you make a regular expression case-insensitive?

15. What does the . character normally match? What does it match if re.DOTALL is passed as the second argument to re.compile()?

16. What is the difference between .* and .*??

17. What is the character class syntax to match all numbers and lowercase letters?

18. If numRegex = re.compile(r'\d+'), what will numRegex.sub('X', '12 drummers, 11 pipers, five rings, 3 hens') return?

19. What does passing re.VERBOSE as the second argument to re.compile() allow you to do?

20. How would you write a regex that matches a number with commas for every three digits? It must match the following:
    - '42'
    - '1,234'
    - '6,368,745'

    but not the following:
    - '12,34,567' (which has only two digits between the commas)
    - '1234' (which lacks commas)

21. How would you write a regex that matches the full name of someone whose last name is Nakamoto? You can assume that the first name that comes before it will always be one word that begins with a capital letter. The regex must match the following:

- 'Satoshi Nakamoto'
- 'Alice Nakamoto'
- 'RoboCop Nakamoto'

but not the following:

- 'satoshi Nakamoto' (where the first name is not capitalized)
- 'Mr. Nakamoto' (where the preceding word has a nonletter character)
- 'Nakamoto' (which has no first name)
- 'Satoshi nakamoto' (where Nakamoto is not capitalized)

22. How would you write a regex that matches a sentence where the first word is either *Alice, Bob,* or *Carol*; the second word is either *eats, pets,* or *throws*; the third word is *apples, cats,* or *baseballs*; and the sentence ends with a period? This regex should be case-insensitive. It must match the following:

- 'Alice eats apples.'
- 'Bob pets cats.'
- 'Carol throws baseballs.'
- 'Alice throws Apples.'
- 'BOB EATS CATS.'

but not the following:

- 'RoboCop eats apples.'
- 'ALICE THROWS FOOTBALLS.'
- 'Carol eats 7 cats.'

Practice Projects

For practice, write programs to do the following tasks.

Strong Password Detection

Write a function that uses regular expressions to make sure the password string it is passed is strong. A strong password is defined as one that is at least eight characters long, contains both uppercase and lowercase characters, and has at least one digit. You may need to test the string against multiple regex patterns to validate its strength.

Regex Version of strip()

Write a function that takes a string and does the same thing as the strip() string method. If no other arguments are passed other than the string to strip, then whitespace characters will be removed from the beginning and end of the string. Otherwise, the characters specified in the second argument to the function will be removed from the string.

8

READING AND
WRITING FILES

Variables are a fine way to store data while
your program is running, but if you want
your data to persist even after your program
has finished, you need to save it to a file. You
can think of a file's contents as a single string value,
potentially gigabytes in size. In this chapter, you will
learn how to use Python to create, read, and save files
on the hard drive.

Files and File Paths

A file has two key properties: a *filename* (usually written as one word) and
a *path*. The path specifies the location of a file on the computer. For example,
there is a file on my Windows 7 laptop with the filename *project.docx* in the
path *C:\Users\asweigart\Documents*. The part of the filename after the last
period is called the file's *extension* and tells you a file's type. *project.docx* is a
Word document, and *Users*, *asweigart*, and *Documents* all refer to *folders* (also

called *directories*). Folders can contain files and other folders. For example, *project.docx* is in the *Documents* folder, which is inside the *asweigart* folder, which is inside the *Users* folder. Figure 8-1 shows this folder organization.

The *C:* part of the path is the *root folder*, which contains all other folders. On Windows, the root folder is named *C:* and is also called the *C: drive*. On OS X and Linux, the root folder is /. In this book, I'll be using the Windows-style root folder, *C:*. If you are entering the interactive shell examples on OS X or Linux, enter / instead.

Figure 8-1: A file in a hierarchy of folders

Additional *volumes*, such as a DVD drive or USB thumb drive, will appear differently on different operating systems. On Windows, they appear as new, lettered root drives, such as *D:* or *E:*. On OS X, they appear as new folders under the */Volumes* folder. On Linux, they appear as new folders under the */mnt* ("mount") folder. Also note that while folder names and filenames are not case sensitive on Windows and OS X, they are case sensitive on Linux.

Backslash on Windows and Forward Slash on OS X and Linux

On Windows, paths are written using backslashes (\) as the separator between folder names. OS X and Linux, however, use the forward slash (/) as their path separator. If you want your programs to work on all operating systems, you will have to write your Python scripts to handle both cases.

Fortunately, this is simple to do with the os.path.join() function. If you pass it the string values of individual file and folder names in your path, os.path.join() will return a string with a file path using the correct path separators. Enter the following into the interactive shell:

```
>>> import os
>>> os.path.join('usr', 'bin', 'spam')
'usr\\bin\\spam'
```

I'm running these interactive shell examples on Windows, so os.path .join('usr', 'bin', 'spam') returned 'usr\\bin\\spam'. (Notice that the backslashes are doubled because each backslash needs to be escaped by another backslash character.) If I had called this function on OS X or Linux, the string would have been 'usr/bin/spam'.

The os.path.join() function is helpful if you need to create strings for filenames. These strings will be passed to several of the file-related functions introduced in this chapter. For example, the following example joins names from a list of filenames to the end of a folder's name:

```
>>> myFiles = ['accounts.txt', 'details.csv', 'invite.docx']
>>> for filename in myFiles:
```

```
        print(os.path.join('C:\\Users\\asweigart', filename))
C:\Users\asweigart\accounts.txt
C:\Users\asweigart\details.csv
C:\Users\asweigart\invite.docx
```

The Current Working Directory

Every program that runs on your computer has a *current working directory*, or *cwd*. Any filenames or paths that do not begin with the root folder are assumed to be under the current working directory. You can get the current working directory as a string value with the os.getcwd() function and change it with os.chdir(). Enter the following into the interactive shell:

```
>>> import os
>>> os.getcwd()
'C:\\Python34'
>>> os.chdir('C:\\Windows\\System32')
>>> os.getcwd()
'C:\\Windows\\System32'
```

Here, the current working directory is set to *C:\Python34*, so the filename *project.docx* refers to *C:\Python34\project.docx*. When we change the current working directory to *C:\Windows*, *project.docx* is interpreted as *C:\Windows\project.docx*.

Python will display an error if you try to change to a directory that does not exist.

```
>>> os.chdir('C:\\ThisFolderDoesNotExist')
Traceback (most recent call last):
  File "<pyshell#18>", line 1, in <module>
    os.chdir('C:\\ThisFolderDoesNotExist')
FileNotFoundError: [WinError 2] The system cannot find the file specified:
'C:\\ThisFolderDoesNotExist'
```

NOTE *While folder is the more modern name for directory, note that current working directory (or just working directory) is the standard term, not current working folder.*

Absolute vs. Relative Paths

There are two ways to specify a file path.

- An *absolute path*, which always begins with the root folder
- A *relative path*, which is relative to the program's current working directory

There are also the *dot* (.) and *dot-dot* (..) folders. These are not real folders but special names that can be used in a path. A single period ("dot") for a folder name is shorthand for "this directory." Two periods ("dot-dot") means "the parent folder."

Figure 8-2 is an example of some folders and files. When the current working directory is set to *C:\bacon*, the relative paths for the other folders and files are set as they are in the figure.

Figure 8-2: The relative paths for folders and files in the working directory C:\bacon

The .\ at the start of a relative path is optional. For example, *.\spam.txt* and *spam.txt* refer to the same file.

Creating New Folders with os.makedirs()

Your programs can create new folders (directories) with the os.makedirs() function. Enter the following into the interactive shell:

```
>>> import os
>>> os.makedirs('C:\\delicious\\walnut\\waffles')
```

This will create not just the *C:\delicious* folder but also a *walnut* folder inside *C:\delicious* and a *waffles* folder inside *C:\delicious\walnut*. That is, os.makedirs() will create any necessary intermediate folders in order to ensure that the full path exists. Figure 8-3 shows this hierarchy of folders.

Figure 8-3: The result of
os.makedirs('C:\\delicious
\\walnut\\waffles')

The os.path Module

The os.path module contains many helpful functions related to filenames and file paths. For instance, you've already used os.path.join() to build paths in a way that will work on any operating system. Since os.path is a module inside the os module, you can import it by simply running import os. Whenever your programs need to work with files, folders, or file paths, you can refer to the short examples in this section. The full documentation for the os.path module is on the Python website at *http://docs.python.org/3/library/os.path.html*.

> **NOTE** *Most of the examples that follow in this section will require the os module, so remember to import it at the beginning of any script you write and any time you restart IDLE. Otherwise, you'll get a* NameError: name 'os' is not defined *error message.*

Handling Absolute and Relative Paths

The os.path module provides functions for returning the absolute path of a relative path and for checking whether a given path is an absolute path.

- Calling os.path.abspath(*path*) will return a string of the absolute path of the argument. This is an easy way to convert a relative path into an absolute one.
- Calling os.path.isabs(*path*) will return True if the argument is an absolute path and False if it is a relative path.
- Calling os.path.relpath(*path*, *start*) will return a string of a relative path from the *start* path to *path*. If *start* is not provided, the current working directory is used as the start path.

Try these functions in the interactive shell:

```
>>> os.path.abspath('.')
'C:\\Python34'
>>> os.path.abspath('.\\Scripts')
'C:\\Python34\\Scripts'
>>> os.path.isabs('.')
False
>>> os.path.isabs(os.path.abspath('.'))
True
```

Since *C:\Python34* was the working directory when os.path.abspath() was called, the "single-dot" folder represents the absolute path 'C:\\Python34'.

> **NOTE** *Since your system probably has different files and folders on it than mine, you won't be able to follow every example in this chapter exactly. Still, try to follow along using folders that exist on your computer.*

Enter the following calls to os.path.relpath() into the interactive shell:

```
>>> os.path.relpath('C:\\Windows', 'C:\\')
'Windows'
>>> os.path.relpath('C:\\Windows', 'C:\\spam\\eggs')
'..\\..\\Windows'
>>> os.getcwd()
'C:\\Python34'
```

Calling os.path.dirname(*path*) will return a string of everything that comes before the last slash in the path argument. Calling os.path.basename(*path*) will return a string of everything that comes after the last slash in the path argument. The dir name and base name of a path are outlined in Figure 8-4.

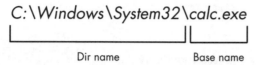

Dir name   Base name

Figure 8-4: The base name follows the last slash in a path and is the same as the filename. The dir name is everything before the last slash.

For example, enter the following into the interactive shell:

```
>>> path = 'C:\\Windows\\System32\\calc.exe'
>>> os.path.basename(path)
'calc.exe'
>>> os.path.dirname(path)
'C:\\Windows\\System32'
```

If you need a path's dir name and base name together, you can just call os.path.split() to get a tuple value with these two strings, like so:

```
>>> calcFilePath = 'C:\\Windows\\System32\\calc.exe'
>>> os.path.split(calcFilePath)
('C:\\Windows\\System32', 'calc.exe')
```

Notice that you could create the same tuple by calling os.path.dirname() and os.path.basename() and placing their return values in a tuple.

```
>>> (os.path.dirname(calcFilePath), os.path.basename(calcFilePath))
('C:\\Windows\\System32', 'calc.exe')
```

But os.path.split() is a nice shortcut if you need both values.

Also, note that os.path.split() does *not* take a file path and return a list of strings of each folder. For that, use the split() string method and split on the string in os.sep. Recall from earlier that the os.sep variable is set to the correct folder-separating slash for the computer running the program.

For example, enter the following into the interactive shell:

```
>>> calcFilePath.split(os.path.sep)
['C:', 'Windows', 'System32', 'calc.exe']
```

On OS X and Linux systems, there will be a blank string at the start of the returned list:

```
>>> '/usr/bin'.split(os.path.sep)
['', 'usr', 'bin']
```

The split() string method will work to return a list of each part of the path. It will work on any operating system if you pass it os.path.sep.

Finding File Sizes and Folder Contents

Once you have ways of handling file paths, you can then start gathering information about specific files and folders. The os.path module provides functions for finding the size of a file in bytes and the files and folders inside a given folder.

- Calling os.path.getsize(*path*) will return the size in bytes of the file in the *path* argument.

- Calling os.listdir(*path*) will return a list of filename strings for each file in the *path* argument. (Note that this function is in the os module, not os.path.)

Here's what I get when I try these functions in the interactive shell:

```
>>> os.path.getsize('C:\\Windows\\System32\\calc.exe')
776192
>>> os.listdir('C:\\Windows\\System32')
['0409', '12520437.cpx', '12520850.cpx', '5U877.ax', 'aaclient.dll',
--snip--
'xwtpdui.dll', 'xwtpw32.dll', 'zh-CN', 'zh-HK', 'zh-TW', 'zipfldr.dll']
```

As you can see, the *calc.exe* program on my computer is 776,192 bytes in size, and I have a lot of files in *C:\Windows\system32*. If I want to find the total size of all the files in this directory, I can use os.path.getsize() and os.listdir() together.

```
>>> totalSize = 0
>>> for filename in os.listdir('C:\\Windows\\System32'):
        totalSize = totalSize + os.path.getsize(os.path.join('C:\\Windows\\System32', filename))

>>> print(totalSize)
1117846456
```

As I loop over each filename in the *C:\Windows\System32* folder, the totalSize variable is incremented by the size of each file. Notice how when I call os.path.getsize(), I use os.path.join() to join the folder name with the current filename. The integer that os.path.getsize() returns is added to the value of totalSize. After looping through all the files, I print totalSize to see the total size of the *C:\Windows\System32* folder.

Checking Path Validity

Many Python functions will crash with an error if you supply them with a path that does not exist. The os.path module provides functions to check whether a given path exists and whether it is a file or folder.

- Calling os.path.exists(*path*) will return True if the file or folder referred to in the argument exists and will return False if it does not exist.

- Calling os.path.isfile(*path*) will return True if the path argument exists and is a file and will return False otherwise.

- Calling os.path.isdir(*path*) will return True if the path argument exists and is a folder and will return False otherwise.

Here's what I get when I try these functions in the interactive shell:

```
>>> os.path.exists('C:\\Windows')
True
>>> os.path.exists('C:\\some_made_up_folder')
False
>>> os.path.isdir('C:\\Windows\\System32')
True
>>> os.path.isfile('C:\\Windows\\System32')
False
>>> os.path.isdir('C:\\Windows\\System32\\calc.exe')
False
>>> os.path.isfile('C:\\Windows\\System32\\calc.exe')
True
```

You can determine whether there is a DVD or flash drive currently attached to the computer by checking for it with the os.path.exists() function. For instance, if I wanted to check for a flash drive with the volume named *D:* on my Windows computer, I could do that with the following:

```
>>> os.path.exists('D:\\')
False
```

Oops! It looks like I forgot to plug in my flash drive.

The File Reading/Writing Process

Once you are comfortable working with folders and relative paths, you'll be able to specify the location of files to read and write. The functions covered in the next few sections will apply to plaintext files. *Plaintext files* contain only basic text characters and do not include font, size, or color information. Text files with the *.txt* extension or Python script files with the *.py* extension are examples of plaintext files. These can be opened with Windows's Notepad or OS X's TextEdit application. Your programs can easily read the contents of plaintext files and treat them as an ordinary string value.

Binary files are all other file types, such as word processing documents, PDFs, images, spreadsheets, and executable programs. If you open a binary file in Notepad or TextEdit, it will look like scrambled nonsense, like in Figure 8-5.

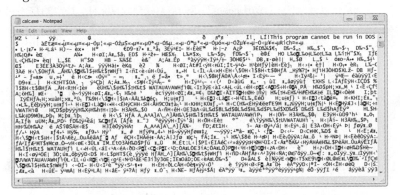

Figure 8-5: The Windows calc.exe *program opened in Notepad*

Since every different type of binary file must be handled in its own way, this book will not go into reading and writing raw binary files directly. Fortunately, many modules make working with binary files easier—you will explore one of them, the shelve module, later in this chapter.

There are three steps to reading or writing files in Python.

1. Call the open() function to return a File object.
2. Call the read() or write() method on the File object.
3. Close the file by calling the close() method on the File object.

Opening Files with the open() Function

To open a file with the open() function, you pass it a string path indicating the file you want to open; it can be either an absolute or relative path. The open() function returns a File object.

Try it by creating a text file named *hello.txt* using Notepad or TextEdit. Type **Hello world!** as the content of this text file and save it in your user home folder. Then, if you're using Windows, enter the following into the interactive shell:

```
>>> helloFile = open('C:\\Users\\your_home_folder\\hello.txt')
```

If you're using OS X, enter the following into the interactive shell instead:

```
>>> helloFile = open('/Users/your_home_folder/hello.txt')
```

Make sure to replace *your_home_folder* with your computer username. For example, my username is *asweigart*, so I'd enter `'C:\\Users\\asweigart\\hello.txt'` on Windows.

Both these commands will open the file in "reading plaintext" mode, or *read mode* for short. When a file is opened in read mode, Python lets you only read data from the file; you can't write or modify it in any way. Read mode is the default mode for files you open in Python. But if you don't want to rely on Python's defaults, you can explicitly specify the mode by passing the string value `'r'` as a second argument to `open()`. So `open('/Users/asweigart/hello.txt', 'r')` and `open('/Users/asweigart/hello.txt')` do the same thing.

The call to `open()` returns a `File` object. A `File` object represents a file on your computer; it is simply another type of value in Python, much like the lists and dictionaries you're already familiar with. In the previous example, you stored the `File` object in the variable `helloFile`. Now, whenever you want to read from or write to the file, you can do so by calling methods on the `File` object in `helloFile`.

Reading the Contents of Files

Now that you have a `File` object, you can start reading from it. If you want to read the entire contents of a file as a string value, use the `File` object's `read()` method. Let's continue with the *hello.txt* File object you stored in `helloFile` . Enter the following into the interactive shell:

```
>>> helloContent = helloFile.read()
>>> helloContent
'Hello world!'
```

If you think of the contents of a file as a single large string value, the `read()` method returns the string that is stored in the file.

Alternatively, you can use the `readlines()` method to get a *list* of string values from the file, one string for each line of text. For example, create a file named *sonnet29.txt* in the same directory as *hello.txt* and write the following text in it:

```
When, in disgrace with fortune and men's eyes,
I all alone beweep my outcast state,
And trouble deaf heaven with my bootless cries,
And look upon myself and curse my fate,
```

Make sure to separate the four lines with line breaks. Then enter the following into the interactive shell:

```
>>> sonnetFile = open('sonnet29.txt')
>>> sonnetFile.readlines()
[When, in disgrace with fortune and men's eyes,\n', ' I all alone beweep my
outcast state,\n', 'And trouble deaf heaven with my bootless cries,\n', 'And
look upon myself and curse my fate,']
```

Note that each of the string values ends with a newline character, \n , except for the last line of the file. A list of strings is often easier to work with than a single large string value.

Writing to Files

Python allows you to write content to a file in a way similar to how the print() function "writes" strings to the screen. You can't write to a file you've opened in read mode, though. Instead, you need to open it in "write plaintext" mode or "append plaintext" mode, or *write mode* and *append mode* for short.

Write mode will overwrite the existing file and start from scratch, just like when you overwrite a variable's value with a new value. Pass 'w' as the second argument to open() to open the file in write mode. Append mode, on the other hand, will append text to the end of the existing file. You can think of this as appending to a list in a variable, rather than overwriting the variable altogether. Pass 'a' as the second argument to open() to open the file in append mode.

If the filename passed to open() does not exist, both write and append mode will create a new, blank file. After reading or writing a file, call the close() method before opening the file again.

Let's put these concepts together. Enter the following into the interactive shell:

```
>>> baconFile = open('bacon.txt', 'w')
>>> baconFile.write('Hello world!\n')
13
>>> baconFile.close()
>>> baconFile = open('bacon.txt', 'a')
>>> baconFile.write('Bacon is not a vegetable.')
25
>>> baconFile.close()
>>> baconFile = open('bacon.txt')
>>> content = baconFile.read()
>>> baconFile.close()
>>> print(content)
Hello world!
Bacon is not a vegetable.
```

First, we open *bacon.txt* in write mode. Since there isn't a *bacon.txt* yet, Python creates one. Calling write() on the opened file and passing write() the string argument 'Hello world! /n' writes the string to the file and returns the number of characters written, including the newline. Then we close the file.

To add text to the existing contents of the file instead of replacing the string we just wrote, we open the file in append mode. We write 'Bacon is not a vegetable.' to the file and close it. Finally, to print the file contents to the screen, we open the file in its default read mode, call read(), store the resulting File object in content, close the file, and print content.

Note that the write() method does not automatically add a newline character to the end of the string like the print() function does. You will have to add this character yourself.

Saving Variables with the shelve Module

You can save variables in your Python programs to binary shelf files using the shelve module. This way, your program can restore data to variables from the hard drive. The shelve module will let you add Save and Open features to your program. For example, if you ran a program and entered some configuration settings, you could save those settings to a shelf file and then have the program load them the next time it is run.

Enter the following into the interactive shell:

```
>>> import shelve
>>> shelfFile = shelve.open('mydata')
>>> cats = ['Zophie', 'Pooka', 'Simon']
>>> shelfFile['cats'] = cats
>>> shelfFile.close()
```

To read and write data using the shelve module, you first import shelve. Call shelve.open() and pass it a filename, and then store the returned shelf value in a variable. You can make changes to the shelf value as if it were a dictionary. When you're done, call close() on the shelf value. Here, our shelf value is stored in shelfFile. We create a list cats and write shelfFile['cats'] = cats to store the list in shelfFile as a value associated with the key 'cats' (like in a dictionary). Then we call close() on shelfFile.

After running the previous code on Windows, you will see three new files in the current working directory: *mydata.bak*, *mydata.dat*, and *mydata.dir*. On OS X, only a single *mydata.db* file will be created.

These binary files contain the data you stored in your shelf. The format of these binary files is not important; you only need to know what the shelve module does, not how it does it. The module frees you from worrying about how to store your program's data to a file.

Your programs can use the shelve module to later reopen and retrieve the data from these shelf files. Shelf values don't have to be opened in read or write mode—they can do both once opened. Enter the following into the interactive shell:

```
>>> shelfFile = shelve.open('mydata')
>>> type(shelfFile)
<class 'shelve.DbfilenameShelf'>
>>> shelfFile['cats']
['Zophie', 'Pooka', 'Simon']
>>> shelfFile.close()
```

Here, we open the shelf files to check that our data was stored correctly. Entering shelfFile['cats'] returns the same list that we stored earlier, so we know that the list is correctly stored, and we call close().

Just like dictionaries, shelf values have `keys()` and `values()` methods that will return list-like values of the keys and values in the shelf. Since these methods return list-like values instead of true lists, you should pass them to the `list()` function to get them in list form. Enter the following into the interactive shell:

```
>>> shelfFile = shelve.open('mydata')
>>> list(shelfFile.keys())
['cats']
>>> list(shelfFile.values())
[['Zophie', 'Pooka', 'Simon']]
>>> shelfFile.close()
```

Plaintext is useful for creating files that you'll read in a text editor such as Notepad or TextEdit, but if you want to save data from your Python programs, use the `shelve` module.

Saving Variables with the pprint.pformat() Function

Recall from "Pretty Printing" on page 111 that the `pprint.pprint()` function will "pretty print" the contents of a list or dictionary to the screen, while the `pprint.pformat()` function will return this same text as a string instead of printing it. Not only is this string formatted to be easy to read, but it is also syntactically correct Python code. Say you have a dictionary stored in a variable and you want to save this variable and its contents for future use. Using `pprint.pformat()` will give you a string that you can write to *.py* file. This file will be your very own module that you can import whenever you want to use the variable stored in it.

For example, enter the following into the interactive shell:

```
>>> import pprint
>>> cats = [{'name': 'Zophie', 'desc': 'chubby'}, {'name': 'Pooka', 'desc': 'fluffy'}]
>>> pprint.pformat(cats)
"[{'desc': 'chubby', 'name': 'Zophie'}, {'desc': 'fluffy', 'name': 'Pooka'}]"
>>> fileObj = open('myCats.py', 'w')
>>> fileObj.write('cats = ' + pprint.pformat(cats) + '\n')
83
>>> fileObj.close()
```

Here, we import pprint to let us use `pprint.pformat()`. We have a list of dictionaries, stored in a variable cats. To keep the list in cats available even after we close the shell, we use `pprint.pformat()` to return it as a string. Once we have the data in cats as a string, it's easy to write the string to a file, which we'll call *myCats.py*.

The modules that an import statement imports are themselves just Python scripts. When the string from `pprint.pformat()` is saved to a *.py* file, the file is a module that can be imported just like any other.

And since Python scripts are themselves just text files with the *.py* file extension, your Python programs can even generate other Python programs. You can then import these files into scripts.

```
>>> import myCats
>>> myCats.cats
[{'name': 'Zophie', 'desc': 'chubby'}, {'name': 'Pooka', 'desc': 'fluffy'}]
>>> myCats.cats[0]
{'name': 'Zophie', 'desc': 'chubby'}
>>> myCats.cats[0]['name']
'Zophie'
```

The benefit of creating a *.py* file (as opposed to saving variables with the shelve module) is that because it is a text file, the contents of the file can be read and modified by anyone with a simple text editor. For most applications, however, saving data using the shelve module is the preferred way to save variables to a file. Only basic data types such as integers, floats, strings, lists, and dictionaries can be written to a file as simple text. File objects, for example, cannot be encoded as text.

Project: Generating Random Quiz Files

Say you're a geography teacher with 35 students in your class and you want to give a pop quiz on US state capitals. Alas, your class has a few bad eggs in it, and you can't trust the students not to cheat. You'd like to randomize the order of questions so that each quiz is unique, making it impossible for anyone to crib answers from anyone else. Of course, doing this by hand would be a lengthy and boring affair. Fortunately, you know some Python.

Here is what the program does:

- Creates 35 different quizzes.
- Creates 50 multiple-choice questions for each quiz, in random order.
- Provides the correct answer and three random wrong answers for each question, in random order.
- Writes the quizzes to 35 text files.
- Writes the answer keys to 35 text files.

This means the code will need to do the following:

- Store the states and their capitals in a dictionary.
- Call open(), write(), and close() for the quiz and answer key text files.
- Use random.shuffle() to randomize the order of the questions and multiple-choice options.

Step 1: Store the Quiz Data in a Dictionary

The first step is to create a skeleton script and fill it with your quiz data. Create a file named *randomQuizGenerator.py*, and make it look like the following:

```python
#! python3
# randomQuizGenerator.py - Creates quizzes with questions and answers in
# random order, along with the answer key.

❶ import random

# The quiz data. Keys are states and values are their capitals.
❷ capitals = {'Alabama': 'Montgomery', 'Alaska': 'Juneau', 'Arizona': 'Phoenix',
'Arkansas': 'Little Rock', 'California': 'Sacramento', 'Colorado': 'Denver',
'Connecticut': 'Hartford', 'Delaware': 'Dover', 'Florida': 'Tallahassee',
'Georgia': 'Atlanta', 'Hawaii': 'Honolulu', 'Idaho': 'Boise', 'Illinois':
'Springfield', 'Indiana': 'Indianapolis', 'Iowa': 'Des Moines', 'Kansas':
'Topeka', 'Kentucky': 'Frankfort', 'Louisiana': 'Baton Rouge', 'Maine':
'Augusta', 'Maryland': 'Annapolis', 'Massachusetts': 'Boston', 'Michigan':
'Lansing', 'Minnesota': 'Saint Paul', 'Mississippi': 'Jackson', 'Missouri':
'Jefferson City', 'Montana': 'Helena', 'Nebraska': 'Lincoln', 'Nevada':
'Carson City', 'New Hampshire': 'Concord', 'New Jersey': 'Trenton', 'New
Mexico': 'Santa Fe', 'New York': 'Albany', 'North Carolina': 'Raleigh',
'North Dakota': 'Bismarck', 'Ohio': 'Columbus', 'Oklahoma': 'Oklahoma City',
'Oregon': 'Salem', 'Pennsylvania': 'Harrisburg', 'Rhode Island': 'Providence',
'South Carolina': 'Columbia', 'South Dakota': 'Pierre', 'Tennessee':
'Nashville', 'Texas': 'Austin', 'Utah': 'Salt Lake City', 'Vermont':
'Montpelier', 'Virginia': 'Richmond', 'Washington': 'Olympia', 'West
Virginia': 'Charleston', 'Wisconsin': 'Madison', 'Wyoming': 'Cheyenne'}

# Generate 35 quiz files.
❸ for quizNum in range(35):
    # TODO: Create the quiz and answer key files.

    # TODO: Write out the header for the quiz.

    # TODO: Shuffle the order of the states.

    # TODO: Loop through all 50 states, making a question for each.
```

Since this program will be randomly ordering the questions and answers, you'll need to import the random module ❶ to make use of its functions. The capitals variable ❷ contains a dictionary with US states as keys and their capitals as values. And since you want to create 35 quizzes, the code that actually generates the quiz and answer key files (marked with TODO comments for now) will go inside a for loop that loops 35 times ❸. (This number can be changed to generate any number of quiz files.)

Step 2: Create the Quiz File and Shuffle the Question Order

Now it's time to start filling in those TODOs.

The code in the loop will be repeated 35 times—once for each quiz—so you have to worry about only one quiz at a time within the loop. First you'll create the actual quiz file. It needs to have a unique filename and should also have some kind of standard header in it, with places for the student to fill in a name, date, and class period. Then you'll need to get a list of states in randomized order, which can be used later to create the questions and answers for the quiz.

Add the following lines of code to *randomQuizGenerator.py*:

```
#! python3
# randomQuizGenerator.py - Creates quizzes with questions and answers in
# random order, along with the answer key.

--snip--

# Generate 35 quiz files.
for quizNum in range(35):
    # Create the quiz and answer key files.
❶    quizFile = open('capitalsquiz%s.txt' % (quizNum + 1), 'w')
❷    answerKeyFile = open('capitalsquiz_answers%s.txt' % (quizNum + 1), 'w')

    # Write out the header for the quiz.
❸    quizFile.write('Name:\n\nDate:\n\nPeriod:\n\n')
    quizFile.write((' ' * 20) + 'State Capitals Quiz (Form %s)' % (quizNum + 1))
    quizFile.write('\n\n')

    # Shuffle the order of the states.
    states = list(capitals.keys())
❹    random.shuffle(states)

    # TODO: Loop through all 50 states, making a question for each.
```

The filenames for the quizzes will be *capitalsquiz<N>.txt*, where *<N>* is a unique number for the quiz that comes from quizNum, the for loop's counter. The answer key for *capitalsquiz<N>.txt* will be stored in a text file named *capitalsquiz_answers<N>.txt*. Each time through the loop, the %s placeholder in 'capitalsquiz%s.txt' and 'capitalsquiz_answers%s.txt' will be replaced by (quizNum + 1), so the first quiz and answer key created will be *capitalsquiz1.txt* and *capitalsquiz_answers1.txt*. These files will be created with calls to the open() function at ❶ and ❷, with 'w' as the second argument to open them in write mode.

The write() statements at ❸ create a quiz header for the student to fill out. Finally, a randomized list of US states is created with the help of the random.shuffle() function ❹, which randomly reorders the values in any list that is passed to it.

Step 3: Create the Answer Options

Now you need to generate the answer options for each question, which will be multiple choice from A to D. You'll need to create another for loop—this one to generate the content for each of the 50 questions on the quiz. Then there will be a third for loop nested inside to generate the multiple-choice options for each question. Make your code look like the following:

```python
#! python3
# randomQuizGenerator.py - Creates quizzes with questions and answers in
# random order, along with the answer key.

--snip--

    # Loop through all 50 states, making a question for each.
    for questionNum in range(50):

        # Get right and wrong answers.
❶      correctAnswer = capitals[states[questionNum]]
❷      wrongAnswers = list(capitals.values())
❸      del wrongAnswers[wrongAnswers.index(correctAnswer)]
❹      wrongAnswers = random.sample(wrongAnswers, 3)
❺      answerOptions = wrongAnswers + [correctAnswer]
❻      random.shuffle(answerOptions)

        # TODO: Write the question and answer options to the quiz file.

        # TODO: Write the answer key to a file.
```

The correct answer is easy to get—it's stored as a value in the capitals dictionary ❶. This loop will loop through the states in the shuffled states list, from states[0] to states[49], find each state in capitals, and store that state's corresponding capital in correctAnswer.

The list of possible wrong answers is trickier. You can get it by duplicating *all* the values in the capitals dictionary ❷, deleting the correct answer ❸, and selecting three random values from this list ❹. The random.sample() function makes it easy to do this selection. Its first argument is the list you want to select from; the second argument is the number of values you want to select. The full list of answer options is the combination of these three wrong answers with the correct answers ❺. Finally, the answers need to be randomized ❻ so that the correct response isn't always choice D.

Step 4: Write Content to the Quiz and Answer Key Files

All that is left is to write the question to the quiz file and the answer to the answer key file. Make your code look like the following:

```python
#! python3
# randomQuizGenerator.py - Creates quizzes with questions and answers in
# random order, along with the answer key.

--snip--
```

```
     # Loop through all 50 states, making a question for each.
     for questionNum in range(50):
         --snip--

         # Write the question and the answer options to the quiz file.
         quizFile.write('%s. What is the capital of %s?\n' % (questionNum + 1,
             states[questionNum]))
❶       for i in range(4):
❷           quizFile.write('    %s. %s\n' % ('ABCD'[i], answerOptions[i]))
         quizFile.write('\n')

         # Write the answer key to a file.
❸       answerKeyFile.write('%s. %s\n' % (questionNum + 1, 'ABCD'[
             answerOptions.index(correctAnswer)]))
     quizFile.close()
     answerKeyFile.close()
```

A for loop that goes through integers 0 to 3 will write the answer options in the answerOptions list ❶. The expression 'ABCD'[i] at ❷ treats the string 'ABCD' as an array and will evaluate to 'A','B', 'C', and then 'D' on each respective iteration through the loop.

In the final line ❸, the expression answerOptions.index(correctAnswer) will find the integer index of the correct answer in the randomly ordered answer options, and 'ABCD'[answerOptions.index(correctAnswer)] will evaluate to the correct answer's letter to be written to the answer key file.

After you run the program, this is how your *capitalsquiz1.txt* file will look, though of course your questions and answer options may be different from those shown here, depending on the outcome of your random.shuffle() calls:

```
Name:

Date:

Period:

               State Capitals Quiz (Form 1)

1. What is the capital of West Virginia?
    A. Hartford
    B. Santa Fe
    C. Harrisburg
    D. Charleston

2. What is the capital of Colorado?
    A. Raleigh
    B. Harrisburg
    C. Denver
    D. Lincoln

--snip--
```

The corresponding *capitalsquiz_answers1.txt* text file will look like this:

```
1. D
2. C
3. A
4. C
--snip--
```

Project: Multiclipboard

Say you have the boring task of filling out many forms in a web page or software with several text fields. The clipboard saves you from typing the same text over and over again. But only one thing can be on the clipboard at a time. If you have several different pieces of text that you need to copy and paste, you have to keep highlighting and copying the same few things over and over again.

You can write a Python program to keep track of multiple pieces of text. This "multiclipboard" will be named *mcb.pyw* (since "mcb" is shorter to type than "multiclipboard"). The *.pyw* extension means that Python won't show a Terminal window when it runs this program. (See Appendix B for more details.)

The program will save each piece of clipboard text under a keyword. For example, when you run `py mcb.pyw save spam`, the current contents of the clipboard will be saved with the keyword *spam*. This text can later be loaded to the clipboard again by running `py mcb.pyw spam`. And if the user forgets what keywords they have, they can run `py mcb.pyw list` to copy a list of all keywords to the clipboard.

Here's what the program does:

- The command line argument for the keyword is checked.
- If the argument is save, then the clipboard contents are saved to the keyword.
- If the argument is list, then all the keywords are copied to the clipboard.
- Otherwise, the text for the keyword is copied to the clipboard.

This means the code will need to do the following:

- Read the command line arguments from sys.argv.
- Read and write to the clipboard.
- Save and load to a shelf file.

If you use Windows, you can easily run this script from the Run... window by creating a batch file named *mcb.bat* with the following content:

```
@pyw.exe C:\Python34\mcb.pyw %*
```

Step 1: Comments and Shelf Setup

Let's start by making a skeleton script with some comments and basic setup. Make your code look like the following:

```
#! python3
# mcb.pyw - Saves and loads pieces of text to the clipboard.
❶ # Usage: py.exe mcb.pyw save <keyword> - Saves clipboard to keyword.
  #        py.exe mcb.pyw <keyword> - Loads keyword to clipboard.
  #        py.exe mcb.pyw list - Loads all keywords to clipboard.

❷ import shelve, pyperclip, sys

❸ mcbShelf = shelve.open('mcb')

  # TODO: Save clipboard content.

  # TODO: List keywords and load content.

  mcbShelf.close()
```

It's common practice to put general usage information in comments at the top of the file ❶. If you ever forget how to run your script, you can always look at these comments for a reminder. Then you import your modules ❷. Copying and pasting will require the pyperclip module, and reading the command line arguments will require the sys module. The shelve module will also come in handy: Whenever the user wants to save a new piece of clipboard text, you'll save it to a shelf file. Then, when the user wants to paste the text back to their clipboard, you'll open the shelf file and load it back into your program. The shelf file will be named with the prefix *mcb* ❸.

Step 2: Save Clipboard Content with a Keyword

The program does different things depending on whether the user wants to save text to a keyword, load text into the clipboard, or list all the existing keywords. Let's deal with that first case. Make your code look like the following:

```
#! python3
# mcb.pyw - Saves and loads pieces of text to the clipboard.
--snip--

  # Save clipboard content.
❶ if len(sys.argv) == 3 and sys.argv[1].lower() == 'save':
❷     mcbShelf[sys.argv[2]] = pyperclip.paste()
  elif len(sys.argv) == 2:
❸     # TODO: List keywords and load content.

  mcbShelf.close()
```

If the first command line argument (which will always be at index 1 of the sys.argv list) is 'save' ❶, the second command line argument is the keyword for the current content of the clipboard. The keyword will be used as the key for mcbShelf, and the value will be the text currently on the clipboard ❷.

If there is only one command line argument, you will assume it is either 'list' or a keyword to load content onto the clipboard. You will implement that code later. For now, just put a TODO comment there ❸.

Step 3: List Keywords and Load a Keyword's Content

Finally, let's implement the two remaining cases: The user wants to load clipboard text in from a keyword, or they want a list of all available keywords. Make your code look like the following:

```python
#! python3
# mcb.pyw - Saves and loads pieces of text to the clipboard.
--snip--

# Save clipboard content.
if len(sys.argv) == 3 and sys.argv[1].lower() == 'save':
        mcbShelf[sys.argv[2]] = pyperclip.paste()
elif len(sys.argv) == 2:
    # List keywords and load content.
    if sys.argv[1].lower() == 'list':
        pyperclip.copy(str(list(mcbShelf.keys())))
    elif sys.argv[1] in mcbShelf:
        pyperclip.copy(mcbShelf[sys.argv[1]])

mcbShelf.close()
```

(with markers ❶, ❷, ❸ pointing to the `if sys.argv[1].lower() == 'list':`, `pyperclip.copy(str(list(mcbShelf.keys())))`, and `pyperclip.copy(mcbShelf[sys.argv[1]])` lines respectively)

If there is only one command line argument, first let's check whether it's 'list' ❶. If so, a string representation of the list of shelf keys will be copied to the clipboard ❷. The user can paste this list into an open text editor to read it.

Otherwise, you can assume the command line argument is a keyword. If this keyword exists in the mcbShelf shelf as a key, you can load the value onto the clipboard ❸.

And that's it! Launching this program has different steps depending on what operating system your computer uses. See Appendix B for details for your operating system.

Recall the password locker program you created in Chapter 6 that stored the passwords in a dictionary. Updating the passwords required changing the source code of the program. This isn't ideal because average users don't feel comfortable changing source code to update their software. Also, every time you modify the source code to a program, you run the risk of accidentally introducing new bugs. By storing the data for a program in a different place than the code, you can make your programs easier for others to use and more resistant to bugs.

Summary

Files are organized into folders (also called directories), and a path describes the location of a file. Every program running on your computer has a current working directory, which allows you to specify file paths relative to the current location instead of always typing the full (or absolute) path. The os.path module has many functions for manipulating file paths.

Your programs can also directly interact with the contents of text files. The open() function can open these files to read in their contents as one large string (with the read() method) or as a list of strings (with the readlines() method). The open() function can open files in write or append mode to create new text files or add to existing text files, respectively.

In previous chapters, you used the clipboard as a way of getting large amounts of text into a program, rather than typing it all in. Now you can have your programs read files directly from the hard drive, which is a big improvement, since files are much less volatile than the clipboard.

In the next chapter, you will learn how to handle the files themselves, by copying them, deleting them, renaming them, moving them, and more.

Practice Questions

1.   What is a relative path relative to?
2.   What does an absolute path start with?
3.   What do the os.getcwd() and os.chdir() functions do?
4.   What are the . and .. folders?
5.   In *C:\bacon\eggs\spam.txt*, which part is the dir name, and which part is the base name?
6.   What are the three "mode" arguments that can be passed to the open() function?
7.   What happens if an existing file is opened in write mode?
8.   What is the difference between the read() and readlines() methods?
9.   What data structure does a shelf value resemble?

Practice Projects

For practice, design and write the following programs.

Extending the Multiclipboard

Extend the multiclipboard program in this chapter so that it has a delete <keyword> command line argument that will delete a keyword from the shelf. Then add a delete command line argument that will delete *all* keywords.

Mad Libs

Create a Mad Libs program that reads in text files and lets the user add their own text anywhere the word *ADJECTIVE, NOUN, ADVERB,* or *VERB* appears in the text file. For example, a text file may look like this:

```
The ADJECTIVE panda walked to the NOUN and then VERB. A nearby NOUN was
unaffected by these events.
```

The program would find these occurrences and prompt the user to replace them.

```
Enter an adjective:
silly
Enter a noun:
chandelier
Enter a verb:
screamed
Enter a noun:
pickup truck
```

The following text file would then be created:

```
The silly panda walked to the chandelier and then screamed. A nearby pickup
truck was unaffected by these events.
```

The results should be printed to the screen and saved to a new text file.

Regex Search

Write a program that opens all *.txt* files in a folder and searches for any line that matches a user-supplied regular expression. The results should be printed to the screen.

9

ORGANIZING FILES

In the previous chapter, you learned how to create and write to new files in Python. Your programs can also organize preexisting files on the hard drive. Maybe you've had the experience of going through a folder full of dozens, hundreds, or even thousands of files and copying, renaming, moving, or compressing them all by hand. Or consider tasks such as these:

- Making copies of all PDF files (and *only* the PDF files) in every sub-folder of a folder
- Removing the leading zeros in the filenames for every file in a folder of hundreds of files named *spam001.txt, spam002.txt, spam003.txt,* and so on
- Compressing the contents of several folders into one ZIP file (which could be a simple backup system)

All this boring stuff is just begging to be automated in Python. By programming your computer to do these tasks, you can transform it into a quick-working file clerk who never makes mistakes.

As you begin working with files, you may find it helpful to be able to quickly see what the extension (*.txt*, *.pdf*, *.jpg*, and so on) of a file is. With OS X and Linux, your file browser most likely shows extensions automatically. With Windows, file extensions may be hidden by default. To show extensions, go to **Start ▸ Control Panel ▸ Appearance and Personalization ▸ Folder Options**. On the View tab, under Advanced Settings, uncheck the **Hide extensions for known file types** checkbox.

The shutil Module

The shutil (or shell utilities) module has functions to let you copy, move, rename, and delete files in your Python programs. To use the shutil functions, you will first need to use import shutil.

Copying Files and Folders

The shutil module provides functions for copying files, as well as entire folders.

Calling shutil.copy(*source*, *destination*) will copy the file at the path *source* to the folder at the path *destination*. (Both *source* and *destination* are strings.) If *destination* is a filename, it will be used as the new name of the copied file. This function returns a string of the path of the copied file.

Enter the following into the interactive shell to see how shutil.copy() works:

```
>>> import shutil, os
>>> os.chdir('C:\\')
❶ >>> shutil.copy('C:\\spam.txt', 'C:\\delicious')
'C:\\delicious\\spam.txt'
❷ >>> shutil.copy('eggs.txt', 'C:\\delicious\\eggs2.txt')
'C:\\delicious\\eggs2.txt'
```

The first shutil.copy() call copies the file at *C:\spam.txt* to the folder *C:\delicious*. The return value is the path of the newly copied file. Note that since a folder was specified as the destination ❶, the original *spam.txt* filename is used for the new, copied file's filename. The second shutil.copy() call ❷ also copies the file at *C:\eggs.txt* to the folder *C:\delicious* but gives the copied file the name *eggs2.txt*.

While shutil.copy() will copy a single file, shutil.copytree() will copy an entire folder and every folder and file contained in it. Calling shutil.copytree(*source*, *destination*) will copy the folder at the path *source*, along with all of its files and subfolders, to the folder at the path *destination*. The *source* and *destination* parameters are both strings. The function returns a string of the path of the copied folder.

Enter the following into the interactive shell:

```
>>> import shutil, os
>>> os.chdir('C:\\')
>>> shutil.copytree('C:\\bacon', 'C:\\bacon_backup')
'C:\\bacon_backup'
```

The shutil.copytree() call creates a new folder named *bacon_backup* with the same content as the original *bacon* folder. You have now safely backed up your precious, precious bacon.

Moving and Renaming Files and Folders

Calling shutil.move(*source*, *destination*) will move the file or folder at the path *source* to the path *destination* and will return a string of the absolute path of the new location.

If *destination* points to a folder, the *source* file gets moved into *destination* and keeps its current filename. For example, enter the following into the interactive shell:

```
>>> import shutil
>>> shutil.move('C:\\bacon.txt', 'C:\\eggs')
'C:\\eggs\\bacon.txt'
```

Assuming a folder named *eggs* already exists in the *C:* directory, this shutil.move() calls says, "Move *C:\bacon.txt* into the folder *C:\eggs*."

If there had been a *bacon.txt* file already in *C:\eggs*, it would have been overwritten. Since it's easy to accidentally overwrite files in this way, you should take some care when using move().

The *destination* path can also specify a filename. In the following example, the *source* file is moved *and* renamed.

```
>>> shutil.move('C:\\bacon.txt', 'C:\\eggs\\new_bacon.txt')
'C:\\eggs\\new_bacon.txt'
```

This line says, "Move *C:\bacon.txt* into the folder *C:\eggs*, and while you're at it, rename that *bacon.txt* file to *new_bacon.txt*."

Both of the previous examples worked under the assumption that there was a folder *eggs* in the *C:* directory. But if there is no *eggs* folder, then move() will rename *bacon.txt* to a file named *eggs*.

```
>>> shutil.move('C:\\bacon.txt', 'C:\\eggs')
'C:\\eggs'
```

Here, move() can't find a folder named *eggs* in the *C:* directory and so assumes that *destination* must be specifying a filename, not a folder. So the *bacon.txt* text file is renamed to *eggs* (a text file without the *.txt* file extension)—probably not what you wanted! This can be a tough-to-spot bug in your programs since the move() call can happily do something that might be quite different from what you were expecting. This is yet another reason to be careful when using move().

Finally, the folders that make up the destination must already exist, or else Python will throw an exception. Enter the following into the interactive shell:

```
>>> shutil.move('spam.txt', 'c:\\does_not_exist\\eggs\\ham')
Traceback (most recent call last):
  File "C:\Python34\lib\shutil.py", line 521, in move
    os.rename(src, real_dst)
FileNotFoundError: [WinError 3] The system cannot find the path specified:
'spam.txt' -> 'c:\\does_not_exist\\eggs\\ham'

During handling of the above exception, another exception occurred:

Traceback (most recent call last):
  File "<pyshell#29>", line 1, in <module>
    shutil.move('spam.txt', 'c:\\does_not_exist\\eggs\\ham')
  File "C:\Python34\lib\shutil.py", line 533, in move
    copy2(src, real_dst)
  File "C:\Python34\lib\shutil.py", line 244, in copy2
    copyfile(src, dst, follow_symlinks=follow_symlinks)
  File "C:\Python34\lib\shutil.py", line 108, in copyfile
    with open(dst, 'wb') as fdst:
FileNotFoundError: [Errno 2] No such file or directory: 'c:\\does_not_exist\\
eggs\\ham'
```

Python looks for *eggs* and *ham* inside the directory *does_not_exist*. It doesn't find the nonexistent directory, so it can't move *spam.txt* to the path you specified.

Permanently Deleting Files and Folders

You can delete a single file or a single empty folder with functions in the os module, whereas to delete a folder and all of its contents, you use the shutil module.

- Calling os.unlink(*path*) will delete the file at *path*.
- Calling os.rmdir(*path*) will delete the folder at *path*. This folder must be empty of any files or folders.
- Calling shutil.rmtree(*path*) will remove the folder at *path*, and all files and folders it contains will also be deleted.

Be careful when using these functions in your programs! It's often a good idea to first run your program with these calls commented out and with print() calls added to show the files that would be deleted. Here is a Python program that was intended to delete files that have the *.txt* file extension but has a typo (highlighted in bold) that causes it to delete *.rxt* files instead:

```
import os
for filename in os.listdir():
    if filename.endswith('.rxt'):
        os.unlink(filename)
```

If you had any important files ending with *.rxt*, they would have been accidentally, permanently deleted. Instead, you should have first run the program like this:

```
import os
for filename in os.listdir():
    if filename.endswith('.rxt'):
        #os.unlink(filename)
        print(filename)
```

Now the os.unlink() call is commented, so Python ignores it. Instead, you will print the filename of the file that would have been deleted. Running this version of the program first will show you that you've accidentally told the program to delete *.rxt* files instead of *.txt* files.

Once you are certain the program works as intended, delete the print(filename) line and uncomment the os.unlink(filename) line. Then run the program again to actually delete the files.

Safe Deletes with the send2trash Module

Since Python's built-in shutil.rmtree() function irreversibly deletes files and folders, it can be dangerous to use. A much better way to delete files and folders is with the third-party send2trash module. You can install this module by running pip install send2trash from a Terminal window. (See Appendix A for a more in-depth explanation of how to install third-party modules.)

Using send2trash is much safer than Python's regular delete functions, because it will send folders and files to your computer's trash or recycle bin instead of permanently deleting them. If a bug in your program deletes something with send2trash you didn't intend to delete, you can later restore it from the recycle bin.

After you have installed send2trash, enter the following into the interactive shell:

```
>>> import send2trash
>>> baconFile = open('bacon.txt', 'a')    # creates the file
>>> baconFile.write('Bacon is not a vegetable.')
25
>>> baconFile.close()
>>> send2trash.send2trash('bacon.txt')
```

In general, you should always use the send2trash.send2trash() function to delete files and folders. But while sending files to the recycle bin lets you recover them later, it will not free up disk space like permanently deleting them does. If you want your program to free up disk space, use the os and shutil functions for deleting files and folders. Note that the send2trash() function can only send files to the recycle bin; it cannot pull files out of it.

Walking a Directory Tree

Say you want to rename every file in some folder and also every file in every subfolder of that folder. That is, you want to walk through the directory tree, touching each file as you go. Writing a program to do this could get tricky; fortunately, Python provides a function to handle this process for you.

Let's look at the *C:\delicious* folder with its contents, shown in Figure 9-1.

Figure 9-1: An example folder that
contains three folders and four files

Here is an example program that uses the os.walk() function on the directory tree from Figure 9-1:

```
import os

for folderName, subfolders, filenames in os.walk('C:\\delicious'):
    print('The current folder is ' + folderName)

    for subfolder in subfolders:
        print('SUBFOLDER OF ' + folderName + ': ' + subfolder)
```

```
    for filename in filenames:
        print('FILE INSIDE ' + folderName + ': '+ filename)

    print('')
```

The os.walk() function is passed a single string value: the path of a folder. You can use os.walk() in a for loop statement to walk a directory tree, much like how you can use the range() function to walk over a range of numbers. Unlike range(), the os.walk() function will return three values on each iteration through the loop:

1. A string of the current folder's name
2. A list of strings of the folders in the current folder
3. A list of strings of the files in the current folder

(By current folder, I mean the folder for the current iteration of the for loop. The current working directory of the program is *not* changed by os.walk().)

Just like you can choose the variable name i in the code for i in range(10):, you can also choose the variable names for the three values listed earlier. I usually use the names foldername, subfolders, and filenames.

When you run this program, it will output the following:

```
The current folder is C:\delicious
SUBFOLDER OF C:\delicious: cats
SUBFOLDER OF C:\delicious: walnut
FILE INSIDE C:\delicious: spam.txt

The current folder is C:\delicious\cats
FILE INSIDE C:\delicious\cats: catnames.txt
FILE INSIDE C:\delicious\cats: zophie.jpg

The current folder is C:\delicious\walnut
SUBFOLDER OF C:\delicious\walnut: waffles

The current folder is C:\delicious\walnut\waffles
FILE INSIDE C:\delicious\walnut\waffles: butter.txt.
```

Since os.walk() returns lists of strings for the subfolder and filename variables, you can use these lists in their own for loops. Replace the print() function calls with your own custom code. (Or if you don't need one or both of them, remove the for loops.)

Compressing Files with the zipfile Module

You may be familiar with ZIP files (with the *.zip* file extension), which can hold the compressed contents of many other files. Compressing a file reduces its size, which is useful when transferring it over the Internet. And since a ZIP file can also contain multiple files and subfolders, it's a handy way to package several files into one. This single file, called an *archive file*, can then be, say, attached to an email.

Your Python programs can both create and open (or *extract*) ZIP files using functions in the zipfile module. Say you have a ZIP file named *example.zip* that has the contents shown in Figure 9-2.

You can download this ZIP file from *http://nostarch.com/automatestuff/* or just follow along using a ZIP file already on your computer.

Figure 9-2: The contents of example.zip

Reading ZIP Files

To read the contents of a ZIP file, first you must create a ZipFile object (note the capital letters *Z* and *F*). ZipFile objects are conceptually similar to the File objects you saw returned by the open() function in the previous chapter: They are values through which the program interacts with the file. To create a ZipFile object, call the zipfile.ZipFile() function, passing it a string of the *.zip* file's filename. Note that zipfile is the name of the Python module, and ZipFile() is the name of the function.

For example, enter the following into the interactive shell:

```
>>> import zipfile, os
>>> os.chdir('C:\\')     # move to the folder with example.zip
>>> exampleZip = zipfile.ZipFile('example.zip')
>>> exampleZip.namelist()
['spam.txt', 'cats/', 'cats/catnames.txt', 'cats/zophie.jpg']
>>> spamInfo = exampleZip.getinfo('spam.txt')
>>> spamInfo.file_size
13908
>>> spamInfo.compress_size
3828
❶ >>> 'Compressed file is %sx smaller!' % (round(spamInfo.file_size / spamInfo
.compress_size, 2))
'Compressed file is 3.63x smaller!'
>>> exampleZip.close()
```

A ZipFile object has a namelist() method that returns a list of strings for all the files and folders contained in the ZIP file. These strings can be passed to the getinfo() ZipFile method to return a ZipInfo object about that particular file. ZipInfo objects have their own attributes, such as file_size and compress_size in bytes, which hold integers of the original file size and compressed file size, respectively. While a ZipFile object represents an entire archive file, a ZipInfo object holds useful information about a *single file* in the archive.

The command at ❶ calculates how efficiently *example.zip* is compressed by dividing the original file size by the compressed file size and prints this information using a string formatted with %s.

Extracting from ZIP Files

The extractall() method for ZipFile objects extracts all the files and folders from a ZIP file into the current working directory.

```
>>> import zipfile, os
>>> os.chdir('C:\\')       # move to the folder with example.zip
>>> exampleZip = zipfile.ZipFile('example.zip')
❶ >>> exampleZip.extractall()
>>> exampleZip.close()
```

After running this code, the contents of *example.zip* will be extracted to *C:*. Optionally, you can pass a folder name to extractall() to have it extract the files into a folder other than the current working directory. If the folder passed to the extractall() method does not exist, it will be created. For instance, if you replaced the call at ❶ with exampleZip.extractall('C:\\ delicious'), the code would extract the files from *example.zip* into a newly created *C:\delicious* folder.

The extract() method for ZipFile objects will extract a single file from the ZIP file. Continue the interactive shell example:

```
>>> exampleZip.extract('spam.txt')
'C:\\spam.txt'
>>> exampleZip.extract('spam.txt', 'C:\\some\\new\\folders')
'C:\\some\\new\\folders\\spam.txt'
>>> exampleZip.close()
```

The string you pass to extract() must match one of the strings in the list returned by namelist(). Optionally, you can pass a second argument to extract() to extract the file into a folder other than the current working directory. If this second argument is a folder that doesn't yet exist, Python will create the folder. The value that extract() returns is the absolute path to which the file was extracted.

Creating and Adding to ZIP Files

To create your own compressed ZIP files, you must open the ZipFile object in *write mode* by passing 'w' as the second argument. (This is similar to opening a text file in write mode by passing 'w' to the open() function.)

When you pass a path to the write() method of a ZipFile object, Python will compress the file at that path and add it into the ZIP file. The write() method's first argument is a string of the filename to add. The second argument is the *compression type* parameter, which tells the computer what algorithm it should use to compress the files; you can always just set this value to zipfile.ZIP_DEFLATED. (This specifies the *deflate* compression algorithm, which works well on all types of data.) Enter the following into the interactive shell:

```
>>> import zipfile
>>> newZip = zipfile.ZipFile('new.zip', 'w')
>>> newZip.write('spam.txt', compress_type=zipfile.ZIP_DEFLATED)
>>> newZip.close()
```

This code will create a new ZIP file named *new.zip* that has the compressed contents of *spam.txt*.

Keep in mind that, just as with writing to files, write mode will erase all existing contents of a ZIP file. If you want to simply add files to an existing ZIP file, pass 'a' as the second argument to zipfile.ZipFile() to open the ZIP file in *append mode*.

Project: Renaming Files with American-Style Dates to European-Style Dates

Say your boss emails you thousands of files with American-style dates (MM-DD-YYYY) in their names and needs them renamed to European-style dates (DD-MM-YYYY). This boring task could take all day to do by hand! Let's write a program to do it instead.

Here's what the program does:

- It searches all the filenames in the current working directory for American-style dates.
- When one is found, it renames the file with the month and day swapped to make it European-style.

This means the code will need to do the following:

- Create a regex that can identify the text pattern of American-style dates.
- Call os.listdir() to find all the files in the working directory.
- Loop over each filename, using the regex to check whether it has a date.
- If it has a date, rename the file with shutil.move().

For this project, open a new file editor window and save your code as *renameDates.py*.

Step 1: Create a Regex for American-Style Dates

The first part of the program will need to import the necessary modules and create a regex that can identify MM-DD-YYYY dates. The to-do comments will remind you what's left to write in this program. Typing them as TODO makes them easy to find using IDLE's CTRL-F find feature. Make your code look like the following:

```
#! python3
# renameDates.py - Renames filenames with American MM-DD-YYYY date format
# to European DD-MM-YYYY.

❶ import shutil, os, re

   # Create a regex that matches files with the American date format.
❷ datePattern = re.compile(r"""^(.*?) # all text before the date
       ((0|1)?\d)-                    # one or two digits for the month
```

```
      ((0|1|2|3)?\d)-            # one or two digits for the day
      ((19|20)\d\d)             # four digits for the year
      (.*?)$                    # all text after the date
❸    """, re.VERBOSE)
```

```
# TODO: Loop over the files in the working directory.

# TODO: Skip files without a date.

# TODO: Get the different parts of the filename.

# TODO: Form the European-style filename.

# TODO: Get the full, absolute file paths.

# TODO: Rename the files.
```

From this chapter, you know the shutil.move() function can be used to rename files: Its arguments are the name of the file to rename and the new filename. Because this function exists in the shutil module, you must import that module ❶.

But before renaming the files, you need to identify which files you want to rename. Filenames with dates such as *spam4-4-1984.txt* and *01-03-2014eggs.zip* should be renamed, while filenames without dates such as *littlebrother.epub* can be ignored.

You can use a regular expression to identify this pattern. After importing the re module at the top, call re.compile() to create a Regex object ❷. Passing re.VERBOSE for the second argument ❸ will allow whitespace and comments in the regex string to make it more readable.

The regular expression string begins with ^(.*?) to match any text at the beginning of the filename that might come before the date. The ((0|1)?\d) group matches the month. The first digit can be either 0 or 1, so the regex matches 12 for December but also 02 for February. This digit is also optional so that the month can be 04 or 4 for April. The group for the day is ((0|1|2|3)?\d) and follows similar logic; 3, 03, and 31 are all valid numbers for days. (Yes, this regex will accept some invalid dates such as 4-31-2014, 2-29-2013, and 0-15-2014. Dates have a lot of thorny special cases that can be easy to miss. But for simplicity, the regex in this program works well enough.)

While 1885 is a valid year, you can just look for years in the 20th or 21st century. This will keep your program from accidentally matching nondate filenames with a date-like format, such as *10-10-1000.txt*.

The (.*?)$ part of the regex will match any text that comes after the date.

Step 2: Identify the Date Parts from the Filenames

Next, the program will have to loop over the list of filename strings returned from os.listdir() and match them against the regex. Any files that do not have a date in them should be skipped. For filenames that have a date, the matched text will be stored in several variables. Fill in the first three TODOs in your program with the following code:

```
#! python3
# renameDates.py - Renames filenames with American MM-DD-YYYY date format
# to European DD-MM-YYYY.

--snip--

# Loop over the files in the working directory.
for amerFilename in os.listdir('.'):
    mo = datePattern.search(amerFilename)

    # Skip files without a date.
❶    if mo == None:
❷        continue

❸    # Get the different parts of the filename.
    beforePart = mo.group(1)
    monthPart  = mo.group(2)
    dayPart    = mo.group(4)
    yearPart   = mo.group(6)
    afterPart  = mo.group(8)

--snip--
```

If the Match object returned from the search() method is None ❶, then the filename in amerFilename does not match the regular expression. The continue statement ❷ will skip the rest of the loop and move on to the next filename.

Otherwise, the various strings matched in the regular expression groups are stored in variables named beforePart, monthPart, dayPart, yearPart, and afterPart ❸. The strings in these variables will be used to form the European-style filename in the next step.

To keep the group numbers straight, try reading the regex from the beginning and count up each time you encounter an opening parenthesis. Without thinking about the code, just write an outline of the regular expression. This can help you visualize the groups. For example:

```
datePattern = re.compile(r"""^(1)    # all text before the date
    (2 (3) )-                        # one or two digits for the month
    (4 (5) )-                        # one or two digits for the day
    (6 (7) )                         # four digits for the year
    (8)$                             # all text after the date
    """, re.VERBOSE)
```

Here, the numbers **1** through **8** represent the groups in the regular expression you wrote. Making an outline of the regular expression, with just the parentheses and group numbers, can give you a clearer understanding of your regex before you move on with the rest of the program.

Step 3: Form the New Filename and Rename the Files

As the final step, concatenate the strings in the variables made in the previous step with the European-style date: The date comes before the month. Fill in the three remaining TODOs in your program with the following code:

```python
#! python3
# renameDates.py - Renames filenames with American MM-DD-YYYY date format
# to European DD-MM-YYYY.

--snip--

    # Form the European-style filename.
❶    euroFilename = beforePart + dayPart + '-' + monthPart + '-' + yearPart +
                     afterPart

    # Get the full, absolute file paths.
    absWorkingDir = os.path.abspath('.')
    amerFilename = os.path.join(absWorkingDir, amerFilename)
    euroFilename = os.path.join(absWorkingDir, euroFilename)

    # Rename the files.
❷    print('Renaming "%s" to "%s"...' % (amerFilename, euroFilename))
❸    #shutil.move(amerFilename, euroFilename)   # uncomment after testing
```

Store the concatenated string in a variable named euroFilename ❶. Then, pass the original filename in amerFilename and the new euroFilename variable to the shutil.move() function to rename the file ❸.

This program has the shutil.move() call commented out and instead prints the filenames that will be renamed ❷. Running the program like this first can let you double-check that the files are renamed correctly. Then you can uncomment the shutil.move() call and run the program again to actually rename the files.

Ideas for Similar Programs

There are many other reasons why you might want to rename a large number of files.

- To add a prefix to the start of the filename, such as adding *spam_* to rename *eggs.txt* to *spam_eggs.txt*
- To change filenames with European-style dates to American-style dates
- To remove the zeros from files such as *spam0042.txt*

Project: Backing Up a Folder into a ZIP File

Say you're working on a project whose files you keep in a folder named *C:\AlsPythonBook*. You're worried about losing your work, so you'd like to create ZIP file "snapshots" of the entire folder. You'd like to keep different versions, so you want the ZIP file's filename to increment each time it is made; for example, *AlsPythonBook_1.zip*, *AlsPythonBook_2.zip*,

AlsPythonBook_3.zip, and so on. You could do this by hand, but it is rather annoying, and you might accidentally misnumber the ZIP files' names. It would be much simpler to run a program that does this boring task for you.

For this project, open a new file editor window and save it as *backupToZip.py*.

Step 1: Figure Out the ZIP File's Name

The code for this program will be placed into a function named backupToZip(). This will make it easy to copy and paste the function into other Python programs that need this functionality. At the end of the program, the function will be called to perform the backup. Make your program look like this:

```python
#! python3
# backupToZip.py - Copies an entire folder and its contents into
# a ZIP file whose filename increments.

❶ import zipfile, os

def backupToZip(folder):
    # Backup the entire contents of "folder" into a ZIP file.

    folder = os.path.abspath(folder)    # make sure folder is absolute

    # Figure out the filename this code should use based on
    # what files already exist.
❷   number = 1
❸   while True:
        zipFilename = os.path.basename(folder) + '_' + str(number) + '.zip'
        if not os.path.exists(zipFilename):
            break
        number = number + 1

❹   # TODO: Create the ZIP file.

    # TODO: Walk the entire folder tree and compress the files in each folder.
    print('Done.')

backupToZip('C:\\delicious')
```

Do the basics first: Add the shebang (#!) line, describe what the program does, and import the zipfile and os modules ❶.

Define a backupToZip() function that takes just one parameter, folder. This parameter is a string path to the folder whose contents should be backed up. The function will determine what filename to use for the ZIP file it will create; then the function will create the file, walk the folder folder, and add each of the subfolders and files to the ZIP file. Write TODO comments for these steps in the source code to remind yourself to do them later ❹.

The first part, naming the ZIP file, uses the base name of the absolute path of folder. If the folder being backed up is *C:\delicious*, the ZIP file's name should be *delicious_N.zip*, where $N = 1$ is the first time you run the program, $N = 2$ is the second time, and so on.

You can determine what *N* should be by checking whether *delicious_1.zip* already exists, then checking whether *delicious_2.zip* already exists, and so on. Use a variable named number for *N* ❷, and keep incrementing it inside the loop that calls os.path.exists() to check whether the file exists ❸. The first nonexistent filename found will cause the loop to break, since it will have found the filename of the new zip.

Step 2: Create the New ZIP File

Next let's create the ZIP file. Make your program look like the following:

```python
#! python3
# backupToZip.py - Copies an entire folder and its contents into
# a ZIP file whose filename increments.

--snip--
    while True:
        zipFilename = os.path.basename(folder) + '_' + str(number) + '.zip'
        if not os.path.exists(zipFilename):
            break
        number = number + 1

    # Create the ZIP file.
    print('Creating %s...' % (zipFilename))
❶  backupZip = zipfile.ZipFile(zipFilename, 'w')

    # TODO: Walk the entire folder tree and compress the files in each folder.
    print('Done.')

backupToZip('C:\\delicious')
```

Now that the new ZIP file's name is stored in the zipFilename variable, you can call zipfile.ZipFile() to actually create the ZIP file ❶. Be sure to pass 'w' as the second argument so that the ZIP file is opened in write mode.

Step 3: Walk the Directory Tree and Add to the ZIP File

Now you need to use the os.walk() function to do the work of listing every file in the folder and its subfolders. Make your program look like the following:

```python
#! python3
# backupToZip.py - Copies an entire folder and its contents into
# a ZIP file whose filename increments.

--snip--

    # Walk the entire folder tree and compress the files in each folder.
❶  for foldername, subfolders, filenames in os.walk(folder):
        print('Adding files in %s...' % (foldername))
        # Add the current folder to the ZIP file.
❷      backupZip.write(foldername)
```

```
                 # Add all the files in this folder to the ZIP file.
❸            for filename in filenames:
                 newBase = os.path.basename(folder) + '_'
                 if filename.startswith(newBase) and filename.endswith('.zip'):
                     continue    # don't backup the backup ZIP files
                 backupZip.write(os.path.join(foldername, filename))
         backupZip.close()
         print('Done.')


backupToZip('C:\\delicious')
```

You can use os.walk() in a for loop ❶, and on each iteration it will return the iteration's current folder name, the subfolders in that folder, and the filenames in that folder.

In the for loop, the folder is added to the ZIP file ❷. The nested for loop can go through each filename in the filenames list ❸. Each of these is added to the ZIP file, except for previously made backup ZIPs.

When you run this program, it will produce output that will look something like this:

```
Creating delicious_1.zip...
Adding files in C:\delicious...
Adding files in C:\delicious\cats...
Adding files in C:\delicious\waffles...
Adding files in C:\delicious\walnut...
Adding files in C:\delicious\walnut\waffles...
Done.
```

The second time you run it, it will put all the files in *C:\delicious* into a ZIP file named *delicious_2.zip*, and so on.

Ideas for Similar Programs

You can walk a directory tree and add files to compressed ZIP archives in several other programs. For example, you can write programs that do the following:

- Walk a directory tree and archive just files with certain extensions, such as *.txt* or *.py*, and nothing else
- Walk a directory tree and archive every file except the *.txt* and *.py* ones
- Find the folder in a directory tree that has the greatest number of files or the folder that uses the most disk space

Summary

Even if you are an experienced computer user, you probably handle files manually with the mouse and keyboard. Modern file explorers make it easy to work with a few files. But sometimes you'll need to perform a task that would take hours using your computer's file explorer.

The os and shutil modules offer functions for copying, moving, renaming, and deleting files. When deleting files, you might want to use the send2trash module to move files to the recycle bin or trash rather than permanently deleting them. And when writing programs that handle files, it's a good idea to comment out the code that does the actual copy/move/rename/delete and add a print() call instead so you can run the program and verify exactly what it will do.

Often you will need to perform these operations not only on files in one folder but also on every folder in that folder, every folder in those folders, and so on. The os.walk() function handles this trek across the folders for you so that you can concentrate on what your program needs to do with the files in them.

The zipfile module gives you a way of compressing and extracting files in .zip archives through Python. Combined with the file-handling functions of os and shutil, zipfile makes it easy to package up several files from anywhere on your hard drive. These .zip files are much easier to upload to websites or send as email attachments than many separate files.

Previous chapters of this book have provided source code for you to copy. But when you write your own programs, they probably won't come out perfectly the first time. The next chapter focuses on some Python modules that will help you analyze and debug your programs so that you can quickly get them working correctly.

Practice Questions

1. What is the difference between shutil.copy() and shutil.copytree()?

2. What function is used to rename files?

3. What is the difference between the delete functions in the send2trash and shutil modules?

4. ZipFile objects have a close() method just like File objects' close() method. What ZipFile method is equivalent to File objects' open() method?

Practice Projects

For practice, write programs to do the following tasks.

Selective Copy

Write a program that walks through a folder tree and searches for files with a certain file extension (such as .pdf or .jpg). Copy these files from whatever location they are in to a new folder.

Deleting Unneeded Files

It's not uncommon for a few unneeded but humongous files or folders to take up the bulk of the space on your hard drive. If you're trying to free up room on your computer, you'll get the most bang for your buck by deleting the most massive of the unwanted files. But first you have to find them.

Write a program that walks through a folder tree and searches for exceptionally large files or folders—say, ones that have a file size of more than 100MB. (Remember, to get a file's size, you can use os.path.getsize() from the os module.) Print these files with their absolute path to the screen.

Filling in the Gaps

Write a program that finds all files with a given prefix, such as *spam001.txt*, *spam002.txt*, and so on, in a single folder and locates any gaps in the numbering (such as if there is a *spam001.txt* and *spam003.txt* but no *spam002.txt*). Have the program rename all the later files to close this gap.

As an added challenge, write another program that can insert gaps into numbered files so that a new file can be added.

10

DEBUGGING

Now that you know enough to write more complicated programs, you may start finding not-so-simple bugs in them. This chapter covers some tools and techniques for finding the root cause of bugs in your program to help you fix bugs faster and with less effort.

To paraphrase an old joke among programmers, "Writing code accounts for 90 percent of programming. Debugging code accounts for the other 90 percent."

Your computer will do only what you tell it to do; it won't read your mind and do what you *intended* it to do. Even professional programmers create bugs all the time, so don't feel discouraged if your program has a problem.

Fortunately, there are a few tools and techniques to identify what exactly your code is doing and where it's going wrong. First, you will look at logging and assertions, two features that can help you detect bugs early. In general, the earlier you catch bugs, the easier they will be to fix.

Second, you will look at how to use the debugger. The debugger is a feature of IDLE that executes a program one instruction at a time, giving you a chance to inspect the values in variables while your code runs, and track how the values change over the course of your program. This is much slower than running the program at full speed, but it is helpful to see the actual values in a program while it runs, rather than deducing what the values might be from the source code.

Raising Exceptions

Python raises an exception whenever it tries to execute invalid code. In Chapter 3, you read about how to handle Python's exceptions with try and except statements so that your program can recover from exceptions that you anticipated. But you can also raise your own exceptions in your code. Raising an exception is a way of saying, "Stop running the code in this function and move the program execution to the except statement."

Exceptions are raised with a raise statement. In code, a raise statement consists of the following:

- The raise keyword
- A call to the Exception() function
- A string with a helpful error message passed to the Exception() function

For example, enter the following into the interactive shell:

```
>>> raise Exception('This is the error message.')
Traceback (most recent call last):
  File "<pyshell#191>", line 1, in <module>
    raise Exception('This is the error message.')
Exception: This is the error message.
```

If there are no try and except statements covering the raise statement that raised the exception, the program simply crashes and displays the exception's error message.

Often it's the code that calls the function, not the function itself, that knows how to handle an exception. So you will commonly see a raise statement inside a function and the try and except statements in the code calling the function. For example, open a new file editor window, enter the following code, and save the program as *boxPrint.py*:

```
def boxPrint(symbol, width, height):
    if len(symbol) != 1:
❶       raise Exception('Symbol must be a single character string.')
    if width <= 2:
❷       raise Exception('Width must be greater than 2.')
    if height <= 2:
❸       raise Exception('Height must be greater than 2.')
```

```
        print(symbol * width)
        for i in range(height - 2):
            print(symbol + (' ' * (width - 2)) + symbol)
        print(symbol * width)

for sym, w, h in (('*', 4, 4), ('O', 20, 5), ('x', 1, 3), ('ZZ', 3, 3)):
    try:
        boxPrint(sym, w, h)
❹  except Exception as err:
❺      print('An exception happened: ' + str(err))
```

Here we've defined a boxPrint() function that takes a character, a width, and a height, and uses the character to make a little picture of a box with that width and height. This box shape is printed to the screen.

Say we want the character to be a single character, and the width and height to be greater than 2. We add if statements to raise exceptions if these requirements aren't satisfied. Later, when we call boxPrint() with various arguments, our try/except will handle invalid arguments.

This program uses the except Exception as err form of the except statement ❹. If an Exception object is returned from boxPrint() ❶❷❸, this except statement will store it in a variable named err. The Exception object can then be converted to a string by passing it to str() to produce a user-friendly error message ❺. When you run this *boxPrint.py*, the output will look like this:

```
****
*  *
*  *
****
OOOOOOOOOOOOOOOOOOOO
O                  O
O                  O
O                  O
OOOOOOOOOOOOOOOOOOOO
An exception happened: Width must be greater than 2.
An exception happened: Symbol must be a single character string.
```

Using the try and except statements, you can handle errors more gracefully instead of letting the entire program crash.

Getting the Traceback as a String

When Python encounters an error, it produces a treasure trove of error information called the *traceback*. The traceback includes the error message, the line number of the line that caused the error, and the sequence of the function calls that led to the error. This sequence of calls is called the *call stack*.

Open a new file editor window in IDLE, enter the following program, and save it as *errorExample.py*:

```
def spam():
    bacon()
```

```
def bacon():
    raise Exception('This is the error message.')

spam()
```

When you run *errorExample.py*, the output will look like this:

```
Traceback (most recent call last):
  File "errorExample.py", line 7, in <module>
    spam()
  File "errorExample.py", line 2, in spam
    bacon()
  File "errorExample.py", line 5, in bacon
    raise Exception('This is the error message.')
Exception: This is the error message.
```

From the traceback, you can see that the error happened on line 5, in the bacon() function. This particular call to bacon() came from line 2, in the spam() function, which in turn was called on line 7. In programs where functions can be called from multiple places, the call stack can help you determine which call led to the error.

The traceback is displayed by Python whenever a raised exception goes unhandled. But you can also obtain it as a string by calling traceback.format_exc(). This function is useful if you want the information from an exception's traceback but also want an except statement to gracefully handle the exception. You will need to import Python's traceback module before calling this function.

For example, instead of crashing your program right when an exception occurs, you can write the traceback information to a log file and keep your program running. You can look at the log file later, when you're ready to debug your program. Enter the following into the interactive shell:

```
>>> import traceback
>>> try:
        raise Exception('This is the error message.')
except:
        errorFile = open('errorInfo.txt', 'w')
        errorFile.write(traceback.format_exc())
        errorFile.close()
        print('The traceback info was written to errorInfo.txt.')

116
The traceback info was written to errorInfo.txt.
```

The 116 is the return value from the write() method, since 116 characters were written to the file. The traceback text was written to *errorInfo.txt*.

```
Traceback (most recent call last):
  File "<pyshell#28>", line 2, in <module>
Exception: This is the error message.
```

Assertions

An *assertion* is a sanity check to make sure your code isn't doing something obviously wrong. These sanity checks are performed by assert statements. If the sanity check fails, then an AssertionError exception is raised. In code, an assert statement consists of the following:

- The assert keyword
- A condition (that is, an expression that evaluates to True or False)
- A comma
- A string to display when the condition is False

For example, enter the following into the interactive shell:

```
>>> podBayDoorStatus = 'open'
>>> assert podBayDoorStatus == 'open', 'The pod bay doors need to be "open".'
>>> podBayDoorStatus = 'I\'m sorry, Dave. I\'m afraid I can\'t do that.'
>>> assert podBayDoorStatus == 'open', 'The pod bay doors need to be "open".'
Traceback (most recent call last):
  File "<pyshell#10>", line 1, in <module>
    assert podBayDoorStatus == 'open', 'The pod bay doors need to be "open".'
AssertionError: The pod bay doors need to be "open".
```

Here we've set podBayDoorStatus to 'open', so from now on, we fully expect the value of this variable to be 'open'. In a program that uses this variable, we might have written a lot of code under the assumption that the value is 'open'—code that depends on its being 'open' in order to work as we expect. So we add an assertion to make sure we're right to assume podBayDoorStatus is 'open'. Here, we include the message 'The pod bay doors need to be "open".' so it'll be easy to see what's wrong if the assertion fails.

Later, say we make the obvious mistake of assigning podBayDoorStatus another value, but don't notice it among many lines of code. The assertion catches this mistake and clearly tells us what's wrong.

In plain English, an assert statement says, "I assert that this condition holds true, and if not, there is a bug somewhere in the program." Unlike exceptions, your code should *not* handle assert statements with try and except; if an assert fails, your program *should* crash. By failing fast like this, you shorten the time between the original cause of the bug and when you first notice the bug. This will reduce the amount of code you will have to check before finding the code that's causing the bug.

Assertions are for programmer errors, not user errors. For errors that can be recovered from (such as a file not being found or the user entering invalid data), raise an exception instead of detecting it with an assert statement.

Using an Assertion in a Traffic Light Simulation

Say you're building a traffic light simulation program. The data structure representing the stoplights at an intersection is a dictionary with keys 'ns' and 'ew', for the stoplights facing north-south and east-west, respectively. The values at these keys will be one of the strings 'green', 'yellow', or 'red'. The code would look something like this:

```
market_2nd = {'ns': 'green', 'ew': 'red'}
mission_16th = {'ns': 'red', 'ew': 'green'}
```

These two variables will be for the intersections of Market Street and 2nd Street, and Mission Street and 16th Street. To start the project, you want to write a switchLights() function, which will take an intersection dictionary as an argument and switch the lights.

At first, you might think that switchLights() should simply switch each light to the next color in the sequence: Any 'green' values should change to 'yellow', 'yellow' values should change to 'red', and 'red' values should change to 'green'. The code to implement this idea might look like this:

```
def switchLights(stoplight):
    for key in stoplight.keys():
        if stoplight[key] == 'green':
            stoplight[key] = 'yellow'
        elif stoplight[key] == 'yellow':
            stoplight[key] = 'red'
        elif stoplight[key] == 'red':
            stoplight[key] = 'green'

switchLights(market_2nd)
```

You may already see the problem with this code, but let's pretend you wrote the rest of the simulation code, thousands of lines long, without noticing it. When you finally do run the simulation, the program doesn't crash—but your virtual cars do!

Since you've already written the rest of the program, you have no idea where the bug could be. Maybe it's in the code simulating the cars or in the code simulating the virtual drivers. It could take hours to trace the bug back to the switchLights() function.

But if while writing switchLights() you had added an assertion to check that *at least one of the lights is always red*, you might have included the following at the bottom of the function:

```
assert 'red' in stoplight.values(), 'Neither light is red! ' + str(stoplight)
```

With this assertion in place, your program would crash with this error message:

```
Traceback (most recent call last):
  File "carSim.py", line 14, in <module>
    switchLights(market_2nd)
  File "carSim.py", line 13, in switchLights
    assert 'red' in stoplight.values(), 'Neither light is red! ' + str(stoplight)
❶ AssertionError: Neither light is red! {'ns': 'yellow', 'ew': 'green'}
```

The important line here is the AssertionError ❶. While your program crashing is not ideal, it immediately points out that a sanity check failed: Neither direction of traffic has a red light, meaning that traffic could be going both ways. By failing fast early in the program's execution, you can save yourself a lot of future debugging effort.

Logging

If you've ever put a print() statement in your code to output some variable's value while your program is running, you've used a form of *logging* to debug your code. Logging is a great way to understand what's happening in your program and in what order its happening. Python's logging module makes it easy to create a record of custom messages that you write. These log messages will describe when the program execution has reached the logging function call and list any variables you have specified at that point in time. On the other hand, a missing log message indicates a part of the code was skipped and never executed.

Using the logging Module

To enable the logging module to display log messages on your screen as your program runs, copy the following to the top of your program (but under the #! python shebang line):

```
import logging
logging.basicConfig(level=logging.DEBUG, format=' %(asctime)s -  %(levelname)s
-  %(message)s')
```

You don't need to worry too much about how this works, but basically, when Python logs an event, it creates a LogRecord object that holds information about that event. The logging module's basicConfig() function lets you specify what details about the LogRecord object you want to see and how you want those details displayed.

Say you wrote a function to calculate the *factorial* of a number. In mathematics, factorial 4 is $1 \times 2 \times 3 \times 4$, or 24. Factorial 7 is $1 \times 2 \times 3 \times 4 \times 5 \times 6 \times 7$, or 5,040. Open a new file editor window and enter the following code. It has a bug in it, but you will also enter several log messages to help yourself figure out what is going wrong. Save the program as *factorialLog.py*.

```
import logging
logging.basicConfig(level=logging.DEBUG, format=' %(asctime)s -  %(levelname)s
-  %(message)s')
logging.debug('Start of program')

def factorial(n):
    logging.debug('Start of factorial(%s%%)'  % (n))
    total = 1
    for i in range(n + 1):
        total *= i
        logging.debug('i is ' + str(i) + ', total is ' + str(total))
```

```
    logging.debug('End of factorial(%s%%)' % (n))
    return total

print(factorial(5))
logging.debug('End of program')
```

Here, we use the `logging.debug()` function when we want to print log information. This `debug()` function will call `basicConfig()`, and a line of information will be printed. This information will be in the format we specified in `basicConfig()` and will include the messages we passed to `debug()`. The `print(factorial(5))` call is part of the original program, so the result is displayed even if logging messages are disabled.

The output of this program looks like this:

```
2015-05-23 16:20:12,664 - DEBUG - Start of program
2015-05-23 16:20:12,664 - DEBUG - Start of factorial(5)
2015-05-23 16:20:12,665 - DEBUG - i is 0, total is 0
2015-05-23 16:20:12,668 - DEBUG - i is 1, total is 0
2015-05-23 16:20:12,670 - DEBUG - i is 2, total is 0
2015-05-23 16:20:12,673 - DEBUG - i is 3, total is 0
2015-05-23 16:20:12,675 - DEBUG - i is 4, total is 0
2015-05-23 16:20:12,678 - DEBUG - i is 5, total is 0
2015-05-23 16:20:12,680 - DEBUG - End of factorial(5)
0
2015-05-23 16:20:12,684 - DEBUG - End of program
```

The `factorial()` function is returning 0 as the factorial of 5, which isn't right. The `for` loop should be multiplying the value in `total` by the numbers from 1 to 5. But the log messages displayed by `logging.debug()` show that the `i` variable is starting at 0 instead of 1. Since zero times anything is zero, the rest of the iterations also have the wrong value for `total`. Logging messages provide a trail of breadcrumbs that can help you figure out when things started to go wrong.

Change the `for i in range(n + 1):` line to `for i in range(1, n + 1):`, and run the program again. The output will look like this:

```
2015-05-23 17:13:40,650 - DEBUG - Start of program
2015-05-23 17:13:40,651 - DEBUG - Start of factorial(5)
2015-05-23 17:13:40,651 - DEBUG - i is 1, total is 1
2015-05-23 17:13:40,654 - DEBUG - i is 2, total is 2
2015-05-23 17:13:40,656 - DEBUG - i is 3, total is 6
2015-05-23 17:13:40,659 - DEBUG - i is 4, total is 24
2015-05-23 17:13:40,661 - DEBUG - i is 5, total is 120
2015-05-23 17:13:40,661 - DEBUG - End of factorial(5)
120
2015-05-23 17:13:40,666 - DEBUG - End of program
```

The `factorial(5)` call correctly returns 120. The log messages showed what was going on inside the loop, which led straight to the bug.

You can see that the `logging.debug()` calls printed out not just the strings passed to them but also a timestamp and the word *DEBUG*.

Don't Debug with print()

Typing `import logging` and `logging.basicConfig(level=logging.DEBUG, format= '%(asctime)s - %(levelname)s - %(message)s')` is somewhat unwieldy. You may want to use `print()` calls instead, but don't give in to this temptation! Once you're done debugging, you'll end up spending a lot of time removing `print()` calls from your code for each log message. You might even accidentally remove some `print()` calls that were being used for nonlog messages. The nice thing about log messages is that you're free to fill your program with as many as you like, and you can always disable them later by adding a single `logging.disable(logging.CRITICAL)` call. Unlike `print()`, the `logging` module makes it easy to switch between showing and hiding log messages.

Log messages are intended for the programmer, not the user. The user won't care about the contents of some dictionary value you need to see to help with debugging; use a log message for something like that. For messages that the user will want to see, like *File not found* or *Invalid input, please enter a number*, you should use a `print()` call. You don't want to deprive the user of useful information after you've disabled log messages.

Logging Levels

Logging levels provide a way to categorize your log messages by importance. There are five logging levels, described in Table 10-1 from least to most important. Messages can be logged at each level using a different logging function.

Table 10-1: Logging Levels in Python

Level	Logging Function	Description
DEBUG	`logging.debug()`	The lowest level. Used for small details. Usually you care about these messages only when diagnosing problems.
INFO	`logging.info()`	Used to record information on general events in your program or confirm that things are working at their point in the program.
WARNING	`logging.warning()`	Used to indicate a potential problem that doesn't prevent the program from working but might do so in the future.
ERROR	`logging.error()`	Used to record an error that caused the program to fail to do something.
CRITICAL	`logging.critical()`	The highest level. Used to indicate a fatal error that has caused or is about to cause the program to stop running entirely.

Your logging message is passed as a string to these functions. The logging levels are suggestions. Ultimately, it is up to you to decide which category your log message falls into. Enter the following into the interactive shell:

```
>>> import logging
>>> logging.basicConfig(level=logging.DEBUG, format=' %(asctime)s -
%(levelname)s - %(message)s')
>>> logging.debug('Some debugging details.')
2015-05-18 19:04:26,901 - DEBUG - Some debugging details.
>>> logging.info('The logging module is working.')
2015-05-18 19:04:35,569 - INFO - The logging module is working.
>>> logging.warning('An error message is about to be logged.')
2015-05-18 19:04:56,843 - WARNING - An error message is about to be logged.
>>> logging.error('An error has occurred.')
2015-05-18 19:05:07,737 - ERROR - An error has occurred.
>>> logging.critical('The program is unable to recover!')
2015-05-18 19:05:45,794 - CRITICAL - The program is unable to recover!
```

The benefit of logging levels is that you can change what priority of logging message you want to see. Passing logging.DEBUG to the basicConfig() function's level keyword argument will show messages from all the logging levels (DEBUG being the lowest level). But after developing your program some more, you may be interested only in errors. In that case, you can set basicConfig()'s level argument to logging.ERROR. This will show only ERROR and CRITICAL messages and skip the DEBUG, INFO, and WARNING messages.

Disabling Logging

After you've debugged your program, you probably don't want all these log messages cluttering the screen. The logging.disable() function disables these so that you don't have to go into your program and remove all the logging calls by hand. You simply pass logging.disable() a logging level, and it will suppress all log messages at that level or lower. So if you want to disable logging entirely, just add logging.disable(logging.CRITICAL) to your program. For example, enter the following into the interactive shell:

```
>>> import logging
>>> logging.basicConfig(level=logging.INFO, format=' %(asctime)s -
%(levelname)s - %(message)s')
>>> logging.critical('Critical error! Critical error!')
2015-05-22 11:10:48,054 - CRITICAL - Critical error! Critical error!
>>> logging.disable(logging.CRITICAL)
>>> logging.critical('Critical error! Critical error!')
>>> logging.error('Error! Error!')
```

Since logging.disable() will disable all messages after it, you will probably want to add it near the import logging line of code in your program. This way, you can easily find it to comment out or uncomment that call to enable or disable logging messages as needed.

Logging to a File

Instead of displaying the log messages to the screen, you can write them to a text file. The logging.basicConfig() function takes a filename keyword argument, like so:

```
import logging
logging.basicConfig(filename='myProgramLog.txt', level=logging.DEBUG, format='
%(asctime)s -  %(levelname)s -  %(message)s')
```

The log messages will be saved to *myProgramLog.txt*. While logging messages are helpful, they can clutter your screen and make it hard to read the program's output. Writing the logging messages to a file will keep your screen clear and store the messages so you can read them after running the program. You can open this text file in any text editor, such as Notepad or TextEdit.

IDLE's Debugger

The *debugger* is a feature of IDLE that allows you to execute your program one line at a time. The debugger will run a single line of code and then wait for you to tell it to continue. By running your program "under the debugger" like this, you can take as much time as you want to examine the values in the variables at any given point during the program's lifetime. This is a valuable tool for tracking down bugs.

To enable IDLE's debugger, click **Debug ▶ Debugger** in the interactive shell window. This will bring up the Debug Control window, which looks like Figure 10-1.

Figure 10-1: The Debug Control window

When the Debug Control window appears, select all four of the **Stack**, **Locals**, **Source**, and **Globals** checkboxes so that the window shows the full set of debug information. While the Debug Control window is displayed, any time you run a program from the file editor, the debugger will pause execution before the first instruction and display the following:

- The line of code that is about to be executed
- A list of all local variables and their values
- A list of all global variables and their values

You'll notice that in the list of global variables there are several variables you haven't defined, such as __builtins__, __doc__, __file__, and so on. These are variables that Python automatically sets whenever it runs a program. The meaning of these variables is beyond the scope of this book, and you can comfortably ignore them.

The program will stay paused until you press one of the five buttons in the Debug Control window: Go, Step, Over, Out, or Quit.

Go

Clicking the Go button will cause the program to execute normally until it terminates or reaches a *breakpoint*. (Breakpoints are described later in this chapter.) If you are done debugging and want the program to continue normally, click the **Go** button.

Step

Clicking the Step button will cause the debugger to execute the next line of code and then pause again. The Debug Control window's list of global and local variables will be updated if their values change. If the next line of code is a function call, the debugger will "step into" that function and jump to the first line of code of that function.

Over

Clicking the Over button will execute the next line of code, similar to the Step button. However, if the next line of code is a function call, the Over button will "step over" the code in the function. The function's code will be executed at full speed, and the debugger will pause as soon as the function call returns. For example, if the next line of code is a print() call, you don't really care about code inside the built-in print() function; you just want the string you pass it printed to the screen. For this reason, using the Over button is more common than the Step button.

Out

Clicking the Out button will cause the debugger to execute lines of code at full speed until it returns from the current function. If you have stepped into a function call with the Step button and now simply want to keep executing instructions until you get back out, click the **Out** button to "step out" of the current function call.

Quit

If you want to stop debugging entirely and not bother to continue executing the rest of the program, click the **Quit** button. The Quit button will immediately terminate the program. If you want to run your program normally again, select **Debug ▸ Debugger** again to disable the debugger.

Debugging a Number Adding Program

Open a new file editor window and enter the following code:

```python
print('Enter the first number to add:')
first = input()
print('Enter the second number to add:')
second = input()
print('Enter the third number to add:')
third = input()
print('The sum is ' + first + second + third)
```

Save it as *buggyAddingProgram.py* and run it first without the debugger enabled. The program will output something like this:

```
Enter the first number to add:
5
Enter the second number to add:
3
Enter the third number to add:
42
The sum is 5342
```

The program hasn't crashed, but the sum is obviously wrong. Let's enable the Debug Control window and run it again, this time under the debugger.

When you press F5 or select **Run ▸ Run Module** (with **Debug ▸ Debugger** enabled and all four checkboxes on the Debug Control window checked), the program starts in a paused state on line 1. The debugger will always pause on the line of code it is about to execute. The Debug Control window will look like Figure 10-2.

Figure 10-2: The Debug Control window when the program
first starts under the debugger

Click the **Over** button once to execute the first print() call. You should
use Over instead of Step here, since you don't want to step into the code for
the print() function. The Debug Control window will update to line 2, and
line 2 in the file editor window will be highlighted, as shown in Figure 10-3.
This shows you where the program execution currently is.

Figure 10-3: The Debug Control window after clicking Over

Click **Over** again to execute the input() function call, and the buttons in the Debug Control window will disable themselves while IDLE waits for you to type something for the input() call into the interactive shell window. Enter **5** and press Return. The Debug Control window buttons will be reenabled.

Keep clicking **Over**, entering **3** and **42** as the next two numbers, until the debugger is on line 7, the final print() call in the program. The Debug Control window should look like Figure 10-4. You can see in the Globals section that the first, second, and third variables are set to string values '5', '3', and '42' instead of integer values 5, 3, and 42. When the last line is executed, these strings are concatenated instead of added together, causing the bug.

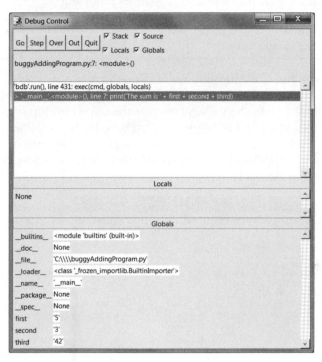

Figure 10-4: The Debug Control window on the last line. The variables are set to strings, causing the bug.

Stepping through the program with the debugger is helpful but can also be slow. Often you'll want the program to run normally until it reaches a certain line of code. You can configure the debugger to do this with breakpoints.

Breakpoints

A *breakpoint* can be set on a specific line of code and forces the debugger to pause whenever the program execution reaches that line. Open a new file editor window and enter the following program, which simulates flipping a coin 1,000 times. Save it as *coinFlip.py*.

```
import random
heads = 0
for i in range(1, 1001):
❶    if random.randint(0, 1) == 1:
         heads = heads + 1
     if i == 500:
❷        print('Halfway done!')
print('Heads came up ' + str(heads) + ' times.')
```

The `random.randint(0, 1)` call ❶ will return 0 half of the time and 1 the other half of the time. This can be used to simulate a 50/50 coin flip where 1 represents heads. When you run this program without the debugger, it quickly outputs something like the following:

```
Halfway done!
Heads came up 490 times.
```

If you ran this program under the debugger, you would have to click the Over button thousands of times before the program terminated. If you were interested in the value of `heads` at the halfway point of the program's execution, when 500 of 1000 coin flips have been completed, you could instead just set a breakpoint on the line `print('Halfway done!')` ❷. To set a breakpoint, right-click the line in the file editor and select **Set Breakpoint**, as shown in Figure 10-5.

Figure 10-5: Setting a breakpoint

You don't want to set a breakpoint on the `if` statement line, since the `if` statement is executed on every single iteration through the loop. By setting the breakpoint on the code in the `if` statement, the debugger breaks only when the execution enters the `if` clause.

The line with the breakpoint will be highlighted in yellow in the file editor. When you run the program under the debugger, it will start in a paused state at the first line, as usual. But if you click Go, the program will run at full speed until it reaches the line with the breakpoint set on it. You can then click Go, Over, Step, or Out to continue as normal.

If you want to remove a breakpoint, right-click the line in the file editor and select **Clear Breakpoint** from the menu. The yellow highlighting will go away, and the debugger will not break on that line in the future.

Summary

Assertions, exceptions, logging, and the debugger are all valuable tools to find and prevent bugs in your program. Assertions with the Python assert statement are a good way to implement "sanity checks" that give you an early warning when a necessary condition doesn't hold true. Assertions are only for errors that the program shouldn't try to recover from and should fail fast. Otherwise, you should raise an exception.

An exception can be caught and handled by the try and except statements. The logging module is a good way to look into your code while it's running and is much more convenient to use than the print() function because of its different logging levels and ability to log to a text file.

The debugger lets you step through your program one line at a time. Alternatively, you can run your program at normal speed and have the debugger pause execution whenever it reaches a line with a breakpoint set. Using the debugger, you can see the state of any variable's value at any point during the program's lifetime.

These debugging tools and techniques will help you write programs that work. Accidentally introducing bugs into your code is a fact of life, no matter how many years of coding experience you have.

Practice Questions

1. Write an assert statement that triggers an AssertionError if the variable spam is an integer less than 10.

2. Write an assert statement that triggers an AssertionError if the variables eggs and bacon contain strings that are the same as each other, even if their cases are different (that is, 'hello' and 'hello' are considered the same, and 'goodbye' and 'GOODbye' are also considered the same).

3. Write an assert statement that *always* triggers an AssertionError.

4. What are the two lines that your program must have in order to be able to call logging.debug()?

5. What are the two lines that your program must have in order to have logging.debug() send a logging message to a file named *programLog.txt*?

6. What are the five logging levels?

7. What line of code can you add to disable all logging messages in your program?

8. Why is using logging messages better than using print() to display the same message?

9. What are the differences between the Step, Over, and Out buttons in the Debug Control window?

10. After you click Go in the Debug Control window, when will the debugger stop?

11. What is a breakpoint?

12. How do you set a breakpoint on a line of code in IDLE?

Practice Project

For practice, write a program that does the following.

Debugging Coin Toss

The following program is meant to be a simple coin toss guessing game. The player gets two guesses (it's an easy game). However, the program has several bugs in it. Run through the program a few times to find the bugs that keep the program from working correctly.

```python
import random
guess = ''
while guess not in ('heads', 'tails'):
    print('Guess the coin toss! Enter heads or tails:')
    guess = input()
toss = random.randint(0, 1) # 0 is tails, 1 is heads
if toss == guess:
    print('You got it!')
else:
    print('Nope! Guess again!')
    guesss = input()
    if toss == guess:
        print('You got it!')
    else:
        print('Nope. You are really bad at this game.')
```

11

WEB SCRAPING

In those rare, terrifying moments when I'm without Wi-Fi, I realize just how much of what I do on the computer is really what I do on the Internet. Out of sheer habit I'll find myself trying to check email, read friends' Twitter feeds, or answer the question, "Did Kurtwood Smith have any major roles before he was in the original 1987 *RoboCop*?"[1]

Since so much work on a computer involves going on the Internet, it'd be great if your programs could get online. *Web scraping* is the term for using a program to download and process content from the Web. For example, Google runs many web scraping programs to index web pages for its search engine. In this chapter, you will learn about several modules that make it easy to scrape web pages in Python.

---

1. The answer is no.

webbrowser Comes with Python and opens a browser to a specific page.

Requests Downloads files and web pages from the Internet.

Beautiful Soup Parses HTML, the format that web pages are written in.

Selenium Launches and controls a web browser. Selenium is able to fill in forms and simulate mouse clicks in this browser.

Project: mapIt.py with the webbrowser Module

The `webbrowser` module's `open()` function can launch a new browser to a specified URL. Enter the following into the interactive shell:

```
>>> import webbrowser
>>> webbrowser.open('http://inventwithpython.com/')
```

A web browser tab will open to the URL *http://inventwithpython.com/*. This is about the only thing the `webbrowser` module can do. Even so, the `open()` function does make some interesting things possible. For example, it's tedious to copy a street address to the clipboard and bring up a map of it on Google Maps. You could take a few steps out of this task by writing a simple script to automatically launch the map in your browser using the contents of your clipboard. This way, you only have to copy the address to a clipboard and run the script, and the map will be loaded for you.

This is what your program does:

- Gets a street address from the command line arguments or clipboard.
- Opens the web browser to the Google Maps page for the address.

This means your code will need to do the following:

- Read the command line arguments from `sys.argv`.
- Read the clipboard contents.
- Call the `webbrowser.open()` function to open the web browser.

Open a new file editor window and save it as *mapIt.py*.

Step 1: Figure Out the URL

Based on the instructions in Appendix B, set up *mapIt.py* so that when you run it from the command line, like so . . .

```
C:\> mapit 870 Valencia St, San Francisco, CA 94110
```

. . . the script will use the command line arguments instead of the clipboard. If there are no command line arguments, then the program will know to use the contents of the clipboard.

First you need to figure out what URL to use for a given street address. When you load *http://maps.google.com/* in the browser and search for an address, the URL in the address bar looks something like this: *https:// www.google.com/maps/place/870+Valencia+St/@37.7590311,-122.4215096,17z/ data=!3m1!4b1!4m2!3m1!1s0x808f7e3dadc07a37:0xc86b0b2bb93b73d8.*

The address is in the URL, but there's a lot of additional text there as well. Websites often add extra data to URLs to help track visitors or customize sites. But if you try just going to *https://www.google.com/maps/place/870+ Valencia+St+San+Francisco+CA/,* you'll find that it still brings up the correct page. So your program can be set to open a web browser to `'https:// www.google.com/maps/place/`*your_address_string*`'` (where *your_address_string* is the address you want to map).

Step 2: Handle the Command Line Arguments

Make your code look like this:

```
#! python3
# mapIt.py - Launches a map in the browser using an address from the
# command line or clipboard.

import webbrowser, sys
if len(sys.argv) > 1:
    # Get address from command line.
    address = ' '.join(sys.argv[1:])

# TODO: Get address from clipboard.
```

After the program's `#!` shebang line, you need to import the `webbrowser` module for launching the browser and import the sys module for reading the potential command line arguments. The `sys.argv` variable stores a list of the program's filename and command line arguments. If this list has more than just the filename in it, then `len(sys.argv)` evaluates to an integer greater than 1, meaning that command line arguments have indeed been provided.

Command line arguments are usually separated by spaces, but in this case, you want to interpret all of the arguments as a single string. Since `sys.argv` is a list of strings, you can pass it to the `join()` method, which returns a single string value. You don't want the program name in this string, so instead of `sys.argv`, you should pass `sys.argv[1:]` to chop off the first element of the array. The final string that this expression evaluates to is stored in the address variable.

If you run the program by entering this into the command line . . .

```
mapit 870 Valencia St, San Francisco, CA 94110
```

. . . the `sys.argv` variable will contain this list value:

```
['mapIt.py', '870', 'Valencia', 'St, ', 'San', 'Francisco, ', 'CA', '94110']
```

The address variable will contain the string `'870 Valencia St, San Francisco, CA 94110'`.

Step 3: Handle the Clipboard Content and Launch the Browser

Make your code look like the following:

```python
#! python3
# mapIt.py - Launches a map in the browser using an address from the
# command line or clipboard.

import webbrowser, sys, pyperclip
if len(sys.argv) > 1:
    # Get address from command line.
    address = ' '.join(sys.argv[1:])
else:
    # Get address from clipboard.
    address = pyperclip.paste()

webbrowser.open('https://www.google.com/maps/place/' + address)
```

If there are no command line arguments, the program will assume the address is stored on the clipboard. You can get the clipboard content with pyperclip.paste() and store it in a variable named address. Finally, to launch a web browser with the Google Maps URL, call webbrowser.open().

While some of the programs you write will perform huge tasks that save you hours, it can be just as satisfying to use a program that conveniently saves you a few seconds each time you perform a common task, such as getting a map of an address. Table 11-1 compares the steps needed to display a map with and without *mapIt.py*.

Table 11-1: Getting a Map with and Without *mapIt.py*

Manually getting a map	Using *mapIt.py*
Highlight the address.	Highlight the address.
Copy the address.	Copy the address.
Open the web browser.	Run *mapIt.py*.
Go to *http://maps.google.com/*.	
Click the address text field.	
Paste the address.	
Press ENTER.	

See how *mapIt.py* makes this task less tedious?

Ideas for Similar Programs

As long as you have a URL, the webbrowser module lets users cut out the step of opening the browser and directing themselves to a website. Other programs could use this functionality to do the following:

- Open all links on a page in separate browser tabs.
- Open the browser to the URL for your local weather.
- Open several social network sites that you regularly check.

Downloading Files from the Web with the requests Module

The requests module lets you easily download files from the Web without having to worry about complicated issues such as network errors, connection problems, and data compression. The requests module doesn't come with Python, so you'll have to install it first. From the command line, run **pip install requests**. (Appendix A has additional details on how to install third-party modules.)

The requests module was written because Python's urllib2 module is too complicated to use. In fact, take a permanent marker and black out this entire paragraph. Forget I ever mentioned urllib2. If you need to download things from the Web, just use the requests module.

Next, do a simple test to make sure the requests module installed itself correctly. Enter the following into the interactive shell:

```
>>> import requests
```

If no error messages show up, then the requests module has been successfully installed.

Downloading a Web Page with the requests.get() Function

The requests.get() function takes a string of a URL to download. By calling type() on requests.get()'s return value, you can see that it returns a Response object, which contains the response that the web server gave for your request. I'll explain the Response object in more detail later, but for now, enter the following into the interactive shell while your computer is connected to the Internet:

```
>>> import requests
❶ >>> res = requests.get('https://automatetheboringstuff.com/files/rj.txt')
>>> type(res)
<class 'requests.models.Response'>
❷ >>> res.status_code == requests.codes.ok
True
>>> len(res.text)
178981
>>> print(res.text[:250])
The Project Gutenberg EBook of Romeo and Juliet, by William Shakespeare

This eBook is for the use of anyone anywhere at no cost and with
almost no restrictions whatsoever.  You may copy it, give it away or
re-use it under the terms of the Proje
```

The URL goes to a text web page for the entire play of *Romeo and Juliet*, provided on this book's site ❶. You can tell that the request for this web page succeeded by checking the status_code attribute of the Response object.

If it is equal to the value of requests.codes.ok, then everything went fine ❷. (Incidentally, the status code for "OK" in the HTTP protocol is 200. You may already be familiar with the 404 status code for "Not Found.")

If the request succeeded, the downloaded web page is stored as a string in the Response object's text variable. This variable holds a large string of the entire play; the call to len(res.text) shows you that it is more than 178,000 characters long. Finally, calling print(res.text[:250]) displays only the first 250 characters.

Checking for Errors

As you've seen, the Response object has a status_code attribute that can be checked against requests.codes.ok to see whether the download succeeded. A simpler way to check for success is to call the raise_for_status() method on the Response object. This will raise an exception if there was an error downloading the file and will do nothing if the download succeeded. Enter the following into the interactive shell:

```
>>> res = requests.get('http://inventwithpython.com/page_that_does_not_exist')
>>> res.raise_for_status()
Traceback (most recent call last):
  File "<pyshell#138>", line 1, in <module>
    res.raise_for_status()
  File "C:\Python34\lib\site-packages\requests\models.py", line 773, in raise_for_status
    raise HTTPError(http_error_msg, response=self)
requests.exceptions.HTTPError: 404 Client Error: Not Found
```

The raise_for_status() method is a good way to ensure that a program halts if a bad download occurs. This is a good thing: You want your program to stop as soon as some unexpected error happens. If a failed download *isn't* a deal breaker for your program, you can wrap the raise_for_status() line with try and except statements to handle this error case without crashing.

```
import requests
res = requests.get('http://inventwithpython.com/page_that_does_not_exist')
try:
    res.raise_for_status()
except Exception as exc:
    print('There was a problem: %s' % (exc))
```

This raise_for_status() method call causes the program to output the following:

```
There was a problem: 404 Client Error: Not Found
```

Always call raise_for_status() after calling requests.get(). You want to be sure that the download has actually worked before your program continues.

Saving Downloaded Files to the Hard Drive

From here, you can save the web page to a file on your hard drive with the standard open() function and write() method. There are some slight differences, though. First, you must open the file in *write binary* mode by passing the string 'wb' as the second argument to open(). Even if the page is in plaintext (such as the *Romeo and Juliet* text you downloaded earlier), you need to write binary data instead of text data in order to maintain the *Unicode encoding* of the text.

UNICODE ENCODINGS

Unicode encodings are beyond the scope of this book, but you can learn more about them from these web pages:

- Joel on Software: The Absolute Minimum Every Software Developer Absolutely, Positively Must Know About Unicode and Character Sets (No Excuses!): *http://www.joelonsoftware.com/articles/Unicode.html*

- Pragmatic Unicode: *http://nedbatchelder.com/text/unipain.html*

To write the web page to a file, you can use a for loop with the Response object's iter_content() method.

```
>>> import requests
>>> res = requests.get('https://automatetheboringstuff.com/files/rj.txt')
>>> res.raise_for_status()
>>> playFile = open('RomeoAndJuliet.txt', 'wb')
>>> for chunk in res.iter_content(100000):
        playFile.write(chunk)

100000
78981
>>> playFile.close()
```

The iter_content() method returns "chunks" of the content on each iteration through the loop. Each chunk is of the *bytes* data type, and you get to specify how many bytes each chunk will contain. One hundred thousand bytes is generally a good size, so pass 100000 as the argument to iter_content().

The file *RomeoAndJuliet.txt* will now exist in the current working directory. Note that while the filename on the website was *rj.txt*, the file on your hard drive has a different filename. The requests module simply handles downloading the contents of web pages. Once the page is downloaded, it is simply data in your program. Even if you were to lose your Internet connection after downloading the web page, all the page data would still be on your computer.

The write() method returns the number of bytes written to the file. In the previous example, there were 100,000 bytes in the first chunk, and the remaining part of the file needed only 78,981 bytes.

To review, here's the complete process for downloading and saving a file:

1. Call requests.get() to download the file.
2. Call open() with 'wb' to create a new file in write binary mode.
3. Loop over the Response object's iter_content() method.
4. Call write() on each iteration to write the content to the file.
5. Call close() to close the file.

That's all there is to the requests module! The for loop and iter_content() stuff may seem complicated compared to the open()/write()/close() workflow you've been using to write text files, but it's to ensure that the requests module doesn't eat up too much memory even if you download massive files. You can learn about the requests module's other features from *http://requests.readthedocs.org/*.

HTML

Before you pick apart web pages, you'll learn some HTML basics. You'll also see how to access your web browser's powerful developer tools, which will make scraping information from the Web much easier.

Resources for Learning HTML

Hypertext Markup Language (HTML) is the format that web pages are written in. This chapter assumes you have some basic experience with HTML, but if you need a beginner tutorial, I suggest one of the following sites:

- *http://htmldog.com/guides/html/beginner/*
- *http://www.codecademy.com/tracks/web/*
- *https://developer.mozilla.org/en-US/learn/html/*

A Quick Refresher

In case it's been a while since you've looked at any HTML, here's a quick overview of the basics. An HTML file is a plaintext file with the *.html* file extension. The text in these files is surrounded by *tags*, which are words enclosed in angle brackets. The tags tell the browser how to format the web page. A starting tag and closing tag can enclose some text to form an *element*. The *text* (or *inner HTML*) is the content between the starting and closing tags. For example, the following HTML will display *Hello world!* in the browser, with *Hello* in bold:

```
<strong>Hello</strong> world!
```

This HTML will look like Figure 11-1 in a browser.

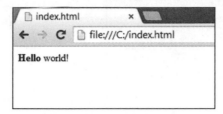

Figure 11-1: Hello world! rendered in the browser

The opening `<strong>` tag says that the enclosed text will appear in bold. The closing `</strong>` tags tells the browser where the end of the bold text is.

There are many different tags in HTML. Some of these tags have extra properties in the form of *attributes* within the angle brackets. For example, the `<a>` tag encloses text that should be a link. The URL that the text links to is determined by the `href` attribute. Here's an example:

```
Al's free <a href="http://inventwithpython.com">Python books</a>.
```

This HTML will look like Figure 11-2 in a browser.

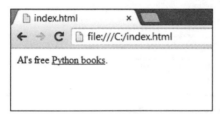

Figure 11-2: The link rendered in the browser

Some elements have an `id` attribute that is used to uniquely identify the element in the page. You will often instruct your programs to seek out an element by its `id` attribute, so figuring out an element's `id` attribute using the browser's developer tools is a common task in writing web scraping programs.

Viewing the Source HTML of a Web Page

You'll need to look at the HTML source of the web pages that your programs will work with. To do this, right-click (or CTRL-click on OS X) any web page in your web browser, and select **View Source** or **View page source** to see the HTML text of the page (see Figure 11-3). This is the text your browser actually receives. The browser knows how to display, or *render*, the web page from this HTML.

Figure 11-3: Viewing the source of a web page

I highly recommend viewing the source HTML of some of your favorite sites. It's fine if you don't fully understand what you are seeing when you look at the source. You won't need HTML mastery to write simple web scraping programs—after all, you won't be writing your own websites. You just need enough knowledge to pick out data from an existing site.

Opening Your Browser's Developer Tools

In addition to viewing a web page's source, you can look through a page's HTML using your browser's developer tools. In Chrome and Internet Explorer for Windows, the developer tools are already installed, and you can press F12 to make them appear (see Figure 11-4). Pressing F12 again will make the developer tools disappear. In Chrome, you can also bring up the developer tools by selecting View ▸ Developer ▸ Developer Tools. In OS X, pressing ⌘-OPTION-I will open Chrome's Developer Tools.

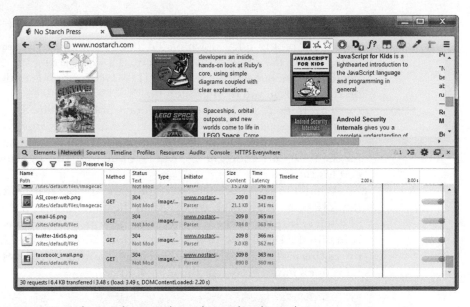

Figure 11-4: The Developer Tools window in the Chrome browser

In Firefox, you can bring up the Web Developer Tools Inspector by pressing CTRL-SHIFT-C on Windows and Linux or by pressing ⌘-OPTION-C on OS X. The layout is almost identical to Chrome's developer tools.

In Safari, open the Preferences window, and on the Advanced pane check the **Show Develop menu in the menu bar** option. After it has been enabled, you can bring up the developer tools by pressing ⌘-OPTION-I.

After enabling or installing the developer tools in your browser, you can right-click any part of the web page and select **Inspect Element** from the context menu to bring up the HTML responsible for that part of the page. This will be helpful when you begin to parse HTML for your web scraping programs.

DON'T USE REGULAR EXPRESSIONS TO PARSE HTML

Locating a specific piece of HTML in a string seems like a perfect case for regular expressions. However, I advise you against it. There are many different ways that HTML can be formatted and still be considered valid HTML, but trying to capture all these possible variations in a regular expression can be tedious and error prone. A module developed specifically for parsing HTML, such as Beautiful Soup, will be less likely to result in bugs.

You can find an extended argument for why you shouldn't to parse HTML with regular expressions at *http://stackoverflow.com/a/1732454/1893164/*.

Using the Developer Tools to Find HTML Elements

Once your program has downloaded a web page using the requests module, you will have the page's HTML content as a single string value. Now you need to figure out which part of the HTML corresponds to the information on the web page you're interested in.

This is where the browser's developer tools can help. Say you want to write a program to pull weather forecast data from *http://weather.gov/*. Before writing any code, do a little research. If you visit the site and search for the 94105 ZIP code, the site will take you to a page showing the forecast for that area.

What if you're interested in scraping the temperature information for that ZIP code? Right-click where it is on the page (or CONTROL-click on OS X) and select **Inspect Element** from the context menu that appears. This will bring up the Developer Tools window, which shows you the HTML that produces this particular part of the web page. Figure 11-5 shows the developer tools open to the HTML of the temperature.

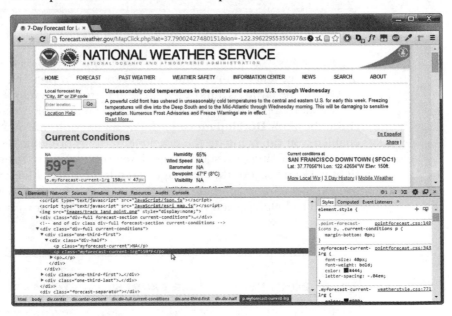

Figure 11-5: Inspecting the element that holds the temperature text with the developer tools

From the developer tools, you can see that the HTML responsible for the temperature part of the web page is <p class="myforecast-current -lrg">59°F</p>. This is exactly what you were looking for! It seems that the temperature information is contained inside a <p> element with the myforecast-current-lrg class. Now that you know what you're looking for, the BeautifulSoup module will help you find it in the string.

Parsing HTML with the BeautifulSoup Module

Beautiful Soup is a module for extracting information from an HTML page (and is much better for this purpose than regular expressions). The BeautifulSoup module's name is bs4 (for Beautiful Soup, version 4). To install it, you will need to run pip install beautifulsoup4 from the command line. (Check out Appendix A for instructions on installing third-party modules.) While beautifulsoup4 is the name used for installation, to import Beautiful Soup you run import bs4.

For this chapter, the Beautiful Soup examples will *parse* (that is, analyze and identify the parts of) an HTML file on the hard drive. Open a new file editor window in IDLE, enter the following, and save it as *example.html*. Alternatively, download it from *http://nostarch.com/automatestuff/*.

```
<!-- This is the example.html example file. -->

<html><head><title>The Website Title</title></head>
<body>
<p>Download my <strong>Python</strong> book from <a href="http://
inventwithpython.com">my website</a>.</p>
<p class="slogan">Learn Python the easy way!</p>
<p>By <span id="author">Al Sweigart</span></p>
</body></html>
```

As you can see, even a simple HTML file involves many different tags and attributes, and matters quickly get confusing with complex websites. Thankfully, Beautiful Soup makes working with HTML much easier.

Creating a BeautifulSoup Object from HTML

The bs4.BeautifulSoup() function needs to be called with a string containing the HTML it will parse. The bs4.BeautifulSoup() function returns is a BeautifulSoup object. Enter the following into the interactive shell while your computer is connected to the Internet:

```
>>> import requests, bs4
>>> res = requests.get('http://nostarch.com')
>>> res.raise_for_status()
>>> noStarchSoup = bs4.BeautifulSoup(res.text)
>>> type(noStarchSoup)
<class 'bs4.BeautifulSoup'>
```

This code uses requests.get() to download the main page from the No Starch Press website and then passes the text attribute of the response to bs4.BeautifulSoup(). The BeautifulSoup object that it returns is stored in a variable named noStarchSoup.

You can also load an HTML file from your hard drive by passing a File object to `bs4.BeautifulSoup()`. Enter the following into the interactive shell (make sure the *example.html* file is in the working directory):

```
>>> exampleFile = open('example.html')
>>> exampleSoup = bs4.BeautifulSoup(exampleFile)
>>> type(exampleSoup)
<class 'bs4.BeautifulSoup'>
```

Once you have a `BeautifulSoup` object, you can use its methods to locate specific parts of an HTML document.

Finding an Element with the select() Method

You can retrieve a web page element from a `BeautifulSoup` object by calling the `select()`method and passing a string of a CSS *selector* for the element you are looking for. Selectors are like regular expressions: They specify a pattern to look for, in this case, in HTML pages instead of general text strings.

A full discussion of CSS selector syntax is beyond the scope of this book (there's a good selector tutorial in the resources at *http://nostarch.com/ automatestuff/*), but here's a short introduction to selectors. Table 11-2 shows examples of the most common CSS selector patterns.

Table 11-2: Examples of CSS Selectors

Selector passed to the `select()` method	Will match . . .
`soup.select('div')`	All elements named `<div>`
`soup.select('#author')`	The element with an id attribute of author
`soup.select('.notice')`	All elements that use a CSS class attribute named notice
`soup.select('div span')`	All elements named `<span>` that are within an element named `<div>`
`soup.select('div > span')`	All elements named `<span>` that are *directly* within an element named `<div>`, with no other element in between
`soup.select('input[name]')`	All elements named `<input>` that have a name attribute with any value
`soup.select('input[type="button"]')`	All elements named `<input>` that have an attribute named type with value button

The various selector patterns can be combined to make sophisticated matches. For example, `soup.select('p #author')` will match any element that has an id attribute of author, as long as it is also inside a `<p>` element.

The `select()` method will return a list of `Tag` objects, which is how Beautiful Soup represents an HTML element. The list will contain one `Tag` object for every match in the `BeautifulSoup` object's HTML. Tag values can be passed to the `str()` function to show the HTML tags they represent.

Tag values also have an attrs attribute that shows all the HTML attributes of the tag as a dictionary. Using the *example.html* file from earlier, enter the following into the interactive shell:

```
>>> import bs4
>>> exampleFile = open('example.html')
>>> exampleSoup = bs4.BeautifulSoup(exampleFile.read())
>>> elems = exampleSoup.select('#author')
>>> type(elems)
<class 'list'>
>>> len(elems)
1
>>> type(elems[0])
<class 'bs4.element.Tag'>
>>> elems[0].getText()
'Al Sweigart'
>>> str(elems[0])
'<span id="author">Al Sweigart</span>'
>>> elems[0].attrs
{'id': 'author'}
```

This code will pull the element with id="author" out of our example HTML. We use select('#author') to return a list of all the elements with id="author". We store this list of **Tag** objects in the variable elems, and len(elems) tells us there is one **Tag** object in the list; there was one match. Calling getText() on the element returns the element's text, or inner HTML. The text of an element is the content between the opening and closing tags: in this case, 'Al Sweigart'.

Passing the element to str() returns a string with the starting and closing tags and the element's text. Finally, attrs gives us a dictionary with the element's attribute, 'id', and the value of the id attribute, 'author'.

You can also pull all the <p> elements from the BeautifulSoup object. Enter this into the interactive shell:

```
>>> pElems = exampleSoup.select('p')
>>> str(pElems[0])
'<p>Download my <strong>Python</strong> book from <a href="http://
inventwithpython.com">my website</a>.</p>'
>>> pElems[0].getText()
'Download my Python book from my website.'
>>> str(pElems[1])
'<p class="slogan">Learn Python the easy way!</p>'
>>> pElems[1].getText()
'Learn Python the easy way!'
>>> str(pElems[2])
'<p>By <span id="author">Al Sweigart</span></p>'
>>> pElems[2].getText()
'By Al Sweigart'
```

This time, select() gives us a list of three matches, which we store in pElems. Using str() on pElems[0], pElems[1], and pElems[2] shows you each element as a string, and using getText() on each element shows you its text.

Getting Data from an Element's Attributes

The get() method for Tag objects makes it simple to access attribute values from an element. The method is passed a string of an attribute name and returns that attribute's value. Using *example.html*, enter the following into the interactive shell:

```
>>> import bs4
>>> soup = bs4.BeautifulSoup(open('example.html'))
>>> spanElem = soup.select('span')[0]
>>> str(spanElem)
'<span id="author">Al Sweigart</span>'
>>> spanElem.get('id')
'author'
>>> spanElem.get('some_nonexistent_addr') == None
True
>>> spanElem.attrs
{'id': 'author'}
```

Here we use select() to find any <span> elements and then store the first matched element in spanElem. Passing the attribute name 'id' to get() returns the attribute's value, 'author'.

Project: "I'm Feeling Lucky" Google Search

Whenever I search a topic on Google, I don't look at just one search result at a time. By middle-clicking a search result link (or clicking while holding CTRL), I open the first several links in a bunch of new tabs to read later. I search Google often enough that this workflow—opening my browser, searching for a topic, and middle-clicking several links one by one—is tedious. It would be nice if I could simply type a search term on the command line and have my computer automatically open a browser with all the top search results in new tabs. Let's write a script to do this.

This is what your program does:

- Gets search keywords from the command line arguments.
- Retrieves the search results page.
- Opens a browser tab for each result.

This means your code will need to do the following:

- Read the command line arguments from sys.argv.
- Fetch the search result page with the requests module.
- Find the links to each search result.
- Call the webbrowser.open() function to open the web browser.

Open a new file editor window and save it as *lucky.py*.

Step 1: Get the Command Line Arguments and Request the Search Page

Before coding anything, you first need to know the URL of the search result page. By looking at the browser's address bar after doing a Google search, you can see that the result page has a URL like *https://www.google.com/search?q=SEARCH_TERM_HERE*. The requests module can download this page and then you can use Beautiful Soup to find the search result links in the HTML. Finally, you'll use the webbrowser module to open those links in browser tabs.

Make your code look like the following:

```python
#! python3
# lucky.py - Opens several Google search results.

import requests, sys, webbrowser, bs4

print('Googling...')    # display text while downloading the Google page
res = requests.get('http://google.com/search?q=' + ' '.join(sys.argv[1:]))
res.raise_for_status()

# TODO: Retrieve top search result links.

# TODO: Open a browser tab for each result.
```

The user will specify the search terms using command line arguments when they launch the program. These arguments will be stored as strings in a list in sys.argv.

Step 2: Find All the Results

Now you need to use Beautiful Soup to extract the top search result links from your downloaded HTML. But how do you figure out the right selector for the job? For example, you can't just search for all <a> tags, because there are lots of links you don't care about in the HTML. Instead, you must inspect the search result page with the browser's developer tools to try to find a selector that will pick out only the links you want.

After doing a Google search for *Beautiful Soup*, you can open the browser's developer tools and inspect some of the link elements on the page. They look incredibly complicated, something like this: <a href="/url?sa=t&rct=j&q=&esrc=s&source=web&cd=1&cad=rja&uact=8&ved=0CCgQFjAA&url=http%3A%2F%2Fwww.crummy.com%2Fsoftware%2FBeautifulSoup%2F&ei=LHBVU_XDD9KVyAShmYDwCw&usg=AFQjCNHAxwplurFOBqg5cehWQEVKi-TuLQ&sig2=sdZu6WVlBlVSDrwhtworMA" onmousedown="return rwt(this,'','','1','AFQjCNHAxwplurFOBqg5cehWQEVKi-TuLQ','sdZu6WVlBlVSDrwhtworMA','0CCgQFjAA','','',event)" data-href="http://www.crummy.com/software/BeautifulSoup/">Beautiful Soup: We called him Tortoise because he taught us.</a>.

It doesn't matter that the element looks incredibly complicated. You just need to find the pattern that all the search result links have. But this <a> element doesn't have anything that easily distinguishes it from the nonsearch result <a> elements on the page.

Make your code look like the following:

```python
#! python3
# lucky.py - Opens several google search results.

import requests, sys, webbrowser, bs4

--snip--

# Retrieve top search result links.
soup = bs4.BeautifulSoup(res.text)

# Open a browser tab for each result.
linkElems = soup.select('.r a')
```

If you look up a little from the `<a>` element, though, there is an element like this: `<h3 class="r">`. Looking through the rest of the HTML source, it looks like the r class is used only for search result links. You don't have to know what the CSS class r is or what it does. You're just going to use it as a marker for the `<a>` element you are looking for. You can create a `BeautifulSoup` object from the downloaded page's HTML text and then use the selector `'.r a'` to find all `<a>` elements that are within an element that has the r CSS class.

Step 3: Open Web Browsers for Each Result

Finally, we'll tell the program to open web browser tabs for our results. Add the following to the end of your program:

```python
#! python3
# lucky.py - Opens several google search results.

import requests, sys, webbrowser, bs4

--snip--

# Open a browser tab for each result.
linkElems = soup.select('.r a')
numOpen = min(5, len(linkElems))
for i in range(numOpen):
    webbrowser.open('http://google.com' + linkElems[i].get('href'))
```

By default, you open the first five search results in new tabs using the `webbrowser` module. However, the user may have searched for something that turned up fewer than five results. The `soup.select()` call returns a list of all the elements that matched your `'.r a'` selector, so the number of tabs you want to open is either 5 or the length of this list (whichever is smaller).

The built-in Python function `min()` returns the smallest of the integer or float arguments it is passed. (There is also a built-in `max()` function that returns the largest argument it is passed.) You can use `min()` to find out whether there are fewer than five links in the list and store the number of links to open in a variable named `numOpen`. Then you can run through a `for` loop by calling `range(numOpen)`.

On each iteration of the loop, you use `webbrowser.open()` to open a new tab in the web browser. Note that the `href` attribute's value in the returned `<a>` elements do not have the initial `http://google.com` part, so you have to concatenate that to the `href` attribute's string value.

Now you can instantly open the first five Google results for, say, *Python programming tutorials* by running `lucky python programming tutorials` on the command line! (See Appendix B for how to easily run programs on your operating system.)

Ideas for Similar Programs

The benefit of tabbed browsing is that you can easily open links in new tabs to peruse later. A program that automatically opens several links at once can be a nice shortcut to do the following:

- Open all the product pages after searching a shopping site such as Amazon
- Open all the links to reviews for a single product
- Open the result links to photos after performing a search on a photo site such as Flickr or Imgur

Project: Downloading All XKCD Comics

Blogs and other regularly updating websites usually have a front page with the most recent post as well as a Previous button on the page that takes you to the previous post. Then that post will also have a Previous button, and so on, creating a trail from the most recent page to the first post on the site. If you wanted a copy of the site's content to read when you're not online, you could manually navigate over every page and save each one. But this is pretty boring work, so let's write a program to do it instead.

XKCD is a popular geek webcomic with a website that fits this structure (see Figure 11-6). The front page at *http://xkcd.com/* has a Prev button that guides the user back through prior comics. Downloading each comic by hand would take forever, but you can write a script to do this in a couple of minutes.

Here's what your program does:

- Loads the XKCD home page.
- Saves the comic image on that page.
- Follows the Previous Comic link.
- Repeats until it reaches the first comic.

Figure 11-6: XKCD, "a webcomic of romance, sarcasm, math, and language"

This means your code will need to do the following:

- Download pages with the requests module.
- Find the URL of the comic image for a page using Beautiful Soup.
- Download and save the comic image to the hard drive with iter_content().
- Find the URL of the Previous Comic link, and repeat.

Open a new file editor window and save it as *downloadXkcd.py*.

Step 1: Design the Program

If you open the browser's developer tools and inspect the elements on the page, you'll find the following:

- The URL of the comic's image file is given by the href attribute of an <img> element.
- The <img> element is inside a <div id="comic"> element.
- The Prev button has a rel HTML attribute with the value prev.
- The first comic's Prev button links to the *http://xkcd.com/#* URL, indicating that there are no more previous pages.

Make your code look like the following:

```
#! python3
# downloadXkcd.py - Downloads every single XKCD comic.

import requests, os, bs4

url = 'http://xkcd.com'              # starting url
os.makedirs('xkcd', exist_ok=True)   # store comics in ./xkcd
```

```
while not url.endswith('#'):
    # TODO: Download the page.

    # TODO: Find the URL of the comic image.

    # TODO: Download the image.

    # TODO: Save the image to ./xkcd.

    # TODO: Get the Prev button's url.

print('Done.')
```

You'll have a url variable that starts with the value `'http://xkcd.com'` and repeatedly update it (in a for loop) with the URL of the current page's Prev link. At every step in the loop, you'll download the comic at url. You'll know to end the loop when url ends with `'#'`.

You will download the image files to a folder in the current working directory named *xkcd*. The call `os.makedirs()` ensures that this folder exists, and the `exist_ok=True` keyword argument prevents the function from throwing an exception if this folder already exists. The rest of the code is just comments that outline the rest of your program.

Step 2: Download the Web Page

Let's implement the code for downloading the page. Make your code look like the following:

```
#! python3
# downloadXkcd.py - Downloads every single XKCD comic.

import requests, os, bs4

url = 'http://xkcd.com'                    # starting url
os.makedirs('xkcd', exist_ok=True)         # store comics in ./xkcd
while not url.endswith('#'):
    # Download the page.
    print('Downloading page %s...' % url)
    res = requests.get(url)
    res.raise_for_status()

    soup = bs4.BeautifulSoup(res.text)

    # TODO: Find the URL of the comic image.

    # TODO: Download the image.

    # TODO: Save the image to ./xkcd.

    # TODO: Get the Prev button's url.

print('Done.')
```

First, print url so that the user knows which URL the program is about to download; then use the requests module's request.get() function to download it. As always, you immediately call the Response object's raise_for_status() method to throw an exception and end the program if something went wrong with the download. Otherwise, you create a BeautifulSoup object from the text of the downloaded page.

Step 3: Find and Download the Comic Image

Make your code look like the following:

```
#! python3
# downloadXkcd.py - Downloads every single XKCD comic.

import requests, os, bs4

--snip--

    # Find the URL of the comic image.
    comicElem = soup.select('#comic img')
    if comicElem == []:
        print('Could not find comic image.')
    else:
        comicUrl = 'http:' + comicElem[0].get('src')
        # Download the image.
        print('Downloading image %s...' % (comicUrl))
        res = requests.get(comicUrl)
        res.raise_for_status()

    # TODO: Save the image to ./xkcd.

    # TODO: Get the Prev button's url.

print('Done.')
```

From inspecting the XKCD home page with your developer tools, you know that the <img> element for the comic image is inside a <div> element with the id attribute set to comic, so the selector '#comic img' will get you the correct <img> element from the BeautifulSoup object.

A few XKCD pages have special content that isn't a simple image file. That's fine; you'll just skip those. If your selector doesn't find any elements, then soup.select('#comic img') will return a blank list. When that happens, the program can just print an error message and move on without downloading the image.

Otherwise, the selector will return a list containing one <img> element. You can get the src attribute from this <img> element and pass it to requests.get() to download the comic's image file.

Step 4: Save the Image and Find the Previous Comic

Make your code look like the following:

```python
#! python3
# downloadXkcd.py - Downloads every single XKCD comic.

import requests, os, bs4

--snip--

        # Save the image to ./xkcd.
        imageFile = open(os.path.join('xkcd', os.path.basename(comicUrl)), 'wb')
        for chunk in res.iter_content(100000):
            imageFile.write(chunk)
        imageFile.close()

    # Get the Prev button's url.
    prevLink = soup.select('a[rel="prev"]')[0]
    url = 'http://xkcd.com' + prevLink.get('href')

print('Done.')
```

At this point, the image file of the comic is stored in the res variable. You need to write this image data to a file on the hard drive.

You'll need a filename for the local image file to pass to open(). The comicUrl will have a value like 'http://imgs.xkcd.com/comics/heartbleed _explanation.png'—which you might have noticed looks a lot like a file path. And in fact, you can call os.path.basename() with comicUrl, and it will return just the last part of the URL, 'heartbleed_explanation.png'. You can use this as the filename when saving the image to your hard drive. You join this name with the name of your xkcd folder using os.path.join() so that your program uses backslashes (\) on Windows and forward slashes (/) on OS X and Linux. Now that you finally have the filename, you can call open() to open a new file in 'wb' "write binary" mode.

Remember from earlier in this chapter that to save files you've downloaded using Requests, you need to loop over the return value of the iter_content() method. The code in the for loop writes out chunks of the image data (at most 100,000 bytes each) to the file and then you close the file. The image is now saved to your hard drive.

Afterward, the selector 'a[rel="prev"]' identifies the <a> element with the rel attribute set to prev, and you can use this <a> element's href attribute to get the previous comic's URL, which gets stored in url. Then the while loop begins the entire download process again for this comic.

The output of this program will look like this:

```
Downloading page http://xkcd.com...
Downloading image http://imgs.xkcd.com/comics/phone_alarm.png...
Downloading page http://xkcd.com/1358/...
```

```
Downloading image http://imgs.xkcd.com/comics/nro.png...
Downloading page http://xkcd.com/1357/...
Downloading image http://imgs.xkcd.com/comics/free_speech.png...
Downloading page http://xkcd.com/1356/...
Downloading image http://imgs.xkcd.com/comics/orbital_mechanics.png...
Downloading page http://xkcd.com/1355/...
Downloading image http://imgs.xkcd.com/comics/airplane_message.png...
Downloading page http://xkcd.com/1354/...
Downloading image http://imgs.xkcd.com/comics/heartbleed_explanation.png...
--snip--
```

This project is a good example of a program that can automatically follow links in order to scrape large amounts of data from the Web. You can learn about Beautiful Soup's other features from its documentation at *http://www.crummy.com/software/BeautifulSoup/bs4/doc/*.

Ideas for Similar Programs

Downloading pages and following links are the basis of many web crawling programs. Similar programs could also do the following:

- Back up an entire site by following all of its links.
- Copy all the messages off a web forum.
- Duplicate the catalog of items for sale on an online store.

The requests and BeautifulSoup modules are great as long as you can figure out the URL you need to pass to requests.get(). However, sometimes this isn't so easy to find. Or perhaps the website you want your program to navigate requires you to log in first. The selenium module will give your programs the power to perform such sophisticated tasks.

Controlling the Browser with the selenium Module

The selenium module lets Python directly control the browser by programmatically clicking links and filling in login information, almost as though there is a human user interacting with the page. Selenium allows you to interact with web pages in a much more advanced way than Requests and Beautiful Soup; but because it launches a web browser, it is a bit slower and hard to run in the background if, say, you just need to download some files from the Web.

Appendix A has more detailed steps on installing third-party modules.

Starting a Selenium-Controlled Browser

For these examples, you'll need the Firefox web browser. This will be the browser that you control. If you don't already have Firefox, you can download it for free from *http://getfirefox.com/*.

Importing the modules for Selenium is slightly tricky. Instead of `import selenium`, you need to run `from selenium import webdriver`. (The exact reason why the `selenium` module is set up this way is beyond the scope of this book.) After that, you can launch the Firefox browser with Selenium. Enter the following into the interactive shell:

```
>>> from selenium import webdriver
>>> browser = webdriver.Firefox()
>>> type(browser)
<class 'selenium.webdriver.firefox.webdriver.WebDriver'>
>>> browser.get('http://inventwithpython.com')
```

You'll notice when `webdriver.Firefox()` is called, the Firefox web browser starts up. Calling `type()` on the value `webdriver.Firefox()` reveals it's of the `WebDriver` data type. And calling `browser.get('http://inventwithpython.com')` directs the browser to *http://inventwithpython.com/*. Your browser should look something like Figure 11-7.

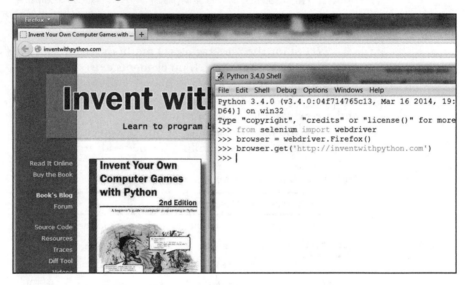

Figure 11-7: After calling `webdriver.Firefox()` and `get()` in IDLE, the Firefox browser appears.

Finding Elements on the Page

WebDriver objects have quite a few methods for finding elements on a page. They are divided into the `find_element_*` and `find_elements_*` methods. The `find_element_*` methods return a single `WebElement` object, representing the first element on the page that matches your query. The `find_elements_*` methods return a list of `WebElement_*` objects for *every* matching element on the page.

Table 11-3 shows several examples of `find_element_*` and `find_elements_*` methods being called on a `WebDriver` object that's stored in the variable `browser`.

Table 11-3: Selenium's WebDriver Methods for Finding Elements

Method name	WebElement object/list returned
browser.find_element_by_class_name(*name*) browser.find_elements_by_class_name(*name*)	Elements that use the CSS class *name*
browser.find_element_by_css_selector(*selector*) browser.find_elements_by_css_selector(*selector*)	Elements that match the CSS *selector*
browser.find_element_by_id(*id*) browser.find_elements_by_id(*id*)	Elements with a matching *id* attribute value
browser.find_element_by_link_text(*text*) browser.find_elements_by_link_text(*text*)	<a> elements that completely match the *text* provided
browser.find_element_by_partial_link_text(*text*) browser.find_elements_by_partial_link_text(*text*)	<a> elements that contain the *text* provided
browser.find_element_by_name(*name*) browser.find_elements_by_name(*name*)	Elements with a matching *name* attribute value
browser.find_element_by_tag_name(*name*) browser.find_elements_by_tag_name(*name*)	Elements with a matching tag *name* (case insensitive; an <a> element is matched by 'a' and 'A')

Except for the *_by_tag_name() methods, the arguments to all the methods are case sensitive. If no elements exist on the page that match what the method is looking for, the selenium module raises a NoSuchElement exception. If you do not want this exception to crash your program, add try and except statements to your code.

Once you have the WebElement object, you can find out more about it by reading the attributes or calling the methods in Table 11-4.

Table 11-4: WebElement Attributes and Methods

Attribute or method	Description
tag_name	The tag name, such as 'a' for an <a> element
get_attribute(*name*)	The value for the element's name attribute
text	The text within the element, such as 'hello' in hello
clear()	For text field or text area elements, clears the text typed into it
is_displayed()	Returns True if the element is visible; otherwise returns False
is_enabled()	For input elements, returns True if the element is enabled; otherwise returns False
is_selected()	For checkbox or radio button elements, returns True if the element is selected; otherwise returns False
location	A dictionary with keys 'x' and 'y' for the position of the element in the page

For example, open a new file editor and enter the following program:

```
from selenium import webdriver
browser = webdriver.Firefox()
browser.get('http://inventwithpython.com')
```

```
try:
    elem = browser.find_element_by_class_name('bookcover')
    print('Found <%s> element with that class name!' % (elem.tag_name))
except:
    print('Was not able to find an element with that name.')
```

Here we open Firefox and direct it to a URL. On this page, we try to find elements with the class name 'bookcover', and if such an element is found, we print its tag name using the tag_name attribute. If no such element was found, we print a different message.

This program will output the following:

```
Found <img> element with that class name!
```

We found an element with the class name 'bookcover' and the tag name 'img'.

Clicking the Page

WebElement objects returned from the find_element_* and find_elements_* methods have a click() method that simulates a mouse click on that element. This method can be used to follow a link, make a selection on a radio button, click a Submit button, or trigger whatever else might happen when the element is clicked by the mouse. For example, enter the following into the interactive shell:

```
>>> from selenium import webdriver
>>> browser = webdriver.Firefox()
>>> browser.get('http://inventwithpython.com')
>>> linkElem = browser.find_element_by_link_text('Read It Online')
>>> type(linkElem)
<class 'selenium.webdriver.remote.webelement.WebElement'>
>>> linkElem.click()      # follows the "Read It Online" link
```

This opens Firefox to *http://inventwithpython.com/*, gets the WebElement object for the <a> element with the text *Read It Online*, and then simulates clicking that <a> element. It's just like if you clicked the link yourself; the browser then follows that link.

Filling Out and Submitting Forms

Sending keystrokes to text fields on a web page is a matter of finding the <input> or <textarea> element for that text field and then calling the send_keys() method. For example, enter the following into the interactive shell:

```
>>> from selenium import webdriver
>>> browser = webdriver.Firefox()
>>> browser.get('https://gmail.com')
>>> emailElem = browser.find_element_by_id('Email')
>>> emailElem.send_keys('your_real_email_here@gmail.com')
>>> nextButtonElem = browser.find_element_by_id('next')
```

```
>>> nextButtonElem.click()
>>> passwordElem = browser.find_element_by_id('Passwd')
>>> passwordElem.send_keys('your_real_password_here')
>>> passwordElem.submit()
```

As long as Gmail hasn't changed the id of the Username and Password text fields since this book was published, the previous code will fill in those text fields with the provided text. (You can always use the browser's inspector to verify the id.) Calling the submit() method on any element will have the same result as clicking the Submit button for the form that element is in. (You could have just as easily called emailElem.submit(), and the code would have done the same thing.)

Sending Special Keys

Selenium has a module for keyboard keys that are impossible to type into a string value, which function much like escape characters. These values are stored in attributes in the selenium.webdriver.common.keys module. Since that is such a long module name, it's much easier to run from selenium.webdriver.common.keys import Keys at the top of your program; if you do, then you can simply write Keys anywhere you'd normally have to write selenium.webdriver.common.keys. Table 11-5 lists the commonly used Keys variables.

Table 11-5: Commonly Used Variables in the selenium.webdriver.common.keys Module

Attributes	Meanings
Keys.DOWN, Keys.UP, Keys.LEFT, Keys.RIGHT	The keyboard arrow keys
Keys.ENTER, Keys.RETURN	The ENTER and RETURN keys
Keys.HOME, Keys.END, Keys.PAGE_DOWN, Keys.PAGE_UP	The HOME, END, PAGEDOWN, and PAGEUP keys
Keys.ESCAPE, Keys.BACK_SPACE, Keys.DELETE	The ESC, BACKSPACE, and DELETE keys
Keys.F1, Keys.F2, . . . , Keys.F12	The F1 to F12 keys at the top of the keyboard
Keys.TAB	The TAB key

For example, if the cursor is not currently in a text field, pressing the HOME and END keys will scroll the browser to the top and bottom of the page, respectively. Enter the following into the interactive shell, and notice how the send_keys() calls scroll the page:

```
>>> from selenium import webdriver
>>> from selenium.webdriver.common.keys import Keys
>>> browser = webdriver.Firefox()
>>> browser.get('http://nostarch.com')
>>> htmlElem = browser.find_element_by_tag_name('html')
>>> htmlElem.send_keys(Keys.END)     # scrolls to bottom
>>> htmlElem.send_keys(Keys.HOME)    # scrolls to top
```

The <html> tag is the base tag in HTML files: The full content of the HTML file is enclosed within the <html> and </html> tags. Calling browser .find_element_by_tag_name('html') is a good place to send keys to the general web page. This would be useful if, for example, new content is loaded once you've scrolled to the bottom of the page.

Clicking Browser Buttons

Selenium can simulate clicks on various browser buttons as well through the following methods:

browser.back()   Clicks the Back button.

browser.forward()   Clicks the Forward button.

browser.refresh()   Clicks the Refresh/Reload button.

browser.quit()   Clicks the Close Window button.

More Information on Selenium

Selenium can do much more beyond the functions described here. It can modify your browser's cookies, take screenshots of web pages, and run custom JavaScript. To learn more about these features, you can visit the Selenium documentation at *http://selenium-python.readthedocs.org/*.

Summary

Most boring tasks aren't limited to the files on your computer. Being able to programmatically download web pages will extend your programs to the Internet. The requests module makes downloading straightforward, and with some basic knowledge of HTML concepts and selectors, you can utilize the BeautifulSoup module to parse the pages you download.

But to fully automate any web-based tasks, you need direct control of your web browser through the selenium module. The selenium module will allow you to log in to websites and fill out forms automatically. Since a web browser is the most common way to send and receive information over the Internet, this is a great ability to have in your programmer toolkit.

Practice Questions

1. Briefly describe the differences between the webbrowser, requests, BeautifulSoup, and selenium modules.

2. What type of object is returned by requests.get()? How can you access the downloaded content as a string value?

3. What Requests method checks that the download worked?

4. How can you get the HTTP status code of a Requests response?

5. How do you save a Requests response to a file?

6. What is the keyboard shortcut for opening a browser's developer tools?

7. How can you view (in the developer tools) the HTML of a specific element on a web page?

8. What is the CSS selector string that would find the element with an `id` attribute of `main`?

9. What is the CSS selector string that would find the elements with a CSS class of `highlight`?

10. What is the CSS selector string that would find all the `<div>` elements inside another `<div>` element?

11. What is the CSS selector string that would find the `<button>` element with a `value` attribute set to `favorite`?

12. Say you have a Beautiful Soup `Tag` object stored in the variable `spam` for the element `<div>Hello world!</div>`. How could you get a string `'Hello world!'` from the `Tag` object?

13. How would you store all the attributes of a Beautiful Soup `Tag` object in a variable named `linkElem`?

14. Running `import selenium` doesn't work. How do you properly import the selenium module?

15. What's the difference between the `find_element_*` and `find_elements_*` methods?

16. What methods do Selenium's `WebElement` objects have for simulating mouse clicks and keyboard keys?

17. You could call `send_keys(Keys.ENTER)` on the Submit button's `WebElement` object, but what is an easier way to submit a form with Selenium?

18. How can you simulate clicking a browser's Forward, Back, and Refresh buttons with Selenium?

Practice Projects

For practice, write programs to do the following tasks.

Command Line Emailer

Write a program that takes an email address and string of text on the command line and then, using Selenium, logs into your email account and sends an email of the string to the provided address. (You might want to set up a separate email account for this program.)

This would be a nice way to add a notification feature to your programs. You could also write a similar program to send messages from a Facebook or Twitter account.

Image Site Downloader

Write a program that goes to a photo-sharing site like Flickr or Imgur, searches for a category of photos, and then downloads all the resulting images. You could write a program that works with any photo site that has a search feature.

2048

2048 is a simple game where you combine tiles by sliding them up, down, left, or right with the arrow keys. You can actually get a fairly high score by repeatedly sliding in an up, right, down, and left pattern over and over again. Write a program that will open the game at *https://gabrielecirulli .github.io/2048/* and keep sending up, right, down, and left keystrokes to automatically play the game.

Link Verification

Write a program that, given the URL of a web page, will attempt to download every linked page on the page. The program should flag any pages that have a 404 "Not Found" status code and print them out as broken links.

12

WORKING WITH EXCEL SPREADSHEETS

Excel is a popular and powerful spreadsheet application for Windows. The `openpyxl` module allows your Python programs to read and modify Excel spreadsheet files. For example, you might have the boring task of copying certain data from one spreadsheet and pasting it into another one. Or you might have to go through thousands of rows and pick out just a handful of them to make small edits based on some criteria. Or you might have to look through hundreds of spreadsheets of department budgets, searching for any that are in the red. These are exactly the sort of boring, mindless spreadsheet tasks that Python can do for you.

Although Excel is proprietary software from Microsoft, there are free alternatives that run on Windows, OS X, and Linux. Both LibreOffice Calc and OpenOffice Calc work with Excel's *.xlsx* file format for spreadsheets, which means the `openpyxl` module can work on spreadsheets from these applications as well. You can download the software from *https://www.libreoffice .org/* and *http://www.openoffice.org/*, respectively. Even if you already have

Excel installed on your computer, you may find these programs easier to use. The screenshots in this chapter, however, are all from Excel 2010 on Windows 7.

Excel Documents

First, let's go over some basic definitions: An Excel spreadsheet document is called a *workbook*. A single workbook is saved in a file with the *.xlsx* extension. Each workbook can contain multiple *sheets* (also called *worksheets*). The sheet the user is currently viewing (or last viewed before closing Excel) is called the *active sheet*.

Each sheet has *columns* (addressed by letters starting at *A*) and *rows* (addressed by numbers starting at 1). A box at a particular column and row is called a *cell*. Each cell can contain a number or text value. The grid of cells with data makes up a sheet.

Installing the openpyxl Module

Python does not come with OpenPyXL, so you'll have to install it. Follow the instructions for installing third-party modules in Appendix A; the name of the module is openpyxl. To test whether it is installed correctly, enter the following into the interactive shell:

```
>>> import openpyxl
```

If the module was correctly installed, this should produce no error messages. Remember to import the openpyxl module before running the interactive shell examples in this chapter, or you'll get a NameError: name 'openpyxl' is not defined error.

This book covers version 2.3.3 of OpenPyXL, but new versions are regularly released by the OpenPyXL team. Don't worry, though: New versions should stay backward compatible with the instructions in this book for quite some time. If you have a newer version and want to see what additional features may be available to you, you can check out the full documentation for OpenPyXL at *http://openpyxl.readthedocs.org/*.

Reading Excel Documents

The examples in this chapter will use a spreadsheet named *example.xlsx* stored in the root folder. You can either create the spreadsheet yourself or download it from *http://nostarch.com/automatestuff/*. Figure 12-1 shows the tabs for the three default sheets named *Sheet1*, *Sheet2*, and *Sheet3* that Excel automatically provides for new workbooks. (The number of default sheets created may vary between operating systems and spreadsheet programs.)

Figure 12-1: The tabs for a workbook's sheets are in the lower-left corner of Excel.

Sheet 1 in the example file should look like Table 12-1. (If you didn't download *example.xlsx* from the website, you should enter this data into the sheet yourself.)

Table 12-1: The *example.xlsx* Spreadsheet

	A	B	C
1	4/5/2015 1:34:02 PM	Apples	73
2	4/5/2015 3:41:23 AM	Cherries	85
3	4/6/2015 12:46:51 PM	Pears	14
4	4/8/2015 8:59:43 AM	Oranges	52
5	4/10/2015 2:07:00 AM	Apples	152
6	4/10/2015 6:10:37 PM	Bananas	23
7	4/10/2015 2:40:46 AM	Strawberries	98

Now that we have our example spreadsheet, let's see how we can manipulate it with the openpyxl module.

Opening Excel Documents with OpenPyXL

Once you've imported the openpyxl module, you'll be able to use the openpyxl .load_workbook() function. Enter the following into the interactive shell:

```
>>> import openpyxl
>>> wb = openpyxl.load_workbook('example.xlsx')
>>> type(wb)
<class 'openpyxl.workbook.workbook.Workbook'>
```

The openpyxl.load_workbook() function takes in the filename and returns a value of the workbook data type. This Workbook object represents the Excel file, a bit like how a File object represents an opened text file.

Remember that *example.xlsx* needs to be in the current working directory in order for you to work with it. You can find out what the current working directory is by importing os and using os.getcwd(), and you can change the current working directory using os.chdir().

Getting Sheets from the Workbook

You can get a list of all the sheet names in the workbook by calling the get_sheet_names() method. Enter the following into the interactive shell:

```
>>> import openpyxl
>>> wb = openpyxl.load_workbook('example.xlsx')
>>> wb.get_sheet_names()
['Sheet1', 'Sheet2', 'Sheet3']
>>> sheet = wb.get_sheet_by_name('Sheet3')
>>> sheet
<Worksheet "Sheet3">
>>> type(sheet)
<class 'openpyxl.worksheet.worksheet.Worksheet'>
>>> sheet.title
'Sheet3'
>>> anotherSheet = wb.active
>>> anotherSheet
<Worksheet "Sheet1">
```

Each sheet is represented by a Worksheet object, which you can obtain by passing the sheet name string to the get_sheet_by_name() workbook method. Finally, you can use the active attribute of a Workbook object to get the workbook's active sheet. The active sheet is the sheet that's on top when the workbook is opened in Excel. Once you have the Worksheet object, you can get its name from the title attribute.

Getting Cells from the Sheets

Once you have a Worksheet object, you can access a Cell object by its name. Enter the following into the interactive shell:

```
>>> import openpyxl
>>> wb = openpyxl.load_workbook('example.xlsx')
>>> sheet = wb.get_sheet_by_name('Sheet1')
>>> sheet['A1']
<Cell Sheet1.A1>
>>> sheet['A1'].value
datetime.datetime(2015, 4, 5, 13, 34, 2)
>>> c = sheet['B1']
>>> c.value
'Apples'
>>> 'Row ' + str(c.row) + ', Column ' + c.column + ' is ' + c.value
'Row 1, Column B is Apples'
>>> 'Cell ' + c.coordinate + ' is ' + c.value
'Cell B1 is Apples'
>>> sheet['C1'].value
73
```

The Cell object has a value attribute that contains, unsurprisingly, the value stored in that cell. Cell objects also have row, column, and coordinate attributes that provide location information for the cell.

Here, accessing the value attribute of our `Cell` object for cell B1 gives us the string `'Apples'`. The `row` attribute gives us the integer 1, the `column` attribute gives us `'B'`, and the `coordinate` attribute gives us `'B1'`.

OpenPyXL will automatically interpret the dates in column A and return them as `datetime` values rather than strings. The `datetime` data type is explained further in Chapter 16.

Specifying a column by letter can be tricky to program, especially because after column Z, the columns start by using two letters: AA, AB, AC, and so on. As an alternative, you can also get a cell using the sheet's `cell()` method and passing integers for its `row` and `column` keyword arguments. The first row or column integer is 1, not 0. Continue the interactive shell example by entering the following:

```
>>> sheet.cell(row=1, column=2)
<Cell Sheet1.B1>
>>> sheet.cell(row=1, column=2).value
'Apples'
>>> for i in range(1, 8, 2):
        print(i, sheet.cell(row=i, column=2).value)

1 Apples
3 Pears
5 Apples
7 Strawberries
```

As you can see, using the sheet's `cell()` method and passing it `row=1` and `column=2` gets you a `Cell` object for cell B1, just like specifying `sheet['B1']` did. Then, using the `cell()` method and its keyword arguments, you can write a `for` loop to print the values of a series of cells.

Say you want to go down column B and print the value in every cell with an odd row number. By passing 2 for the `range()` function's "step" parameter, you can get cells from every second row (in this case, all the odd-numbered rows). The `for` loop's `i` variable is passed for the `row` keyword argument to the `cell()` method, while 2 is always passed for the `column` keyword argument. Note that the integer 2, not the string `'B'`, is passed.

You can determine the size of the sheet with the `Worksheet` object's `max_row` and `max_column` attributes. Enter the following into the interactive shell:

```
>>> import openpyxl
>>> wb = openpyxl.load_workbook('example.xlsx')
>>> sheet = wb.get_sheet_by_name('Sheet1')
>>> sheet.max_row
7
>>> sheet.max_column
3
```

Note that the `max_column` attribute is an integer rather than the letter that appears in Excel.

Converting Between Column Letters and Numbers

To convert from letters to numbers, call the openpyxl.cell.column_index_from
_string() function. To convert from numbers to letters, call the openpyxl.cell
.get_column_letter() function. Enter the following into the interactive shell:

```
>>> import openpyxl
>>> from openpyxl.cell import get_column_letter, column_index_from_string
>>> get_column_letter(1)
'A'
>>> get_column_letter(2)
'B'
>>> get_column_letter(27)
'AA'
>>> get_column_letter(900)
'AHP'
>>> wb = openpyxl.load_workbook('example.xlsx')
>>> sheet = wb.get_sheet_by_name('Sheet1')
>>> get_column_letter(sheet.max_column)
'C'
>>> column_index_from_string('A')
1
>>> column_index_from_string('AA')
27
```

After you import these two functions from the openpyxl.cell module, you can call get_column_letter() and pass it an integer like 27 to figure out what the letter name of the 27th column is. The function column_index_string() does the reverse: You pass it the letter name of a column, and it tells you what number that column is. You don't need to have a workbook loaded to use these functions. If you want, you can load a workbook, get a Worksheet object, and use a Worksheet attribute like max_column to get an integer. Then, you can pass that integer to get_column_letter().

Getting Rows and Columns from the Sheets

You can slice Worksheet objects to get all the Cell objects in a row, column, or rectangular area of the spreadsheet. Then you can loop over all the cells in the slice. Enter the following into the interactive shell:

```
>>> import openpyxl
>>> wb = openpyxl.load_workbook('example.xlsx')
>>> sheet = wb.get_sheet_by_name('Sheet1')
>>> tuple(sheet['A1':'C3'])
((<Cell Sheet1.A1>, <Cell Sheet1.B1>, <Cell Sheet1.C1>), (<Cell Sheet1.A2>,
<Cell Sheet1.B2>, <Cell Sheet1.C2>), (<Cell Sheet1.A3>, <Cell Sheet1.B3>,
<Cell Sheet1.C3>))
❶ >>> for rowOfCellObjects in sheet['A1':'C3']:
❷        for cellObj in rowOfCellObjects:
             print(cellObj.coordinate, cellObj.value)
          print('--- END OF ROW ---')
```

```
A1 2015-04-05 13:34:02
B1 Apples
C1 73
--- END OF ROW ---
A2 2015-04-05 03:41:23
B2 Cherries
C2 85
--- END OF ROW ---
A3 2015-04-06 12:46:51
B3 Pears
C3 14
--- END OF ROW ---
```

Here, we specify that we want the `Cell` objects in the rectangular area from A1 to C3, and we get a `Generator` object containing the `Cell` objects in that area. To help us visualize this `Generator` object, we can use `tuple()` on it to display its `Cell` objects in a tuple.

This tuple contains three tuples: one for each row, from the top of the desired area to the bottom. Each of these three inner tuples contains the `Cell` objects in one row of our desired area, from the leftmost cell to the right. So overall, our slice of the sheet contains all the `Cell` objects in the area from A1 to C3, starting from the top-left cell and ending with the bottom-right cell.

To print the values of each cell in the area, we use two for loops. The outer for loop goes over each row in the slice ❶. Then, for each row, the nested for loop goes through each cell in that row ❷.

To access the values of cells in a particular row or column, you can also use a `Worksheet` object's rows and columns attribute. Enter the following into the interactive shell:

```
>>> import openpyxl
>>> wb = openpyxl.load_workbook('example.xlsx')
>>> sheet = wb.active
>>> sheet.columns[1]
(<Cell Sheet1.B1>, <Cell Sheet1.B2>, <Cell Sheet1.B3>, <Cell Sheet1.B4>,
<Cell Sheet1.B5>, <Cell Sheet1.B6>, <Cell Sheet1.B7>)
>>> for cellObj in sheet.columns[1]:
        print(cellObj.value)

Apples
Cherries
Pears
Oranges
Apples
Bananas
Strawberries
```

Using the rows attribute on a `Worksheet` object will give you a tuple of tuples. Each of these inner tuples represents a row, and contains the `Cell` objects in that row. The columns attribute also gives you a tuple of tuples, with each of the inner tuples containing the `Cell` objects in a particular column. For *example.xlsx*, since there are 7 rows and 3 columns, `rows` gives us a tuple of 7 tuples (each containing 3 Cell objects), and `columns` gives us a tuple of 3 tuples (each containing 7 Cell objects).

To access one particular tuple, you can refer to it by its index in the larger tuple. For example, to get the tuple that represents column B, you use `sheet.columns[1]`. To get the tuple containing the Cell objects in column A, you'd use `sheet.columns[0]`. Once you have a tuple representing one row or column, you can loop through its Cell objects and print their values.

Workbooks, Sheets, Cells

As a quick review, here's a rundown of all the functions, methods, and data types involved in reading a cell out of a spreadsheet file:

1. Import the `openpyxl` module.
2. Call the `openpyxl.load_workbook()` function.
3. Get a Workbook object.
4. Use the `active` attribute or call the `get_sheet_by_name()` workbook method.
5. Get a Worksheet object.
6. Use indexing or the `cell()` sheet method with `row` and `column` keyword arguments.
7. Get a Cell object.
8. Read the Cell object's `value` attribute.

Project: Reading Data from a Spreadsheet

Say you have a spreadsheet of data from the 2010 US Census and you have the boring task of going through its thousands of rows to count both the total population and the number of census tracts for each county. (A census tract is simply a geographic area defined for the purposes of the census.) Each row represents a single census tract. We'll name the spreadsheet file *censuspopdata.xlsx*, and you can download it from *http://nostarch.com/automatestuff/*. Its contents look like Figure 12-2.

	A	B	C	D	E
1	CensusTract	State	County	POP2010	
9841	06075010500	CA	San Francisco	2685	
9842	06075010600	CA	San Francisco	3894	
9843	06075010700	CA	San Francisco	5592	
9844	06075010800	CA	San Francisco	4578	
9845	06075010900	CA	San Francisco	4320	
9846	06075011000	CA	San Francisco	4827	
9847	06075011100	CA	San Francisco	5164	

Population by Census Tract

Ready

Figure 12-2: The censuspopdata.xlsx spreadsheet

Even though Excel can calculate the sum of multiple selected cells, you'd still have to select the cells for each of the 3,000-plus counties. Even if it takes just a few seconds to calculate a county's population by hand, this would take hours to do for the whole spreadsheet.

In this project, you'll write a script that can read from the census spreadsheet file and calculate statistics for each county in a matter of seconds.

This is what your program does:

- Reads the data from the Excel spreadsheet.
- Counts the number of census tracts in each county.
- Counts the total population of each county.
- Prints the results.

This means your code will need to do the following:

- Open and read the cells of an Excel document with the openpyxl module.
- Calculate all the tract and population data and store it in a data structure.
- Write the data structure to a text file with the *.py* extension using the pprint module.

Step 1: Read the Spreadsheet Data

There is just one sheet in the *censuspopdata.xlsx* spreadsheet, named 'Population by Census Tract', and each row holds the data for a single census tract. The columns are the tract number (A), the state abbreviation (B), the county name (C), and the population of the tract (D).

Open a new file editor window and enter the following code. Save the file as *readCensusExcel.py*.

```
#! python3
# readCensusExcel.py - Tabulates population and number of census tracts for
# each county.

❶ import openpyxl, pprint
  print('Opening workbook...')
❷ wb = openpyxl.load_workbook('censuspopdata.xlsx')
❸ sheet = wb.get_sheet_by_name('Population by Census Tract')
  countyData = {}

  # TODO: Fill in countyData with each county's population and tracts.
  print('Reading rows...')
❹ for row in range(2, sheet.max_row + 1):
      # Each row in the spreadsheet has data for one census tract.
      state  = sheet['B' + str(row)].value
      county = sheet['C' + str(row)].value
      pop    = sheet['D' + str(row)].value

  # TODO: Open a new text file and write the contents of countyData to it.
```

This code imports the openpyxl module, as well as the pprint module that you'll use to print the final county data ❶. Then it opens the *censuspopdata .xlsx* file ❷, gets the sheet with the census data ❸, and begins iterating over its rows ❹.

Note that you've also created a variable named countyData, which will contain the populations and number of tracts you calculate for each county. Before you can store anything in it, though, you should determine exactly how you'll structure the data inside it.

Step 2: Populate the Data Structure

The data structure stored in countyData will be a dictionary with state abbreviations as its keys. Each state abbreviation will map to another dictionary, whose keys are strings of the county names in that state. Each county name will in turn map to a dictionary with just two keys, 'tracts' and 'pop'. These keys map to the number of census tracts and population for the county. For example, the dictionary will look similar to this:

```
{'AK': {'Aleutians East': {'pop': 3141, 'tracts': 1},
        'Aleutians West': {'pop': 5561, 'tracts': 2},
        'Anchorage': {'pop': 291826, 'tracts': 55},
        'Bethel': {'pop': 17013, 'tracts': 3},
        'Bristol Bay': {'pop': 997, 'tracts': 1},
        --snip--
```

If the previous dictionary were stored in countyData, the following expressions would evaluate like this:

```
>>> countyData['AK']['Anchorage']['pop']
291826
>>> countyData['AK']['Anchorage']['tracts']
55
```

More generally, the countyData dictionary's keys will look like this:

```
countyData[state abbrev][county]['tracts']
countyData[state abbrev][county]['pop']
```

Now that you know how countyData will be structured, you can write the code that will fill it with the county data. Add the following code to the bottom of your program:

```
#! python 3
# readCensusExcel.py - Tabulates population and number of census tracts for
# each county.

--snip--
```

```
for row in range(2, sheet.max_row + 1):
    # Each row in the spreadsheet has data for one census tract.
    state  = sheet['B' + str(row)].value
    county = sheet['C' + str(row)].value
    pop    = sheet['D' + str(row)].value

    # Make sure the key for this state exists.
❶   countyData.setdefault(state, {})
    # Make sure the key for this county in this state exists.
❷   countyData[state].setdefault(county, {'tracts': 0, 'pop': 0})

    # Each row represents one census tract, so increment by one.
❸   countyData[state][county]['tracts'] += 1
    # Increase the county pop by the pop in this census tract.
❹   countyData[state][county]['pop'] += int(pop)

# TODO: Open a new text file and write the contents of countyData to it.
```

The last two lines of code perform the actual calculation work, incrementing the value for tracts ❸ and increasing the value for pop ❹ for the current county on each iteration of the for loop.

The other code is there because you cannot add a county dictionary as the value for a state abbreviation key until the key itself exists in countyData. (That is, countyData['AK']['Anchorage']['tracts'] += 1 will cause an error if the 'AK' key doesn't exist yet.) To make sure the state abbreviation key exists in your data structure, you need to call the setdefault() method to set a value if one does not already exist for state ❶.

Just as the countyData dictionary needs a dictionary as the value for each state abbreviation key, each of *those* dictionaries will need its own dictionary as the value for each county key ❷. And each of *those* dictionaries in turn will need keys 'tracts' and 'pop' that start with the integer value 0. (If you ever lose track of the dictionary structure, look back at the example dictionary at the start of this section.)

Since setdefault() will do nothing if the key already exists, you can call it on every iteration of the for loop without a problem.

Step 3: Write the Results to a File

After the for loop has finished, the countyData dictionary will contain all of the population and tract information keyed by county and state. At this point, you could program more code to write this to a text file or another Excel spreadsheet. For now, let's just use the pprint.pformat() function to write the countyData dictionary value as a massive string to a file named *census2010.py*. Add the following code to the bottom of your program (making sure to keep it unindented so that it stays outside the for loop):

```
#! python 3
# readCensusExcel.py - Tabulates population and number of census tracts for
# each county.
```

```
--snip--

for row in range(2, sheet.max_row + 1):
--snip--

# Open a new text file and write the contents of countyData to it.
print('Writing results...')
resultFile = open('census2010.py', 'w')
resultFile.write('allData = ' + pprint.pformat(countyData))
resultFile.close()
print('Done.')
```

The pprint.pformat() function produces a string that itself is format-ted as valid Python code. By outputting it to a text file named *census2010.py*, you've generated a Python program from your Python program! This may seem complicated, but the advantage is that you can now import *census2010.py* just like any other Python module. In the interactive shell, change the cur-rent working directory to the folder with your newly created *census2010.py* file (on my laptop, this is *C:\Python34*), and then import it:

```
>>> import os
>>> os.chdir('C:\\Python34')
>>> import census2010
>>> census2010.allData['AK']['Anchorage']
{'pop': 291826, 'tracts': 55}
>>> anchoragePop = census2010.allData['AK']['Anchorage']['pop']
>>> print('The 2010 population of Anchorage was ' + str(anchoragePop))
The 2010 population of Anchorage was 291826
```

The *readCensusExcel.py* program was throwaway code: Once you have its results saved to *census2010.py*, you won't need to run the program again. Whenever you need the county data, you can just run import census2010.

Calculating this data by hand would have taken hours; this program did it in a few seconds. Using OpenPyXL, you will have no trouble extract-ing information that is saved to an Excel spreadsheet and performing calcu-lations on it. You can download the complete program from *http://nostarch .com/automatestuff/*.

Ideas for Similar Programs

Many businesses and offices use Excel to store various types of data, and it's not uncommon for spreadsheets to become large and unwieldy. Any program that parses an Excel spreadsheet has a similar structure: It loads the spreadsheet file, preps some variables or data structures, and then loops through each of the rows in the spreadsheet. Such a program could do the following:

- Compare data across multiple rows in a spreadsheet.
- Open multiple Excel files and compare data between spreadsheets.

- Check whether a spreadsheet has blank rows or invalid data in any cells and alert the user if it does.

- Read data from a spreadsheet and use it as the input for your Python programs.

Writing Excel Documents

OpenPyXL also provides ways of writing data, meaning that your programs can create and edit spreadsheet files. With Python, it's simple to create spreadsheets with thousands of rows of data.

Creating and Saving Excel Documents

Call the openpyxl.Workbook() function to create a new, blank Workbook object. Enter the following into the interactive shell:

```
>>> import openpyxl
>>> wb = openpyxl.Workbook()
>>> wb.get_sheet_names()
['Sheet']
>>> sheet = wb.active
>>> sheet.title
'Sheet'
>>> sheet.title = 'Spam Bacon Eggs Sheet'
>>> wb.get_sheet_names()
['Spam Bacon Eggs Sheet']
```

The workbook will start off with a single sheet named *Sheet*. You can change the name of the sheet by storing a new string in its title attribute.

Any time you modify the Workbook object or its sheets and cells, the spreadsheet file will not be saved until you call the save() workbook method. Enter the following into the interactive shell (with *example.xlsx* in the current working directory):

```
>>> import openpyxl
>>> wb = openpyxl.load_workbook('example.xlsx')
>>> sheet = wb.active
>>> sheet.title = 'Spam Spam Spam'
>>> wb.save('example_copy.xlsx')
```

Here, we change the name of our sheet. To save our changes, we pass a filename as a string to the save() method. Passing a different filename than the original, such as 'example_copy.xlsx', saves the changes to a copy of the spreadsheet.

Whenever you edit a spreadsheet you've loaded from a file, you should always save the new, edited spreadsheet to a different filename than the original. That way, you'll still have the original spreadsheet file to work with in case a bug in your code caused the new, saved file to have incorrect or corrupt data.

Creating and Removing Sheets

Sheets can be added to and removed from a workbook with the create_sheet() and remove_sheet() methods. Enter the following into the interactive shell:

```
>>> import openpyxl
>>> wb = openpyxl.Workbook()
>>> wb.get_sheet_names()
['Sheet']
>>> wb.create_sheet()
<Worksheet "Sheet1">
>>> wb.get_sheet_names()
['Sheet', 'Sheet1']
>>> wb.create_sheet(index=0, title='First Sheet')
<Worksheet "First Sheet">
>>> wb.get_sheet_names()
['First Sheet', 'Sheet', 'Sheet1']
>>> wb.create_sheet(index=2, title='Middle Sheet')
<Worksheet "Middle Sheet">
>>> wb.get_sheet_names()
['First Sheet', 'Sheet', 'Middle Sheet', 'Sheet1']
```

The create_sheet() method returns a new Worksheet object named SheetX, which by default is set to be the last sheet in the workbook. Optionally, the index and name of the new sheet can be specified with the index and title keyword arguments.

Continue the previous example by entering the following:

```
>>> wb.get_sheet_names()
['First Sheet', 'Sheet', 'Middle Sheet', 'Sheet1']
>>> wb.remove_sheet(wb.get_sheet_by_name('Middle Sheet'))
>>> wb.remove_sheet(wb.get_sheet_by_name('Sheet1'))
>>> wb.get_sheet_names()
['First Sheet', 'Sheet']
```

The remove_sheet() method takes a Worksheet object, not a string of the sheet name, as its argument. If you know only the name of a sheet you want to remove, call get_sheet_by_name() and pass its return value into remove_sheet().

Remember to call the save() method to save the changes after adding sheets to or removing sheets from the workbook.

Writing Values to Cells

Writing values to cells is much like writing values to keys in a dictionary. Enter this into the interactive shell:

```
>>> import openpyxl
>>> wb = openpyxl.Workbook()
>>> sheet = wb.get_sheet_by_name('Sheet')
>>> sheet['A1'] = 'Hello world!'
>>> sheet['A1'].value
'Hello world!'
```

If you have the cell's coordinate as a string, you can use it just like a dictionary key on the Worksheet object to specify which cell to write to.

Project: Updating a Spreadsheet

In this project, you'll write a program to update cells in a spreadsheet of produce sales. Your program will look through the spreadsheet, find specific kinds of produce, and update their prices. Download this spreadsheet from *http://nostarch.com/automatestuff/*. Figure 12-3 shows what the spreadsheet looks like.

⊿	A	B	C	D	E
1	**PRODUCE**	**COST PER POUND**	**POUNDS SOLD**	**TOTAL**	
2	Potatoes	0.86	21.6	18.58	
3	Okra	2.26	38.6	87.24	
4	Fava beans	2.69	32.8	88.23	
5	Watermelon	0.66	27.3	18.02	
6	Garlic	1.19	4.9	5.83	
7	Parsnips	2.27	1.1	2.5	
8	Asparagus	2.49	37.9	94.37	
9	Avocados	3.23	9.2	29.72	
10	Celery	3.07	28.9	88.72	
11	Okra	2.26	40	90.4	

Figure 12-3: A spreadsheet of produce sales

Each row represents an individual sale. The columns are the type of produce sold (A), the cost per pound of that produce (B), the number of pounds sold (C), and the total revenue from the sale (D). The TOTAL column is set to the Excel formula *=ROUND(B3*C3, 2)*, which multiplies the cost per pound by the number of pounds sold and rounds the result to the nearest cent. With this formula, the cells in the TOTAL column will automatically update themselves if there is a change in column B or C.

Now imagine that the prices of garlic, celery, and lemons were entered incorrectly, leaving you with the boring task of going through thousands of rows in this spreadsheet to update the cost per pound for any garlic, celery, and lemon rows. You can't do a simple find-and-replace for the price because there might be other items with the same price that you don't want to mistakenly "correct." For thousands of rows, this would take hours to do by hand. But you can write a program that can accomplish this in seconds.

Your program does the following:

- Loops over all the rows.
- If the row is for garlic, celery, or lemons, changes the price.

This means your code will need to do the following:

- Open the spreadsheet file.
- For each row, check whether the value in column A is Celery, Garlic, or Lemon.
- If it is, update the price in column B.
- Save the spreadsheet to a new file (so that you don't lose the old spreadsheet, just in case).

Step 1: Set Up a Data Structure with the Update Information

The prices that you need to update are as follows:

Celery	1.19
Garlic	3.07
Lemon	1.27

You could write code like this:

```
if produceName == 'Celery':
    cellObj = 1.19
if produceName == 'Garlic':
    cellObj = 3.07
if produceName == 'Lemon':
    cellObj = 1.27
```

Having the produce and updated price data hardcoded like this is a bit inelegant. If you needed to update the spreadsheet again with different prices or different produce, you would have to change a lot of the code. Every time you change code, you risk introducing bugs.

A more flexible solution is to store the corrected price information in a dictionary and write your code to use this data structure. In a new file editor window, enter the following code:

```
#! python3
# updateProduce.py - Corrects costs in produce sales spreadsheet.

import openpyxl

wb = openpyxl.load_workbook('produceSales.xlsx')
sheet = wb.get_sheet_by_name('Sheet')

# The produce types and their updated prices
PRICE_UPDATES = {'Garlic': 3.07,
                 'Celery': 1.19,
                 'Lemon': 1.27}

# TODO: Loop through the rows and update the prices.
```

Save this as *updateProduce.py*. If you need to update the spreadsheet again, you'll need to update only the PRICE_UPDATES dictionary, not any other code.

Step 2: Check All Rows and Update Incorrect Prices

The next part of the program will loop through all the rows in the spreadsheet. Add the following code to the bottom of *updateProduce.py*:

```
#! python3
# updateProduce.py - Corrects costs in produce sales spreadsheet.

--snip--

# Loop through the rows and update the prices.
❶ for rowNum in range(2, sheet.max_row):      # skip the first row
❷     produceName = sheet.cell(row=rowNum, column=1).value
❸     if produceName in PRICE_UPDATES:
           sheet.cell(row=rowNum, column=2).value = PRICE_UPDATES[produceName]

❹ wb.save('updatedProduceSales.xlsx')
```

We loop through the rows starting at row 2, since row 1 is just the header ❶. The cell in column 1 (that is, column A) will be stored in the variable produceName ❷. If produceName exists as a key in the PRICE_UPDATES dictionary ❸, then you know this is a row that must have its price corrected. The correct price will be in PRICE_UPDATES[produceName].

Notice how clean using PRICE_UPDATES makes the code. Only one if statement, rather than code like if produceName == 'Garlic': , is necessary for every type of produce to update. And since the code uses the PRICE_UPDATES dictionary instead of hardcoding the produce names and updated costs into the for loop, you modify only the PRICE_UPDATES dictionary and not the code if the produce sales spreadsheet needs additional changes.

After going through the entire spreadsheet and making changes, the code saves the Workbook object to *updatedProduceSales.xlsx* ❹. It doesn't overwrite the old spreadsheet just in case there's a bug in your program and the updated spreadsheet is wrong. After checking that the updated spreadsheet looks right, you can delete the old spreadsheet.

You can download the complete source code for this program from *http://nostarch.com/automatestuff/*.

Ideas for Similar Programs

Since many office workers use Excel spreadsheets all the time, a program that can automatically edit and write Excel files could be really useful. Such a program could do the following:

- Read data from one spreadsheet and write it to parts of other spreadsheets.
- Read data from websites, text files, or the clipboard and write it to a spreadsheet.
- Automatically "clean up" data in spreadsheets. For example, it could use regular expressions to read multiple formats of phone numbers and edit them to a single, standard format.

Setting the Font Style of Cells

Styling certain cells, rows, or columns can help you emphasize important areas in your spreadsheet. In the produce spreadsheet, for example, your program could apply bold text to the potato, garlic, and parsnip rows. Or perhaps you want to italicize every row with a cost per pound greater than $5. Styling parts of a large spreadsheet by hand would be tedious, but your programs can do it instantly.

To customize font styles in cells, important, import the Font() function from the openpyxl.styles module.

```
from openpyxl.styles import Font
```

This allows you to type Font() instead of openpyxl.styles.Font(). (See "Importing Modules" on page 57 to review this style of import statement.)

Here's an example that creates a new workbook and sets cell A1 to have a 24-point, italicized font. Enter the following into the interactive shell:

```
>>> import openpyxl
>>> from openpyxl.styles import Font
>>> wb = openpyxl.Workbook()
>>> sheet = wb.get_sheet_by_name('Sheet')
❶ >>> italic24Font = Font(size=24, italic=True)
❷ >>> sheet['A1'].font = italic24Font
>>> sheet['A1'] = 'Hello world!'
>>> wb.save('styled.xlsx')
```

In this example, Font(size=24, italic=True) returns a Font object, which is stored in italic24Font ❶. The keyword arguments to Font(), size and italic, configure the Font object's styling information. And when sheet['A1'].font is assigned the italic24Font object ❷, all that font styling information gets applied to cell A1.

Font Objects

To set font attributes, you pass keyword arguments to Font(). Table 12-2 shows the possible keyword arguments for the Font() function.

Table 12-2: Keyword Arguments for Font Objects

Keyword argument	Data type	Description
name	String	The font name, such as 'Calibri' or 'Times New Roman'
size	Integer	The point size
bold	Boolean	True, for bold font
italic	Boolean	True, for italic font

You can call Font() to create a Font object and store that Font object in a variable. You then assign that variable to a Cell object's font attribute. For example, this code creates various font styles:

```
>>> import openpyxl
>>> from openpyxl.styles import Font
>>> wb = openpyxl.Workbook()
>>> sheet = wb.get_sheet_by_name('Sheet')

>>> fontObj1 = Font(name='Times New Roman', bold=True)
>>> sheet['A1'].font = fontObj1
>>> sheet['A1'] = 'Bold Times New Roman'

>>> fontObj2 = Font(size=24, italic=True)
>>> sheet['B3'].font = fontObj2
>>> sheet['B3'] = '24 pt Italic'

>>> wb.save('styles.xlsx')
```

Here, we store a Font object in fontObj1 and then set the A1 Cell object's font attribute to fontObj1. We repeat the process with another Font object to set the font of a second cell. After you run this code, the styles of the A1 and B3 cells in the spreadsheet will be set to custom font styles, as shown in Figure 12-4.

Figure 12-4: A spreadsheet with custom font styles

For cell A1, we set the font name to 'Times New Roman' and set bold to true, so our text appears in bold Times New Roman. We didn't specify a size, so the openpyxl default, 11, is used. In cell B3, our text is italic, with a size of 24; we didn't specify a font name, so the openpyxl default, Calibri, is used.

Formulas

Formulas, which begin with an equal sign, can configure cells to contain values calculated from other cells. In this section, you'll use the openpyxl module to programmatically add formulas to cells, just like any normal value. For example:

```
>>> sheet['B9'] = '=SUM(B1:B8)'
```

This will store *=SUM(B1:B8)* as the value in cell B9. This sets the B9 cell to a formula that calculates the sum of values in cells B1 to B8. You can see this in action in Figure 12-5.

Figure 12-5: Cell B9 contains the formula =SUM(B1:B8), which adds the cells B1 to B8.

A formula is set just like any other text value in a cell. Enter the following into the interactive shell:

```
>>> import openpyxl
>>> wb = openpyxl.Workbook()
>>> sheet = wb.active
>>> sheet['A1'] = 200
>>> sheet['A2'] = 300
>>> sheet['A3'] = '=SUM(A1:A2)'
>>> wb.save('writeFormula.xlsx')
```

The cells in A1 and A2 are set to 200 and 300, respectively. The value in cell A3 is set to a formula that sums the values in A1 and A2. When the spreadsheet is opened in Excel, A3 will display its value as 500.

Excel formulas offer a level of programmability for spreadsheets but can quickly become unmanageable for complicated tasks. For example, even if you're deeply familiar with Excel formulas, it's a headache to try to decipher what *=IFERROR(TRIM(IF(LEN(VLOOKUP(F7, Sheet2!$A$1:$B$10000, 2, FALSE))>0,SUBSTITUTE(VLOOKUP(F7, Sheet2!$A$1:$B$10000, 2, FALSE), " ", "")),"")), "")* actually does. Python code is much more readable.

Adjusting Rows and Columns

In Excel, adjusting the sizes of rows and columns is as easy as clicking and dragging the edges of a row or column header. But if you need to set a row or column's size based on its cells' contents or if you want to set sizes in a large number of spreadsheet files, it will be much quicker to write a Python program to do it.

Rows and columns can also be hidden entirely from view. Or they can be "frozen" in place so that they are always visible on the screen and appear on every page when the spreadsheet is printed (which is handy for headers).

Setting Row Height and Column Width

Worksheet objects have row_dimensions and column_dimensions attributes that control row heights and column widths. Enter this into the interactive shell:

```
>>> import openpyxl
>>> wb = openpyxl.Workbook()
>>> sheet = wb.active
>>> sheet['A1'] = 'Tall row'
>>> sheet['B2'] = 'Wide column'
>>> sheet.row_dimensions[1].height = 70
>>> sheet.column_dimensions['B'].width = 20
>>> wb.save('dimensions.xlsx')
```

A sheet's row_dimensions and column_dimensions are dictionary-like values; row_dimensions contains RowDimension objects and column_dimensions contains ColumnDimension objects. In row_dimensions, you can access one of the objects using the number of the row (in this case, 1 or 2). In column_dimensions, you can access one of the objects using the letter of the column (in this case, A or B).

The *dimensions.xlsx* spreadsheet looks like Figure 12-6.

Figure 12-6: Row 1 and column B set to larger heights and widths

Once you have the RowDimension object, you can set its height. Once you have the ColumnDimension object, you can set its width. The row height can be set to an integer or float value between 0 and 409. This value represents the height measured in *points*, where one point equals 1/72 of an inch. The default row height is 12.75. The column width can be set to an integer or float value between 0 and 255. This value represents the number of characters at the default font size (11 point) that can be displayed in the cell. The default column width is 8.43 characters. Columns with widths of 0 or rows with heights of 0 are hidden from the user.

Merging and Unmerging Cells

A rectangular area of cells can be merged into a single cell with the merge_cells() sheet method. Enter the following into the interactive shell:

```
>>> import openpyxl
>>> wb = openpyxl.Workbook()
>>> sheet = wb.active
>>> sheet.merge_cells('A1:D3')
>>> sheet['A1'] = 'Twelve cells merged together.'
>>> sheet.merge_cells('C5:D5')
>>> sheet['C5'] = 'Two merged cells.'
>>> wb.save('merged.xlsx')
```

The argument to merge_cells() is a single string of the top-left and bottom-right cells of the rectangular area to be merged: 'A1:D3' merges 12 cells into a single cell. To set the value of these merged cells, simply set the value of the top-left cell of the merged group.

When you run this code, *merged.xlsx* will look like Figure 12-7.

Figure 12-7: Merged cells in a spreadsheet

To unmerge cells, call the unmerge_cells() sheet method. Enter this into the interactive shell.

```
>>> import openpyxl
>>> wb = openpyxl.load_workbook('merged.xlsx')
>>> sheet = wb.active
>>> sheet.unmerge_cells('A1:D3')
>>> sheet.unmerge_cells('C5:D5')
>>> wb.save('merged.xlsx')
```

If you save your changes and then take a look at the spreadsheet, you'll see that the merged cells have gone back to being individual cells.

Freeze Panes

For spreadsheets too large to be displayed all at once, it's helpful to "freeze" a few of the top rows or leftmost columns onscreen. Frozen column or row headers, for example, are always visible to the user even as they scroll through the spreadsheet. These are known as *freeze panes*. In OpenPyXL, each Worksheet object has a freeze_panes attribute that can be set to a Cell object or a string of a cell's coordinates. Note that all rows above and all columns to the left of this cell will be frozen, but the row and column of the cell itself will not be frozen.

To unfreeze all panes, set freeze_panes to None or 'A1'. Table 12-3 shows which rows and columns will be frozen for some example settings of freeze_panes.

Table 12-3: Frozen Pane Examples

freeze_panes **setting**	**Rows and columns frozen**
sheet.freeze_panes = 'A2'	Row 1
sheet.freeze_panes = 'B1'	Column A
sheet.freeze_panes = 'C1'	Columns A and B
sheet.freeze_panes = 'C2'	Row 1 and columns A and B
sheet.freeze_panes = 'A1' or sheet.freeze_panes = None	No frozen panes

Make sure you have the produce sales spreadsheet from *http://nostarch .com/automatestuff/*. Then enter the following into the interactive shell:

```
>>> import openpyxl
>>> wb = openpyxl.load_workbook('produceSales.xlsx')
>>> sheet = wb.active
>>> sheet.freeze_panes = 'A2'
>>> wb.save('freezeExample.xlsx')
```

If you set the freeze_panes attribute to 'A2', row 1 will always be viewable, no matter where the user scrolls in the spreadsheet. You can see this in Figure 12-8.

Figure 12-8: With freeze_panes set to 'A2', row 1 is always visible even as the user scrolls down.

Charts

OpenPyXL supports creating bar, line, scatter, and pie charts using the data in a sheet's cells. To make a chart, you need to do the following:

1. Create a `Reference` object from a rectangular selection of cells.
2. Create a `Series` object by passing in the `Reference` object.
3. Create a `Chart` object.
4. Append the `Series` object to the `Chart` object.
5. Add the `Chart` object to the `Worksheet` object, optionally specifying which cell should be the top-left corner of the chart.

The `Reference` object requires some explaining. `Reference` objects are created by calling the `openpyxl.chart.Reference()` function and passing three arguments:

1. The `Worksheet` object containing your chart data.
2. A tuple of two integers, representing the top-left cell of the rectangular selection of cells containing your chart data: The first integer in the tuple is the row, and the second is the column. Note that 1 is the first row, not 0.
3. A tuple of two integers, representing the bottom-right cell of the rectangular selection of cells containing your chart data: The first integer in the tuple is the row, and the second is the column.

Figure 12-9 shows some sample coordinate arguments.

Figure 12-9: From left to right: (1, 1), (10, 1); (3, 2), (6, 4); (5, 3), (5, 3)

Enter this interactive shell example to create a bar chart and add it to the spreadsheet:

```
>>> import openpyxl
>>> wb = openpyxl.Workbook()
>>> sheet = wb.active
```

```
>>> for i in range(1, 11):              # create some data in column A
        sheet['A' + str(i)] = i

>>> refObj = openpyxl.chart.Reference(sheet, min_col=1, min_row=1, max_col=1,
        max_row=10)

>>> seriesObj = openpyxl.chart.Series(refObj, title='First series')

>>> chartObj = openpyxl.chart.BarChart()
>>> chartObj.title = 'My Chart'
>>> chartObj.append(seriesObj)

>>> sheet.add_chart(chartObj, 'C5')
>>> wb.save('sampleChart.xlsx')
```

This produces a spreadsheet that looks like Figure 12-10.

Figure 12-10: A spreadsheet with a chart added

We've created a bar chart by calling openpyxl.chart.BarChart(). You can also create line charts, scatter charts, and pie charts by calling openpyxl.chart.LineChart(), openpyxl.chart.ScatterChart(), and openpyxl.chart.PieChart().

Unfortunately, in the current version of OpenPyXL (2.3.3), the load_workbook() function does not load charts in Excel files. Even if the Excel file has charts, the loaded Workbook object will not include them. If you load a Workbook object and immediately save it to the same *.xlsx* filename, you will effectively remove the charts from it.

Summary

Often the hard part of processing information isn't the processing itself but simply getting the data in the right format for your program. But once you have your spreadsheet loaded into Python, you can extract and manipulate its data much faster than you could by hand.

You can also generate spreadsheets as output from your programs. So if colleagues need your text file or PDF of thousands of sales contacts transferred to a spreadsheet file, you won't have to tediously copy and paste it all into Excel.

Equipped with the openpyxl module and some programming knowledge, you'll find processing even the biggest spreadsheets a piece of cake.

Practice Questions

For the following questions, imagine you have a Workbook object in the variable wb, a Worksheet object in sheet, a Cell object in cell, a Comment object in comm, and an Image object in img.

1. What does the openpyxl.load_workbook() function return?

2. What does the get_sheet_names() workbook method return?

3. How would you retrieve the Worksheet object for a sheet named 'Sheet1'?

4. How would you retrieve the Worksheet object for the workbook's active sheet?

5. How would you retrieve the value in the cell C5?

6. How would you set the value in the cell C5 to "Hello"?

7. How would you retrieve the cell's row and column as integers?

8. What do the sheet.max_column and sheet.max_row sheet attributes hold, and what is the data type of these attributes?

9. If you needed to get the integer index for column 'M', what function would you need to call?

10. If you needed to get the string name for column 14, what function would you need to call?

11. How can you retrieve a tuple of all the Cell objects from A1 to F1?

12. How would you save the workbook to the filename *example.xlsx*?

13. How do you set a formula in a cell?

14. If you want to retrieve the result of a cell's formula instead of the cell's formula itself, what must you do first?

15. How would you set the height of row 5 to 100?

16. How would you hide column C?

17. Name a few features that OpenPyXL 2.3.3 does not load from a spreadsheet file.

18. What is a freeze pane?

19. What five functions and methods do you have to call to create a bar chart?

Practice Projects

For practice, write programs that perform the following tasks.

Multiplication Table Maker

Create a program *multiplicationTable.py* that takes a number *N* from the command line and creates an *N×N* multiplication table in an Excel spreadsheet. For example, when the program is run like this:

```
py multiplicationTable.py 6
```

. . . it should create a spreadsheet that looks like Figure 12-11.

	A	B	C	D	E	F	G	H
1		1	2	3	4	5	6	
2	1	1	2	3	4	5	6	
3	2	2	4	6	8	10	12	
4	3	3	6	9	12	15	18	
5	4	4	8	12	16	20	24	
6	5	5	10	15	20	25	30	
7	6	6	12	18	24	30	36	
8								
9								

Figure 12-11: A multiplication table generated in a spreadsheet

Row 1 and column A should be used for labels and should be in bold.

Blank Row Inserter

Create a program *blankRowInserter.py* that takes two integers and a filename string as command line arguments. Let's call the first integer *N* and the second integer *M*. Starting at row *N*, the program should insert *M* blank rows into the spreadsheet. For example, when the program is run like this:

```
python blankRowInserter.py 3 2 myProduce.xlsx
```

. . . the "before" and "after" spreadsheets should look like Figure 12-12.

Figure 12-12: Before (left) and after (right) the two blank rows are inserted at row 3

You can write this program by reading in the contents of the spreadsheet. Then, when writing out the new spreadsheet, use a for loop to copy the first *N* lines. For the remaining lines, add *M* to the row number in the output spreadsheet.

Spreadsheet Cell Inverter

Write a program to invert the row and column of the cells in the spreadsheet. For example, the value at row 5, column 3 will be at row 3, column 5 (and vice versa). This should be done for all cells in the spreadsheet. For example, the "before" and "after" spreadsheets would look something like Figure 12-13.

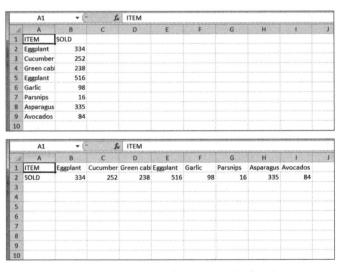

Figure 12-13: The spreadsheet before (top) and after (bottom) inversion

You can write this program by using nested for loops to read in the spreadsheet's data into a list of lists data structure. This data structure could have sheetData[x][y] for the cell at column x and row y. Then, when writing out the new spreadsheet, use sheetData[y][x] for the cell at column x and row y.

Text Files to Spreadsheet

Write a program to read in the contents of several text files (you can make the text files yourself) and insert those contents into a spreadsheet, with one line of text per row. The lines of the first text file will be in the cells of column A, the lines of the second text file will be in the cells of column B, and so on.

Use the `readlines()` File object method to return a list of strings, one string per line in the file. For the first file, output the first line to column 1, row 1. The second line should be written to column 1, row 2, and so on. The next file that is read with `readlines()` will be written to column 2, the next file to column 3, and so on.

Spreadsheet to Text Files

Write a program that performs the tasks of the previous program in reverse order: The program should open a spreadsheet and write the cells of column A into one text file, the cells of column B into another text file, and so on.

13

WORKING WITH PDF
AND WORD DOCUMENTS

PDF and Word documents are binary files, which makes them much more complex than plaintext files. In addition to text, they store lots of font, color, and layout information. If you want your programs to read or write to PDFs or Word documents, you'll need to do more than simply pass their filenames to open().

Fortunately, there are Python modules that make it easy for you to interact with PDFs and Word documents. This chapter will cover two such modules: PyPDF2 and Python-Docx.

PDF Documents

PDF stands for *Portable Document Format* and uses the *.pdf* file extension. Although PDFs support many features, this chapter will focus on the two things you'll be doing most often with them: reading text content from PDFs and crafting new PDFs from existing documents.

The module you'll use to work with PDFs is PyPDF2. To install it, run pip install PyPDF2 from the command line. This module name is case sensitive, so make sure the *y* is lowercase and everything else is uppercase. (Check out Appendix A for full details about installing third-party modules.) If the module was installed correctly, running import PyPDF2 in the interactive shell shouldn't display any errors.

THE PROBLEMATIC PDF FORMAT

While PDF files are great for laying out text in a way that's easy for people to print and read, they're not straightforward for software to parse into plaintext. As such, PyPDF2 might make mistakes when extracting text from a PDF and may even be unable to open some PDFs at all. There isn't much you can do about this, unfortunately. PyPDF2 may simply be unable to work with some of your particular PDF files. That said, I haven't found any PDF files so far that can't be opened with PyPDF2.

Extracting Text from PDFs

PyPDF2 does not have a way to extract images, charts, or other media from PDF documents, but it can extract text and return it as a Python string. To start learning how PyPDF2 works, we'll use it on the example PDF shown in Figure 13-1.

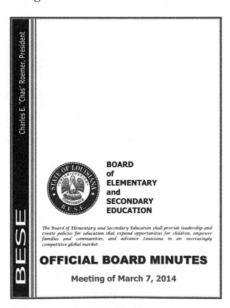

Figure 13-1: The PDF page that we will be extracting text from

Download this PDF from *http://nostarch.com/automatestuff/*, and enter the following into the interactive shell:

```
>>> import PyPDF2
>>> pdfFileObj = open('meetingminutes.pdf', 'rb')
>>> pdfReader = PyPDF2.PdfFileReader(pdfFileObj)
❶ >>> pdfReader.numPages
19
❷ >>> pageObj = pdfReader.getPage(0)
❸ >>> pageObj.extractText()
'OOFFFFIICCIIAALL  BBOOAARRDD MMIINNUUTTEESS   Meeting of March 7, 2015
\n    The Board of Elementary and Secondary Education shall provide leadership
and create policies for education that expand opportunities for children,
empower families and communities, and advance Louisiana in an increasingly
competitive global market. BOARD  of ELEMENTARY and  SECONDARY EDUCATION  '
```

First, import the PyPDF2 module. Then open *meetingminutes.pdf* in read binary mode and store it in pdfFileObj. To get a PdfFileReader object that represents this PDF, call PyPDF2.PdfFileReader() and pass it pdfFileObj. Store this PdfFileReader object in pdfReader.

The total number of pages in the document is stored in the numPages attribute of a PdfFileReader object ❶. The example PDF has 19 pages, but let's extract text from only the first page.

To extract text from a page, you need to get a Page object, which represents a single page of a PDF, from a PdfFileReader object. You can get a Page object by calling the getPage() method ❷ on a PdfFileReader object and passing it the page number of the page you're interested in—in our case, 0.

PyPDF2 uses a *zero-based index* for getting pages: The first page is page 0, the second is page 1, and so on. This is always the case, even if pages are numbered differently within the document. For example, say your PDF is a three-page excerpt from a longer report, and its pages are numbered 42, 43, and 44. To get the first page of this document, you would want to call pdfReader.getPage(0), not getPage(42) or getPage(1).

Once you have your Page object, call its extractText() method to return a string of the page's text ❸. The text extraction isn't perfect: The text *Charles E. "Chas" Roemer, President* from the PDF is absent from the string returned by extractText(), and the spacing is sometimes off. Still, this approximation of the PDF text content may be good enough for your program.

Decrypting PDFs

Some PDF documents have an encryption feature that will keep them from being read until whoever is opening the document provides a password. Enter the following into the interactive shell with the PDF you downloaded, which has been encrypted with the password *rosebud*:

```
>>> import PyPDF2
>>> pdfReader = PyPDF2.PdfFileReader(open('encrypted.pdf', 'rb'))
❶ >>> pdfReader.isEncrypted
True
```

```
>>> pdfReader.getPage(0)
```
❷ Traceback (most recent call last):
  File "<pyshell#173>", line 1, in <module>
    pdfReader.getPage()
  --*snip*--
  File "C:\Python34\lib\site-packages\PyPDF2\pdf.py", line 1173, in getObject
    raise utils.PdfReadError("file has not been decrypted")
PyPDF2.utils.PdfReadError: file has not been decrypted
❸ >>> pdfReader.decrypt('rosebud')
1
```
>>> pageObj = pdfReader.getPage(0)
```

All PdfFileReader objects have an isEncrypted attribute that is True if the PDF is encrypted and False if it isn't ❶. Any attempt to call a function that reads the file before it has been decrypted with the correct password will result in an error ❷.

To read an encrypted PDF, call the decrypt() function and pass the password as a string ❸. After you call decrypt() with the correct password, you'll see that calling getPage() no longer causes an error. If given the wrong password, the decrypt() function will return 0 and getPage() will continue to fail. Note that the decrypt() method decrypts only the PdfFileReader object, not the actual PDF file. After your program terminates, the file on your hard drive remains encrypted. Your program will have to call decrypt() again the next time it is run.

Creating PDFs

PyPDF2's counterpart to PdfFileReader objects is PdfFileWriter objects, which can create new PDF files. But PyPDF2 cannot write arbitrary text to a PDF like Python can do with plaintext files. Instead, PyPDF2's PDF-writing capabilities are limited to copying pages from other PDFs, rotating pages, overlaying pages, and encrypting files.

PyPDF2 doesn't allow you to directly edit a PDF. Instead, you have to create a new PDF and then copy content over from an existing document. The examples in this section will follow this general approach:

1. Open one or more existing PDFs (the source PDFs) into PdfFileReader objects.

2. Create a new PdfFileWriter object.

3. Copy pages from the PdfFileReader objects into the PdfFileWriter object.

4. Finally, use the PdfFileWriter object to write the output PDF.

Creating a PdfFileWriter object creates only a value that represents a PDF document in Python. It doesn't create the actual PDF file. For that, you must call the PdfFileWriter's write() method.

The write() method takes a regular File object that has been opened in *write-binary* mode. You can get such a File object by calling Python's open() function with two arguments: the string of what you want the PDF's filename to be and 'wb' to indicate the file should be opened in write-binary mode.

If this sounds a little confusing, don't worry—you'll see how this works in the following code examples.

Copying Pages

You can use PyPDF2 to copy pages from one PDF document to another. This allows you to combine multiple PDF files, cut unwanted pages, or reorder pages.

Download *meetingminutes.pdf* and *meetingminutes2.pdf* from *http://nostarch .com/automatestuff/* and place the PDFs in the current working directory. Enter the following into the interactive shell:

```
>>> import PyPDF2
>>> pdf1File = open('meetingminutes.pdf', 'rb')
>>> pdf2File = open('meetingminutes2.pdf', 'rb')
❶ >>> pdf1Reader = PyPDF2.PdfFileReader(pdf1File)
❷ >>> pdf2Reader = PyPDF2.PdfFileReader(pdf2File)
❸ >>> pdfWriter = PyPDF2.PdfFileWriter()

>>> for pageNum in range(pdf1Reader.numPages):
❹       pageObj = pdf1Reader.getPage(pageNum)
❺       pdfWriter.addPage(pageObj)

>>> for pageNum in range(pdf2Reader.numPages):
❹       pageObj = pdf2Reader.getPage(pageNum)
❺       pdfWriter.addPage(pageObj)

❻ >>> pdfOutputFile = open('combinedminutes.pdf', 'wb')
>>> pdfWriter.write(pdfOutputFile)
>>> pdfOutputFile.close()
>>> pdf1File.close()
>>> pdf2File.close()
```

Open both PDF files in read binary mode and store the two resulting File objects in pdf1File and pdf2File. Call PyPDF2.PdfFileReader() and pass it pdf1File to get a PdfFileReader object for *meetingminutes.pdf* ❶. Call it again and pass it pdf2File to get a PdfFileReader object for *meetingminutes2.pdf* ❷. Then create a new PdfFileWriter object, which represents a blank PDF document ❸.

Next, copy all the pages from the two source PDFs and add them to the PdfFileWriter object. Get the Page object by calling getPage() on a PdfFileReader object ❹. Then pass that Page object to your PdfFileWriter's addPage() method ❺. These steps are done first for pdf1Reader and then again for pdf2Reader. When you're done copying pages, write a new PDF called *combinedminutes.pdf* by passing a File object to the PdfFileWriter's write() method ❻.

NOTE *PyPDF2 cannot insert pages in the middle of a PdfFileWriter object; the addPage() method will only add pages to the end.*

You have now created a new PDF file that combines the pages from *meetingminutes.pdf* and *meetingminutes2.pdf* into a single document. Remember that the File object passed to PyPDF2.PdfFileReader() needs to be opened in read-binary mode by passing 'rb' as the second argument to open(). Likewise, the File object passed to PyPDF2.PdfFileWriter() needs to be opened in write-binary mode with 'wb'.

Rotating Pages

The pages of a PDF can also be rotated in 90-degree increments with the rotateClockwise() and rotateCounterClockwise() methods. Pass one of the integers 90, 180, or 270 to these methods. Enter the following into the interactive shell, with the *meetingminutes.pdf* file in the current working directory:

```
>>> import PyPDF2
>>> minutesFile = open('meetingminutes.pdf', 'rb')
>>> pdfReader = PyPDF2.PdfFileReader(minutesFile)
❶ >>> page = pdfReader.getPage(0)
❷ >>> page.rotateClockwise(90)
{'/Contents': [IndirectObject(961, 0), IndirectObject(962, 0),
--snip--
}
>>> pdfWriter = PyPDF2.PdfFileWriter()
>>> pdfWriter.addPage(page)
❸ >>> resultPdfFile = open('rotatedPage.pdf', 'wb')
>>> pdfWriter.write(resultPdfFile)
>>> resultPdfFile.close()
>>> minutesFile.close()
```

Here we use getPage(0) to select the first page of the PDF ❶, and then we call rotateClockwise(90) on that page ❷. We write a new PDF with the rotated page and save it as *rotatedPage.pdf* ❸.

The resulting PDF will have one page, rotated 90 degrees clockwise, as in Figure 13-2. The return values from rotateClockwise() and rotateCounterClockwise() contain a lot of information that you can ignore.

Figure 13-2: The rotatedPage.pdf file with the page
rotated 90 degrees clockwise

Overlaying Pages

PyPDF2 can also overlay the contents of one page over another, which is
useful for adding a logo, timestamp, or watermark to a page. With Python,
it's easy to add watermarks to multiple files and only to pages your program
specifies.

Download *watermark.pdf* from *http://nostarch.com/automatestuff/* and place
the PDF in the current working directory along with *meetingminutes.pdf*. Then
enter the following into the interactive shell:

```
   >>> import PyPDF2
   >>> minutesFile = open('meetingminutes.pdf', 'rb')
❶ >>> pdfReader = PyPDF2.PdfFileReader(minutesFile)
❷ >>> minutesFirstPage = pdfReader.getPage(0)
❸ >>> pdfWatermarkReader = PyPDF2.PdfFileReader(open('watermark.pdf', 'rb'))
❹ >>> minutesFirstPage.mergePage(pdfWatermarkReader.getPage(0))
❺ >>> pdfWriter = PyPDF2.PdfFileWriter()
❻ >>> pdfWriter.addPage(minutesFirstPage)

❼ >>> for pageNum in range(1, pdfReader.numPages):
           pageObj = pdfReader.getPage(pageNum)
           pdfWriter.addPage(pageObj)
```

```
>>> resultPdfFile = open('watermarkedCover.pdf', 'wb')
>>> pdfWriter.write(resultPdfFile)
>>> minutesFile.close()
>>> resultPdfFile.close()
```

Here we make a `PdfFileReader` object of *meetingminutes.pdf* ❶. We call `getPage(0)` to get a `Page` object for the first page and store this object in `minutesFirstPage` ❷. We then make a `PdfFileReader` object for *watermark.pdf* ❸ and call `mergePage()` on `minutesFirstPage` ❹. The argument we pass to `mergePage()` is a `Page` object for the first page of *watermark.pdf*.

Now that we've called `mergePage()` on `minutesFirstPage`, `minutesFirstPage` represents the watermarked first page. We make a `PdfFileWriter` object ❺ and add the watermarked first page ❻. Then we loop through the rest of the pages in *meetingminutes.pdf* and add them to the `PdfFileWriter` object ❼. Finally, we open a new PDF called *watermarkedCover.pdf* and write the contents of the PdfFileWriter to the new PDF.

Figure 13-3 shows the results. Our new PDF, *watermarkedCover.pdf*, has all the contents of the *meetingminutes.pdf*, and the first page is watermarked.

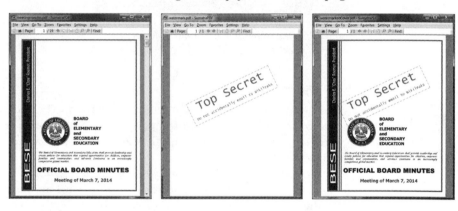

Figure 13-3: The original PDF (left), the watermark PDF (center), and the merged PDF (right)

Encrypting PDFs

A `PdfFileWriter` object can also add encryption to a PDF document. Enter the following into the interactive shell:

```
>>> import PyPDF2
>>> pdfFile = open('meetingminutes.pdf', 'rb')
>>> pdfReader = PyPDF2.PdfFileReader(pdfFile)
>>> pdfWriter = PyPDF2.PdfFileWriter()
>>> for pageNum in range(pdfReader.numPages):
        pdfWriter.addPage(pdfReader.getPage(pageNum))

❶ >>> pdfWriter.encrypt('swordfish')
>>> resultPdf = open('encryptedminutes.pdf', 'wb')
>>> pdfWriter.write(resultPdf)
>>> resultPdf.close()
```

Before calling the write() method to save to a file, call the encrypt() method and pass it a password string ❶. PDFs can have a *user password* (allowing you to view the PDF) and an *owner password* (allowing you to set permissions for printing, commenting, extracting text, and other features). The user password and owner password are the first and second arguments to encrypt(), respectively. If only one string argument is passed to encrypt(), it will be used for both passwords.

In this example, we copied the pages of *meetingminutes.pdf* to a PdfFileWriter object. We encrypted the PdfFileWriter with the password *swordfish*, opened a new PDF called *encryptedminutes.pdf*, and wrote the contents of the PdfFileWriter to the new PDF. Before anyone can view *encryptedminutes.pdf*, they'll have to enter this password. You may want to delete the original, unencrypted *meetingminutes.pdf* file after ensuring its copy was correctly encrypted.

Project: Combining Select Pages from Many PDFs

Say you have the boring job of merging several dozen PDF documents into a single PDF file. Each of them has a cover sheet as the first page, but you don't want the cover sheet repeated in the final result. Even though there are lots of free programs for combining PDFs, many of them simply merge entire files together. Let's write a Python program to customize which pages you want in the combined PDF.

At a high level, here's what the program will do:

- Find all PDF files in the current working directory.
- Sort the filenames so the PDFs are added in order.
- Write each page, excluding the first page, of each PDF to the output file.

In terms of implementation, your code will need to do the following:

- Call os.listdir() to find all the files in the working directory and remove any non-PDF files.
- Call Python's sort() list method to alphabetize the filenames.
- Create a PdfFileWriter object for the output PDF.
- Loop over each PDF file, creating a PdfFileReader object for it.
- Loop over each page (except the first) in each PDF file.
- Add the pages to the output PDF.
- Write the output PDF to a file named *allminutes.pdf*.

For this project, open a new file editor window and save it as *combinePdfs.py*.

Step 1: Find All PDF Files

First, your program needs to get a list of all files with the *.pdf* extension in the current working directory and sort them. Make your code look like the following:

```python
#! python3
# combinePdfs.py - Combines all the PDFs in the current working directory into
# into a single PDF.

❶ import PyPDF2, os

   # Get all the PDF filenames.
   pdfFiles = []
   for filename in os.listdir('.'):
       if filename.endswith('.pdf'):
❷         pdfFiles.append(filename)
❸ pdfFiles.sort(key = str.lower)

❹ pdfWriter = PyPDF2.PdfFileWriter()

   # TODO: Loop through all the PDF files.

   # TODO: Loop through all the pages (except the first) and add them.

   # TODO: Save the resulting PDF to a file.
```

After the shebang line and the descriptive comment about what the program does, this code imports the os and PyPDF2 modules ❶. The os.listdir('.') call will return a list of every file in the current working directory. The code loops over this list and adds only those files with the *.pdf* extension to pdfFiles ❷. Afterward, this list is sorted in alphabetical order with the key = str.lower keyword argument to sort() ❸.

A PdfFileWriter object is created to hold the combined PDF pages ❹. Finally, a few comments outline the rest of the program.

Step 2: Open Each PDF

Now the program must read each PDF file in pdfFiles. Add the following to your program:

```python
#! python3
# combinePdfs.py - Combines all the PDFs in the current working directory into
# a single PDF.

import PyPDF2, os

# Get all the PDF filenames.
pdfFiles = []
--snip--
```

```
# Loop through all the PDF files.
for filename in pdfFiles:
    pdfFileObj = open(filename, 'rb')
    pdfReader = PyPDF2.PdfFileReader(pdfFileObj)
    # TODO: Loop through all the pages (except the first) and add them.

# TODO: Save the resulting PDF to a file.
```

For each PDF, the loop opens a filename in read-binary mode by calling open() with 'rb' as the second argument. The open() call returns a File object, which gets passed to PyPDF2.PdfFileReader() to create a PdfFileReader object for that PDF file.

Step 3: Add Each Page

For each PDF, you'll want to loop over every page except the first. Add this code to your program:

```
#! python3
# combinePdfs.py - Combines all the PDFs in the current working directory into
# a single PDF.

import PyPDF2, os

--snip--

# Loop through all the PDF files.
for filename in pdfFiles:
--snip--
    # Loop through all the pages (except the first) and add them.
❶   for pageNum in range(1, pdfReader.numPages):
        pageObj = pdfReader.getPage(pageNum)
        pdfWriter.addPage(pageObj)

# TODO: Save the resulting PDF to a file.
```

The code inside the for loop copies each Page object individually to the PdfFileWriter object. Remember, you want to skip the first page. Since PyPDF2 considers 0 to be the first page, your loop should start at 1 ❶ and then go up to, but not include, the integer in pdfReader.numPages.

Step 4: Save the Results

After these nested for loops are done looping, the pdfWriter variable will contain a PdfFileWriter object with the pages for all the PDFs combined. The last step is to write this content to a file on the hard drive. Add this code to your program:

```
#! python3
# combinePdfs.py - Combines all the PDFs in the current working directory into
# a single PDF.
```

```
import PyPDF2, os

--snip--

# Loop through all the PDF files.
for filename in pdfFiles:
--snip--
    # Loop through all the pages (except the first) and add them.
    for pageNum in range(1, pdfReader.numPages):
    --snip--

# Save the resulting PDF to a file.
pdfOutput = open('allminutes.pdf', 'wb')
pdfWriter.write(pdfOutput)
pdfOutput.close()
```

Passing `'wb'` to open() opens the output PDF file, *allminutes.pdf*, in write-binary mode. Then, passing the resulting File object to the write() method creates the actual PDF file. A call to the close() method finishes the program.

Ideas for Similar Programs

Being able to create PDFs from the pages of other PDFs will let you make programs that can do the following:

- Cut out specific pages from PDFs.
- Reorder pages in a PDF.
- Create a PDF from only those pages that have some specific text, identified by extractText().

Word Documents

Python can create and modify Word documents, which have the *.docx* file extension, with the python-docx module. You can install the module by running pip install python-docx. (Appendix A has full details on installing third-party modules.)

NOTE   *When using pip to first install Python-Docx, be sure to install python-docx, not docx. The installation name docx is for a different module that this book does not cover. However, when you are going to import the python-docx module, you'll need to run import docx, not import python-docx.*

If you don't have Word, LibreOffice Writer and OpenOffice Writer are both free alternative applications for Windows, OS X, and Linux that can be used to open *.docx* files. You can download them from *https://www.libreoffice.org* and *http://openoffice.org*, respectively. The full documentation for Python-Docx is available at *https://python-docx.readthedocs.org/*. Although there is a version of Word for OS X, this chapter will focus on Word for Windows.

Compared to plaintext, *.docx* files have a lot of structure. This structure is represented by three different data types in Python-Docx. At the highest level, a Document object represents the entire document. The Document object contains a list of Paragraph objects for the paragraphs in the document. (A new paragraph begins whenever the user presses ENTER or RETURN while typing in a Word document.) Each of these Paragraph objects contains a list of one or more Run objects. The single-sentence paragraph in Figure 13-4 has four runs.

A plain paragraph with some **bold** and some *italic*

|_____||_____||_____||_____|
                 Run   Run   Run   Run

Figure 13-4: The Run objects identified in a Paragraph object

The text in a Word document is more than just a string. It has font, size, color, and other styling information associated with it. A *style* in Word is a collection of these attributes. A Run object is a contiguous run of text with the same style. A new Run object is needed whenever the text style changes.

Reading Word Documents

Let's experiment with the python-docx module. Download *demo.docx* from *http://nostarch.com/automatestuff/* and save the document to the working directory. Then enter the following into the interactive shell:

```
>>> import docx
❶ >>> doc = docx.Document('demo.docx')
❷ >>> len(doc.paragraphs)
7
❸ >>> doc.paragraphs[0].text
'Document Title'
❹ >>> doc.paragraphs[1].text
'A plain paragraph with some bold and some italic'
❺ >>> len(doc.paragraphs[1].runs)
4
❻ >>> doc.paragraphs[1].runs[0].text
'A plain paragraph with some '
❼ >>> doc.paragraphs[1].runs[1].text
'bold'
❽ >>> doc.paragraphs[1].runs[2].text
' and some '
❾ >>> doc.paragraphs[1].runs[3].text
'italic'
```

At ❶, we open a *.docx* file in Python, call docx.Document(), and pass the filename *demo.docx*. This will return a Document object, which has a paragraphs attribute that is a list of Paragraph objects. When we call len() on doc.paragraphs, it returns 7, which tells us that there are seven Paragraph objects in this document ❷. Each of these Paragraph objects has a text attribute that contains a string of the text in that paragraph (without the style information). Here, the first text attribute contains 'DocumentTitle' ❸, and the second contains 'A plain paragraph with some bold and some italic' ❹.

Each Paragraph object also has a runs attribute that is a list of Run objects. Run objects also have a text attribute, containing just the text in that particular run. Let's look at the text attributes in the second Paragraph object, 'A plain paragraph with some bold and some italic'. Calling len() on this Paragraph object tells us that there are four Run objects ❺. The first run object contains 'A plain paragraph with some ' ❻. Then, the text change to a bold style, so 'bold' starts a new Run object ❼. The text returns to an unbolded style after that, which results in a third Run object, ' and some ' ❽. Finally, the fourth and last Run object contains 'italic' in an italic style ❾.

With Python-Docx, your Python programs will now be able to read the text from a *.docx* file and use it just like any other string value.

Getting the Full Text from a .docx File

If you care only about the text, not the styling information, in the Word document, you can use the getText() function. It accepts a filename of a *.docx* file and returns a single string value of its text. Open a new file editor window and enter the following code, saving it as *readDocx.py*:

```
#! python3

import docx

def getText(filename):
    doc = docx.Document(filename)
    fullText = []
    for para in doc.paragraphs:
        fullText.append(para.text)
    return '\n'.join(fullText)
```

The getText() function opens the Word document, loops over all the Paragraph objects in the paragraphs list, and then appends their text to the list in fullText. After the loop, the strings in fullText are joined together with newline characters.

The *readDocx.py* program can be imported like any other module. Now if you just need the text from a Word document, you can enter the following:

```
>>> import readDocx
>>> print(readDocx.getText('demo.docx'))
Document Title
A plain paragraph with some bold and some italic
Heading, level 1
Intense quote
first item in unordered list
first item in ordered list
```

You can also adjust getText() to modify the string before returning it. For example, to indent each paragraph, replace the append() call in *readDocx.py* with this:

```
fullText.append('    ' + para.text)
```

To add a double space in between paragraphs, change the join() call code to this:

```
return '\n\n'.join(fullText)
```

As you can see, it takes only a few lines of code to write functions that will read a *.docx* file and return a string of its content to your liking.

Styling Paragraph and Run Objects

In Word for Windows, you can see the styles by pressing CTRL-ALT-SHIFT-S to display the Styles pane, which looks like Figure 13-5. On OS X, you can view the Styles pane by clicking the **View ▸ Styles** menu item.

Figure 13-5: Display the Styles pane by pressing CTRL-ALT-SHIFT-S on Windows.

Word and other word processors use styles to keep the visual presentation of similar types of text consistent and easy to change. For example, perhaps you want to set body paragraphs in 11-point, Times New Roman, left-justified, ragged-right text. You can create a style with these settings and assign it to all body paragraphs. Then, if you later want to change the presentation of all body paragraphs in the document, you can just change the style, and all those paragraphs will be automatically updated.

For Word documents, there are three types of styles: *Paragraph styles* can be applied to Paragraph objects, *character styles* can be applied to Run objects, and *linked styles* can be applied to both kinds of objects. You can give both Paragraph and Run objects styles by setting their style attribute to a string. This string should be the name of a style. If style is set to None, then there will be no style associated with the Paragraph or Run object.

The string values for the default Word styles are as follows:

'Normal'	'Heading5'	'ListBullet'	'ListParagraph'
'BodyText'	'Heading6'	'ListBullet2'	'MacroText'
'BodyText2'	'Heading7'	'ListBullet3'	'NoSpacing'
'BodyText3'	'Heading8'	'ListContinue'	'Quote'
'Caption'	'Heading9'	'ListContinue2'	'Subtitle'
'Heading1'	'IntenseQuote'	'ListContinue3'	'TOCHeading'
'Heading2'	'List'	'ListNumber'	'Title'
'Heading3'	'List2'	'ListNumber2'	
'Heading4'	'List3'	'ListNumber3'	

When setting the style attribute, do not use spaces in the style name. For example, while the style name may be Subtle Emphasis, you should set the style attribute to the string value 'SubtleEmphasis' instead of 'Subtle Emphasis'. Including spaces will cause Word to misread the style name and not apply it.

When using a linked style for a Run object, you will need to add 'Char' to the end of its name. For example, to set the Quote linked style for a Paragraph object, you would use paragraphObj.style = 'Quote', but for a Run object, you would use runObj.style = 'QuoteChar'.

In the current version of Python-Docx (0.7.4), the only styles that can be used are the default Word styles and the styles in the opened *.docx*. New styles cannot be created—though this may change in future versions of Python-Docx.

Creating Word Documents with Nondefault Styles

If you want to create Word documents that use styles beyond the default ones, you will need to open Word to a blank Word document and create the styles yourself by clicking the **New Style** button at the bottom of the Styles pane (Figure 13-6 shows this on Windows).

This will open the Create New Style from Formatting dialog, where you can enter the new style. Then, go back into the interactive shell and open this blank Word document with docx.Document(), using it as the base for your Word document. The name you gave this style will now be available to use with Python-Docx.

Figure 13-6: The New Style button (left) and the Create New Style from Formatting dialog (right)

Run Attributes

Runs can be further styled using text attributes. Each attribute can be set to one of three values: True (the attribute is always enabled, no matter what other styles are applied to the run), False (the attribute is always disabled), or None (defaults to whatever the run's style is set to).

Table 13-1 lists the text attributes that can be set on Run objects.

Table 13-1: Run Object text Attributes

Attribute	Description
bold	The text appears in bold.
italic	The text appears in italic.
underline	The text is underlined.
strike	The text appears with strikethrough.
double_strike	The text appears with double strikethrough.
all_caps	The text appears in capital letters.
small_caps	The text appears in capital letters, with lowercase letters two points smaller.
shadow	The text appears with a shadow.
outline	The text appears outlined rather than solid.
rtl	The text is written right-to-left.
imprint	The text appears pressed into the page.
emboss	The text appears raised off the page in relief.

For example, to change the styles of *demo.docx*, enter the following into the interactive shell:

```
>>> doc = docx.Document('demo.docx')
>>> doc.paragraphs[0].text
'Document Title'
>>> doc.paragraphs[0].style
'Title'
>>> doc.paragraphs[0].style = 'Normal'
>>> doc.paragraphs[1].text
'A plain paragraph with some bold and some italic'
>>> (doc.paragraphs[1].runs[0].text, doc.paragraphs[1].runs[1].text, doc.
paragraphs[1].runs[2].text, doc.paragraphs[1].runs[3].text)
('A plain paragraph with some ', 'bold', ' and some ', 'italic')
>>> doc.paragraphs[1].runs[0].style = 'QuoteChar'
>>> doc.paragraphs[1].runs[1].underline = True
>>> doc.paragraphs[1].runs[3].underline = True
>>> doc.save('restyled.docx')
```

Here, we use the text and style attributes to easily see what's in the paragraphs in our document. We can see that it's simple to divide a paragraph into runs and access each run individually. So we get the first, second, and fourth runs in the second paragraph, style each run, and save the results to a new document.

The words *Document Title* at the top of *restyled.docx* will have the Normal style instead of the Title style, the Run object for the text *A plain paragraph with some* will have the QuoteChar style, and the two Run objects for the words *bold* and *italic* will have their underline attributes set to True. Figure 13-7 shows how the styles of paragraphs and runs look in *restyled.docx*.

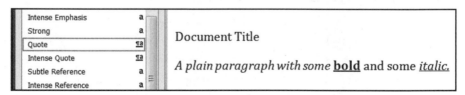

Figure 13-7: The restyled.docx file

You can find more complete documentation on Python-Docx's use of styles at *https://python-docx.readthedocs.org/en/latest/user/styles.html*.

Writing Word Documents

Enter the following into the interactive shell:

```
>>> import docx
>>> doc = docx.Document()
>>> doc.add_paragraph('Hello world!')
<docx.text.Paragraph object at 0x0000000003B56F60>
>>> doc.save('helloworld.docx')
```

To create your own *.docx* file, call docx.Document() to return a new, blank Word Document object. The add_paragraph() document method adds a new paragraph of text to the document and returns a reference to the Paragraph object that was added. When you're done adding text, pass a filename string to the save() document method to save the Document object to a file.

This will create a file named *helloworld.docx* in the current working directory that, when opened, looks like Figure 13-8.

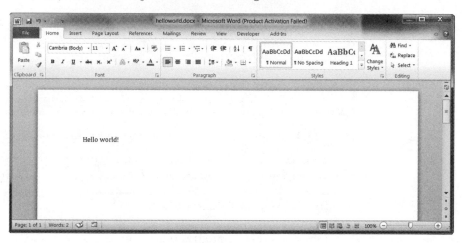

Figure 13-8: The Word document created using add_paragraph('Hello world!')

You can add paragraphs by calling the add_paragraph() method again with the new paragraph's text. Or to add text to the end of an existing paragraph, you can call the paragraph's add_run() method and pass it a string. Enter the following into the interactive shell:

```
>>> import docx
>>> doc = docx.Document()
>>> doc.add_paragraph('Hello world!')
<docx.text.Paragraph object at 0x000000000366AD30>
>>> paraObj1 = doc.add_paragraph('This is a second paragraph.')
>>> paraObj2 = doc.add_paragraph('This is a yet another paragraph.')
>>> paraObj1.add_run(' This text is being added to the second paragraph.')
<docx.text.Run object at 0x0000000003A2C860>
>>> doc.save('multipleParagraphs.docx')
```

The resulting document will look like Figure 13-9. Note that the text *This text is being added to the second paragraph.* was added to the Paragraph object in paraObj1, which was the second paragraph added to doc. The add_paragraph() and add_run() functions return paragraph and Run objects, respectively, to save you the trouble of extracting them as a separate step.

Keep in mind that as of Python-Docx version 0.5.3, new Paragraph objects can be added only to the end of the document, and new Run objects can be added only to the end of a Paragraph object.

The save() method can be called again to save the additional changes you've made.

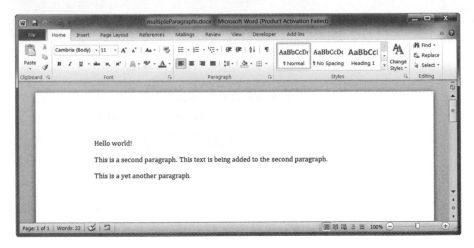

Figure 13-9: The document with multiple Paragraph *and* Run *objects added*

Both add_paragraph() and add_run() accept an optional second argument that is a string of the Paragraph or Run object's style. For example:

```
>>> doc.add_paragraph('Hello world!', 'Title')
```

This line adds a paragraph with the text *Hello world!* in the Title style.

Adding Headings

Calling add_heading() adds a paragraph with one of the heading styles. Enter the following into the interactive shell:

```
>>> doc = docx.Document()
>>> doc.add_heading('Header 0', 0)
<docx.text.Paragraph object at 0x00000000036CB3C8>
>>> doc.add_heading('Header 1', 1)
<docx.text.Paragraph object at 0x00000000036CB630>
>>> doc.add_heading('Header 2', 2)
<docx.text.Paragraph object at 0x00000000036CB828>
>>> doc.add_heading('Header 3', 3)
<docx.text.Paragraph object at 0x00000000036CB2E8>
>>> doc.add_heading('Header 4', 4)
<docx.text.Paragraph object at 0x00000000036CB3C8>
>>> doc.save('headings.docx')
```

The arguments to add_heading() are a string of the heading text and an integer from 0 to 4. The integer 0 makes the heading the Title style, which is used for the top of the document. Integers 1 to 4 are for various heading levels, with 1 being the main heading and 4 the lowest subheading. The add_heading() function returns a Paragraph object to save you the step of extracting it from the Document object as a separate step.

The resulting *headings.docx* file will look like Figure 13-10.

Header 0

Header 1

Header 2

Header 3

Header 4

Figure 13-10: The headings.docx *document with headings 0 to 4*

Adding Line and Page Breaks

To add a line break (rather than starting a whole new paragraph), you can call the add_break() method on the Run object you want to have the break appear after. If you want to add a page break instead, you need to pass the value docx.text.WD_BREAK.PAGE as a lone argument to add_break(), as is done in the middle of the following example:

```
>>> doc = docx.Document()
>>> doc.add_paragraph('This is on the first page!')
<docx.text.Paragraph object at 0x0000000003785518>
❶ >>> doc.paragraphs[0].runs[0].add_break(docx.text.WD_BREAK.PAGE)
>>> doc.add_paragraph('This is on the second page!')
<docx.text.Paragraph object at 0x00000000037855F8>
>>> doc.save('twoPage.docx')
```

This creates a two-page Word document with *This is on the first page!* on the first page and *This is on the second page!* on the second. Even though there was still plenty of space on the first page after the text *This is on the first page!*, we forced the next paragraph to begin on a new page by inserting a page break after the first run of the first paragraph ❶.

Adding Pictures

Document objects have an add_picture() method that will let you add an image to the end of the document. Say you have a file *zophie.png* in the current working directory. You can add *zophie.png* to the end of your document with a width of 1 inch and height of 4 centimeters (Word can use both imperial and metric units) by entering the following:

```
>>> doc.add_picture('zophie.png', width=docx.shared.Inches(1),
height=docx.shared.Cm(4))
<docx.shape.InlineShape object at 0x00000000036C7D30>
```

The first argument is a string of the image's filename. The optional `width` and `height` keyword arguments will set the width and height of the image in the document. If left out, the width and height will default to the normal size of the image.

You'll probably prefer to specify an image's height and width in familiar units such as inches and centimeters, so you can use the `docx.shared.Inches()` and `docx.shared.Cm()` functions when you're specifying the `width` and `height` keyword arguments.

Summary

Text information isn't just for plaintext files; in fact, it's pretty likely that you deal with PDFs and Word documents much more often. You can use the `PyPDF2` module to read and write PDF documents. Unfortunately, reading text from PDF documents might not always result in a perfect translation to a string because of the complicated PDF file format, and some PDFs might not be readable at all. In these cases, you're out of luck unless future updates to PyPDF2 support additional PDF features.

Word documents are more reliable, and you can read them with the python-docx module. You can manipulate text in Word documents via `Paragraph` and `Run` objects. These objects can also be given styles, though they must be from the default set of styles or styles already in the document. You can add new paragraphs, headings, breaks, and pictures to the document, though only to the end.

Many of the limitations that come with working with PDFs and Word documents are because these formats are meant to be nicely displayed for human readers, rather than easy to parse by software. The next chapter takes a look at two other common formats for storing information: JSON and CSV files. These formats are designed to be used by computers, and you'll see that Python can work with these formats much more easily.

Practice Questions

1. A string value of the PDF filename is *not* passed to the `PyPDF2`
   `.PdfFileReader()` function. What do you pass to the function instead?
2. What modes do the `File` objects for `PdfFileReader()` and `PdfFileWriter()` need to be opened in?
3. How do you acquire a `Page` object for page 5 from a `PdfFileReader` object?
4. What `PdfFileReader` variable stores the number of pages in the PDF document?
5. If a `PdfFileReader` object's PDF is encrypted with the password `swordfish`, what must you do before you can obtain `Page` objects from it?
6. What methods do you use to rotate a page?
7. What method returns a `Document` object for a file named *demo.docx*?

8. What is the difference between a Paragraph object and a Run object?

9. How do you obtain a list of Paragraph objects for a Document object that's stored in a variable named doc?

10. What type of object has bold, underline, italic, strike, and outline variables?

11. What is the difference between setting the bold variable to True, False, or None?

12. How do you create a Document object for a new Word document?

13. How do you add a paragraph with the text 'Hello there!' to a Document object stored in a variable named doc?

14. What integers represent the levels of headings available in Word documents?

Practice Projects

For practice, write programs that do the following.

PDF Paranoia

Using the os.walk() function from Chapter 9, write a script that will go through every PDF in a folder (and its subfolders) and encrypt the PDFs using a password provided on the command line. Save each encrypted PDF with an _encrypted.pdf suffix added to the original filename. Before deleting the original file, have the program attempt to read and decrypt the file to ensure that it was encrypted correctly.

Then, write a program that finds all encrypted PDFs in a folder (and its subfolders) and creates a decrypted copy of the PDF using a provided password. If the password is incorrect, the program should print a message to the user and continue to the next PDF.

Custom Invitations as Word Documents

Say you have a text file of guest names. This *guests.txt* file has one name per line, as follows:

```
Prof. Plum
Miss Scarlet
Col. Mustard
Al Sweigart
RoboCop
```

Write a program that would generate a Word document with custom invitations that look like Figure 13-11.

Since Python-Docx can use only those styles that already exist in the Word document, you will have to first add these styles to a blank Word file and then open that file with Python-Docx. There should be one invitation per page in the resulting Word document, so call add_break() to add a page break after the last paragraph of each invitation. This way, you will need to open only one Word document to print all of the invitations at once.

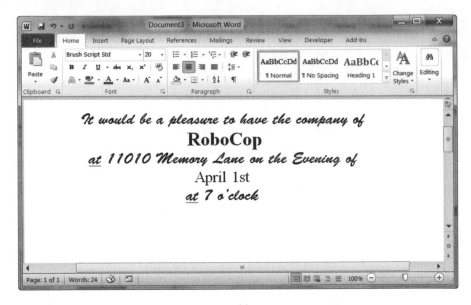

Figure 13-11: The Word document generated by your custom invite script

You can download a sample *guests.txt* file from *http://nostarch.com/ automatestuff/*.

Brute-Force PDF Password Breaker

Say you have an encrypted PDF that you have forgotten the password to, but you remember it was a single English word. Trying to guess your forgotten password is quite a boring task. Instead you can write a program that will decrypt the PDF by trying every possible English word until it finds one that works. This is called a *brute-force password attack*. Download the text file *dictionary.txt* from *http://nostarch.com/automatestuff/*. This *dictionary file* contains over 44,000 English words with one word per line.

Using the file-reading skills you learned in Chapter 8, create a list of word strings by reading this file. Then loop over each word in this list, passing it to the decrypt() method. If this method returns the integer 0, the password was wrong and your program should continue to the next password. If decrypt() returns 1, then your program should break out of the loop and print the hacked password. You should try both the uppercase and lowercase form of each word. (On my laptop, going through all 88,000 uppercase and lowercase words from the dictionary file takes a couple of minutes. This is why you shouldn't use a simple English word for your passwords.)

14

WORKING WITH CSV FILES AND JSON DATA

In Chapter 13, you learned how to extract text from PDF and Word documents. These files were in a binary format, which required special Python modules to access their data. CSV and JSON files, on the other hand, are just plaintext files. You can view them in a text editor, such as IDLE's file editor. But Python also comes with the special csv and json modules, each providing functions to help you work with these file formats.

CSV stands for "comma-separated values," and CSV files are simplified spreadsheets stored as plaintext files. Python's csv module makes it easy to parse CSV files.

JSON (pronounced "JAY-sawn" or "Jason"—it doesn't matter how because either way people will say you're pronouncing it wrong) is a format that stores information as JavaScript source code in plaintext files.

(JSON is short for JavaScript Object Notation.) You don't need to know the JavaScript programming language to use JSON files, but the JSON format is useful to know because it's used in many web applications.

The csv Module

Each line in a CSV file represents a row in the spreadsheet, and commas separate the cells in the row. For example, the spreadsheet *example.xlsx* from *http://nostarch.com/automatestuff/* would look like this in a CSV file:

```
4/5/2015 13:34,Apples,73
4/5/2015 3:41,Cherries,85
4/6/2015 12:46,Pears,14
4/8/2015 8:59,Oranges,52
4/10/2015 2:07,Apples,152
4/10/2015 18:10,Bananas,23
4/10/2015 2:40,Strawberries,98
```

I will use this file for this chapter's interactive shell examples. You can download *example.csv* from *http://nostarch.com/automatestuff/* or enter the text into a text editor and save it as *example.csv*.

CSV files are simple, lacking many of the features of an Excel spreadsheet. For example, CSV files

- Don't have types for their values—everything is a string
- Don't have settings for font size or color
- Don't have multiple worksheets
- Can't specify cell widths and heights
- Can't have merged cells
- Can't have images or charts embedded in them

The advantage of CSV files is simplicity. CSV files are widely supported by many types of programs, can be viewed in text editors (including IDLE's file editor), and are a straightforward way to represent spreadsheet data. The CSV format is exactly as advertised: It's just a text file of comma-separated values.

Since CSV files are just text files, you might be tempted to read them in as a string and then process that string using the techniques you learned in Chapter 8. For example, since each cell in a CSV file is separated by a comma, maybe you could just call the split() method on each line of text to get the values. But not every comma in a CSV file represents the boundary between two cells. CSV files also have their own set of escape characters to allow commas and other characters to be included *as part of the values*. The split() method doesn't handle these escape characters. Because of these potential pitfalls, you should always use the csv module for reading and writing CSV files.

Reader Objects

To read data from a CSV file with the csv module, you need to create a Reader object. A Reader object lets you iterate over lines in the CSV file. Enter the following into the interactive shell, with *example.csv* in the current working directory:

```
❶ >>> import csv
❷ >>> exampleFile = open('example.csv')
❸ >>> exampleReader = csv.reader(exampleFile)
❹ >>> exampleData = list(exampleReader)
❺ >>> exampleData
[['4/5/2015 13:34', 'Apples', '73'], ['4/5/2015 3:41', 'Cherries', '85'],
['4/6/2015 12:46', 'Pears', '14'], ['4/8/2015 8:59', 'Oranges', '52'],
['4/10/2015 2:07', 'Apples', '152'], ['4/10/2015 18:10', 'Bananas', '23'],
['4/10/2015 2:40', 'Strawberries', '98']]
```

The csv module comes with Python, so we can import it ❶ without having to install it first.

To read a CSV file with the csv module, first open it using the open() function ❷, just as you would any other text file. But instead of calling the read() or readlines() method on the File object that open() returns, pass it to the csv.reader() function ❸. This will return a Reader object for you to use. Note that you don't pass a filename string directly to the csv.reader() function.

The most direct way to access the values in the Reader object is to convert it to a plain Python list by passing it to list() ❹. Using list() on this Reader object returns a list of lists, which you can store in a variable like exampleData. Entering exampleData in the shell displays the list of lists ❺.

Now that you have the CSV file as a list of lists, you can access the value at a particular row and column with the expression exampleData[row][col], where row is the index of one of the lists in exampleData, and col is the index of the item you want from that list. Enter the following into the interactive shell:

```
>>> exampleData[0][0]
'4/5/2015 13:34'
>>> exampleData[0][1]
'Apples'
>>> exampleData[0][2]
'73'
>>> exampleData[1][1]
'Cherries'
>>> exampleData[6][1]
'Strawberries'
```

exampleData[0][0] goes into the first list and gives us the first string, exampleData[0][2] goes into the first list and gives us the third string, and so on.

Reading Data from Reader Objects in a for Loop

For large CSV files, you'll want to use the Reader object in a for loop. This avoids loading the entire file into memory at once. For example, enter the following into the interactive shell:

```
>>> import csv
>>> exampleFile = open('example.csv')
>>> exampleReader = csv.reader(exampleFile)
>>> for row in exampleReader:
        print('Row #' + str(exampleReader.line_num) + ' ' + str(row))

Row #1 ['4/5/2015 13:34', 'Apples', '73']
Row #2 ['4/5/2015 3:41', 'Cherries', '85']
Row #3 ['4/6/2015 12:46', 'Pears', '14']
Row #4 ['4/8/2015 8:59', 'Oranges', '52']
Row #5 ['4/10/2015 2:07', 'Apples', '152']
Row #6 ['4/10/2015 18:10', 'Bananas', '23']
Row #7 ['4/10/2015 2:40', 'Strawberries', '98']
```

After you import the csv module and make a Reader object from the CSV file, you can loop through the rows in the Reader object. Each row is a list of values, with each value representing a cell.

The print() function call prints the number of the current row and the contents of the row. To get the row number, use the Reader object's line_num variable, which contains the number of the current line.

The Reader object can be looped over only once. To reread the CSV file, you must call csv.reader to create a Reader object.

Writer Objects

A Writer object lets you write data to a CSV file. To create a Writer object, you use the csv.writer() function. Enter the following into the interactive shell:

```
>>> import csv
❶ >>> outputFile = open('output.csv', 'w', newline='')
❷ >>> outputWriter = csv.writer(outputFile)
>>> outputWriter.writerow(['spam', 'eggs', 'bacon', 'ham'])
21
>>> outputWriter.writerow(['Hello, world!', 'eggs', 'bacon', 'ham'])
32
>>> outputWriter.writerow([1, 2, 3.141592, 4])
16
>>> outputFile.close()
```

First, call open() and pass it 'w' to open a file in write mode ❶. This will create the object you can then pass to csv.writer() ❷ to create a Writer object.

On Windows, you'll also need to pass a blank string for the open() function's newline keyword argument. For technical reasons beyond the scope of this book, if you forget to set the newline argument, the rows in *output.csv* will be double-spaced, as shown in Figure 14-1.

Figure 14-1: If you forget the `newline=''` keyword argument in open(), the CSV file will be double-spaced.

The `writerow()` method for `Writer` objects takes a list argument. Each value in the list is placed in its own cell in the output CSV file. The return value of `writerow()` is the number of characters written to the file for that row (including newline characters).

This code produces an *output.csv* file that looks like this:

```
spam,eggs,bacon,ham
"Hello, world!",eggs,bacon,ham
1,2,3.141592,4
```

Notice how the `Writer` object automatically escapes the comma in the value `'Hello, world!'` with double quotes in the CSV file. The `csv` module saves you from having to handle these special cases yourself.

The delimiter and lineterminator Keyword Arguments

Say you want to separate cells with a tab character instead of a comma and you want the rows to be double-spaced. You could enter something like the following into the interactive shell:

```
>>> import csv
>>> csvFile = open('example.tsv', 'w', newline='')
❶ >>> csvWriter = csv.writer(csvFile, delimiter='\t', lineterminator='\n\n')
>>> csvWriter.writerow(['apples', 'oranges', 'grapes'])
24
>>> csvWriter.writerow(['eggs', 'bacon', 'ham'])
17
>>> csvWriter.writerow(['spam', 'spam', 'spam', 'spam', 'spam', 'spam'])
32
>>> csvFile.close()
```

This changes the delimiter and line terminator characters in your file. The *delimiter* is the character that appears between cells on a row. By default, the delimiter for a CSV file is a comma. The *line terminator* is the character that comes at the end of a row. By default, the line terminator is a newline. You can change characters to different values by using the delimiter and lineterminator keyword arguments with csv.writer().

Passing delimiter='\t' and lineterminator='\n\n' ❶ changes the character between cells to a tab and the character between rows to two newlines. We then call writerow() three times to give us three rows.

This produces a file named *example.tsv* with the following contents:

apples	oranges	grapes			
eggs	bacon	ham			
spam	spam	spam	spam	spam	spam

Now that our cells are separated by tabs, we're using the file extension *.tsv*, for tab-separated values.

Project: Removing the Header from CSV Files

Say you have the boring job of removing the first line from several hundred CSV files. Maybe you'll be feeding them into an automated process that requires just the data and not the headers at the top of the columns. You *could* open each file in Excel, delete the first row, and resave the file—but that would take hours. Let's write a program to do it instead.

The program will need to open every file with the *.csv* extension in the current working directory, read in the contents of the CSV file, and rewrite the contents without the first row to a file of the same name. This will replace the old contents of the CSV file with the new, headless contents.

WARNING *As always, whenever you write a program that modifies files, be sure to back up the files, first just in case your program does not work the way you expect it to. You don't want to accidentally erase your original files.*

At a high level, the program must do the following:

- Find all the CSV files in the current working directory.
- Read in the full contents of each file.
- Write out the contents, skipping the first line, to a new CSV file.

At the code level, this means the program will need to do the following:

- Loop over a list of files from os.listdir(), skipping the non-CSV files.
- Create a CSV Reader object and read in the contents of the file, using the line_num attribute to figure out which line to skip.
- Create a CSV Writer object and write out the read-in data to the new file.

For this project, open a new file editor window and save it as *removeCsvHeader.py*.

Step 1: Loop Through Each CSV File

The first thing your program needs to do is loop over a list of all CSV filenames for the current working directory. Make your *removeCsvHeader.py* look like this:

```python
#! python3
# removeCsvHeader.py - Removes the header from all CSV files in the current
# working directory.

import csv, os

os.makedirs('headerRemoved', exist_ok=True)

# Loop through every file in the current working directory.
for csvFilename in os.listdir('.'):
    if not csvFilename.endswith('.csv'):
❶        continue    # skip non-csv files

    print('Removing header from ' + csvFilename + '...')

    # TODO: Read the CSV file in (skipping first row).

    # TODO: Write out the CSV file.
```

The os.makedirs() call will create a headerRemoved folder where all the headless CSV files will be written. A for loop on os.listdir('.') gets you partway there, but it will loop over *all* files in the working directory, so you'll need to add some code at the start of the loop that skips filenames that don't end with .csv. The continue statement ❶ makes the for loop move on to the next filename when it comes across a non-CSV file.

Just so there's *some* output as the program runs, print out a message saying which CSV file the program is working on. Then, add some TODO comments for what the rest of the program should do.

Step 2: Read in the CSV File

The program doesn't remove the first line from the CSV file. Rather, it creates a new copy of the CSV file without the first line. Since the copy's filename is the same as the original filename, the copy will overwrite the original.

The program will need a way to track whether it is currently looping on the first row. Add the following to *removeCsvHeader.py*.

```python
#! python3
# removeCsvHeader.py - Removes the header from all CSV files in the current
# working directory.

--snip--
```

```
# Read the CSV file in (skipping first row).
csvRows = []
csvFileObj = open(csvFilename)
readerObj = csv.reader(csvFileObj)
for row in readerObj:
    if readerObj.line_num == 1:
        continue    # skip first row
    csvRows.append(row)
csvFileObj.close()

# TODO: Write out the CSV file.
```

The Reader object's line_num attribute can be used to determine which line in the CSV file it is currently reading. Another for loop will loop over the rows returned from the CSV Reader object, and all rows but the first will be appended to csvRows.

As the for loop iterates over each row, the code checks whether readerObj.line_num is set to 1. If so, it executes a continue to move on to the next row without appending it to csvRows. For every row afterward, the condition will be always be False, and the row will be appended to csvRows.

Step 3: Write Out the CSV File Without the First Row

Now that csvRows contains all rows but the first row, the list needs to be written out to a CSV file in the *headerRemoved* folder. Add the following to *removeCsvHeader.py*:

```
#! python3
# removeCsvHeader.py - Removes the header from all CSV files in the current
# working directory.
--snip--

# Loop through every file in the current working directory.
❶ for csvFilename in os.listdir('.'):
    if not csvFilename.endswith('.csv'):
        continue    # skip non-CSV files

    --snip--

    # Write out the CSV file.
    csvFileObj = open(os.path.join('headerRemoved', csvFilename), 'w',
                newline='')
    csvWriter = csv.writer(csvFileObj)
    for row in csvRows:
        csvWriter.writerow(row)
    csvFileObj.close()
```

The CSV Writer object will write the list to a CSV file in headerRemoved using csvFilename (which we also used in the CSV reader). This will overwrite the original file.

Once we create the `Writer` object, we loop over the sublists stored in csvRows and write each sublist to the file.

After the code is executed, the outer for loop ❶ will loop to the next filename from os.listdir('.'). When that loop is finished, the program will be complete.

To test your program, download *removeCsvHeader.zip* from *http://nostarch .com/automatestuff/* and unzip it to a folder. Run the *removeCsvHeader.py* program in that folder. The output will look like this:

```
Removing header from NAICS_data_1048.csv...
Removing header from NAICS_data_1218.csv...
--snip--
Removing header from NAICS_data_9834.csv...
Removing header from NAICS_data_9986.csv...
```

This program should print a filename each time it strips the first line from a CSV file.

Ideas for Similar Programs

The programs that you could write for CSV files are similar to the kinds you could write for Excel files, since they're both spreadsheet files. You could write programs to do the following:

- Compare data between different rows in a CSV file or between multiple CSV files.
- Copy specific data from a CSV file to an Excel file, or vice versa.
- Check for invalid data or formatting mistakes in CSV files and alert the user to these errors.
- Read data from a CSV file as input for your Python programs.

JSON and APIs

JavaScript Object Notation is a popular way to format data as a single human-readable string. JSON is the native way that JavaScript programs write their data structures and usually resembles what Python's pprint() function would produce. You don't need to know JavaScript in order to work with JSON-formatted data.

Here's an example of data formatted as JSON:

```
{"name": "Zophie", "isCat": true,
 "miceCaught": 0, "napsTaken": 37.5,
 "felineIQ": null}
```

JSON is useful to know, because many websites offer JSON content as a way for programs to interact with the website. This is known as providing an *application programming interface (API)*. Accessing an API is the same as accessing any other web page via a URL. The difference is that the data returned by an API is formatted (with JSON, for example) for machines; APIs aren't easy for people to read.

Many websites make their data available in JSON format. Facebook, Twitter, Yahoo, Google, Tumblr, Wikipedia, Flickr, Data.gov, Reddit, IMDb, Rotten Tomatoes, LinkedIn, and many other popular sites offer APIs for programs to use. Some of these sites require registration, which is almost always free. You'll have to find documentation for what URLs your program needs to request in order to get the data you want, as well as the general format of the JSON data structures that are returned. This documentation should be provided by whatever site is offering the API; if they have a "Developers" page, look for the documentation there.

Using APIs, you could write programs that do the following:

- Scrape raw data from websites. (Accessing APIs is often more convenient than downloading web pages and parsing HTML with Beautiful Soup.)

- Automatically download new posts from one of your social network accounts and post them to another account. For example, you could take your Tumblr posts and post them to Facebook.

- Create a "movie encyclopedia" for your personal movie collection by pulling data from IMDb, Rotten Tomatoes, and Wikipedia and putting it into a single text file on your computer.

You can see some examples of JSON APIs in the resources at *http:// nostarch.com/automatestuff/*.

The json Module

Python's json module handles all the details of translating between a string with JSON data and Python values for the json.loads() and json.dumps() functions. JSON can't store *every* kind of Python value. It can contain values of only the following data types: strings, integers, floats, Booleans, lists, dictionaries, and NoneType. JSON cannot represent Python-specific objects, such as File objects, CSV Reader or Writer objects, Regex objects, or Selenium WebElement objects.

Reading JSON with the loads() Function

To translate a string containing JSON data into a Python value, pass it to the json.loads() function. (The name means "load string," not "loads.") Enter the following into the interactive shell:

```
>>> stringOfJsonData = '{"name": "Zophie", "isCat": true, "miceCaught": 0,
"felineIQ": null}'
>>> import json
>>> jsonDataAsPythonValue = json.loads(stringOfJsonData)
>>> jsonDataAsPythonValue
{'isCat': True, 'miceCaught': 0, 'name': 'Zophie', 'felineIQ': None}
```

After you import the json module, you can call loads() and pass it a string of JSON data. Note that JSON strings always use double quotes. It will return that data as a Python dictionary. Python dictionaries are not ordered, so the key-value pairs may appear in a different order when you print jsonDataAsPythonValue.

Writing JSON with the dumps() Function

The json.dumps() function (which means "dump string," not "dumps") will translate a Python value into a string of JSON-formatted data. Enter the following into the interactive shell:

```
>>> pythonValue = {'isCat': True, 'miceCaught': 0, 'name': 'Zophie',
'felineIQ': None}
>>> import json
>>> stringOfJsonData = json.dumps(pythonValue)
>>> stringOfJsonData
'{"isCat": true, "felineIQ": null, "miceCaught": 0, "name": "Zophie" }'
```

The value can only be one of the following basic Python data types: dictionary, list, integer, float, string, Boolean, or None.

Project: Fetching Current Weather Data

Checking the weather seems fairly trivial: Open your web browser, click the address bar, type the URL to a weather website (or search for one and then click the link), wait for the page to load, look past all the ads, and so on.

Actually, there are a lot of boring steps you could skip if you had a program that downloaded the weather forecast for the next few days and printed it as plaintext. This program uses the requests module from Chapter 11 to download data from the Web.

Overall, the program does the following:

- Reads the requested location from the command line.
- Downloads JSON weather data from OpenWeatherMap.org.
- Converts the string of JSON data to a Python data structure.
- Prints the weather for today and the next two days.

So the code will need to do the following:

- Join strings in sys.argv to get the location.
- Call requests.get() to download the weather data.
- Call json.loads() to convert the JSON data to a Python data structure.
- Print the weather forecast.

For this project, open a new file editor window and save it as *quickWeather.py*.

Step 1: Get Location from the Command Line Argument

The input for this program will come from the command line. Make *quickWeather.py* look like this:

```
#! python3
# quickWeather.py - Prints the weather for a location from the command line.

import json, requests, sys

# Compute location from command line arguments.
if len(sys.argv) < 2:
    print('Usage: quickWeather.py location')
    sys.exit()
location = ' '.join(sys.argv[1:])

# TODO: Download the JSON data from OpenWeatherMap.org's API.

# TODO: Load JSON data into a Python variable.
```

In Python, command line arguments are stored in the sys.argv list. After the #! shebang line and import statements, the program will check that there is more than one command line argument. (Recall that sys.argv will always have at least one element, sys.argv[0], which contains the Python script's filename.) If there is only one element in the list, then the user didn't provide a location on the command line, and a "usage" message will be provided to the user before the program ends.

Command line arguments are split on spaces. The command line argument San Francisco, CA would make sys.argv hold ['quickWeather.py', 'San', 'Francisco,', 'CA']. Therefore, call the join() method to join all the strings except for the first in sys.argv. Store this joined string in a variable named location.

Step 2: Download the JSON Data

OpenWeatherMap.org provides real-time weather information in JSON format. First you must sign up for a free API key on the site. (This key is used to limit how frequently you make requests on their server to keep their bandwidth costs down.) Your program simply has to download the page at *http://api.openweathermap.org/data/2.5/forecast/daily?q=<Location>&cnt=3& APPID=<API key>*, where *<Location>* is the name of the city whose weather you want and *<API key>* is your personal API key. Add the following to *quickWeather.py*.

```
#! python3
# quickWeather.py - Prints the weather for a location from the command line.

--snip--

# Download the JSON data from OpenWeatherMap.org's API.
url ='http://api.openweathermap.org/data/2.5/forecast/daily?q=%s&cnt=3' % (location)
response = requests.get(url)
```

```
response.raise_for_status()

# TODO: Load JSON data into a Python variable.
```

We have location from our command line arguments. To make the URL we want to access, we use the %s placeholder and insert whatever string is stored in location into that spot in the URL string. We store the result in url and pass url to requests.get(). The requests.get() call returns a Response object, which you can check for errors by calling raise_for_status(). If no exception is raised, the downloaded text will be in response.text.

Step 3: Load JSON Data and Print Weather

The response.text member variable holds a large string of JSON-formatted data. To convert this to a Python value, call the json.loads() function. The JSON data will look something like this:

```
{'city': {'coord': {'lat': 37.7771, 'lon': -122.42},
          'country': 'United States of America',
          'id': '5391959',
          'name': 'San Francisco',
          'population': 0},
 'cnt': 3,
 'cod': '200',
 'list': [{'clouds': 0,
           'deg': 233,
           'dt': 1402344000,
           'humidity': 58,
           'pressure': 1012.23,
           'speed': 1.96,
           'temp': {'day': 302.29,
                    'eve': 296.46,
                    'max': 302.29,
                    'min': 289.77,
                    'morn': 294.59,
                    'night': 289.77},
           'weather': [{'description': 'sky is clear',
                        'icon': '01d',
--snip--
```

You can see this data by passing weatherData to pprint.pprint(). You may want to check *http://openweathermap.org/* for more documentation on what these fields mean. For example, the online documentation will tell you that the 302.29 after 'day' is the daytime temperature in Kelvin, not Celsius or Fahrenheit.

The weather descriptions you want are after 'main' and 'description'. To neatly print them out, add the following to *quickWeather.py*.

```
! python3
# quickWeather.py - Prints the weather for a location from the command line.

--snip--
```

```
# Load JSON data into a Python variable.
weatherData = json.loads(response.text)

# Print weather descriptions.
❶ w = weatherData['list']
print('Current weather in %s:' % (location))
print(w[0]['weather'][0]['main'], '-', w[0]['weather'][0]['description'])
print()
print('Tomorrow:')
print(w[1]['weather'][0]['main'], '-', w[1]['weather'][0]['description'])
print()
print('Day after tomorrow:')
print(w[2]['weather'][0]['main'], '-', w[2]['weather'][0]['description'])
```

Notice how the code stores weatherData['list'] in the variable w to save you some typing ❶. You use w[0], w[1], and w[2] to retrieve the dictionaries for today, tomorrow, and the day after tomorrow's weather, respectively. Each of these dictionaries has a 'weather' key, which contains a list value. You're interested in the first list item, a nested dictionary with several more keys, at index 0. Here, we print the values stored in the 'main' and 'description' keys, separated by a hyphen.

When this program is run with the command line argument quickWeather.py San Francisco, CA, the output looks something like this:

```
Current weather in San Francisco, CA:
Clear - sky is clear

Tomorrow:
Clouds - few clouds

Day after tomorrow:
Clear - sky is clear
```

(The weather is one of the reasons I like living in San Francisco!)

Ideas for Similar Programs

Accessing weather data can form the basis for many types of programs. You can create similar programs to do the following:

- Collect weather forecasts for several campsites or hiking trails to see which one will have the best weather.
- Schedule a program to regularly check the weather and send you a frost alert if you need to move your plants indoors. (Chapter 15 covers scheduling, and Chapter 16 explains how to send email.)
- Pull weather data from multiple sites to show all at once, or calculate and show the average of the multiple weather predictions.

Summary

CSV and JSON are common plaintext formats for storing data. They are easy for programs to parse while still being human readable, so they are often used for simple spreadsheets or web app data. The csv and json modules greatly simplify the process of reading and writing to CSV and JSON files.

The last few chapters have taught you how to use Python to parse information from a wide variety of file formats. One common task is taking data from a variety of formats and parsing it for the particular information you need. These tasks are often specific to the point that commercial software is not optimally helpful. By writing your own scripts, you can make the computer handle large amounts of data presented in these formats.

In Chapter 15, you'll break away from data formats and learn how to make your programs communicate with you by sending emails and text messages.

Practice Questions

1. What are some features Excel spreadsheets have that CSV spreadsheets don't?

2. What do you pass to csv.reader() and csv.writer() to create Reader and Writer objects?

3. What modes do File objects for reader and Writer objects need to be opened in?

4. What method takes a list argument and writes it to a CSV file?

5. What do the delimiter and lineterminator keyword arguments do?

6. What function takes a string of JSON data and returns a Python data structure?

7. What function takes a Python data structure and returns a string of JSON data?

Practice Project

For practice, write a program that does the following.

Excel-to-CSV Converter

Excel can save a spreadsheet to a CSV file with a few mouse clicks, but if you had to convert hundreds of Excel files to CSVs, it would take hours of clicking. Using the openpyxl module from Chapter 12, write a program that reads all the Excel files in the current working directory and outputs them as CSV files.

A single Excel file might contain multiple sheets; you'll have to create one CSV file per *sheet*. The filenames of the CSV files should be *<excel filename>_<sheet title>.csv*, where *<excel filename>* is the filename of the Excel file without the file extension (for example, 'spam_data', not 'spam_data.xlsx') and *<sheet title>* is the string from the Worksheet object's title variable.

This program will involve many nested for loops. The skeleton of the program will look something like this:

```
for excelFile in os.listdir('.'):
    # Skip non-xlsx files, load the workbook object.
    for sheetName in wb.get_sheet_names():
        # Loop through every sheet in the workbook.
        sheet = wb.get_sheet_by_name(sheetName)

        # Create the CSV filename from the Excel filename and sheet title.
        # Create the csv.writer object for this CSV file.

        # Loop through every row in the sheet.
        for rowNum in range(1, sheet.max_row + 1):
            rowData = []    # append each cell to this list
            # Loop through each cell in the row.
            for colNum in range(1, sheet.max_column + 1):
                # Append each cell's data to rowData.

            # Write the rowData list to the CSV file.

        csvFile.close()
```

Download the ZIP file *excelSpreadsheets.zip* from *http://nostarch.com/ automatestuff/*, and unzip the spreadsheets into the same directory as your program. You can use these as the files to test the program on.

15

KEEPING TIME, SCHEDULING TASKS, AND LAUNCHING PROGRAMS

Running programs while you're sitting at your computer is fine, but it's also useful to have programs run without your direct supervision. Your computer's clock can schedule programs to run code at some specified time and date or at regular intervals. For example, your program could scrape a website every hour to check for changes or do a CPU-intensive task at 4 AM while you sleep. Python's `time` and `datetime` modules provide these functions.

You can also write programs that launch other programs on a schedule by using the `subprocess` and `threading` modules. Often, the fastest way to program is to take advantage of applications that other people have already written.

The time Module

Your computer's system clock is set to a specific date, time, and time zone. The built-in time module allows your Python programs to read the system clock for the current time. The time.time() and time.sleep() functions are the most useful in the time module.

The time.time() Function

The *Unix epoch* is a time reference commonly used in programming: 12 AM on January 1, 1970, Coordinated Universal Time (UTC). The time.time() function returns the number of seconds since that moment as a float value. (Recall that a float is just a number with a decimal point.) This number is called an *epoch timestamp*. For example, enter the following into the interactive shell:

```
>>> import time
>>> time.time()
1425063955.068649
```

Here I'm calling time.time() on February 27, 2015, at 11:05 Pacific Standard Time, or 7:05 PM UTC. The return value is how many seconds have passed between the Unix epoch and the moment time.time() was called.

NOTE *The interactive shell examples will yield dates and times for when I wrote this chapter in February 2015. Unless you're a time traveler, your dates and times will be different.*

Epoch timestamps can be used to *profile* code, that is, measure how long a piece of code takes to run. If you call time.time() at the beginning of the code block you want to measure and again at the end, you can subtract the first timestamp from the second to find the elapsed time between those two calls. For example, open a new file editor window and enter the following program:

```
  import time
❶ def calcProd():
      # Calculate the product of the first 100,000 numbers.
      product = 1
      for i in range(1, 100000):
          product = product * i
      return product

❷ startTime = time.time()
  prod = calcProd()
❸ endTime = time.time()
❹ print('The result is %s digits long.' % (len(str(prod))))
❺ print('Took %s seconds to calculate.' % (endTime - startTime))
```

At ❶, we define a function calcProd() to loop through the integers from 1 to 99,999 and return their product. At ❷, we call time.time() and store it in startTime. Right after calling calcProd(), we call time.time() again and store it in endTime ❸. We end by printing the length of the product returned by calcProd() ❹ and how long it took to run calcProd() ❺.

Save this program as *calcProd.py* and run it. The output will look something like this:

```
The result is 456569 digits long.
Took 2.844162940979004 seconds to calculate.
```

NOTE *Another way to profile your code is to use the cProfile.run() function, which provides a much more informative level of detail than the simple time.time() technique. The cProfile.run() function is explained at* https://docs.python.org/3/library/profile.html.

The time.sleep() Function

If you need to pause your program for a while, call the time.sleep() function and pass it the number of seconds you want your program to stay paused. Enter the following into the interactive shell:

```
>>> import time
>>> for i in range(3):
❶        print('Tick')
❷        time.sleep(1)
❸        print('Tock')
❹        time.sleep(1)

Tick
Tock
Tick
Tock
Tick
Tock
❺ >>> time.sleep(5)
```

The for loop will print Tick ❶, pause for one second ❷, print Tock ❸, pause for one second ❹, print Tick, pause, and so on until Tick and Tock have each been printed three times.

The time.sleep() function will *block*—that is, it will not return and release your program to execute other code—until after the number of seconds you passed to time.sleep() has elapsed. For example, if you enter time.sleep(5) ❺, you'll see that the next prompt (>>>) doesn't appear until five seconds have passed.

Be aware that pressing CTRL-C will not interrupt time.sleep() calls in IDLE. IDLE waits until the entire pause is over before raising the KeyboardInterrupt exception. To work around this problem, instead of having a single time.sleep(30) call to pause for 30 seconds, use a for loop to make 30 calls to time.sleep(1).

```
>>> for i in range(30):
    time.sleep(1)
```

If you press CTRL-C sometime during these 30 seconds, you should see the KeyboardInterrupt exception thrown right away.

Rounding Numbers

When working with times, you'll often encounter float values with many digits after the decimal. To make these values easier to work with, you can shorten them with Python's built-in round() function, which rounds a float to the precision you specify. Just pass in the number you want to round, plus an optional second argument representing how many digits after the decimal point you want to round it to. If you omit the second argument, round() rounds your number to the nearest whole integer. Enter the following into the interactive shell:

```
>>> import time
>>> now = time.time()
>>> now
1425064108.017826
>>> round(now, 2)
1425064108.02
>>> round(now, 4)
1425064108.0178
>>> round(now)
1425064108
```

After importing time and storing time.time() in now, we call round(now, 2) to round now to two digits after the decimal, round(now, 4) to round to four digits after the decimal, and round(now) to round to the nearest integer.

Project: Super Stopwatch

Say you want to track how much time you spend on boring tasks you haven't automated yet. You don't have a physical stopwatch, and it's surprisingly difficult to find a free stopwatch app for your laptop or smartphone that isn't covered in ads and doesn't send a copy of your browser history to marketers. (It says it can do this in the license agreement you agreed to. You did read the license agreement, didn't you?) You can write a simple stopwatch program yourself in Python.

At a high level, here's what your program will do:

- Track the amount of time elapsed between presses of the ENTER key, with each key press starting a new "lap" on the timer.
- Print the lap number, total time, and lap time.

This means your code will need to do the following:

- Find the current time by calling time.time() and store it as a timestamp at the start of the program, as well as at the start of each lap.
- Keep a lap counter and increment it every time the user presses ENTER.
- Calculate the elapsed time by subtracting timestamps.
- Handle the KeyboardInterrupt exception so the user can press CTRL-C to quit.

Open a new file editor window and save it as *stopwatch.py*.

Step 1: Set Up the Program to Track Times

The stopwatch program will need to use the current time, so you'll want to import the time module. Your program should also print some brief instructions to the user before calling input(), so the timer can begin after the user presses ENTER. Then the code will start tracking lap times.

Enter the following code into the file editor, writing a TODO comment as a placeholder for the rest of the code:

```
#! python3
# stopwatch.py - A simple stopwatch program.

import time

# Display the program's instructions.
print('Press ENTER to begin. Afterwards, press ENTER to "click" the stopwatch.
Press Ctrl-C to quit.')
input()                      # press Enter to begin
print('Started.')
startTime = time.time()      # get the first lap's start time
lastTime = startTime
lapNum = 1

# TODO: Start tracking the lap times.
```

Now that we've written the code to display the instructions, start the first lap, note the time, and set our lap count to 1.

Step 2: Track and Print Lap Times

Now let's write the code to start each new lap, calculate how long the previous lap took, and calculate the total time elapsed since starting the stopwatch. We'll display the lap time and total time and increase the lap count for each new lap. Add the following code to your program:

```
#! python3
# stopwatch.py - A simple stopwatch program.

import time

--snip--
```

```
    # Start tracking the lap times.
❶ try:
❷     while True:
            input()
❸           lapTime = round(time.time() - lastTime, 2)
❹           totalTime = round(time.time() - startTime, 2)
❺           print('Lap #%s: %s (%s)' % (lapNum, totalTime, lapTime), end='')
            lapNum += 1
            lastTime = time.time() # reset the last lap time
❻ except KeyboardInterrupt:
        # Handle the Ctrl-C exception to keep its error message from displaying.
        print('\nDone.')
```

If the user presses CTRL-C to stop the stopwatch, the KeyboardInterrupt exception will be raised, and the program will crash if its execution is not a try statement. To prevent crashing, we wrap this part of the program in a try statement ❶. We'll handle the exception in the except clause ❻, so when CTRL-C is pressed and the exception is raised, the program execution moves to the except clause to print Done, instead of the KeyboardInterrupt error message. Until this happens, the execution is inside an infinite loop ❷ that calls input() and waits until the user presses ENTER to end a lap. When a lap ends, we calculate how long the lap took by subtracting the start time of the lap, lastTime, from the current time, time.time() ❸. We calculate the total time elapsed by subtracting the overall start time of the stopwatch, startTime, from the current time ❹.

Since the results of these time calculations will have many digits after the decimal point (such as 4.766272783279419), we use the round() function to round the float value to two digits at ❸ and ❹.

At ❺, we print the lap number, total time elapsed, and the lap time. Since the user pressing ENTER for the input() call will print a newline to the screen, pass end='' to the print() function to avoid double-spacing the output. After printing the lap information, we get ready for the next lap by adding 1 to the count lapNum and setting lastTime to the current time, which is the start time of the next lap.

Ideas for Similar Programs

Time tracking opens up several possibilities for your programs. Although you can download apps to do some of these things, the benefit of writing programs yourself is that they will be free and not bloated with ads and useless features. You could write similar programs to do the following:

- Create a simple timesheet app that records when you type a person's name and uses the current time to clock them in or out.

- Add a feature to your program to display the elapsed time since a process started, such as a download that uses the requests module. (See Chapter 11.)

- Intermittently check how long a program has been running and offer the user a chance to cancel tasks that are taking too long.

The datetime Module

The time module is useful for getting a Unix epoch timestamp to work with. But if you want to display a date in a more convenient format, or do arithmetic with dates (for example, figuring out what date was 205 days ago or what date is 123 days from now), you should use the datetime module.

The datetime module has its own datetime data type. datetime values represent a specific moment in time. Enter the following into the interactive shell:

```
>>> import datetime
❶ >>> datetime.datetime.now()
❷ datetime.datetime(2015, 2, 27, 11, 10, 49, 55, 53)
❸ >>> dt = datetime.datetime(2015, 10, 21, 16, 29, 0)
❹ >>> dt.year, dt.month, dt.day
(2015, 10, 21)
❺ >>> dt.hour, dt.minute, dt.second
(16, 29, 0)
```

Calling datetime.datetime.now() ❶ returns a datetime object ❷ for the current date and time, according to your computer's clock. This object includes the year, month, day, hour, minute, second, and microsecond of the current moment. You can also retrieve a datetime object for a specific moment by using the datetime.datetime() function ❸, passing it integers representing the year, month, day, hour, and second of the moment you want. These integers will be stored in the datetime object's year, month, day ❹, hour, minute, and second ❺ attributes.

A Unix epoch timestamp can be converted to a datetime object with the datetime.datetime.fromtimestamp() function. The date and time of the datetime object will be converted for the local time zone. Enter the following into the interactive shell:

```
>>> datetime.datetime.fromtimestamp(1000000)
datetime.datetime(1970, 1, 12, 5, 46, 40)
>>> datetime.datetime.fromtimestamp(time.time())
datetime.datetime(2015, 2, 27, 11, 13, 0, 604980)
```

Calling datetime.datetime.fromtimestamp() and passing it 1000000 returns a datetime object for the moment 1,000,000 seconds after the Unix epoch. Passing time.time(), the Unix epoch timestamp for the current moment, returns a datetime object for the current moment. So the expressions datetime.datetime.now() and datetime.datetime.fromtimestamp(time.time()) do the same thing; they both give you a datetime object for the present moment.

NOTE *These examples were entered on a computer set to Pacific Standard Time. If you're in another time zone, your results will look different.*

datetime objects can be compared with each other using comparison operators to find out which one precedes the other. The later datetime object is the "greater" value. Enter the following into the interactive shell:

```
❶ >>> halloween2015 = datetime.datetime(2015, 10, 31, 0, 0, 0)
❷ >>> newyears2016 = datetime.datetime(2016, 1, 1, 0, 0, 0)
   >>> oct31_2015 = datetime.datetime(2015, 10, 31, 0, 0, 0)
❸ >>> halloween2015 == oct31_2015
   True
❹ >>> halloween2015 > newyears2016
   False
❺ >>> newyears2016 > halloween2015
   True
   >>> newyears2016 != oct31_2015
   True
```

Make a datetime object for the first moment (midnight) of October 31, 2015 and store it in halloween2015 ❶. Make a datetime object for the first moment of January 1, 2016 and store it in newyears2016 ❷. Then make another object for midnight on October 31, 2015 and store it in oct31_2015. Comparing halloween2015 and oct31_2015 shows that they're equal ❸. Comparing newyears2016 and halloween 2015 shows that newyears2016 is greater (later) than halloween2015 ❹ ❺.

The timedelta Data Type

The datetime module also provides a timedelta data type, which represents a *duration* of time rather than a *moment* in time. Enter the following into the interactive shell:

```
❶ >>> delta = datetime.timedelta(days=11, hours=10, minutes=9, seconds=8)
❷ >>> delta.days, delta.seconds, delta.microseconds
   (11, 36548, 0)
   >>> delta.total_seconds()
   986948.0
   >>> str(delta)
   '11 days, 10:09:08'
```

To create a timedelta object, use the datetime.timedelta() function. The datetime.timedelta() function takes keyword arguments weeks, days, hours, minutes, seconds, milliseconds, and microseconds. There is no month or year keyword argument because "a month" or "a year" is a variable amount of time depending on the particular month or year. A timedelta object has the total duration represented in days, seconds, and microseconds. These numbers are stored in the days, seconds, and microseconds attributes, respectively. The total_seconds() method will return the duration in number of seconds alone. Passing a timedelta object to str() will return a nicely formatted, human-readable string representation of the object.

In this example, we pass keyword arguments to datetime.delta() to specify a duration of 11 days, 10 hours, 9 minutes, and 8 seconds, and store the returned timedelta object in delta ❶. This timedelta object's days attributes stores 11, and its seconds attribute stores 36548 (10 hours, 9 minutes, and 8 seconds, expressed in seconds) ❷. Calling total_seconds() tells us that 11 days, 10 hours, 9 minutes, and 8 seconds is 986,948 seconds. Finally, passing the timedelta object to str() returns a string clearly explaining the duration.

The arithmetic operators can be used to perform *date arithmetic* on datetime values. For example, to calculate the date 1,000 days from now, enter the following into the interactive shell:

```
>>> dt = datetime.datetime.now()
>>> dt
datetime.datetime(2015, 2, 27, 18, 38, 50, 636181)
>>> thousandDays = datetime.timedelta(days=1000)
>>> dt + thousandDays
datetime.datetime(2017, 11, 23, 18, 38, 50, 636181)
```

First, make a datetime object for the current moment and store it in dt. Then make a timedelta object for a duration of 1,000 days and store it in thousandDays. Add dt and thousandDays together to get a datetime object for the date 1,000 days from now. Python will do the date arithmetic to figure out that 1,000 days after February 27, 2015, will be November 23, 2017. This is useful because when you calculate 1,000 days from a given date, you have to remember how many days are in each month and factor in leap years and other tricky details. The datetime module handles all of this for you.

timedelta objects can be added or subtracted with datetime objects or other timedelta objects using the + and - operators. A timedelta object can be multiplied or divided by integer or float values with the * and / operators. Enter the following into the interactive shell:

```
❶ >>> oct21st = datetime.datetime(2015, 10, 21, 16, 29, 0)
❷ >>> aboutThirtyYears = datetime.timedelta(days=365 * 30)
>>> oct21st
datetime.datetime(2015, 10, 21, 16, 29)
>>> oct21st - aboutThirtyYears
datetime.datetime(1985, 10, 28, 16, 29)
>>> oct21st - (2 * aboutThirtyYears)
datetime.datetime(1955, 11, 5, 16, 29)
```

Here we make a datetime object for October 21, 2015 ❶ and a timedelta object for a duration of about 30 years (we're assuming 365 days for each of those years) ❷. Subtracting aboutThirtyYears from oct21st gives us a datetime object for the date 30 years before October 21, 2015. Subtracting 2 * aboutThirtyYears from oct21st returns a datetime object for the date 60 years before October 21, 2015.

Pausing Until a Specific Date

The time.sleep() method lets you pause a program for a certain number of seconds. By using a while loop, you can pause your programs until a specific date. For example, the following code will continue to loop until Halloween 2016:

```
import datetime
import time
halloween2016 = datetime.datetime(2016, 10, 31, 0, 0, 0)
while datetime.datetime.now() < halloween2016:
    time.sleep(1)
```

The time.sleep(1) call will pause your Python program so that the computer doesn't waste CPU processing cycles simply checking the time over and over. Rather, the while loop will just check the condition once per second and continue with the rest of the program after Halloween 2016 (or whenever you program it to stop).

Converting datetime Objects into Strings

Epoch timestamps and datetime objects aren't very friendly to the human eye. Use the strftime() method to display a datetime object as a string. (The *f* in the name of the strftime() function stands for *format*.)

The strftime() method uses directives similar to Python's string formatting. Table 15-1 has a full list of strftime() directives.

Table 15-1: strftime() Directives

strftime directive	Meaning
%Y	Year with century, as in '2014'
%y	Year without century, '00' to '99' (1970 to 2069)
%m	Month as a decimal number, '01' to '12'
%B	Full month name, as in 'November'
%b	Abbreviated month name, as in 'Nov'
%d	Day of the month, '01' to '31'
%j	Day of the year, '001' to '366'
%w	Day of the week, '0' (Sunday) to '6' (Saturday)
%A	Full weekday name, as in 'Monday'
%a	Abbreviated weekday name, as in 'Mon'
%H	Hour (24-hour clock), '00' to '23'
%I	Hour (12-hour clock), '01' to '12'
%M	Minute, '00' to '59'
%S	Second, '00' to '59'
%p	'AM' or 'PM'
%%	Literal '%' character

Pass strftime() a custom format string containing formatting directives (along with any desired slashes, colons, and so on), and strftime() will return the datetime object's information as a formatted string. Enter the following into the interactive shell:

```
>>> oct21st = datetime.datetime(2015, 10, 21, 16, 29, 0)
>>> oct21st.strftime('%Y/%m/%d %H:%M:%S')
'2015/10/21 16:29:00'
>>> oct21st.strftime('%I:%M %p')
'04:29 PM'
>>> oct21st.strftime("%B of '%y")
"October of '15"
```

Here we have a datetime object for October 21, 2015 at 4:29 PM, stored in oct21st. Passing strftime() the custom format string '%Y/%m/%d %H:%M:%S' returns a string containing 2015, 10, and 21 separated by slashes and 16, 29, and 00 separated by colons. Passing '%I:%M% p' returns '04:29 PM', and passing "%B of '%y" returns "October of '15". Note that strftime() doesn't begin with datetime.datetime.

Converting Strings into datetime Objects

If you have a string of date information, such as '2015/10/21 16:29:00' or 'October 21, 2015', and need to convert it to a datetime object, use the datetime.datetime.strptime() function. The strptime() function is the inverse of the strftime() method. A custom format string using the same directives as strftime() must be passed so that strptime() knows how to parse and understand the string. (The *p* in the name of the strptime() function stands for *parse*.)

Enter the following into the interactive shell:

```
❶ >>> datetime.datetime.strptime('October 21, 2015', '%B %d, %Y')
datetime.datetime(2015, 10, 21, 0, 0)
>>> datetime.datetime.strptime('2015/10/21 16:29:00', '%Y/%m/%d %H:%M:%S')
datetime.datetime(2015, 10, 21, 16, 29)
>>> datetime.datetime.strptime("October of '15", "%B of '%y")
datetime.datetime(2015, 10, 1, 0, 0)
>>> datetime.datetime.strptime("November of '63", "%B of '%y")
datetime.datetime(2063, 11, 1, 0, 0)
```

To get a datetime object from the string 'October 21, 2015', pass 'October 21, 2015' as the first argument to strptime() and the custom format string that corresponds to 'October 21, 2015' as the second argument ❶. The string with the date information must match the custom format string exactly, or Python will raise a ValueError exception.

Review of Python's Time Functions

Dates and times in Python can involve quite a few different data types and functions. Here's a review of the three different types of values used to represent time:

- A Unix epoch timestamp (used by the time module) is a float or integer value of the number of seconds since 12 AM on January 1, 1970, UTC.

- A datetime object (of the datetime module) has integers stored in the attributes year, month, day, hour, minute, and second.

- A timedelta object (of the datetime module) represents a time duration, rather than a specific moment.

Here's a review of time functions and their parameters and return values:

- The time.time() function returns an epoch timestamp float value of the current moment.

- The time.sleep(*seconds*) function stops the program for the amount of seconds specified by the *seconds* argument.

- The datetime.datetime(*year, month, day, hour, minute, second*) function returns a datetime object of the moment specified by the arguments. If *hour*, *minute*, or *second* arguments are not provided, they default to 0.

- The datetime.datetime.now() function returns a datetime object of the current moment.

- The datetime.datetime.fromtimestamp(*epoch*) function returns a datetime object of the moment represented by the *epoch* timestamp argument.

- The datetime.timedelta(*weeks, days, hours, minutes, seconds, milliseconds, microseconds*) function returns a timedelta object representing a duration of time. The function's keyword arguments are all optional and do not include *month* or *year*.

- The total_seconds() method for timedelta objects returns the number of seconds the timedelta object represents.

- The strftime(*format*) method returns a string of the time represented by the datetime object in a custom format that's based on the *format* string. See Table 15-1 for the format details.

- The datetime.datetime.strptime(*time_string, format*) function returns a datetime object of the moment specified by *time_string*, parsed using the *format* string argument. See Table 15-1 for the format details.

Multithreading

To introduce the concept of multithreading, let's look at an example situation. Say you want to schedule some code to run after a delay or at a specific time. You could add code like the following at the start of your program:

```
import time, datetime

startTime = datetime.datetime(2029, 10, 31, 0, 0, 0)
while datetime.datetime.now() < startTime:
    time.sleep(1)

print('Program now starting on Halloween 2029')
--snip--
```

This code designates a start time of October 31, 2029, and keeps calling `time.sleep(1)` until the start time arrives. Your program cannot do anything while waiting for the loop of `time.sleep()` calls to finish; it just sits around until Halloween 2029. This is because Python programs by default have a single *thread* of execution.

To understand what a thread of execution is, remember the Chapter 2 discussion of flow control, when you imagined the execution of a program as placing your finger on a line of code in your program and moving to the next line or wherever it was sent by a flow control statement. A *single-threaded* program has only one finger. But a *multithreaded* program has multiple fingers. Each finger still moves to the next line of code as defined by the flow control statements, but the fingers can be at different places in the program, executing different lines of code at the same time. (All of the programs in this book so far have been single threaded.)

Rather than having all of your code wait until the `time.sleep()` function finishes, you can execute the delayed or scheduled code in a separate thread using Python's `threading` module. The separate thread will pause for the `time.sleep` calls. Meanwhile, your program can do other work in the original thread.

To make a separate thread, you first need to make a `Thread` object by calling the `threading.Thread()` function. Enter the following code in a new file and save it as *threadDemo.py*:

```
import threading, time
print('Start of program.')

❶ def takeANap():
    time.sleep(5)
    print('Wake up!')

❷ threadObj = threading.Thread(target=takeANap)
❸ threadObj.start()

print('End of program.')
```

At ❶, we define a function that we want to use in a new thread. To create a Thread object, we call threading.Thread() and pass it the keyword argument target=takeANap ❷. This means the function we want to call in the new thread is takeANap(). Notice that the keyword argument is target=takeANap, not target=takeANap(). This is because you want to pass the takeANap() function itself as the argument, not call takeANap() and pass its return value.

After we store the Thread object created by threading.Thread() in threadObj, we call threadObj.start() ❸ to create the new thread and start executing the target function in the new thread. When this program is run, the output will look like this:

```
Start of program.
End of program.
Wake up!
```

This can be a bit confusing. If print('End of program.') is the last line of the program, you might think that it should be the last thing printed. The reason Wake up! comes after it is that when threadObj.start() is called, the target function for threadObj is run in a new thread of execution. Think of it as a second finger appearing at the start of the takeANap() function. The main thread continues to print('End of program.'). Meanwhile, the new thread that has been executing the time.sleep(5) call, pauses for 5 seconds. After it wakes from its 5-second nap, it prints 'Wake up!' and then returns from the takeANap() function. Chronologically, 'Wake up!' is the last thing printed by the program.

Normally a program terminates when the last line of code in the file has run (or the sys.exit() function is called). But *threadDemo.py* has two threads. The first is the original thread that began at the start of the program and ends after print('End of program.'). The second thread is created when threadObj.start() is called, begins at the start of the takeANap() function, and ends after takeANap() returns.

A Python program will not terminate until all its threads have terminated. When you ran *threadDemo.py*, even though the original thread had terminated, the second thread was still executing the time.sleep(5) call.

Passing Arguments to the Thread's Target Function

If the target function you want to run in the new thread takes arguments, you can pass the target function's arguments to threading.Thread(). For example, say you wanted to run this print() call in its own thread:

```
>>> print('Cats', 'Dogs', 'Frogs', sep=' & ')
Cats & Dogs & Frogs
```

This print() call has three regular arguments, 'Cats', 'Dogs', and 'Frogs', and one keyword argument, sep=' & '. The regular arguments can be passed as a list to the args keyword argument in `threading.Thread()`. The keyword argument can be specified as a dictionary to the kwargs keyword argument in `threading.Thread()`.

Enter the following into the interactive shell:

```
>>> import threading
>>> threadObj = threading.Thread(target=print, args=['Cats', 'Dogs', 'Frogs'],
kwargs={'sep': ' & '})
>>> threadObj.start()
Cats & Dogs & Frogs
```

To make sure the arguments `'Cats'`, `'Dogs'`, and `'Frogs'` get passed to `print()` in the new thread, we pass `args=['Cats', 'Dogs', 'Frogs']` to `threading.Thread()`. To make sure the keyword argument `sep=' & '` gets passed to `print()` in the new thread, we pass `kwargs={'sep': '& '}` to `threading.Thread()`.

The `threadObj.start()` call will create a new thread to call the `print()` function, and it will pass `'Cats'`, `'Dogs'`, and `'Frogs'` as arguments and `' & '` for the sep keyword argument.

This is an incorrect way to create the new thread that calls `print()`:

```
threadObj = threading.Thread(target=print('Cats', 'Dogs', 'Frogs', sep=' & '))
```

What this ends up doing is calling the `print()` function and passing its return value (`print()`'s return value is always `None`) as the target keyword argument. It *doesn't* pass the `print()` function itself. When passing arguments to a function in a new thread, use the `threading.Thread()` function's args and kwargs keyword arguments.

Concurrency Issues

You can easily create several new threads and have them all running at the same time. But multiple threads can also cause problems called *concurrency issues*. These issues happen when threads read and write variables at the same time, causing the threads to trip over each other. Concurrency issues can be hard to reproduce consistently, making them hard to debug.

Multithreaded programming is its own wide subject and beyond the scope of this book. What you have to keep in mind is this: To avoid concurrency issues, never let multiple threads read or write the same variables. When you create a new Thread object, make sure its target function uses only local variables in that function. This will avoid hard-to-debug concurrency issues in your programs.

NOTE *A beginner's tutorial on multithreaded programming is available at* http://nostarch.com/automatestuff/.

Project: Multithreaded XKCD Downloader

In Chapter 11, you wrote a program that downloaded all of the XKCD comic strips from the XKCD website. This was a single-threaded program: It downloaded one comic at a time. Much of the program's running time was spent establishing the network connection to begin the download and writing the downloaded images to the hard drive. If you have a broadband Internet connection, your single-threaded program wasn't fully utilizing the available bandwidth.

A multithreaded program that has some threads downloading comics while others are establishing connections and writing the comic image files to disk uses your Internet connection more efficiently and downloads the collection of comics more quickly. Open a new file editor window and save it as *multidownloadXkcd.py*. You will modify this program to add multithreading. The completely modified source code is available to download from *http://nostarch.com/automatestuff/*.

Step 1: Modify the Program to Use a Function

This program will mostly be the same downloading code from Chapter 11, so I'll skip the explanation for the Requests and BeautifulSoup code. The main changes you need to make are importing the threading module and making a downloadXkcd() function, which takes starting and ending comic numbers as parameters.

For example, calling downloadXkcd(140, 280) would loop over the downloading code to download the comics at *http://xkcd.com/140*, *http://xkcd.com/141*, *http://xkcd.com/142*, and so on, up to *http://xkcd.com/279*. Each thread that you create will call downloadXkcd() and pass a different range of comics to download.

Add the following code to your *multidownloadXkcd.py* program:

```
#! python3
# multidownloadXkcd.py - Downloads XKCD comics using multiple threads.

import requests, os, bs4, threading
❶ os.makedirs('xkcd', exist_ok=True)    # store comics in ./xkcd

❷ def downloadXkcd(startComic, endComic):
❸     for urlNumber in range(startComic, endComic + 1):
           # Download the page.
           print('Downloading page http://xkcd.com/%s...' % (urlNumber))
❹          res = requests.get('http://xkcd.com/%s' % (urlNumber))
           res.raise_for_status()

❺          soup = bs4.BeautifulSoup(res.text)

           # Find the URL of the comic image.
❻          comicElem = soup.select('#comic img')
           if comicElem == []:
               print('Could not find comic image.')
```

```
       else:
❼          comicUrl = comicElem[0].get('src')
           # Download the image.
           print('Downloading image %s...' % (comicUrl))
❽          res = requests.get(comicUrl)
           res.raise_for_status()

           # Save the image to ./xkcd.
           imageFile = open(os.path.join('xkcd', os.path.basename(comicUrl)), 'wb')
           for chunk in res.iter_content(100000):
               imageFile.write(chunk)
           imageFile.close()

# TODO: Create and start the Thread objects.
# TODO: Wait for all threads to end.
```

After importing the modules we need, we make a directory to store comics in ❶ and start defining downloadxkcd() ❷. We loop through all the numbers in the specified range ❸ and download each page ❹. We use Beautiful Soup to look through the HTML of each page ❺ and find the comic image ❻. If no comic image is found on a page, we print a message. Otherwise, we get the URL of the image ❼ and download the image ❽. Finally, we save the image to the directory we created.

Step 2: Create and Start Threads

Now that we've defined downloadXkcd(), we'll create the multiple threads that each call downloadXkcd() to download different ranges of comics from the XKCD website. Add the following code to *multidownloadXkcd.py* after the downloadXkcd() function definition:

```
#! python3
# multidownloadXkcd.py - Downloads XKCD comics using multiple threads.

--snip--

# Create and start the Thread objects.
downloadThreads = []               # a list of all the Thread objects
for i in range(0, 1400, 100):      # loops 14 times, creates 14 threads
    downloadThread = threading.Thread(target=downloadXkcd, args=(i, i + 99))
    downloadThreads.append(downloadThread)
    downloadThread.start()
```

First we make an empy list downloadThreads; the list will help us keep track of the many Thread objects we'll create. Then we start our for loop. Each time through the loop, we create a Thread object with threading.Thread(), append the Thread object to the list, and call start() to start running downloadXkcd() in the new thread. Since the for loop sets the i variable from 0 to 1400 at steps of 100, i will be set to 0 on the first iteration, 100 on the second iteration, 200 on the third, and so on. Since we pass args=(i, i + 99) to threading.Thread(), the two arguments passed to downloadXkcd() will be 0 and 99 on the first iteration, 100 and 199 on the second iteration, 200 and 299 on the third, and so on.

As the Thread object's start() method is called and the new thread begins to run the code inside downloadXkcd(), the main thread will continue to the next iteration of the for loop and create the next thread.

Step 3: Wait for All Threads to End

The main thread moves on as normal while the other threads we create download comics. But say there's some code you don't want to run in the main thread until all the threads have completed. Calling a Thread object's join() method will block until that thread has finished. By using a for loop to iterate over all the Thread objects in the downloadThreads list, the main thread can call the join() method on each of the other threads. Add the following to the bottom of your program:

```python
#! python3
# multidownloadXkcd.py - Downloads XKCD comics using multiple threads.

--snip--

# Wait for all threads to end.
for downloadThread in downloadThreads:
    downloadThread.join()
print('Done.')
```

The 'Done.' string will not be printed until all of the join() calls have returned. If a Thread object has already completed when its join() method is called, then the method will simply return immediately. If you wanted to extend this program with code that runs only after all of the comics downloaded, you could replace the print('Done.') line with your new code.

Launching Other Programs from Python

Your Python program can start other programs on your computer with the Popen() function in the built-in subprocess module. (The *P* in the name of the Popen() function stands for *process*.) If you have multiple instances of an application open, each of those instances is a separate process of the same program. For example, if you open multiple windows of your web browser at the same time, each of those windows is a different process of the web browser program. See Figure 15-1 for an example of multiple calculator processes open at once.

Every process can have multiple threads. Unlike threads, a process cannot directly read and write another process's variables. If you think of a multithreaded program as having multiple fingers following source code, then having multiple processes of the same program open is like having a friend with a separate copy of the program's source code. You are both independently executing the same program.

If you want to start an external program from your Python script, pass the program's filename to subprocess.Popen(). (On Windows, right-click the application's **Start** menu item and select **Properties** to view the application's filename. On OS X, CTRL-click the application and select **Show Package Contents** to find the path to the executable file.) The Popen() function will then immediately return. Keep in mind that the launched program is not run in the same thread as your Python program.

Figure 15-1: Six running processes of the same calculator program

On a Windows computer, enter the following into the interactive shell:

```
>>> import subprocess
>>> subprocess.Popen('C:\\Windows\\System32\\calc.exe')
<subprocess.Popen object at 0x0000000003055A58>
```

On Ubuntu Linux, you would enter the following:

```
>>> import subprocess
>>> subprocess.Popen('/usr/bin/gnome-calculator')
<subprocess.Popen object at 0x7f2bcf93b20>
```

On OS X, the process is slightly different. See "Opening Files with Default Applications" on page 355.

The return value is a Popen object, which has two useful methods: poll() and wait().

You can think of the poll() method as asking your friend if she's finished running the code you gave her. The poll() method will return None if the process is still running at the time poll() is called. If the program has terminated, it will return the process's integer *exit code*. An exit code is used to indicate whether the process terminated without errors (an exit code of 0) or whether an error caused the process to terminate (a nonzero exit code—generally 1, but it may vary depending on the program).

The wait() method is like waiting for your friend to finish working on her code before you keep working on yours. The wait() method will block until the launched process has terminated. This is helpful if you want your program to pause until the user finishes with the other program. The return value of wait() is the process's integer exit code.

On Windows, enter the following into the interactive shell. Note that the wait() call will block until you quit the launched calculator program.

```
❶ >>> calcProc = subprocess.Popen('c:\\Windows\\System32\\calc.exe')
❷ >>> calcProc.poll() == None
   True
❸ >>> calcProc.wait()
   0
   >>> calcProc.poll()
   0
```

Here we open a calculator process ❶. While it's still running, we check if poll() returns None ❷. It should, as the process is still running. Then we close the calculator program and call wait() on the terminated process ❸. wait() and poll() now return 0, indicating that the process terminated without errors.

Passing Command Line Arguments to Popen()

You can pass command line arguments to processes you create with Popen(). To do so, you pass a list as the sole argument to Popen(). The first string in this list will be the executable filename of the program you want to launch; all the subsequent strings will be the command line arguments to pass to the program when it starts. In effect, this list will be the value of sys.argv for the launched program.

Most applications with a graphical user interface (GUI) don't use command line arguments as extensively as command line–based or terminal-based programs do. But most GUI applications will accept a single argument for a file that the applications will immediately open when they start. For example, if you're using Windows, create a simple text file called *C:\hello.txt* and then enter the following into the interactive shell:

```
>>> subprocess.Popen(['C:\\Windows\\notepad.exe', 'C:\\hello.txt'])
<subprocess.Popen object at 0x00000000032DCEB8>
```

This will not only launch the Notepad application but also have it immediately open the *C:\hello.txt* file.

Task Scheduler, launchd, and cron

If you are computer savvy, you may know about Task Scheduler on Windows, launchd on OS X, or the cron scheduler on Linux. These well-documented and reliable tools all allow you to schedule applications to launch at specific times. If you'd like to learn more about them, you can find links to tutorials at *http://nostarch.com/automatestuff/*.

Using your operating system's built-in scheduler saves you from writing your own clock-checking code to schedule your programs. However, use the time.sleep() function if you just need your program to pause briefly. Or instead of using the operating system's scheduler, your code can loop until a certain date and time, calling time.sleep(1) each time through the loop.

Opening Websites with Python

The webbrowser.open() function can launch a web browser from your program to a specific website, rather than opening the browser application with subprocess.Popen(). See "Project: *mapIt.py* with the webbrowser Module" on page 234 for more details.

Running Other Python Scripts

You can launch a Python script from Python just like any other application. You just have to pass the *python.exe* executable to Popen() and the filename of the *.py* script you want to run as its argument. For example, the following would run the *hello.py* script from Chapter 1:

```
>>> subprocess.Popen(['C:\\python34\\python.exe', 'hello.py'])
<subprocess.Popen object at 0x000000000331CF28>
```

Pass Popen() a list containing a string of the Python executable's path and a string of the script's filename. If the script you're launching needs command line arguments, add them to the list after the script's filename. The location of the Python executable on Windows is *C:\python34\python .exe*. On OS X, it is */Library/Frameworks/Python.framework/Versions/3.3/bin/ python3*. On Linux, it is */usr/bin/python3*.

Unlike importing the Python program as a module, when your Python program launches another Python program, the two are run in separate processes and will not be able to share each other's variables.

Opening Files with Default Applications

Double-clicking a *.txt* file on your computer will automatically launch the application associated with the *.txt* file extension. Your computer will have several of these file extension associations set up already. Python can also open files this way with Popen().

Each operating system has a program that performs the equivalent of double-clicking a document file to open it. On Windows, this is the start program. On OS X, this is the open program. On Ubuntu Linux, this is the see program. Enter the following into the interactive shell, passing 'start', 'open', or 'see' to Popen() depending on your system:

```
>>> fileObj = open('hello.txt', 'w')
>>> fileObj.write('Hello world!')
12
```

```
>>> fileObj.close()
>>> import subprocess
>>> subprocess.Popen(['start', 'hello.txt'], shell=True)
```

Here we write `Hello world!` to a new *hello.txt* file. Then we call `Popen()`, passing it a list containing the program name (in this example, `'start'` for Windows) and the filename. We also pass the `shell=True` keyword argument, which is needed only on Windows. The operating system knows all of the file associations and can figure out that it should launch, say, *Notepad.exe* to handle the *hello.txt* file.

On OS X, the open program is used for opening both document files and programs. Enter the following into the interactive shell if you have a Mac:

```
>>> subprocess.Popen(['open', '/Applications/Calculator.app/'])
<subprocess.Popen object at 0x10202ff98>
```

The Calculator app should open.

THE UNIX PHILOSOPHY

Programs well designed to be launched by other programs become more power-ful than their code alone. The *Unix philosophy* is a set of software design prin-ciples established by the programmers of the Unix operating system (on which the modern Linux and OS X are built). It says that it's better to write small, limited-purpose programs that can interoperate, rather than large, feature-rich applica-tions. The smaller programs are easier to understand, and by being interoper-able, they can be the building blocks of much more powerful applications.

Smartphone apps follow this approach as well. If your restaurant app needs to display directions to a café, the developers didn't reinvent the wheel by writ-ing their own map code. The restaurant app simply launches a map app while passing it the café's address, just as your Python code would call a function and pass it arguments.

The Python programs you've been writing in this book mostly fit the Unix philosophy, especially in one important way: They use command line argu-ments rather than `input()` function calls. If all the information your program needs can be supplied up front, it is preferable to have this information passed as command line arguments rather than waiting for the user to type it in. This way, the command line arguments can be entered by a human user or supplied by another program. This interoperable approach will make your programs reusable as part of another program.

The sole exception is that you don't want passwords passed as command line arguments, since the command line may record them as part of its com-mand history feature. Instead, your program should call the `input()` function when it needs you to enter a password.

You can read more about Unix philosophy at *https://en.wikipedia.org/wiki/Unix_philosophy/*.

Project: Simple Countdown Program

Just like it's hard to find a simple stopwatch application, it can be hard to find a simple countdown application. Let's write a countdown program that plays an alarm at the end of the countdown.

At a high level, here's what your program will do:

- Count down from 60.
- Play a sound file (*alarm.wav*) when the countdown reaches zero.

This means your code will need to do the following:

- Pause for one second in between displaying each number in the countdown by calling `time.sleep()`.
- Call `subprocess.Popen()` to open the sound file with the default application.

Open a new file editor window and save it as *countdown.py*.

Step 1: Count Down

This program will require the `time` module for the `time.sleep()` function and the `subprocess` module for the `subprocess.Popen()` function. Enter the following code and save the file as *countdown.py*:

```
#! python3
# countdown.py - A simple countdown script.

import time, subprocess

❶ timeLeft = 60
   while timeLeft > 0:
❷      print(timeLeft, end='')
❸      time.sleep(1)
❹      timeLeft = timeLeft - 1

# TODO: At the end of the countdown, play a sound file.
```

After importing `time` and `subprocess`, make a variable called `timeLeft` to hold the number of seconds left in the countdown ❶. It can start at 60—or you can change the value here to whatever you need or even have it get set from a command line argument.

In a `while` loop, you display the remaining count ❷, pause for one second ❸, and then decrement the `timeLeft` variable ❹ before the loop starts over again. The loop will keep looping as long as `timeLeft` is greater than `0`. After that, the countdown will be over.

Step 2: Play the Sound File

While there are third-party modules to play sound files of various formats, the quick and easy way is to just launch whatever application the user already uses to play sound files. The operating system will figure out from the *.wav* file extension which application it should launch to play the file. This *.wav* file could easily be some other sound file format, such as *.mp3* or *.ogg*.

You can use any sound file that is on your computer to play at the end of the countdown, or you can download *alarm.wav* from *http://nostarch.com/ automatestuff/*.

Add the following to your code:

```python
#! python3
# countdown.py - A simple countdown script.

import time, subprocess

--snip--

# At the end of the countdown, play a sound file.
subprocess.Popen(['start', 'alarm.wav'], shell=True)
```

After the while loop finishes, *alarm.wav* (or the sound file you choose) will play to notify the user that the countdown is over. On Windows, be sure to include 'start' in the list you pass to Popen() and pass the keyword argument shell=True. On OS X, pass 'open' instead of 'start' and remove shell=True.

Instead of playing a sound file, you could save a text file somewhere with a message like *Break time is over!* and use Popen() to open it at the end of the countdown. This will effectively create a pop-up window with a message. Or you could use the webbrowser.open() function to open a specific website at the end of the countdown. Unlike some free countdown application you'd find online, your own countdown program's alarm can be anything you want!

Ideas for Similar Programs

A countdown is a simple delay before continuing the program's execution. This can also be used for other applications and features, such as the following:

- Use time.sleep() to give the user a chance to press CTRL-C to cancel an action, such as deleting files. Your program can print a "Press CTRL-C to cancel" message and then handle any KeyboardInterrupt exceptions with try and except statements.

- For a long-term countdown, you can use timedelta objects to measure the number of days, hours, minutes, and seconds until some point (a birthday? an anniversary?) in the future.

Summary

The Unix epoch (January 1, 1970, at midnight, UTC) is a standard reference time for many programming languages, including Python. While the time.time() function module returns an epoch timestamp (that is, a float value of the number of seconds since the Unix epoch), the datetime module is better for performing date arithmetic and formatting or parsing strings with date information.

The time.sleep() function will block (that is, not return) for a certain number of seconds. It can be used to add pauses to your program. But if you want to schedule your programs to start at a certain time, the instructions at *http://nostarch.com/automatestuff/* can tell you how to use the scheduler already provided by your operating system.

The threading module is used to create multiple threads, which is useful when you need to download multiple files or do other tasks simultaneously. But make sure the thread reads and writes only local variables, or you might run into concurrency issues.

Finally, your Python programs can launch other applications with the subprocess.Popen() function. Command line arguments can be passed to the Popen() call to open specific documents with the application. Alternatively, you can use the start, open, or see program with Popen() to use your computer's file associations to automatically figure out which application to use to open a document. By using the other applications on your computer, your Python programs can leverage their capabilities for your automation needs.

Practice Questions

1. What is the Unix epoch?

2. What function returns the number of seconds since the Unix epoch?

3. How can you pause your program for exactly 5 seconds?

4. What does the round() function return?

5. What is the difference between a datetime object and a timedelta object?

6. Say you have a function named spam(). How can you call this function and run the code inside it in a separate thread?

7. What should you do to avoid concurrency issues with multiple threads?

8. How can you have your Python program run the *calc.exe* program located in the *C:\Windows\System32* folder?

Practice Projects

For practice, write programs that do the following.

Prettified Stopwatch

Expand the stopwatch project from this chapter so that it uses the rjust() and ljust() string methods to "prettify" the output. (These methods were covered in Chapter 6.) Instead of output such as this:

```
Lap #1: 3.56 (3.56)
Lap #2: 8.63 (5.07)
Lap #3: 17.68 (9.05)
Lap #4: 19.11 (1.43)
```

. . . the output will look like this:

```
Lap # 1:    3.56 (  3.56)
Lap # 2:    8.63 (  5.07)
Lap # 3:   17.68 (  9.05)
Lap # 4:   19.11 (  1.43)
```

Note that you will need string versions of the lapNum, lapTime, and totalTime integer and float variables in order to call the string methods on them.

Next, use the pyperclip module introduced in Chapter 6 to copy the text output to the clipboard so the user can quickly paste the output to a text file or email.

Scheduled Web Comic Downloader

Write a program that checks the websites of several web comics and automatically downloads the images if the comic was updated since the program's last visit. Your operating system's scheduler (Scheduled Tasks on Windows, launchd on OS X, and cron on Linux) can run your Python program once a day. The Python program itself can download the comic and then copy it to your desktop so that it is easy to find. This will free you from having to check the website yourself to see whether it has updated. (A list of web comics is available at *http://nostarch.com/automatestuff/*.)

16

SENDING EMAIL
AND TEXT MESSAGES

Checking and replying to email is a huge time sink. Of course, you can't just write a program to handle all your email for you, since each message requires its own response. But you can still automate plenty of email-related tasks once you know how to write programs that can send and receive email.

For example, maybe you have a spreadsheet full of customer records and want to send each customer a different form letter depending on their age and location details. Commercial software might not be able to do this for you; fortunately, you can write your own program to send these emails, saving yourself a lot of time copying and pasting form emails.

You can also write programs to send emails and SMS texts to notify you of things even while you're away from your computer. If you're automating a task that takes a couple of hours to do, you don't want to go back to your computer every few minutes to check on the program's status. Instead, the program can just text your phone when it's done—freeing you to focus on more important things while you're away from your computer.

SMTP

Much like HTTP is the protocol used by computers to send web pages across the Internet, *Simple Mail Transfer Protocol (SMTP)* is the protocol used for sending email. SMTP dictates how email messages should be formatted, encrypted, and relayed between mail servers, and all the other details that your computer handles after you click Send. You don't need to know these technical details, though, because Python's smtplib module simplifies them into a few functions.

SMTP just deals with sending emails to others. A different protocol, called IMAP, deals with retrieving emails sent to you and is described in "IMAP" on page 366.

Sending Email

You may be familiar with sending emails from Outlook or Thunderbird or through a website such as Gmail or Yahoo! Mail. Unfortunately, Python doesn't offer you a nice graphical user interface like those services. Instead, you call functions to perform each major step of SMTP, as shown in the following interactive shell example.

NOTE *Don't enter this example in IDLE; it won't work because* smtp.example.com, bob@example.com, MY_SECRET_PASSWORD, *and* alice@example.com *are just placeholders. This code is just an overview of the process of sending email with Python.*

```
>>> import smtplib
>>> smtpObj = smtplib.SMTP('smtp.example.com', 587)
>>> smtpObj.ehlo()
(250, b'mx.example.com at your service, [216.172.148.131]\nSIZE 35882577\
n8BITMIME\nSTARTTLS\nENHANCEDSTATUSCODES\nCHUNKING')
>>> smtpObj.starttls()
(220, b'2.0.0 Ready to start TLS')
>>> smtpObj.login('bob@example.com', 'MY_SECRET_PASSWORD')
(235, b'2.7.0 Accepted')
>>> smtpObj.sendmail('bob@example.com', 'alice@example.com', 'Subject: So
long.\nDear Alice, so long and thanks for all the fish. Sincerely, Bob')
{}
>>> smtpObj.quit()
(221, b'2.0.0 closing connection ko10sm23097611pbd.52 - gsmtp')
```

In the following sections, we'll go through each step, replacing the placeholders with your information to connect and log in to an SMTP server, send an email, and disconnect from the server.

Connecting to an SMTP Server

If you've ever set up Thunderbird, Outlook, or another program to connect to your email account, you may be familiar with configuring the SMTP server and port. These settings will be different for each email provider, but a web search for *<your provider> smtp settings* should turn up the server and port to use.

The domain name for the SMTP server will usually be the name of your email provider's domain name, with *smtp.* in front of it. For example, Gmail's SMTP server is at *smtp.gmail.com*. Table 16-1 lists some common email providers and their SMTP servers. (The port is an integer value and will almost always be 587, which is used by the command encryption standard, TLS.)

Table 16-1: Email Providers and Their SMTP Servers

Provider	SMTP server domain name
Gmail	*smtp.gmail.com*
Outlook.com/Hotmail.com	*smtp-mail.outlook.com*
Yahoo Mail	*smtp.mail.yahoo.com*
AT&T	*smpt.mail.att.net* (port 465)
Comcast	*smtp.comcast.net*
Verizon	*smtp.verizon.net* (port 465)

Once you have the domain name and port information for your email provider, create an SMTP object by calling smtplib.SMTP(), passing the domain name as a string argument, and passing the port as an integer argument. The SMTP object represents a connection to an SMTP mail server and has methods for sending emails. For example, the following call creates an SMTP object for connecting to Gmail:

```
>>> smtpObj = smtplib.SMTP('smtp.gmail.com', 587)
>>> type(smtpObj)
<class 'smtplib.SMTP'>
```

Entering type(smtpObj) shows you that there's an SMTP object stored in smtpObj. You'll need this SMTP object in order to call the methods that log you in and send emails. If the smptlib.SMTP() call is not successful, your SMTP server might not support TLS on port 587. In this case, you will need to create an SMTP object using smtplib.SMTP_SSL() and port 465 instead.

```
>>> smtpObj = smtplib.SMTP_SSL('smtp.gmail.com', 465)
```

NOTE *If you are not connected to the Internet, Python will raise a* socket.gaierror: [Errno 11004] getaddrinfo failed *or similar exception.*

For your programs, the differences between TLS and SSL aren't important. You only need to know which encryption standard your SMTP server uses so you know how to connect to it. In all of the interactive shell examples that follow, the smtpObj variable will contain an SMTP object returned by the smtplib.SMTP() or smtplib.SMTP_SSL() function.

Sending the SMTP "Hello" Message

Once you have the SMTP object, call its oddly named ehlo() method to "say hello" to the SMTP email server. This greeting is the first step in SMTP and is important for establishing a connection to the server. You don't need to know the specifics of these protocols. Just be sure to call the ehlo() method first thing after getting the SMTP object or else the later method calls will result in errors. The following is an example of an ehlo() call and its return value:

```
>>> smtpObj.ehlo()
(250, b'mx.google.com at your service, [216.172.148.131]\nSIZE 35882577\
n8BITMIME\nSTARTTLS\nENHANCEDSTATUSCODES\nCHUNKING')
```

If the first item in the returned tuple is the integer 250 (the code for "success" in SMTP), then the greeting succeeded.

Starting TLS Encryption

If you are connecting to port 587 on the SMTP server (that is, you're using TLS encryption), you'll need to call the starttls() method next. This required step enables encryption for your connection. If you are connecting to port 465 (using SSL), then encryption is already set up, and you should skip this step.

Here's an example of the starttls() method call:

```
>>> smtpObj.starttls()
(220, b'2.0.0 Ready to start TLS')
```

starttls() puts your SMTP connection in TLS mode. The 220 in the return value tells you that the server is ready.

Logging in to the SMTP Server

Once your encrypted connection to the SMTP server is set up, you can log in with your username (usually your email address) and email password by calling the login() method.

```
>>> smtpObj.login('my_email_address@gmail.com', 'MY_SECRET_PASSWORD')
(235, b'2.7.0 Accepted')
```

Pass a string of your email address as the first argument and a string of your password as the second argument. The 235 in the return value means authentication was successful. Python will raise an `smtplib .SMTPAuthenticationError` exception for incorrect passwords.

WARNING *Be careful about putting passwords in your source code. If anyone ever copies your program, they'll have access to your email account! It's a good idea to call* `input()` *and have the user type in the password. It may be inconvenient to have to enter a password each time you run your program, but this approach will prevent you from leaving your password in an unencrypted file on your computer where a hacker or laptop thief could easily get it.*

Sending an Email

Once you are logged in to your email provider's SMTP server, you can call the `sendmail()` method to actually send the email. The `sendmail()` method call looks like this:

```
>>> smtpObj.sendmail('my_email_address@gmail.com', 'recipient@example.com',
'Subject: So long.\nDear Alice, so long and thanks for all the fish. Sincerely,
Bob')
{}
```

The `sendmail()` method requires three arguments.

- Your email address as a string (for the email's "from" address)
- The recipient's email address as a string or a list of strings for multiple recipients (for the "to" address)
- The email body as a string

The start of the email body string *must* begin with `'Subject: \n'` for the subject line of the email. The `'\n'` newline character separates the subject line from the main body of the email.

The return value from `sendmail()` is a dictionary. There will be one key-value pair in the dictionary for each recipient for whom email delivery *failed*. An empty dictionary means all recipients were *successfully* sent the email.

Disconnecting from the SMTP Server

Be sure to call the quit() method when you are done sending emails. This will disconnect your program from the SMTP server.

```
>>> smtpObj.quit()
(221, b'2.0.0 closing connection ko10sm23097611pbd.52 - gsmtp')
```

The 221 in the return value means the session is ending.

To review all the steps for connecting and logging in to the server, sending email, and disconnection, see "Sending Email" on page 362.

IMAP

Just as SMTP is the protocol for sending email, the *Internet Message Access Protocol (IMAP)* specifies how to communicate with an email provider's server to retrieve emails sent to your email address. Python comes with an imaplib module, but in fact the third-party imapclient module is easier to use. This chapter provides an introduction to using IMAPClient; the full documentation is at *http://imapclient.readthedocs.org/*.

The imapclient module downloads emails from an IMAP server in a rather complicated format. Most likely, you'll want to convert them from this format into simple string values. The pyzmail module does the hard job of parsing these email messages for you. You can find the complete documentation for PyzMail at *http://www.magiksys.net/pyzmail/*.

Install imapclient and pyzmail from a Terminal window. Appendix A has steps on how to install third-party modules.

Retrieving and Deleting Emails with IMAP

Finding and retrieving an email in Python is a multistep process that requires both the imapclient and pyzmail third-party modules. Just to give you an overview, here's a full example of logging in to an IMAP server, searching for emails, fetching them, and then extracting the text of the email messages from them.

```
>>> import imapclient
>>> imapObj = imapclient.IMAPClient('imap.gmail.com', ssl=True)
>>> imapObj.login('my_email_address@gmail.com', 'MY_SECRET_PASSWORD')
'my_email_address@gmail.com Jane Doe authenticated (Success)'
>>> imapObj.select_folder('INBOX', readonly=True)
>>> UIDs = imapObj.search(['SINCE 05-Jul-2014'])
>>> UIDs
[40032, 40033, 40034, 40035, 40036, 40037, 40038, 40039, 40040, 40041]
>>> rawMessages = imapObj.fetch([40041], ['BODY[]', 'FLAGS'])
>>> import pyzmail
>>> message = pyzmail.PyzMessage.factory(rawMessages[40041]['BODY[]'])
>>> message.get_subject()
'Hello!'
```

```
>>> message.get_addresses('from')
[('Edward Snowden', 'esnowden@nsa.gov')]
>>> message.get_addresses('to')
[(Jane Doe', 'jdoe@example.com')]
>>> message.get_addresses('cc')
[]
>>> message.get_addresses('bcc')
[]
>>> message.text_part != None
True
>>> message.text_part.get_payload().decode(message.text_part.charset)
'Follow the money.\r\n\r\n-Ed\r\n'
>>> message.html_part != None
True
>>> message.html_part.get_payload().decode(message.html_part.charset)
'<div dir="ltr"><div>So long, and thanks for all the fish!<br><br></div>-
Al<br></div>\r\n'
>>> imapObj.logout()
```

You don't have to memorize these steps. After we go through each step in detail, you can come back to this overview to refresh your memory.

Connecting to an IMAP Server

Just like you needed an SMTP object to connect to an SMTP server and send email, you need an IMAPClient object to connect to an IMAP server and receive email. First you'll need the domain name of your email provider's IMAP server. This will be different from the SMTP server's domain name. Table 16-2 lists the IMAP servers for several popular email providers.

Table 16-2: Email Providers and Their IMAP Servers

Provider	IMAP server domain name
Gmail	imap.gmail.com
Outlook.com/Hotmail.com	imap-mail.outlook.com
Yahoo Mail	imap.mail.yahoo.com
AT&T	imap.mail.att.net
Comcast	imap.comcast.net
Verizon	incoming.verizon.net

Once you have the domain name of the IMAP server, call the imapclient.IMAPClient() function to create an IMAPClient object. Most email providers require SSL encryption, so pass the ssl=True keyword argument. Enter the following into the interactive shell (using your provider's domain name):

```
>>> import imapclient
>>> imapObj = imapclient.IMAPClient('imap.gmail.com', ssl=True)
```

In all of the interactive shell examples in the following sections, the imapObj variable will contain an IMAPClient object returned from the imapclient.IMAPClient() function. In this context, a *client* is the object that connects to the server.

Logging in to the IMAP Server

Once you have an IMAPClient object, call its login() method, passing in the username (this is usually your email address) and password as strings.

```
>>> imapObj.login('my_email_address@gmail.com', 'MY_SECRET_PASSWORD')
'my_email_address@gmail.com Jane Doe authenticated (Success)'
```

WARNING   *Remember, never write a password directly into your code! Instead, design your program to accept the password returned from input().*

If the IMAP server rejects this username/password combination, Python will raise an imaplib.error exception. For Gmail accounts, you may need to use an application-specific password; for more details, see "Gmail's Application-Specific Passwords" on page 365.

Searching for Email

Once you're logged on, actually retrieving an email that you're interested in is a two-step process. First, you must select a folder you want to search through. Then, you must call the IMAPClient object's search() method, passing in a string of IMAP search keywords.

Selecting a Folder

Almost every account has an INBOX folder by default, but you can also get a list of folders by calling the IMAPClient object's list_folders() method. This returns a list of tuples. Each tuple contains information about a single folder. Continue the interactive shell example by entering the following:

```
>>> import pprint
>>> pprint.pprint(imapObj.list_folders())
[(('\\HasNoChildren',), '/', 'Drafts'),
 (('\\HasNoChildren',), '/', 'Filler'),
 (('\\HasNoChildren',), '/', 'INBOX'),
 (('\\HasNoChildren',), '/', 'Sent'),
--snip--
 (('\\HasNoChildren', '\\Flagged'), '/', '[Gmail]/Starred'),
 (('\\HasNoChildren', '\\Trash'), '/', '[Gmail]/Trash')]
```

This is what your output might look like if you have a Gmail account. (Gmail calls its folders *labels*, but they work the same way as folders.) The three values in each of the tuples—for example, (('\\HasNoChildren',), '/', 'INBOX')—are as follows:

- A tuple of the folder's flags. (Exactly what these flags represent is beyond the scope of this book, and you can safely ignore this field.)
- The delimiter used in the name string to separate parent folders and subfolders.
- The full name of the folder.

To select a folder to search through, pass the folder's name as a string into the IMAPClient object's select_folder() method.

```
>>> imapObj.select_folder('INBOX', readonly=True)
```

You can ignore select_folder()'s return value. If the selected folder does not exist, Python will raise an imaplib.error exception.

The readonly=True keyword argument prevents you from accidentally making changes or deletions to any of the emails in this folder during the subsequent method calls. Unless you *want* to delete emails, it's a good idea to always set readonly to True.

Performing the Search

With a folder selected, you can now search for emails with the IMAPClient object's search() method. The argument to search() is a list of strings, each formatted to the IMAP's search keys. Table 16-3 describes the various search keys.

Table 16-3: IMAP Search Keys

Search key	Meaning
'ALL'	Returns all messages in the folder. You may run in to imaplib size limits if you request all the messages in a large folder. See "Size Limits" on page 371.
'BEFORE *date*', 'ON *date*', 'SINCE *date*'	These three search keys return, respectively, messages that were received by the IMAP server before, on, or after the given *date*. The date must be formatted like 05-Jul-2015. Also, while 'SINCE 05-Jul-2015' will match messages on and after July 5, 'BEFORE 05-Jul-2015' will match only messages before July 5 but not on July 5 itself.
'SUBJECT *string*', 'BODY *string*', 'TEXT *string*'	Returns messages where *string* is found in the subject, body, or either, respectively. If *string* has spaces in it, then enclose it with double quotes: 'TEXT "search with spaces"'.

(continued)

Table 16-3 (continued)

Search key	Meaning

`'FROM string',`
`'TO string',`
`'CC string',`
`'BCC string'`
	Returns all messages where *string* is found in the "from" emailaddress, "to" addresses, "cc" (carbon copy) addresses, or "bcc" (blind carbon copy) addresses, respectively. If there are multiple email addresses in *string*, then separate them with spaces and enclose them all with double quotes:
	`'CC "firstcc@example.com secondcc@example.com"'`.

`'SEEN',` `'UNSEEN'`	Returns all messages with and without the *Seen* flag, respectively. An email obtains the *Seen* flag if it has been accessed with a `fetch()` method call (described later) or if it is clicked when you're checking your email in an email program or web browser. It's more common to say the email has been "read" rather than "seen," but they mean the same thing.
`'ANSWERED',` `'UNANSWERED'`	Returns all messages with and without the *Answered* flag, respectively. A message obtains the *Answered* flag when it is replied to.
`'DELETED',` `'UNDELETED'`	Returns all messages with and without the *Deleted* flag, respectively. Email messages deleted with the `delete_messages()` method are given the *Deleted* flag but are not permanently deleted until the `expunge()` method is called (see "Deleting Emails" on page 375). Note that some email providers, such as Gmail, automatically expunge emails.
`'DRAFT',` `'UNDRAFT'`	Returns all messages with and without the *Draft* flag, respectively. Draft messages are usually kept in a separate `Drafts` folder rather than in the `INBOX` folder.
`'FLAGGED',` `'UNFLAGGED'`	Returns all messages with and without the *Flagged* flag, respectively. This flag is usually used to mark email messages as "Important" or "Urgent."
`'LARGER N',` `'SMALLER N'`	Returns all messages larger or smaller than *N* bytes, respectively.
`'NOT search-key'`	Returns the messages that *search-key* would *not* have returned.
`'OR search-key1 search-key2'`	Returns the messages that match *either* the first or second *search-key*.

Note that some IMAP servers may have slightly different implementations for how they handle their flags and search keys. It may require some experimentation in the interactive shell to see exactly how they behave.

You can pass multiple IMAP search key strings in the list argument to the search() method. The messages returned are the ones that match *all* the search keys. If you want to match *any* of the search keys, use the OR search key. For the NOT and OR search keys, one and two complete search keys follow the NOT and OR, respectively.

Here are some example search() method calls along with their meanings:

`imapObj.search(['ALL'])`   Returns every message in the currently selected folder.

`imapObj.search(['ON 05-Jul-2015'])`   Returns every message sent on July 5, 2015.

```
imapObj.search(['SINCE 01-Jan-2015', 'BEFORE 01-Feb-2015', 'UNSEEN'])
```
Returns every message sent in January 2015 that is unread. (Note that this means *on and after* January 1 and up to *but not including* February 1.)

```
imapObj.search(['SINCE 01-Jan-2015', 'FROM alice@example.com'])
```
Returns every message from *alice@example.com* sent since the start of 2015.

```
imapObj.search(['SINCE 01-Jan-2015', 'NOT FROM alice@example.com'])
```
Returns every message sent from everyone except *alice@example.com* since the start of 2015.

```
imapObj.search(['OR FROM alice@example.com FROM bob@example.com'])
```
Returns every message ever sent from *alice@example.com* or *bob@example.com*.

```
imapObj.search(['FROM alice@example.com', 'FROM bob@example.com'])
```
Trick example! This search will never return any messages, because messages must match *all* search keywords. Since there can be only one "from" address, it is impossible for a message to be from both *alice@example.com* and *bob@example.com*.

The search() method doesn't return the emails themselves but rather unique IDs (UIDs) for the emails, as integer values. You can then pass these UIDs to the fetch() method to obtain the email content.

Continue the interactive shell example by entering the following:

```
>>> UIDs = imapObj.search(['SINCE 05-Jul-2015'])
>>> UIDs
[40032, 40033, 40034, 40035, 40036, 40037, 40038, 40039, 40040, 40041]
```

Here, the list of message IDs (for messages received July 5 onward) returned by search() is stored in UIDs. The list of UIDs returned on your computer will be different from the ones shown here; they are unique to a particular email account. When you later pass UIDs to other function calls, use the UID values you received, not the ones printed in this book's examples.

Size Limits

If your search matches a large number of email messages, Python might raise an exception that says imaplib.error: got more than 10000 bytes. When this happens, you will have to disconnect and reconnect to the IMAP server and try again.

This limit is in place to prevent your Python programs from eating up too much memory. Unfortunately, the default size limit is often too small. You can change this limit from 10,000 bytes to 10,000,000 bytes by running this code:

```
>>> import imaplib
>>> imaplib._MAXLINE = 10000000
```

This should prevent this error message from coming up again. You may want to make these two lines part of every IMAP program you write.

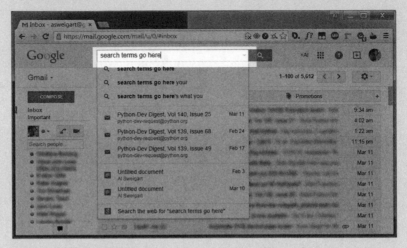
Fetching an Email and Marking It As Read

Once you have a list of UIDs, you can call the IMAPClient object's fetch() method to get the actual email content.

The list of UIDs will be fetch()'s first argument. The second argument should be the list ['BODY[]'], which tells fetch() to download all the body content for the emails specified in your UID list.

Let's continue our interactive shell example.

```
>>> rawMessages = imapObj.fetch(UIDs, ['BODY[]'])
>>> import pprint
>>> pprint.pprint(rawMessages)
{40040: {'BODY[]': 'Delivered-To: my_email_address@gmail.com\r\n'
                    'Received: by 10.76.71.167 with SMTP id '
--snip--
                    '\r\n'
                    '------=_Part_6000970_707736290.1404819487066--\r\n',
         'SEQ': 5430}}
```

Import pprint and pass the return value from fetch(), stored in the variable rawMessages, to pprint.pprint() to "pretty print" it, and you'll see that this return value is a nested dictionary of messages with UIDs as the keys. Each message is stored as a dictionary with two keys: 'BODY[]' and 'SEQ'. The 'BODY[]' key maps to the actual body of the email. The 'SEQ' key is for a *sequence number*, which has a similar role to the UID. You can safely ignore it.

As you can see, the message content in the 'BODY[]' key is pretty unintelligible. It's in a format called RFC 822, which is designed for IMAP servers to read. But you don't need to understand the RFC 822 format; later in this chapter, the pyzmail module will make sense of it for you.

When you selected a folder to search through, you called select_folder() with the readonly=True keyword argument. Doing this will prevent you from accidentally deleting an email—but it also means that emails will not get marked as read if you fetch them with the fetch() method. If you *do* want emails to be marked as read when you fetch them, you will need to pass readonly=False to select_folder(). If the selected folder is already in read-only mode, you can reselect the current folder with another call to select_folder(), this time with the readonly=False keyword argument:

```
>>> imapObj.select_folder('INBOX', readonly=False)
```

Getting Email Addresses from a Raw Message

The raw messages returned from the fetch() method still aren't very useful to people who just want to read their email. The pyzmail module parses these raw messages and returns them as PyzMessage objects, which make the subject, body, "To" field, "From" field, and other sections of the email easily accessible to your Python code.

Continue the interactive shell example with the following (using UIDs from your own email account, not the ones shown here):

```
>>> import pyzmail
>>> message = pyzmail.PyzMessage.factory(rawMessages[40041]['BODY[]'])
```

First, import pyzmail. Then, to create a PyzMessage object of an email, call the pyzmail.PyzMessage.factory() function and pass it the 'BODY[]' section of the raw message. Store the result in message. Now message contains a PyzMessage object, which has several methods that make it easy to get the email's subject line, as well as all sender and recipient addresses. The get_subject() method returns the subject as a simple string value. The get_addresses() method returns a list of addresses for the field you pass it. For example, the method calls might look like this:

```
>>> message.get_subject()
'Hello!'
>>> message.get_addresses('from')
[('Edward Snowden', 'esnowden@nsa.gov')]
>>> message.get_addresses('to')
[(Jane Doe', 'my_email_address@gmail.com')]
>>> message.get_addresses('cc')
[]
>>> message.get_addresses('bcc')
[]
```

Notice that the argument for get_addresses() is 'from', 'to', 'cc', or 'bcc'. The return value of get_addresses() is a list of tuples. Each tuple contains two strings: The first is the name associated with the email address, and the second is the email address itself. If there are no addresses in the requested field, get_addresses() returns a blank list. Here, the 'cc' carbon copy and 'bcc' blind carbon copy fields both contained no addresses and so returned empty lists.

Getting the Body from a Raw Message

Emails can be sent as plaintext, HTML, or both. Plaintext emails contain only text, while HTML emails can have colors, fonts, images, and other features that make the email message look like a small web page. If an email is only plaintext, its PyzMessage object will have its html_part attributes set to None. Likewise, if an email is only HTML, its PyzMessage object will have its text_part attribute set to None.

Otherwise, the text_part or html_part value will have a get_payload() method that returns the email's body as a value of the *bytes* data type. (The bytes data type is beyond the scope of this book.) But this *still* isn't a string value that we can use. Ugh! The last step is to call the decode() method on the bytes value returned by get_payload(). The decode() method takes one argument: the message's character encoding, stored in the text_part.charset or html_part.charset attribute. This, finally, will return the string of the email's body.

Continue the interactive shell example by entering the following:

❶ >>> message.text_part != None
True
>>> message.text_part.get_payload().decode(message.text_part.charset)
❷ 'So long, and thanks for all the fish!\r\n\r\n-Al\r\n'
❸ >>> message.html_part != None
True

❹ >>> message.html_part.get_payload().decode(message.html_part.charset)
' So long, and thanks for all the fish!

 -Al

 \r\n'

The email we're working with has both plaintext and HTML content, so the PyzMessage object stored in message has text_part and html_part attributes not equal to None ❶ ❸. Calling get_payload() on the message's text_part and then calling decode() on the bytes value returns a string of the text version of the email ❷. Using get_payload() and decode() with the message's html_part returns a string of the HTML version of the email ❹.

Deleting Emails

To delete emails, pass a list of message UIDs to the IMAPClient object's delete_messages() method. This marks the emails with the *\Deleted* flag. Calling the expunge() method will permanently delete all emails with the *\Deleted* flag in the currently selected folder. Consider the following interactive shell example:

```
❶ >>> imapObj.select_folder('INBOX', readonly=False)
❷ >>> UIDs = imapObj.search(['ON 09-Jul-2015'])
   >>> UIDs
   [40066]
   >>> imapObj.delete_messages(UIDs)
❸ {40066: ('\\Seen', '\\Deleted')}
   >>> imapObj.expunge()
   ('Success', [(5452, 'EXISTS')])
```

Here we select the inbox by calling select_folder() on the IMAPClient object and passing 'INBOX' as the first argument; we also pass the keyword argument readonly=False so that we can delete emails ❶. We search the inbox for messages received on a specific date and store the returned message IDs in UIDs ❷. Calling delete_message() and passing it UIDs returns a dictionary; each key-value pair is a message ID and a tuple of the message's flags, which should now include *\Deleted* ❸. Calling expunge() then permanently deletes messages with the *\Deleted* flag and returns a success message if there were no problems expunging the emails. Note that some email providers, such as Gmail, automatically expunge emails deleted with delete_messages() instead of waiting for an expunge command from the IMAP client.

Disconnecting from the IMAP Server

When your program has finished retrieving or deleting emails, simply call the IMAPClient's logout() method to disconnect from the IMAP server.

```
>>> imapObj.logout()
```

If your program runs for several minutes or more, the IMAP server may *time out*, or automatically disconnect. In this case, the next method call your program makes on the IMAPClient object will raise an exception like the following:

```
imaplib.abort: socket error: [WinError 10054] An existing connection was
forcibly closed by the remote host
```

In this event, your program will have to call imapclient.IMAPClient() to connect again.

Whew! That's it. There were a lot of hoops to jump through, but you now have a way to get your Python programs to log in to an email account and fetch emails. You can always consult the overview in "Retrieving and Deleting Emails with IMAP" on page 366 whenever you need to remember all of the steps.

Project: Sending Member Dues Reminder Emails

Say you have been "volunteered" to track member dues for the Mandatory Volunteerism Club. This is a truly boring job, involving maintaining a spreadsheet of everyone who has paid each month and emailing reminders to those who haven't. Instead of going through the spreadsheet yourself and copying and pasting the same email to everyone who is behind on dues, let's—you guessed it—write a script that does this for you.

At a high level, here's what your program will do:

- Read data from an Excel spreadsheet.
- Find all members who have not paid dues for the latest month.
- Find their email addresses and send them personalized reminders.

This means your code will need to do the following:

- Open and read the cells of an Excel document with the openpyxl module. (See Chapter 12 for working with Excel files.)
- Create a dictionary of members who are behind on their dues.
- Log in to an SMTP server by calling smtplib.SMTP(), ehlo(), starttls(), and login().
- For all members behind on their dues, send a personalized reminder email by calling the sendmail() method.

Open a new file editor window and save it as *sendDuesReminders.py*.

Step 1: Open the Excel File

Let's say the Excel spreadsheet you use to track membership dues payments looks like Figure 16-2 and is in a file named *duesRecords.xlsx*. You can download this file from *http://nostarch.com/automatestuff/*.

Figure 16-2: The spreadsheet for tracking member dues payments

This spreadsheet has every member's name and email address. Each month has a column tracking members' payment statuses. The cell for each member is marked with the text *paid* once they have paid their dues.

The program will have to open *duesRecords.xlsx* and figure out the column for the latest month by reading the sheet.max_column attribute. (You can consult Chapter 12 for more information on accessing cells in Excel spreadsheet files with the openpyxl module.) Enter the following code into the file editor window:

```
#! python3
# sendDuesReminders.py - Sends emails based on payment status in spreadsheet.

import openpyxl, smtplib, sys

# Open the spreadsheet and get the latest dues status.
❶ wb = openpyxl.load_workbook('duesRecords.xlsx')
❷ sheet = wb.get_sheet_by_name('Sheet1')

❸ lastCol = sheet.max_column
❹ latestMonth = sheet.cell(row=1, column=lastCol).value

# TODO: Check each member's payment status.

# TODO: Log in to email account.

# TODO: Send out reminder emails.
```

After importing the openpyxl, smtplib, and sys modules, we open our *duesRecords.xlsx* file and store the resulting Workbook object in wb ❶. Then we get Sheet 1 and store the resulting Worksheet object in sheet ❷. Now that we have a Worksheet object, we can access rows, columns, and cells. We store the highest column in lastCol ❸, and we then use row number 1 and lastCol to access the cell that should hold the most recent month. We get the value in this cell and store it in latestMonth ❹.

Step 2: Find All Unpaid Members

Once you've determined the column number of the latest month (stored in lastCol), you can loop through all rows after the first row (which has the column headers) to see which members have the text *paid* in the cell for that month's dues. If the member hasn't paid, you can grab the member's name and email address from columns 1 and 2, respectively. This information will go into the unpaidMembers dictionary, which will track all members who haven't paid in the most recent month. Add the following code to *sendDuesReminder.py*.

```python
#! python3
# sendDuesReminders.py - Sends emails based on payment status in spreadsheet.

--snip--

# Check each member's payment status.
unpaidMembers = {}
❶ for r in range(2, sheet.max_row + 1):
❷     payment = sheet.cell(row=r, column=lastCol).value
    if payment != 'paid':
❸         name = sheet.cell(row=r, column=1).value
❹         email = sheet.cell(row=r, column=2).value
❺         unpaidMembers[name] = email
```

This code sets up an empty dictionary unpaidMembers and then loops through all the rows after the first ❶. For each row, the value in the most recent column is stored in payment ❷. If payment is not equal to 'paid', then the value of the first column is stored in name ❸, the value of the second column is stored in email ❹, and name and email are added to unpaidMembers ❺.

Step 3: Send Customized Email Reminders

Once you have a list of all unpaid members, it's time to send them email reminders. Add the following code to your program, except with your real email address and provider information:

```python
#! python3
# sendDuesReminders.py - Sends emails based on payment status in spreadsheet.

--snip--

# Log in to email account.
smtpObj = smtplib.SMTP('smtp.gmail.com', 587)
smtpObj.ehlo()
smtpObj.starttls()
smtpObj.login('my_email_address@gmail.com', sys.argv[1])
```

Create an SMTP object by calling `smtplib.SMTP()` and passing it the domain name and port for your provider. Call `ehlo()` and `starttls()`, and then call `login()` and pass it your email address and `sys.argv[1]`, which will store your password string. You'll enter the password as a command line argument each time you run the program, to avoid saving your password in your source code.

Once your program has logged in to your email account, it should go through the `unpaidMembers` dictionary and send a personalized email to each member's email address. Add the following to *sendDuesReminders.py*:

```python3
#! python3
# sendDuesReminders.py - Sends emails based on payment status in spreadsheet.

--snip--

# Send out reminder emails.
for name, email in unpaidMembers.items():
❶    body = "Subject: %s dues unpaid.\nDear %s,\nRecords show that you have not
paid dues for %s. Please make this payment as soon as possible. Thank you!'" %
(latestMonth, name, latestMonth)
❷    print('Sending email to %s...' % email)
❸    sendmailStatus = smtpObj.sendmail('my_email_address@gmail.com', email, body)

❹    if sendmailStatus != {}:
        print('There was a problem sending email to %s: %s' % (email,
        sendmailStatus))
smtpObj.quit()
```

This code loops through the names and emails in `unpaidMembers`. For each member who hasn't paid, we customize a message with the latest month and the member's name, and store the message in `body` ❶. We print output saying that we're sending an email to this member's email address ❷. Then we call `sendmail()`, passing it the from address and the customized message ❸. We store the return value in `sendmailStatus`.

Remember that the `sendmail()` method will return a nonempty dictionary value if the SMTP server reported an error sending that particular email. The last part of the for loop at ❹ checks if the returned dictionary is nonempty, and if it is, prints the recipient's email address and the returned dictionary.

After the program is done sending all the emails, the `quit()` method is called to disconnect from the SMTP server.

When you run the program, the output will look something like this:

```
Sending email to alice@example.com...
Sending email to bob@example.com...
Sending email to eve@example.com...
```

The recipients will receive an email that looks like Figure 16-3.

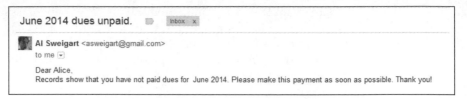

Figure 16-3: An automatically sent email from sendDuesReminders.py

Sending Text Messages with Twilio

Most people are more likely to be near their phones than their computers, so text messages can be a more immediate and reliable way of sending notifications than email. Also, the short length of text messages makes it more likely that a person will get around to reading them.

In this section, you'll learn how to sign up for the free Twilio service and use its Python module to send text messages. Twilio is an *SMS gateway service*, which means it's a service that allows you to send text messages from your programs. Although the free trial account comes with a limited amount of credit and the texts will be prefixed with the words *Sent from a Twilio trial account*, this trial service is probably adequate for your personal programs.

But Twilio isn't the only SMS gateway service. If you prefer not to use Twilio, you can find alternative services by searching online for *free sms gateway*, *python sms api*, or even *twilio alternatives*.

Before signing up for a Twilio account, install the twilio module. Appendix A has more details about installing third-party modules.

NOTE *This section is specific to the United States. Twilio does offer SMS texting services for countries outside of the United States, but those specifics aren't covered in this book. The twilio module and its functions, however, will work the same outside the United States. See http://twilio.com/ for more information.*

Signing Up for a Twilio Account

Go to *http://twilio.com/* and fill out the sign-up form. Once you've signed up for a new account, you'll need to verify a mobile phone number that you want to send texts to. (This verification is necessary to prevent people from using the service to spam random phone numbers with text messages.)

After receiving the text with the verification number, enter it into the Twilio website to prove that you own the mobile phone you are verifying. You will now be able to send texts to this phone number using the twilio module.

Twilio provides your trial account with a phone number to use as the sender of text messages. You will need two more pieces of information: your account SID and the auth (authentication) token. You can find this information on the Dashboard page when you are logged in to your Twilio account. These values act as your Twilio username and password when logging in from a Python program.

Sending Text Messages

Once you've installed the `twilio` module, signed up for a Twilio account, verified your phone number, registered a Twilio phone number, and obtained your account SID and auth token, you will finally be ready to send yourself text messages from your Python scripts.

Compared to all the registration steps, the actual Python code is fairly simple. With your computer connected to the Internet, enter the following into the interactive shell, replacing the `accountSID`, `authToken`, `myTwilioNumber`, and `myCellPhone` variable values with your real information:

```
❶ >>> from twilio.rest import TwilioRestClient
   >>> accountSID = 'ACxxxxxxxxxxxxxxxxxxxxxxxxxxxxxxxxxx'
   >>> authToken  = 'xxxxxxxxxxxxxxxxxxxxxxxxxxxxxxxxxx'
❷ >>> twilioCli = TwilioRestClient(accountSID, authToken)
   >>> myTwilioNumber = '+14955551234'
   >>> myCellPhone = '+14955558888'
❸ >>> message = twilioCli.messages.create(body='Mr. Watson - Come here - I want
   to see you.', from_=myTwilioNumber, to=myCellPhone)
```

A few moments after typing the last line, you should receive a text message that reads *Sent from your Twilio trial account - Mr. Watson - Come here - I want to see you.*

Because of the way the `twilio` module is set up, you need to import it using `from twilio.rest import TwilioRestClient`, not just `import twilio` ❶. Store your account SID in `accountSID` and your auth token in `authToken` and then call `TwilioRestClient()` and pass it `accountSID` and `authToken`. The call to `TwilioRestClient()` returns a `TwilioRestClient` object ❷. This object has a `messages` attribute, which in turn has a `create()` method you can use to send text messages. This is the method that will instruct Twilio's servers to send your text message. After storing your Twilio number and cell phone number in `myTwilioNumber` and `myCellPhone`, respectively, call `create()` and pass it keyword arguments specifying the body of the text message, the sender's number (`myTwilioNumber`), and the recipient's number (`myCellPhone`) ❸.

The `Message` object returned from the `create()` method will have information about the text message that was sent. Continue the interactive shell example by entering the following:

```
>>> message.to
'+14955558888'
>>> message.from_
'+14955551234'
>>> message.body
'Mr. Watson - Come here - I want to see you.'
```

The `to`, `from_`, and `body` attributes should hold your cell phone number, Twilio number, and message, respectively. Note that the sending phone number is in the `from_` attribute—with an underscore at the end—not `from`. This is because `from` is a keyword in Python (you've seen it used in the `from` modulename import * form of import statement, for example), so it cannot be used as an attribute name. Continue the interactive shell example with the following:

```
>>> message.status
'queued'
>>> message.date_created
datetime.datetime(2015, 7, 8, 1, 36, 18)
>>> message.date_sent == None
True
```

The status attribute should give you a string. The date_created and date_sent attributes should give you a datetime object if the message has been created and sent. It may seem odd that the status attribute is set to 'queued' and the date_sent attribute is set to None when you've already received the text message. This is because you captured the Message object in the message variable *before* the text was actually sent. You will need to refetch the Message object in order to see its most up-to-date status and date_sent. Every Twilio message has a unique string ID (SID) that can be used to fetch the latest update of the Message object. Continue the interactive shell example by entering the following:

```
>>> message.sid
'SM09520de7639ba3af137c6fcb7c5f4b51'
❶ >>> updatedMessage = twilioCli.messages.get(message.sid)
>>> updatedMessage.status
'delivered'
>>> updatedMessage.date_sent
datetime.datetime(2015, 7, 8, 1, 36, 18)
```

Entering message.sid show you this message's long SID. By passing this SID to the Twilio client's get() method ❶, you can retrieve a new Message object with the most up-to-date information. In this new Message object, the status and date_sent attributes are correct.

The status attribute will be set to one of the following string values: 'queued', 'sending', 'sent', 'delivered', 'undelivered', or 'failed'. These statuses are self-explanatory, but for more precise details, take a look at the resources at *http://nostarch.com/automatestuff/*.

RECEIVING TEXT MESSAGES WITH PYTHON

Unfortunately, receiving text messages with Twilio is a bit more complicated than sending them. Twilio requires that you have a website running its own web application. That's beyond the scope of this book, but you can find more details in the resources for this book (*http://nostarch.com/automatestuff/*).

Project: "Just Text Me" Module

The person you'll most often text from your programs is probably you. Texting is a great way to send yourself notifications when you're away from your computer. If you've automated a boring task with a program that takes a couple of hours to run, you could have it notify you with a text when it's finished. Or you may have a regularly scheduled program running that sometimes needs to contact you, such as a weather-checking program that texts you a reminder to pack an umbrella.

As a simple example, here's a small Python program with a textmyself() function that sends a message passed to it as a string argument. Open a new file editor window and enter the following code, replacing the account SID, auth token, and phone numbers with your own information. Save it as *textMyself.py*.

```python3
#! python3
# textMyself.py - Defines the textmyself() function that texts a message
# passed to it as a string.

# Preset values:
accountSID = 'ACxxxxxxxxxxxxxxxxxxxxxxxxxxxxxxxxxx'
authToken  = 'xxxxxxxxxxxxxxxxxxxxxxxxxxxxxxxxxx'
myNumber = '+15559998888'
twilioNumber = '+15552225678'

from twilio.rest import TwilioRestClient

❶ def textmyself(message):
❷     twilioCli = TwilioRestClient(accountSID, authToken)
❸     twilioCli.messages.create(body=message, from_=twilioNumber, to=myNumber)
```

This program stores an account SID, auth token, sending number, and receiving number. It then defined textmyself() to take on argument ❶, make a TwilioRestClient object ❷, and call create() with the message you passed ❸.

If you want to make the textmyself() function available to your other programs, simply place the *textMyself.py* file in the same folder as the Python executable (*C:\Python34* on Windows, */usr/local/lib/python3.4* on OS X, and */usr/bin/python3* on Linux). Now you can use the function in your other programs. Whenever you want one of your programs to text you, just add the following:

```
import textmyself
textmyself.textmyself('The boring task is finished.')
```

You need to sign up for Twilio and write the texting code only once. After that, it's just two lines of code to send a text from any of your other programs.

Summary

We communicate with each other on the Internet and over cell phone networks in dozens of different ways, but email and texting predominate. Your programs can communicate through these channels, which gives them powerful new notification features. You can even write programs running on different computers that communicate with one another directly via email, with one program sending emails with SMTP and the other retrieving them with IMAP.

Python's `smtplib` provides functions for using the SMTP to send emails through your email provider's SMTP server. Likewise, the third-party `imapclient` and `pyzmail` modules let you access IMAP servers and retrieve emails sent to you. Although IMAP is a bit more involved than SMTP, it's also quite powerful and allows you to search for particular emails, download them, and parse them to extract the subject and body as string values.

Texting is a bit different from email, since, unlike email, more than just an Internet connection is needed to send SMS texts. Fortunately, services such as Twilio provide modules to allow you to send text messages from your programs. Once you go through an initial setup process, you'll be able to send texts with just a couple lines of code.

With these modules in your skill set, you'll be able to program the specific conditions under which your programs should send notifications or reminders. Now your programs will have reach far beyond the computer they're running on!

Practice Questions

1. What is the protocol for sending email? For checking and receiving email?

2. What four `smtplib` functions/methods must you call to log in to an SMTP server?

3. What two `imapclient` functions/methods must you call to log in to an IMAP server?

4. What kind of argument do you pass to `imapObj.search()`?

5. What do you do if your code gets an error message that says `got more than 10000 bytes`?

6. The `imapclient` module handles connecting to an IMAP server and finding emails. What is one module that handles reading the emails that `imapclient` collects?

7. What three pieces of information do you need from Twilio before you can send text messages?

Practice Projects

For practice, write programs that do the following.

Random Chore Assignment Emailer

Write a program that takes a list of people's email addresses and a list of chores that need to be done and randomly assigns chores to people. Email each person their assigned chores. If you're feeling ambitious, keep a record of each person's previously assigned chores so that you can make sure the program avoids assigning anyone the same chore they did last time. For another possible feature, schedule the program to run once a week automatically.

Here's a hint: If you pass a list to the `random.choice()` function, it will return a randomly selected item from the list. Part of your code could look like this:

```
chores = ['dishes', 'bathroom', 'vacuum', 'walk dog']
randomChore = random.choice(chores)
chores.remove(randomChore)    # this chore is now taken, so remove it
```

Umbrella Reminder

Chapter 11 showed you how to use the `requests` module to scrape data from *http://weather.gov/*. Write a program that runs just before you wake up in the morning and checks whether it's raining that day. If so, have the program text you a reminder to pack an umbrella before leaving the house.

Auto Unsubscriber

Write a program that scans through your email account, finds all the unsubscribe links in all your emails, and automatically opens them in a browser. This program will have to log in to your email provider's IMAP server and download all of your emails. You can use BeautifulSoup (covered in Chapter 11) to check for any instance where the word *unsubscribe* occurs within an HTML link tag.

Once you have a list of these URLs, you can use `webbrowser.open()` to automatically open all of these links in a browser.

You'll still have to manually go through and complete any additional steps to unsubscribe yourself from these lists. In most cases, this involves clicking a link to confirm.

But this script saves you from having to go through all of your emails looking for unsubscribe links. You can then pass this script along to your friends so they can run it on their email accounts. (Just make sure your email password isn't hardcoded in the source code!)

Controlling Your Computer Through Email

Write a program that checks an email account every 15 minutes for any instructions you email it and executes those instructions automatically. For example, BitTorrent is a peer-to-peer downloading system. Using free BitTorrent software such as qBittorrent, you can download large media files on your home computer. If you email the program a (completely legal, not at all piratical) BitTorrent link, the program will eventually check its email, find this message, extract the link, and then launch qBittorrent to start downloading the file. This way, you can have your home computer begin downloads while you're away, and the (completely legal, not at all piratical) download can be finished by the time you return home.

Chapter 15 covers how to launch programs on your computer using the subprocess.Popen() function. For example, the following call would launch the qBittorrent program, along with a torrent file:

```
qbProcess = subprocess.Popen(['C:\\Program Files (x86)\\qBittorrent\\
qbittorrent.exe', 'shakespeare_complete_works.torrent'])
```

Of course, you'll want the program to make sure the emails come from you. In particular, you might want to require that the emails contain a password, since it is fairly trivial for hackers to fake a "from" address in emails. The program should delete the emails it finds so that it doesn't repeat instructions every time it checks the email account. As an extra feature, have the program email or text you a confirmation every time it executes a command. Since you won't be sitting in front of the computer that is running the program, it's a good idea to use the logging functions (see Chapter 10) to write a text file log that you can check if errors come up.

qBittorrent (as well as other BitTorrent applications) has a feature where it can quit automatically after the download completes. Chapter 15 explains how you can determine when a launched application has quit with the wait() method for Popen objects. The wait() method call will block until qBittorrent has stopped, and then your program can email or text you a notification that the download has completed.

There are a lot of possible features you could add to this project. If you get stuck, you can download an example implementation of this program from *http://nostarch.com/automatestuff/*.

17

MANIPULATING IMAGES

If you have a digital camera or even if you just upload photos from your phone to Facebook, you probably cross paths with digital image files all the time. You may know how to use basic graphics software, such as Microsoft Paint or Paintbrush, or even more advanced applications such as Adobe Photoshop. But if you need to edit a massive number of images, editing them by hand can be a lengthy, boring job.

Enter Python. Pillow is a third-party Python module for interacting with image files. The module has several functions that make it easy to crop, resize, and edit the content of an image. With the power to manipulate images the same way you would with software such as Microsoft Paint or Adobe Photoshop, Python can automatically edit hundreds or thousands of images with ease.

Computer Image Fundamentals

In order to manipulate an image, you need to understand the basics of how computers deal with colors and coordinates in images and how you can work with colors and coordinates in Pillow. But before you continue, install the pillow module. See Appendix A for help installing third-party modules.

Colors and RGBA Values

Computer programs often represent a color in an image as an *RGBA value*. An RGBA value is a group of numbers that specify the amount of red, green, blue, and *alpha* (or transparency) in a color. Each of these component values is an integer from 0 (none at all) to 255 (the maximum). These RGBA values are assigned to individual *pixels*; a pixel is the smallest dot of a single color the computer screen can show (as you can imagine, there are millions of pixels on a screen). A pixel's RGB setting tells it precisely what shade of color it should display. Images also have an alpha value to create RGBA values. If an image is displayed on the screen over a background image or desktop wallpaper, the alpha value determines how much of the background you can "see through" the image's pixel.

In Pillow, RGBA values are represented by a tuple of four integer values. For example, the color red is represented by (255, 0, 0, 255). This color has the maximum amount of red, no green or blue, and the maximum alpha value, meaning it is fully opaque. Green is represented by (0, 255, 0, 255), and blue is (0, 0, 255, 255). White, the combination of all colors, is (255, 255, 255, 255), while black, which has no color at all, is (0, 0, 0, 255).

If a color has an alpha value of 0, it is invisible, and it doesn't really matter what the RGB values are. After all, invisible red looks the same as invisible black.

Pillow uses the standard color names that HTML uses. Table 17-1 lists a selection of standard color names and their values.

Table 17-1: Standard Color Names and Their RGBA Values

Name	RGBA value	Name	RGBA value
White	(255, 255, 255, 255)	Red	(255, 0, 0, 255)
Green	(0, 128, 0, 255)	Blue	(0, 0, 255, 255)
Gray	(128, 128, 128, 255)	Yellow	(255, 255, 0, 255)
Black	(0, 0, 0, 255)	Purple	(128, 0, 128, 255)

Pillow offers the ImageColor.getcolor() function so you don't have to memorize RGBA values for the colors you want to use. This function takes a color name string as its first argument, and the string 'RGBA' as its second argument, and it returns an RGBA tuple.

CMYK AND RGB COLORING

In grade school you learned that mixing red, yellow, and blue paints can form other colors; for example, you can mix blue and yellow to make green paint. This is known as the *subtractive color model*, and it applies to dyes, inks, and pigments. This is why color printers have *CMYK* ink cartridges: the *Cyan* (blue), *Magenta* (red), *Yellow*, and *blacK* ink can be mixed together to form any color.

However, the physics of light uses what's called an *additive color model*. When combining light (such as the light given off by your computer screen), red, green, and blue light can be combined to form any other color. This is why *RGB* values represent color in computer programs.

To see how this function works, enter the following into the interactive shell:

```
❶ >>> from PIL import ImageColor
❷ >>> ImageColor.getcolor('red', 'RGBA')
   (255, 0, 0, 255)
❸ >>> ImageColor.getcolor('RED', 'RGBA')
   (255, 0, 0, 255)
   >>> ImageColor.getcolor('Black', 'RGBA')
   (0, 0, 0, 255)
   >>> ImageColor.getcolor('chocolate', 'RGBA')
   (210, 105, 30, 255)
   >>> ImageColor.getcolor('CornflowerBlue', 'RGBA')
   (100, 149, 237, 255)
```

First, you need to import the `ImageColor` module from PIL ❶ (not from Pillow; you'll see why in a moment). The color name string you pass to `ImageColor.getcolor()` is case insensitive, so passing `'red'` ❷ and passing `'RED'` ❸ give you the same RGBA tuple. You can also pass more unusual color names, like `'chocolate'` and `'Cornflower Blue'`.

Pillow supports a huge number of color names, from `'aliceblue'` to `'whitesmoke'`. You can find the full list of more than 100 standard color names in the resources at *http://nostarch.com/automatestuff/*.

Coordinates and Box Tuples

Image pixels are addressed with x- and y-coordinates, which respectively specify a pixel's horizontal and vertical location in an image. The *origin* is the pixel at the top-left corner of the image and is specified with the notation (0, 0). The first zero represents the x-coordinate, which starts at zero at the origin and increases going from left to right. The second zero represents the y-coordinate, which starts at zero at the origin and increases going down the image. This bears repeating: y-coordinates increase going downward, which is the opposite of how you may remember y-coordinates being used in math class. Figure 17-1 demonstrates how this coordinate system works.

Many of Pillow's functions and methods take a *box tuple* argument. This means Pillow is expecting a tuple of four integer coordinates that represent a rectangular region in an image. The four integers are, in order, as follows:

Figure 17-1: The x- and y-coordinates of a 27×26 image of some sort of ancient data storage device

- *Left*: The x-coordinate of the leftmost edge of the box.
- *Top*: The y-coordinate of the top edge of the box.
- *Right*: The x-coordinate of one pixel to the right of the rightmost edge of the box. This integer must be greater than the left integer.
- *Bottom*: The y-coordinate of one pixel lower than the bottom edge of the box. This integer must be greater than the top integer.

Note that the box includes the left and top coordinates and goes up to but does not include the right and bottom coordinates. For example, the box tuple (3, 1, 9, 6) represents all the pixels in the black box in Figure 17-2.

Figure 17-2: The area represented by the box tuple (3, 1, 9, 6)

Manipulating Images with Pillow

Now that you know how colors and coordinates work in Pillow, let's use Pillow to manipulate an image. Figure 17-3 is the image that will be used for all the interactive shell examples in this chapter. You can download it from *http://nostarch.com/automatestuff/*.

Once you have the image file *Zophie.png* in your current working directory, you'll be ready to load the image of Zophie into Python, like so:

```
>>> from PIL import Image
>>> catIm = Image.open('zophie.png')
```

Figure 17-3: My cat Zophie. The camera adds 10 pounds (which is a lot for a cat).

To load the image, you import the `Image` module from Pillow and call `Image.open()`, passing it the image's filename. You can then store the loaded image in a variable like `CatIm`. The module name of Pillow is `PIL` to make it backward compatible with an older module called Python Imaging Library, which is why you must run `from PIL import Image` instead of `from Pillow import Image`. Because of the way Pillow's creators set up the `pillow` module, you must use the `from PIL import Image` form of `import` statement, rather than simply `import PIL`.

If the image file isn't in the current working directory, change the working directory to the folder that contains the image file by calling the `os.chdir()` function.

```
>>> import os
>>> os.chdir('C:\\folder_with_image_file')
```

The `Image.open()` function returns a value of the `Image` object data type, which is how Pillow represents an image as a Python value. You can load an `Image` object from an image file (of any format) by passing the `Image.open()` function a string of the filename. Any changes you make to the `Image` object can be saved to an image file (also of any format) with the `save()` method. All the rotations, resizing, cropping, drawing, and other image manipulations will be done through method calls on this `Image` object.

To shorten the examples in this chapter, I'll assume you've imported Pillow's `Image` module and that you have the Zophie image stored in a variable named `catIm`. Be sure that the *zophie.png* file is in the current working directory so that the `Image.open()` function can find it. Otherwise, you will also have to specify the full absolute path in the string argument to `Image.open()`.

Working with the Image Data Type

An `Image` object has several useful attributes that give you basic information about the image file it was loaded from: its width and height, the filename, and the graphics format (such as JPEG, GIF, or PNG).

For example, enter the following into the interactive shell:

```
>>> from PIL import Image
>>> catIm = Image.open('zophie.png')
>>> catIm.size
❶ (816, 1088)
❷ >>> width, height = catIm.size
❸ >>> width
816
❹ >>> height
1088
>>> catIm.filename
'zophie.png'
>>> catIm.format
'PNG'
>>> catIm.format_description
'Portable network graphics'
❺ >>> catIm.save('zophie.jpg')
```

After making an `Image` object from *Zophie.png* and storing the `Image` object in `catIm`, we can see that the object's `size` attribute contains a tuple of the image's width and height in pixels ❶. We can assign the values in the tuple to `width` and `height` variables ❷ in order to access with `width` ❸ and `height` ❹ individually. The `filename` attribute describes the original file's name. The `format` and `format_description` attributes are strings that describe the image format of the original file (with `format_description` being a bit more verbose).

Finally, calling the save() method and passing it `'zophie.jpg'` saves a new image with the filename *zophie.jpg* to your hard drive ❺. Pillow sees that the file extension is *.jpg* and automatically saves the image using the JPEG image format. Now you should have two images, *zophie.png* and *zophie.jpg*, on your hard drive. While these files are based on the same image, they are not identical because of their different formats.

Pillow also provides the `Image.new()` function, which returns an `Image` object—much like `Image.open()`, except the image represented by `Image.new()`'s object will be blank. The arguments to `Image.new()` are as follows:

- The string `'RGBA'`, which sets the color mode to RGBA. (There are other modes that this book doesn't go into.)

- The size, as a two-integer tuple of the new image's width and height.

- The background color that the image should start with, as a four-integer tuple of an RGBA value. You can use the return value of the ImageColor.getcolor() function for this argument. Alternatively, Image.new() also supports just passing the string of the standard color name.

For example, enter the following into the interactive shell:

```
>>> from PIL import Image
❶ >>> im = Image.new('RGBA', (100, 200), 'purple')
>>> im.save('purpleImage.png')
❷ >>> im2 = Image.new('RGBA', (20, 20))
>>> im2.save('transparentImage.png')
```

Here we create an Image object for an image that's 100 pixels wide and 200 pixels tall, with a purple background ❶. This image is then saved to the file *purpleImage.png*. We call Image.new() again to create another Image object, this time passing (20, 20) for the dimensions and nothing for the background color ❷. Invisible black, (0, 0, 0, 0), is the default color used if no color argument is specified, so the second image has a transparent background; we save this 20×20 transparent square in *transparentImage.png*.

Cropping Images

Cropping an image means selecting a rectangular region inside an image and removing everything outside the rectangle. The crop() method on Image objects takes a box tuple and returns an Image object representing the cropped image. The cropping does not happen in place—that is, the original Image object is left untouched, and the crop() method returns a new Image object. Remeber that a boxed tuple—in this case, the cropped section—includes the left column and top row of pixels but only goes up to and does *not* include the right column and bottom row of pixels.

Enter the following into the interactive shell:

```
>>> croppedIm = catIm.crop((335, 345, 565, 560))
>>> croppedIm.save('cropped.png')
```

This makes a new Image object for the cropped image, stores the object in croppedIm, and then calls save() on croppedIm to save the cropped image in *cropped.png*. The new file *cropped.png* will be created from the original image, like in Figure 17-4.

Figure 17-4: The new image will be just the cropped section of the original image.

Copying and Pasting Images onto Other Images

The copy() method will return a new Image object with the same image as the Image object it was called on. This is useful if you need to make changes to an image but also want to keep an untouched version of the original. For example, enter the following into the interactive shell:

```
>>> catIm = Image.open('zophie.png')
>>> catCopyIm = catIm.copy()
```

The catIm and catCopyIm variables contain two separate Image objects, which both have the same image on them. Now that you have an Image object stored in catCopyIm, you can modify catCopyIm as you like and save it to a new filename, leaving *zophie.png* untouched. For example, let's try modifying catCopyIm with the paste() method.

The paste() method is called on an Image object and pastes another image on top of it. Let's continue the shell example by pasting a smaller image onto catCopyIm.

```
>>> faceIm = catIm.crop((335, 345, 565, 560))
>>> faceIm.size
(230, 215)
>>> catCopyIm.paste(faceIm, (0, 0))
>>> catCopyIm.paste(faceIm, (400, 500))
>>> catCopyIm.save('pasted.png')
```

First we pass crop() a box tuple for the rectangular area in *zophie.png* that contains Zophie's face. This creates an Image object representing a 230×215 crop, which we store in faceIm. Now we can paste faceIm onto catCopyIm. The paste() method takes two arguments: a "source" Image object and a tuple of the x- and y-coordinates where you want to paste the top-left corner of the source Image object onto the main Image object. Here we call paste() twice on catCopyIm, passing (0, 0) the first time and (400, 500) the second time. This pastes faceIm onto catCopyIm twice: once with the top-left corner of faceIm at (0, 0) on catCopyIm, and once with the top-left corner of faceIm at (400, 500). Finally, we save the modified catCopyIm to *pasted.png*. The *pasted.png* image looks like Figure 17-5.

Figure 17-5: Zophie the cat, with her face pasted twice

Note that the paste() method modifies its Image object *in place*; it does not return an Image object with the pasted image. If you want to call paste() but also keep an untouched version of the original image around, you'll need to first copy the image and then call paste() on that copy.

Say you want to tile Zophie's head across the entire image, as in Figure 17-6. You can achieve this effect with just a couple for loops. Continue the interactive shell example by entering the following:

```
>>> catImWidth, catImHeight = catIm.size
>>> faceImWidth, faceImHeight = faceIm.size
❶ >>> catCopyTwo = catIm.copy()
```

```
❷ >>> for left in range(0, catImWidth, faceImWidth):
❸         for top in range(0, catImHeight, faceImHeight):
              print(left, top)
              catCopyTwo.paste(faceIm, (left, top))
0 0
0 215
0 430
0 645
0 860
0 1075
230 0
230 215
--snip--
690 860
690 1075
>>> catCopyTwo.save('tiled.png')
```

Here we store the width of height of catIm in catImWidth and catImHeight. At ❶ we make a copy of catIm and store it in catCopyTwo. Now that we have a copy that we can paste onto, we start looping to paste faceIm onto catCopyTwo. The outer for loop's left variable starts at 0 and increases by faceImWidth(230) ❷. The inner for loop's top variable start at 0 and increases by faceImHeight(215) ❸. These nested for loops produce values for left and top to paste a grid of faceIm images over the catCopyTwo Image object, as in Figure 17-6. To see our nested loops working, we print left and top. After the pasting is complete, we save the modified catCopyTwo to *tiled.png*.

Figure 17-6: Nested for loops used with paste() to duplicate the cat's face (a dupli-cat, if you will).

Resizing an Image

The resize() method is called on an Image object and returns a new Image object of the specified width and height. It accepts a two-integer tuple argument, representing the new width and height of the returned image. Enter the following into the interactive shell:

```
❶ >>> width, height = catIm.size
❷ >>> quartersizedIm = catIm.resize((int(width / 2), int(height / 2)))
   >>> quartersizedIm.save('quartersized.png')
❸ >>> svelteIm = catIm.resize((width, height + 300))
   >>> svelteIm.save('svelte.png')
```

Here we assign the two values in the catIm.size tuple to the variables width and height ❶. Using width and height instead of catIm.size[0] and catIm.size[1] makes the rest of the code more readable.

The first resize() call passes int(width / 2) for the new width and int(height / 2) for the new height ❷, so the Image object returned from resize() will be half the length and width of the original image, or one-quarter of the original image size overall. The resize() method accepts only integers in its tuple argument, which is why you needed to wrap both divisions by 2 in an int() call.

This resizing keeps the same proportions for the width and height. But the new width and height passed to resize() do not have to be proportional to the original image. The svelteIm variable contains an Image object that has the original width but a height that is 300 pixels taller ❸, giving Zophie a more slender look.

Note that the resize() method does not edit the Image object in place but instead returns a new Image object.

Rotating and Flipping Images

Images can be rotated with the rotate() method, which returns a new Image object of the rotated image and leaves the original Image object unchanged. The argument to rotate() is a single integer or float representing the number of degrees to rotate the image counterclockwise. Enter the following into the interactive shell:

```
>>> catIm.rotate(90).save('rotated90.png')
>>> catIm.rotate(180).save('rotated180.png')
>>> catIm.rotate(270).save('rotated270.png')
```

Note how you can *chain* method calls by calling save() directly on the Image object returned from rotate(). The first rotate() and save() call makes a new Image object representing the image rotated counterclockwise by 90 degrees and saves the rotated image to *rotated90.png*. The second and third calls do the same, but with 180 degress and 270 degress. The results look like Figure 17-7.

Figure 17-7: The original image (left) and the image rotated counterclockwise by 90, 180, and 270 degrees

Notice that the width and height of the image change when the image is rotated 90 or 270 degrees. If you rotate an image by some other amount, the original dimensions of the image are maintained. On Windows, a black background is used to fill in any gaps made by the rotation, like in Figure 17-8. On OS X, transparent pixels are used for the gaps instead.

The rotate() method has an optional expand keyword argument that can be set to True to enlarge the dimensions of the image to fit the entire rotated new image. For example, enter the following into the interactive shell:

```
>>> catIm.rotate(6).save('rotated6.png')
>>> catIm.rotate(6, expand=True).save('rotated6_expanded.png')
```

The first call rotates the image 6 degrees and saves it to *rotate6.png* (see the image on the left of Figure 17-8). The second call rotates the image 6 degrees with expand set to True and saves it to *rotate6_expanded.png* (see the image on the right of Figure 17-8).

Figure 17-8: The image rotated 6 degrees normally (left) and with expand=True (right)

You can also get a "mirror flip" of an image with the transpose() method. You must pass either Image.FLIP_LEFT_RIGHT or Image.FLIP_TOP_BOTTOM to the transpose() method. Enter the following into the interactive shell:

```
>>> catIm.transpose(Image.FLIP_LEFT_RIGHT).save('horizontal_flip.png')
>>> catIm.transpose(Image.FLIP_TOP_BOTTOM).save('vertical_flip.png')
```

Like rotate(), transpose() creates a new Image object. Here was pass Image.FLIP_LEFT_RIGHT to flip the image horizontally and then save the result to *horizontal_flip.png*. To flip the image vertically, we pass Image.FLIP_TOP_BOTTOM and save to *vertical_flip.png*. The results look like Figure 17-9.

Figure 17-9: The original image (left), horizontal flip (center), and vertical flip (right)

Changing Individual Pixels

The color of an individual pixel can be retrieved or set with the getpixel() and putpixel() methods. These methods both take a tuple representing the x- and y-coordinates of the pixel. The putpixel() method also takes an additional tuple argument for the color of the pixel. This color argument is a four-integer RGBA tuple or a three-integer RGB tuple. Enter the following into the interactive shell:

```
❶ >>> im = Image.new('RGBA', (100, 100))
❷ >>> im.getpixel((0, 0))
   (0, 0, 0, 0)
❸ >>> for x in range(100):
           for y in range(50):
❹              im.putpixel((x, y), (210, 210, 210))

   >>> from PIL import ImageColor
❺ >>> for x in range(100):
           for y in range(50, 100):
❻              im.putpixel((x, y), ImageColor.getcolor('darkgray', 'RGBA'))
   >>> im.getpixel((0, 0))
   (210, 210, 210, 255)
   >>> im.getpixel((0, 50))
   (169, 169, 169, 255)
   >>> im.save('putPixel.png')
```

At ❶ we make a new image that is a 100×100 transparent square. Calling getpixel() on some coordinates in this image returns (0, 0, 0, 0) because the image is transparent ❷. To color pixels in this image, we can use nested for loops to go through all the pixels in the top half of the image ❸ and color each pixel using putpixel() ❹. Here we pass putpixel() the RGB tuple (210, 210, 210), a light gray.

Say we want to color the bottom half of the image dark gray but don't know the RGB tuple for dark gray. The putpixel() method doesn't accept a standard color name like 'darkgray', so you have to use ImageColor.getcolor() to get a color tuple from 'darkgray'. Loop through the pixels in the bottom half of the image ❺ and pass putpixel() the return value of ImageColor.getcolor() ❻, and you should now have an image that is light gray in its top half and dark gray in the bottom half, as shown in Figure 17-10. You can call getpixel() on some coordinates to confirm that the color at any given pixel is what you expect. Finally, save the image to *putPixel.png*.

Figure 17-10: The putPixel.png *image*

Of course, drawing one pixel at a time onto an image isn't very convenient. If you need to draw shapes, use the ImageDraw functions explained later in this chapter.

Project: Adding a Logo

Say you have the boring job of resizing thousands of images and adding a small logo watermark to the corner of each. Doing this with a basic graphics program such as Paintbrush or Paint would take forever. A fancier graphics application such as Photoshop can do batch processing, but that software costs hundreds of dollars. Let's write a script to do it instead.

Say that Figure 17-11 is the logo you want to add to the bottom-right corner of each image: a black cat icon with a white border, with the rest of the image transparent.

Figure 17-11: The logo to be added to the image.

At a high level, here's what the program should do:

- Load the logo image.
- Loop over all *.png* and *.jpg* files in the working directory.
- Check whether the image is wider or taller than 300 pixels.
- If so, reduce the width or height (whichever is larger) to 300 pixels and scale down the other dimension proportionally.
- Paste the logo image into the corner.
- Save the altered images to another folder.

This means the code will need to do the following:

- Open the *catlogo.png* file as an `Image` object.
- Loop over the strings returned from `os.listdir('.')`.
- Get the width and height of the image from the `size` attribute.
- Calculate the new width and height of the resized image.
- Call the `resize()` method to resize the image.
- Call the `paste()` method to paste the logo.
- Call the `save()` method to save the changes, using the original filename.

Step 1: Open the Logo Image

For this project, open a new file editor window, enter the following code, and save it as *resizeAndAddLogo.py*:

```
#! python3
# resizeAndAddLogo.py - Resizes all images in current working directory to fit
# in a 300x300 square, and adds catlogo.png to the lower-right corner.
```

```
import os
from PIL import Image
```

❶ `SQUARE_FIT_SIZE = 300`
❷ `LOGO_FILENAME = 'catlogo.png'`

❸ `logoIm = Image.open(LOGO_FILENAME)`
❹ `logoWidth, logoHeight = logoIm.size`

```
    # TODO: Loop over all files in the working directory.

    # TODO: Check if image needs to be resized.

    # TODO: Calculate the new width and height to resize to.

    # TODO: Resize the image.

    # TODO: Add the logo.

    # TODO: Save changes.
```

By setting up the SQUARE_FIT_SIZE ❶ and LOGO_FILENAME ❷ constants at the start of the program, we've made it easy to change the program later. Say the logo that you're adding isn't the cat icon, or say you're reducing the output images' largest dimension to something other than 300 pixels. With these constants at the start of the program, you can just open the code, change those values once, and you're done. (Or you can make it so that the values for these constants are taken from the command line arguments.) Without these constants, you'd instead have to search the code for all instances of 300 and 'catlogo.png' and replace them with the values for your new project. In short, using constants makes your program more generalized.

The logo Image object is returned from Image.open() ❸. For readability, logoWidth and logoHeight are assigned to the values from logoIm.size ❹.

The rest of the program is a skeleton of TODO comments for now.

Step 2: Loop Over All Files and Open Images

Now you need to find every *.png* file and *.jpg* file in the current working directory. Note that you don't want to add the logo image to the logo image itself, so the program should skip any image with a filename that's the same as LOGO_FILENAME. Add the following to your code:

```
#! python3
# resizeAndAddLogo.py - Resizes all images in current working directory to fit
# in a 300x300 square, and adds catlogo.png to the lower-right corner.

import os
from PIL import Image

--snip--
```

```
    os.makedirs('withLogo', exist_ok=True)
    # Loop over all files in the working directory.
❶ for filename in os.listdir('.'):
❷     if not (filename.endswith('.png') or filename.endswith('.jpg')) \
           or filename == LOGO_FILENAME:
❸          continue    # skip non-image files and the logo file itself

❹     im = Image.open(filename)
       width, height = im.size
```

--snip--

First, the os.makedirs() call creates a *withLogo* folder to store the finished images with logos, instead of overwriting the original image files. The exist_ok=True keyword argument will keep os.makedirs() from raising an exception if *withLogo* already exists. While looping through all the files in the working directory with os.listdir('.') ❶, the long if statement ❷ checks whether each filename doesn't end with *.png* or *.jpg*. If so—or if the file is the logo image itself—then the loop should skip it and use continue ❸ to go to the next file. If filename *does* end with '.png' or '.jpg' (and isn't the logo file), you can open it as an Image object ❹ and set width and height.

Step 3: Resize the Images

The program should resize the image only if the width or height is larger than SQUARE_FIT_SIZE (300 pixels, in this case), so put all of the resizing code inside an if statement that checks the width and height variables. Add the following code to your program:

```
#! python3
# resizeAndAddLogo.py - Resizes all images in current working directory to fit
# in a 300x300 square, and adds catlogo.png to the lower-right corner.

import os
from PIL import Image

--snip--

    # Check if image needs to be resized.
    if width > SQUARE_FIT_SIZE and height > SQUARE_FIT_SIZE:
        # Calculate the new width and height to resize to.
        if width > height:
❶          height = int((SQUARE_FIT_SIZE / width) * height)
            width = SQUARE_FIT_SIZE
        else:
❷          width = int((SQUARE_FIT_SIZE / height) * width)
            height = SQUARE_FIT_SIZE

        # Resize the image.
        print('Resizing %s...' % (filename))
❸          im = im.resize((width, height))

--snip--
```

If the image does need to be resized, you need to find out whether it is a wide or tall image. If width is greater than height, then the height should be reduced by the same proportion that the width would be reduced ❶. This proportion is the SQUARE_FIT_SIZE value divided by the current width. The new height value is this proportion multiplied by the current height value. Since the division operator returns a float value and resize() requires the dimensions to be integers, remember to convert the result to an integer with the int() function. Finally, the new width value will simply be set to SQUARE_FIT_SIZE.

If the height is greater than or equal to the width (both cases are handled in the else clause), then the same calculation is done, except with the height and width variables swapped ❷.

Once width and height contain the new image dimensions, pass them to the resize() method and store the returned Image object in im ❸.

Step 4: Add the Logo and Save the Changes

Whether or not the image was resized, the logo should still be pasted to the bottom-right corner. Where exactly the logo should be pasted depends on both the size of the image and the size of the logo. Figure 17-12 shows how to calculate the pasting position. The left coordinate for where to paste the logo will be the image width minus the logo width; the top coordinate for where to paste the logo will be the image height minus the logo height.

Figure 17-12: The left and top coordinates for placing the logo in the bottom-right corner should be the image width/height minus the logo width/height.

After your code pastes the logo into the image, it should save the modified Image object. Add the following to your program:

```python3
#! python3
# resizeAndAddLogo.py - Resizes all images in current working directory to fit
# in a 300x300 square, and adds catlogo.png to the lower-right corner.

import os
from PIL import Image
```

```
--snip--

    # Check if image needs to be resized.
    --snip--

    # Add the logo.
❶   print('Adding logo to %s...' % (filename))
❷   im.paste(logoIm, (width - logoWidth, height - logoHeight), logoIm)

    # Save changes.
❸   im.save(os.path.join('withLogo', filename))
```

The new code prints a message telling the user that the logo is being added ❶, pastes logoIm onto im at the calculated coordinates ❷, and saves the changes to a filename in the *withLogo* directory ❸. When you run this program with the *zophie.png* file as the only image in the working directory, the output will look like this:

```
Resizing zophie.png...
Adding logo to zophie.png...
```

The image *zophie.png* will be changed to a 225×300-pixel image that looks like Figure 17-13. Remember that the paste() method will not paste the transparency pixels if you do not pass the logoIm for the third argument as well. This program can automatically resize and "logo-ify" hundreds of images in just a couple minutes.

Figure 17-13: The image zophie.png *resized and the logo added (left). If you forget the third argument, the transparent pixels in the logo will be copied as solid white pixels (right).*

Ideas for Similar Programs

Being able to composite images or modify image sizes in a batch can be useful in many applications. You could write similar programs to do the following:

- Add text or a website URL to images.
- Add timestamps to images.
- Copy or move images into different folders based on their sizes.
- Add a mostly transparent watermark to an image to prevent others from copying it.

Drawing on Images

If you need to draw lines, rectangles, circles, or other simple shapes on an image, use Pillow's ImageDraw module. Enter the following into the interactive shell:

```
>>> from PIL import Image, ImageDraw
>>> im = Image.new('RGBA', (200, 200), 'white')
>>> draw = ImageDraw.Draw(im)
```

First, we import Image and ImageDraw. Then we create a new image, in this case, a 200×200 white image, and store the Image object in im. We pass the Image object to the ImageDraw.Draw() function to receive an ImageDraw object. This object has several methods for drawing shapes and text onto an Image object. Store the ImageDraw object in a variable like draw so you can use it easily in the following example.

Drawing Shapes

The following ImageDraw methods draw various kinds of shapes on the image. The fill and outline parameters for these methods are optional and will default to white if left unspecified.

Points

The point(*xy*, *fill*) method draws individual pixels. The *xy* argument represents a list of the points you want to draw. The list can be a list of x- and y-coordinate tuples, such as [(x, y), (x, y), ...], or a list of x- and y-coordinates without tuples, such as [x1, y1, x2, y2, ...]. The *fill* argument is the color of the points and is either an RGBA tuple or a string of a color name, such as 'red'. The *fill* argument is optional.

Lines

The line(*xy*, *fill*, *width*) method draws a line or series of lines. *xy* is either a list of tuples, such as [(x, y), (x, y), ...], or a list of integers, such as [x1, y1, x2, y2, ...]. Each point is one of the connecting points on the lines you're drawing. The optional *fill* argument is the color of the lines, as an RGBA tuple or color name. The optional *width* argument is the width of the lines and defaults to 1 if left unspecified.

Rectangles

The `rectangle(`*xy, fill, outline*`)` method draws a rectangle. The *xy* argument is a box tuple of the form (*left, top, right, bottom*). The *left* and *top* values specify the x- and y-coordinates of the upper-left corner of the rectangle, while *right* and *bottom* specify the lower-right corner. The optional *fill* argument is the color that will fill the inside of the rectangle. The optional *outline* argument is the color of the rectangle's outline.

Ellipses

The `ellipse(`*xy, fill, outline*`)` method draws an ellipse. If the width and height of the ellipse are identical, this method will draw a circle. The *xy* argument is a box tuple (*left, top, right, bottom*) that represents a box that precisely contains the ellipse. The optional *fill* argument is the color of the inside of the ellipse, and the optional *outline* argument is the color of the ellipse's outline.

Polygons

The `polygon(`*xy, fill, outline*`)` method draws an arbitrary polygon. The *xy* argument is a list of tuples, such as [(x, y), (x, y), ...], or integers, such as [x1, y1, x2, y2, ...], representing the connecting points of the polygon's sides. The last pair of coordinates will be automatically connected to the first pair. The optional *fill* argument is the color of the inside of the polygon, and the optional *outline* argument is the color of the polygon's outline.

Drawing Example

Enter the following into the interactive shell:

```
>>> from PIL import Image, ImageDraw
>>> im = Image.new('RGBA', (200, 200), 'white')
>>> draw = ImageDraw.Draw(im)
❶ >>> draw.line([(0, 0), (199, 0), (199, 199), (0, 199), (0, 0)], fill='black')
❷ >>> draw.rectangle((20, 30, 60, 60), fill='blue')
❸ >>> draw.ellipse((120, 30, 160, 60), fill='red')
❹ >>> draw.polygon(((57, 87), (79, 62), (94, 85), (120, 90), (103, 113)),
    fill='brown')
❺ >>> for i in range(100, 200, 10):
        draw.line([(i, 0), (200, i - 100)], fill='green')

>>> im.save('drawing.png')
```

After making an `Image` object for a 200×200 white image, passing it to `ImageDraw.Draw()` to get an `ImageDraw` object, and storing the `ImageDraw` object in `draw`, you can call drawing methods on `draw`. Here we make a thin, black outline at the edges of the image ❶, a blue rectangle with its top-left corner at (20, 30) and bottom-right corner at (60, 60) ❷, a red ellipse defined by a box from (120, 30) to (160, 60) ❸, a brown polygon with five points ❹, and a pattern of green lines drawn with a for loop ❺. The resulting *drawing.png* file will look like Figure 17-14.

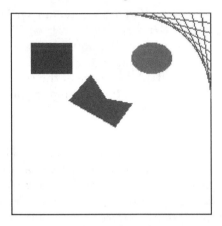

Figure 17-14: The resulting drawing.png *image*

There are several other shape-drawing methods for ImageDraw objects. The full documentation is available at *http://pillow.readthedocs.org/en/latest/reference/ImageDraw.html*.

Drawing Text

The ImageDraw object also has a text() method for drawing text onto an image. The text() method takes four arguments: *xy*, *text*, *fill*, and *font*.

- The *xy* argument is a two-integer tuple specifying the upper-left corner of the text box.
- The *text* argument is the string of text you want to write.
- The optional *fill* argument is the color of the text.
- The optional *font* argument is an ImageFont object, used to set the typeface and size of the text. This is described in more detail in the next section.

Since it's often hard to know in advance what size a block of text will be in a given font, the ImageDraw module also offers a textsize() method. Its first argument is the string of text you want to measure, and its second argument is an optional ImageFont object. The textsize() method will then return a two-integer tuple of the width and height that the text in the given font would be if it were written onto the image. You can use this width and height to help you calculate exactly where you want to put the text on your image.

The first three arguments for text() are straightforward. Before we use text() to draw text onto an image, let's look at the optional fourth argument, the ImageFont object.

Both text() and textsize() take an optional ImageFont object as their final arguments. To create one of these objects, first run the following:

```
>>> from PIL import ImageFont
```

Now that you've imported Pillow's ImageFont module, you can call the ImageFont.truetype() function, which takes two arguments. The first argument is a string for the font's *TrueType file*—this is the actual font file that lives on your hard drive. A TrueType file has the *.ttf* file extension and can usually be found in the following folders:

- On Windows: *C:\Windows\Fonts*
- On OS X: */Library/Fonts* and */System/Library/Fonts*
- On Linux: */usr/share/fonts/truetype*

You don't actually need to enter these paths as part of the TrueType file string because Python knows to automatically search for fonts in these directories. But Python will display an error if it is unable to find the font you specified.

The second argument to ImageFont.truetype() is an integer for the font size in *points* (rather than, say, pixels). Keep in mind that Pillow creates PNG images that are 72 pixels per inch by default, and a point is 1/72 of an inch.

Enter the following into the interactive shell, replacing FONT_FOLDER with the actual folder name your operating system uses:

```
>>> from PIL import Image, ImageDraw, ImageFont
>>> import os
❶ >>> im = Image.new('RGBA', (200, 200), 'white')
❷ >>> draw = ImageDraw.Draw(im)
❸ >>> draw.text((20, 150), 'Hello', fill='purple')
>>> fontsFolder = 'FONT_FOLDER' # e.g. '/Library/Fonts'
❹ >>> arialFont = ImageFont.truetype(os.path.join(fontsFolder, 'arial.ttf'), 32)
❺ >>> draw.text((100, 150), 'Howdy', fill='gray', font=arialFont)
>>> im.save('text.png')
```

After importing Image, ImageDraw, ImageFont, and os, we make an Image object for a new 200×200 white image ❶ and make an ImageDraw object from the Image object ❷. We use text() to draw *Hello* at (20, 150) in purple ❸. We didn't pass the optional fourth argument in this text() call, so the typeface and size of this text aren't customized.

To set a typeface and size, we first store the folder name (like */Library/ Fonts*) in fontsFolder. Then we call ImageFont.truetype(), passing it the *.ttf* file for the font we want, followed by an integer font size ❹. Store the Font object you get from ImageFont.truetype() in a variable like arialFont, and then pass the variable to text() in the final keyword argument. The text() call at ❺ draws *Howdy* at (100, 150) in gray in 32-point Arial.

The resulting *text.png* file will look like Figure 17-15.

Figure 17-15: The resulting text.png *image*

Summary

Images consist of a collection of pixels, and each pixel has an RGBA value for its color and its addressable by x- and y-coordinates. Two common image formats are JPEG and PNG. The pillow module can handle both of these image formats and others.

When an image is loaded into an Image object, its width and height dimensions are stored as a two-integer tuple in the size attribute. Objects of the Image data type also have methods for common image manipulations: crop(), copy(), paste(), resize(), rotate(), and transpose(). To save the Image object to an image file, call the save() method.

If you want your program to draw shapes onto an image, use ImageDraw methods to draw points, lines, rectangles, ellipses, and polygons. The module also provides methods for drawing text in a typeface and font size of your choosing.

Although advanced (and expensive) applications such as Photoshop provide automatic batch processing features, you can use Python scripts to do many of the same modifications for free. In the previous chapters, you wrote Python programs to deal with plaintext files, spreadsheets, PDFs, and other formats. With the pillow module, you've extended your programming powers to processing images as well!

Practice Questions

1. What is an RGBA value?

2. How can you get the RGBA value of 'CornflowerBlue' from the Pillow module?

3. What is a box tuple?

4. What function returns an Image object for, say, an image file named *zophie.png*?

5. How can you find out the width and height of an `Image` object's image?

6. What method would you call to get `Image` object for a 100×100 image, excluding the lower left quarter of it?

7. After making changes to an `Image` object, how could you save it as an image file?

8. What module contains Pillow's shape-drawing code?

9. `Image` objects do not have drawing methods. What kind of object does? How do you get this kind of object?

Practice Projects

For practice, write programs that do the following.

Extending and Fixing the Chapter Project Programs

The *resizeAndAddLogo.py* program in this chapter works with PNG and JPEG files, but Pillow supports many more formats than just these two. Extend *resizeAndAddLogo.py* to process GIF and BMP images as well.

Another small issue is that the program modifies PNG and JPEG files only if their file extensions are set in lowercase. For example, it will process *zophie.png* but not *zophie.PNG*. Change the code so that the file extension check is case insensitive.

Finally, the logo added to the bottom-right corner is meant to be just a small mark, but if the image is about the same size as the logo itself, the result will look like Figure 17-16. Modify *resizeAndAddLogo.py* so that the image must be at least twice the width and height of the logo image before the logo is pasted. Otherwise, it should skip adding the logo.

Figure 17-16: When the image isn't much larger than the logo, the results look ugly.

Identifying Photo Folders on the Hard Drive

I have a bad habit of transferring files from my digital camera to temporary folders somewhere on the hard drive and then forgetting about these folders. It would be nice to write a program that could scan the entire hard drive and find these leftover "photo folders."

Write a program that goes through every folder on your hard drive and finds potential photo folders. Of course, first you'll have to define what you consider a "photo folder" to be; let's say that it's any folder where more than half of the files are photos. And how do you define what files are photos?

First, a photo file must have the file extension *.png* or *.jpg*. Also, photos are large images; a photo file's width and height must both be larger than 500 pixels. This is a safe bet, since most digital camera photos are several thousand pixels in width and height.

As a hint, here's a rough skeleton of what this program might look like:

```
#! python3
# Import modules and write comments to describe this program.

for foldername, subfolders, filenames in os.walk('C:\\'):
    numPhotoFiles = 0
    numNonPhotoFiles = 0
    for filename in filenames:
        # Check if file extension isn't .png or .jpg.
        if TODO:
            numNonPhotoFiles += 1
            continue    # skip to next filename

        # Open image file using Pillow.

        # Check if width & height are larger than 500.
        if TODO:
            # Image is large enough to be considered a photo.
            numPhotoFiles += 1
        else:
            # Image is too small to be a photo.
            numNonPhotoFiles += 1

    # If more than half of files were photos,
    # print the absolute path of the folder.
    if TODO:
        print(TODO)
```

When the program runs, it should print the absolute path of any photo folders to the screen.

Custom Seating Cards

Chapter 13 included a practice project to create custom invitations from a list of guests in a plaintext file. As an additional project, use the `pillow` module to create images for custom seating cards for your guests. For each of the guests listed in the *guests.txt* file from the resources at *http://nostarch.com/automatestuff/*, generate an image file with the guest name and some flowery decoration. A public domain flower image is available in the resources at *http://nostarch.com/automatestuff/*.

To ensure that each seating card is the same size, add a black rectangle on the edges of the invitation image so that when the image is printed out, there will be a guideline for cutting. The PNG files that Pillow produces are set to 72 pixels per inch, so a 4×5-inch card would require a 288×360-pixel image.

18

CONTROLLING THE KEYBOARD AND MOUSE WITH GUI AUTOMATION

Knowing various Python modules for editing spreadsheets, downloading files, and launching programs is useful, but sometimes there just aren't any modules for the applications you need to work with. The ultimate tools for automating tasks on your computer are programs you write that directly control the keyboard and mouse. These programs can control other applications by sending them virtual keystrokes and mouse clicks, just as if you were sitting at your computer and interacting with the applications yourself. This technique is known as *graphical user interface automation*, or *GUI automation* for short. With GUI automation, your programs can do anything that a human user sitting at the computer can do, except spill coffee on the keyboard.

Think of GUI automation as programming a robotic arm. You can program the robotic arm to type at your keyboard and move your mouse for you. This technique is particularly useful for tasks that involve a lot of mindless clicking or filling out of forms.

The pyautogui module has functions for simulating mouse movements, button clicks, and scrolling the mouse wheel. This chapter covers only a subset of PyAutoGUI's features; you can find the full documentation at *http://pyautogui.readthedocs.org/*.

Installing the pyautogui Module

The pyautogui module can send virtual keypresses and mouse clicks to Windows, OS X, and Linux. Depending on which operating system you're using, you may have to install some other modules (called *dependencies*) before you can install PyAutoGUI.

- On Windows, there are no other modules to install.
- On OS X, run `sudo pip3 install pyobjc-framework-Quartz`, `sudo pip3 install pyobjc-core`, and then `sudo pip3 install pyobjc`.
- On Linux, run `sudo pip3 install python3-xlib`, `sudo apt-get install scrot`, `sudo apt-get install python3-tk`, and `sudo apt-get install python3-dev`. (Scrot is a screenshot program that PyAutoGUI uses.)

After these dependencies are installed, run `pip install pyautogui` (or `pip3` on OS X and Linux) to install PyAutoGUI.

Appendix A has complete information on installing third-party modules. To test whether PyAutoGUI has been installed correctly, run `import pyautogui` from the interactive shell and check for any error messages.

Staying on Track

Before you jump in to a GUI automation, you should know how to escape problems that may arise. Python can move your mouse and type keystrokes at an incredible speed. In fact, it might be too fast for other programs to keep up with. Also, if something goes wrong but your program keeps moving the mouse around, it will be hard to tell what exactly the program is doing or how to recover from the problem. Like the enchanted brooms from Disney's *The Sorcerer's Apprentice*, which kept filling—and then overfilling—Mickey's tub with water, your program could get out of control even though it's following your instructions perfectly. Stopping the program can be difficult if the mouse is moving around on its own, preventing you from clicking the IDLE window to close it. Fortunately, there are several ways to prevent or recover from GUI automation problems.

Shutting Down Everything by Logging Out

Perhaps the simplest way to stop an out-of-control GUI automation program is to log out, which will shut down all running programs. On Windows and Linux, the logout hotkey is CTRL-ALT-DEL. On OS X, it is ⌘-SHIFT-OPTION-Q. By logging out, you'll lose any unsaved work, but at least you won't have to wait for a full reboot of the computer.

Pauses and Fail-Safes

You can tell your script to wait after every function call, giving you a short window to take control of the mouse and keyboard if something goes wrong. To do this, set the pyautogui.PAUSE variable to the number of seconds you want it to pause. For example, after setting pyautogui.PAUSE = 1.5, every PyAutoGUI function call will wait one and a half seconds after performing its action. Non-PyAutoGUI instructions will not have this pause.

PyAutoGUI also has a fail-safe feature. Moving the mouse cursor to the upper-left corner of the screen will cause PyAutoGUI to raise the pyautogui .FailSafeException exception. Your program can either handle this exception with try and except statements or let the exception crash your program. Either way, the fail-safe feature will stop the program if you quickly move the mouse as far up and left as you can. You can disable this feature by setting pyautogui.FAILSAFE = False. Enter the following into the interactive shell:

```
>>> import pyautogui
>>> pyautogui.PAUSE = 1
>>> pyautogui.FAILSAFE = True
```

Here we import pyautogui and set pyautogui.PAUSE to 1 for a one-second pause after each function call. We set pyautogui.FAILSAFE to True to enable the fail-safe feature.

Controlling Mouse Movement

In this section, you'll learn how to move the mouse and track its position on the screen using PyAutoGUI, but first you need to understand how PyAutoGUI works with coordinates.

The mouse functions of PyAutoGUI use x- and y-coordinates. Figure 18-1 shows the coordinate system for the computer screen; it's similar to the coordinate system used for images, discussed in Chapter 17. The *origin*, where *x* and *y* are both zero, is at the upper-left corner of the screen. The x-coordinates increase going to the right, and the y-coordinates increase going down. All coordinates are positive integers; there are no negative coordinates.

Figure 18-1: The coordinates of a computer screen with 1920×1080 resolution

Your *resolution* is how many pixels wide and tall your screen is. If your screen's resolution is set to 1920×1080, then the coordinate for the upper-left corner will be (0, 0), and the coordinate for the bottom-right corner will be (1919, 1079).

The pyautogui.size() function returns a two-integer tuple of the screen's width and height in pixels. Enter the following into the interactive shell:

```
>>> import pyautogui
>>> pyautogui.size()
(1920, 1080)
>>> width, height = pyautogui.size()
```

pyautogui.size() returns (1920, 1080) on a computer with a 1920×1080 resolution; depending on your screen's resolution, your return value may be different. You can store the width and height from pyautogui.size() in variables like width and height for better readability in your programs.

Moving the Mouse

Now that you understand screen coordinates, let's move the mouse. The pyautogui.moveTo() function will instantly move the mouse cursor to a specified position on the screen. Integer values for the x- and y-coordinates make up the function's first and second arguments, respectively. An optional duration integer or float keyword argument specifies the number of seconds it should take to move the mouse to the destination. If you leave it out, the default is 0 for instantaneous movement. (All of the duration keyword arguments in PyAutoGUI functions are optional.) Enter the following into the interactive shell:

```
>>> import pyautogui
>>> for i in range(10):
        pyautogui.moveTo(100, 100, duration=0.25)
        pyautogui.moveTo(200, 100, duration=0.25)
        pyautogui.moveTo(200, 200, duration=0.25)
        pyautogui.moveTo(100, 200, duration=0.25)
```

This example moves the mouse cursor clockwise in a square pattern among the four coordinates provided a total of ten times. Each movement takes a quarter of a second, as specified by the duration=0.25 keyword argument. If you hadn't passed a third argument to any of the pyautogui.moveTo() calls, the mouse cursor would have instantly teleported from point to point.

The pyautogui.moveRel() function moves the mouse cursor *relative* to its current position. The following example moves the mouse in the same square pattern, except it begins the square from wherever the mouse happens to be on the screen when the code starts running:

```
>>> import pyautogui
>>> for i in range(10):
        pyautogui.moveRel(100, 0, duration=0.25)
        pyautogui.moveRel(0, 100, duration=0.25)
```

```
pyautogui.moveRel(-100, 0, duration=0.25)
pyautogui.moveRel(0, -100, duration=0.25)
```

pyautogui.moveRel() also takes three arguments: how many pixels to move horizontally to the right, how many pixels to move vertically downward, and (optionally) how long it should take to complete the movement. A negative integer for the first or second argument will cause the mouse to move left or upward, respectively.

Getting the Mouse Position

You can determine the mouse's current position by calling the pyautogui .position() function, which will return a tuple of the mouse cursor's *x* and *y* positions at the time of the function call. Enter the following into the interactive shell, moving the mouse around after each call:

```
>>> pyautogui.position()
(311, 622)
>>> pyautogui.position()
(377, 481)
>>> pyautogui.position()
(1536, 637)
```

Of course, your return values will vary depending on where your mouse cursor is.

Project: "Where Is the Mouse Right Now?"

Being able to determine the mouse position is an important part of setting up your GUI automation scripts. But it's almost impossible to figure out the exact coordinates of a pixel just by looking at the screen. It would be handy to have a program that constantly displays the x- and y-coordinates of the mouse cursor as you move it around.

At a high level, here's what your program should do:

- Display the current x- and y-coordinates of the mouse cursor.
- Update these coordinates as the mouse moves around the screen.

This means your code will need to do the following:

- Call the position() function to fetch the current coordinates.
- Erase the previously printed coordinates by printing \b backspace characters to the screen.
- Handle the KeyboardInterrupt exception so the user can press CTRL-C to quit.

Open a new file editor window and save it as *mouseNow.py*.

Step 1: Import the Module

Start your program with the following:

```
#! python3
# mouseNow.py - Displays the mouse cursor's current position.
import pyautogui
print('Press Ctrl-C to quit.')
#TODO: Get and print the mouse coordinates.
```

The beginning of the program imports the pyautogui module and prints a reminder to the user that they have to press CTRL-C to quit.

Step 2: Set Up the Quit Code and Infinite Loop

You can use an infinite while loop to constantly print the current mouse coordinates from mouse.position(). As for the code that quits the program, you'll need to catch the KeyboardInterrupt exception, which is raised whenever the user presses CTRL-C. If you don't handle this exception, it will display an ugly traceback and error message to the user. Add the following to your program:

```
#! python3
# mouseNow.py - Displays the mouse cursor's current position.
import pyautogui
print('Press Ctrl-C to quit.')
try:
    while True:
        # TODO: Get and print the mouse coordinates.
❶ except KeyboardInterrupt:
❷     print('\nDone.')
```

To handle the exception, enclose the infinite while loop in a try statement. When the user presses CTRL-C, the program execution will move to the except clause ❶ and Done. will be printed in a new line ❷.

Step 3: Get and Print the Mouse Coordinates

The code inside the while loop should get the current mouse coordinates, format them to look nice, and print them. Add the following code to the inside of the while loop:

```
#! python3
# mouseNow.py - Displays the mouse cursor's current position.
import pyautogui
print('Press Ctrl-C to quit.')
--snip--
        # Get and print the mouse coordinates.
        x, y = pyautogui.position()
        positionStr = 'X: ' + str(x).rjust(4) + ' Y: ' + str(y).rjust(4)
--snip--
```

Using the multiple assignment trick, the x and y variables are given the values of the two integers returned in the tuple from pyautogui.position(). By passing x and y to the str() function, you can get string forms of the integer coordinates. The rjust() string method will right-justify them so that they take up the same amount of space, whether the coordinate has one, two, three, or four digits. Concatenating the right-justified string coordinates with 'X: ' and ' Y: ' labels gives us a neatly formatted string, which will be stored in positionStr.

At the end of your program, add the following code:

```
#! python3
# mouseNow.py - Displays the mouse cursor's current position.
--snip--
        print(positionStr, end='')
❶        print('\b' * len(positionStr), end='', flush=True)
```

This actually prints positionStr to the screen. The end='' keyword argument to print() prevents the default newline character from being added to the end of the printed line. It's possible to erase text you've already printed to the screen—but only for the most recent line of text. Once you print a newline character, you can't erase anything printed before it.

To erase text, print the \b backspace escape character. This special character erases a character at the end of the current line on the screen. The line at ❶ uses string replication to produce a string with as many \b characters as the length of the string stored in positionStr, which has the effect of erasing the positionStr string that was last printed.

For a technical reason beyond the scope of this book, always pass flush=True to print() calls that print \b backspace characters. Otherwise, the screen might not update the text as desired.

Since the while loop repeats so quickly, the user won't actually notice that you're deleting and reprinting the whole number on the screen. For example, if the x-coordinate is 563 and the mouse moves one pixel to the right, it will look like only the 3 in 563 is changed to a 4.

When you run the program, there will be only two lines printed. They should look like something like this:

```
Press Ctrl-C to quit.
X:  290 Y:  424
```

The first line displays the instruction to press CTRL-C to quit. The second line with the mouse coordinates will change as you move the mouse around the screen. Using this program, you'll be able to figure out the mouse coordinates for your GUI automation scripts.

Controlling Mouse Interaction

Now that you know how to move the mouse and figure out where it is on the screen, you're ready to start clicking, dragging, and scrolling.

Clicking the Mouse

To send a virtual mouse click to your computer, call the pyautogui.click() method. By default, this click uses the left mouse button and takes place wherever the mouse cursor is currently located. You can pass x- and y-coordinates of the click as optional first and second arguments if you want it to take place somewhere other than the mouse's current position.

If you want to specify which mouse button to use, include the button keyword argument, with a value of 'left', 'middle', or 'right'. For example, pyautogui.click(100, 150, button='left') will click the left mouse button at the coordinates (100, 150), while pyautogui.click(200, 250, button='right') will perform a right-click at (200, 250).

Enter the following into the interactive shell:

```
>>> import pyautogui
>>> pyautogui.click(10, 5)
```

You should see the mouse pointer move to near the top-left corner of your screen and click once. A full "click" is defined as pushing a mouse button down and then releasing it back up without moving the cursor. You can also perform a click by calling pyautogui.mouseDown(), which only pushes the mouse button down, and pyautogui.mouseUp(), which only releases the button. These functions have the same arguments as click(), and in fact, the click() function is just a convenient wrapper around these two function calls.

As a further convenience, the pyautogui.doubleClick() function will perform two clicks with the left mouse button, while the pyautogui.rightClick() and pyautogui.middleClick() functions will perform a click with the right and middle mouse buttons, respectively.

Dragging the Mouse

Dragging means moving the mouse while holding down one of the mouse buttons. For example, you can move files between folders by dragging the folder icons, or you can move appointments around in a calendar app.

PyAutoGUI provides the pyautogui.dragTo() and pyautogui.dragRel() functions to drag the mouse cursor to a new location or a location relative to its current one. The arguments for dragTo() and dragRel() are the same as moveTo() and moveRel(): the x-coordinate/horizontal movement, the y-coordinate/vertical movement, and an optional duration of time. (OS X does not drag correctly when the mouse moves too quickly, so passing a duration keyword argument is recommended.)

To try these functions, open a graphics-drawing application such as Paint on Windows, Paintbrush on OS X, or GNU Paint on Linux. (If you don't have a drawing application, you can use the online one at *http://sumopaint.com/*.) I will use PyAutoGUI to draw in these applications.

With the mouse cursor over the drawing application's canvas and the Pencil or Brush tool selected, enter the following into a new file editor window and save it as *spiralDraw.py*:

```
import pyautogui, time
❶ time.sleep(5)
❷ pyautogui.click()     # click to put drawing program in focus
  distance = 200
  while distance > 0:
❸     pyautogui.dragRel(distance, 0, duration=0.2)    # move right
❹     distance = distance - 5
❺     pyautogui.dragRel(0, distance, duration=0.2)    # move down
❻     pyautogui.dragRel(-distance, 0, duration=0.2)   # move left
      distance = distance - 5
      pyautogui.dragRel(0, -distance, duration=0.2)   # move up
```

When you run this program, there will be a five-second delay ❶ for you to move the mouse cursor over the drawing program's window with the Pencil or Brush tool selected. Then *spiralDraw.py* will take control of the mouse and click to put the drawing program in focus ❷. A window is in *focus* when it has an active blinking cursor, and the actions you take—like typing or, in this case, dragging the mouse—will affect that window. Once the drawing program is in focus, *spiralDraw.py* draws a square spiral pattern like the one in Figure 18-2.

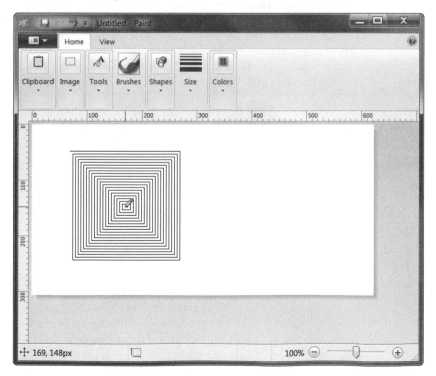

Figure 18-2: The results from the pyautogui.dragRel() example

The distance variable starts at 200, so on the first iteration of the while loop, the first dragRel() call drags the cursor 200 pixels to the right, taking 0.2 seconds ❸. distance is then decreased to 195 ❹, and the second dragRel() call drags the cursor 195 pixels down ❺. The third dragRel() call drags the cursor −195 horizontally (195 to the left) ❻, distance is decreased to 190, and the last dragRel() call drags the cursor 190 pixels up. On each iteration, the mouse is dragged right, down, left, and up, and distance is slightly smaller than it was in the previous iteration. By looping over this code, you can move the mouse cursor to draw a square spiral.

You could draw this spiral by hand (or rather, by mouse), but you'd have to work slowly to be so precise. PyAutoGUI can do it in a few seconds!

NOTE *You could have your code draw the image using the* pillow *module's drawing functions—see Chapter 17 for more information. But using GUI automation allows you to make use of the advanced drawing tools that graphics programs can provide, such as gradients, different brushes, or the fill bucket.*

Scrolling the Mouse

The final PyAutoGUI mouse function is scroll(), which you pass an integer argument for how many units you want to scroll the mouse up or down. The size of a unit varies for each operating system and application, so you'll have to experiment to see exactly how far it scrolls in your particular situation. The scrolling takes place at the mouse cursor's current position. Passing a positive integer scrolls up, and passing a negative integer scrolls down. Run the following in IDLE's interactive shell while the mouse cursor is over the IDLE window:

```
>>> pyautogui.scroll(200)
```

You'll see IDLE briefly scroll upward—and then go back down. The downward scrolling happens because IDLE automatically scrolls down to the bottom after executing an instruction. Enter this code instead:

```
>>> import pyperclip
>>> numbers = ''
>>> for i in range(200):
        numbers = numbers + str(i) + '\n'

>>> pyperclip.copy(numbers)
```

This imports pyperclip and sets up an empty string, numbers. The code then loops through 200 numbers and adds each number to numbers, along with a newline. After pyperclip.copy(numbers), the clipboard will be loaded with 200 lines of numbers. Open a new file editor window and paste the text into it. This will give you a large text window to try scrolling in. Enter the following code into the interactive shell:

```
>>> import time, pyautogui
>>> time.sleep(5); pyautogui.scroll(100)
```

On the second line, you enter two commands separated by a semicolon, which tells Python to run the commands as if they were on separate lines. The only difference is that the interactive shell won't prompt you for input between the two instructions. This is important for this example because we want to the call to `pyautogui.scroll()` to happen automatically after the wait. (Note that while putting two commands on one line can be useful in the interactive shell, you should still have each instruction on a separate line in your programs.)

After pressing ENTER to run the code, you will have five seconds to click the file editor window to put it in focus. Once the pause is over, the `pyautogui.scroll()` call will cause the file editor window to scroll up after the five-second delay.

Working with the Screen

Your GUI automation programs don't have to click and type blindly. PyAutoGUI has screenshot features that can create an image file based on the current contents of the screen. These functions can also return a Pillow Image object of the current screen's appearance. If you've been skipping around in this book, you'll want to read Chapter 17 and install the `pillow` module before continuing with this section.

On Linux computers, the `scrot` program needs to be installed to use the screenshot functions in PyAutoGUI. In a Terminal window, run **sudo apt-get install scrot** to install this program. If you're on Windows or OS X, skip this step and continue with the section.

Getting a Screenshot

To take screenshots in Python, call the `pyautogui.screenshot()` function. Enter the following into the interactive shell:

```
>>> import pyautogui
>>> im = pyautogui.screenshot()
```

The `im` variable will contain the Image object of the screenshot. You can now call methods on the Image object in the `im` variable, just like any other Image object. Enter the following into the interactive shell:

```
>>> im.getpixel((0, 0))
(176, 176, 175)
>>> im.getpixel((50, 200))
(130, 135, 144)
```

Pass `getpixel()` a tuple of coordinates, like (0, 0) or (50, 200), and it'll tell you the color of the pixel at those coordinates in your image. The return value from `getpixel()` is an RGB tuple of three integers for the amount of red, green, and blue in the pixel. (There is no fourth value for alpha, because screenshot images are fully opaque.) This is how your programs can "see" what is currently on the screen.

Analyzing the Screenshot

Say that one of the steps in your GUI automation program is to click a gray button. Before calling the `click()` method, you could take a screenshot and look at the pixel where the script is about to click. If it's not the same gray as the gray button, then your program knows something is wrong. Maybe the window moved unexpectedly, or maybe a pop-up dialog has blocked the button. At this point, instead of continuing—and possibly wreaking havoc by clicking the wrong thing—your program can "see" that it isn't clicking on the right thing and stop itself.

PyAutoGUI's `pixelMatchesColor()` function will return `True` if the pixel at the given x- and y-coordinates on the screen matches the given color. The first and second arguments are integers for the x- and y-coordinates, and the third argument is a tuple of three integers for the RGB color the screen pixel must match. Enter the following into the interactive shell:

```
>>> import pyautogui
>>> im = pyautogui.screenshot()
❶ >>> im.getpixel((50, 200))
(130, 135, 144)
❷ >>> pyautogui.pixelMatchesColor(50, 200, (130, 135, 144))
True
❸ >>> pyautogui.pixelMatchesColor(50, 200, (255, 135, 144))
False
```

After taking a screenshot and using `getpixel()` to get an RGB tuple for the color of a pixel at specific coordinates ❶, pass the same coordinates and RGB tuple to `pixelMatchesColor()` ❷, which should return `True`. Then change a value in the RGB tuple and call `pixelMatchesColor()` again for the same coordinates ❸. This should return `false`. This method can be useful to call whenever your GUI automation programs are about to call `click()`. Note that the color at the given coordinates must *exactly* match. If it is even slightly different—for example, (255, 255, 254) instead of (255, 255, 255)—then `pixelMatchesColor()` will return `False`.

Project: Extending the mouseNow Program

You could extend the *mouseNow.py* project from earlier in this chapter so that it not only gives the x- and y-coordinates of the mouse cursor's current position but also gives the RGB color of the pixel under the cursor. Modify the code inside the `while` loop of *mouseNow.py* to look like this:

```
#! python3
# mouseNow.py - Displays the mouse cursor's current position.
--snip--
        positionStr = 'X: ' + str(x).rjust(4) + ' Y: ' + str(y).rjust(4)
        pixelColor = pyautogui.screenshot().getpixel((x, y))
        positionStr += ' RGB: (' + str(pixelColor[0]).rjust(3)
        positionStr += ', ' + str(pixelColor[1]).rjust(3)
        positionStr += ', ' + str(pixelColor[2]).rjust(3) + ')'
```

```
        print(positionStr, end='')
--snip--
```

Now, when you run *mouseNow.py*, the output will include the RGB color value of the pixel under the mouse cursor.

```
Press Ctrl-C to quit.
X:   406 Y:    17 RGB: (161,   50,   50)
```

This information, along with the pixelMatchesColor() function, should make it easy to add pixel color checks to your GUI automation scripts.

Image Recognition

But what if you do not know beforehand where PyAutoGUI should click? You can use image recognition instead. Give PyAutoGUI an image of what you want to click and let it figure out the coordinates.

For example, if you have previously taken a screenshot to capture the image of a Submit button in *submit.png*, the locateOnScreen() function will return the coordinates where that image is found. To see how locateOnScreen() works, try taking a screenshot of a small area on your screen; then save the image and enter the following into the interactive shell, replacing 'submit.png' with the filename of your screenshot:

```
>>> import pyautogui
>>> pyautogui.locateOnScreen('submit.png')
(643, 745, 70, 29)
```

The four-integer tuple that locateOnScreen() returns has the x-coordinate of the left edge, the y-coordinate of the top edge, the width, and the height for the first place on the screen the image was found. If you're trying this on your computer with your own screenshot, your return value will be different from the one shown here.

If the image cannot be found on the screen, locateOnScreen() will return None. Note that the image on the screen must match the provided image perfectly in order to be recognized. If the image is even a pixel off, locateOnScreen() will return None.

If the image can be found in several places on the screen, locateAllOnScreen() will return a Generator object, which can be passed to list() to return a list of four-integer tuples. There will be one four-integer tuple for each location where the image is found on the screen. Continue the interactive shell example by entering the following (and replacing 'submit.png' with your own image filename):

```
>>> list(pyautogui.locateAllOnScreen('submit.png'))
[(643, 745, 70, 29), (1007, 801, 70, 29)]
```

Each of the four-integer tuples represents an area on the screen. If your image is only found in one area, then using list() and locateAllOnScreen() just returns a list containing one tuple.

Once you have the four-integer tuple for the area on the screen where your image was found, you can click the center of this area by passing the tuple to the center() function to return x- and y-coordinates of the area's center. Enter the following into the interactive shell, replacing the arguments with your own filename, four-integer tuple, and coordinate pair:

```
>>> pyautogui.locateOnScreen('submit.png')
(643, 745, 70, 29)
>>> pyautogui.center((643, 745, 70, 29))
(678, 759)
>>> pyautogui.click((678, 759))
```

Once you have center coordinates from center(), passing the coordinates to click() should click the center of the area on the screen that matches the image you passed to locateOnScreen().

Controlling the Keyboard

PyAutoGUI also has functions for sending virtual keypresses to your computer, which enables you to fill out forms or enter text into applications.

Sending a String from the Keyboard

The pyautogui.typewrite() function sends virtual keypresses to the computer. What these keypresses do depends on what window and text field have focus. You may want to first send a mouse click to the text field you want in order to ensure that it has focus.

As a simple example, let's use Python to automatically type the words *Hello world!* into a file editor window. First, open a new file editor window and position it in the upper-left corner of your screen so that PyAutoGUI will click in the right place to bring it into focus. Next, enter the following into the interactive shell:

```
>>> pyautogui.click(100, 100); pyautogui.typewrite('Hello world!')
```

Notice how placing two commands on the same line, separated by a semicolon, keeps the interactive shell from prompting you for input between running the two instructions. This prevents you from accidentally bringing a new window into focus between the click() and typewrite() calls, which would mess up the example.

Python will first send a virtual mouse click to the coordinates (100, 100), which should click the file editor window and put it in focus. The typewrite() call will send the text *Hello world!* to the window, making it look like Figure 18-3. You now have code that can type for you!

Figure 18-3: Using PyAutoGGUI to click the file editor window and type Hello world! *into it*

By default, the `typewrite()` function will type the full string instantly. However, you can pass an optional second argument to add a short pause between each character. This second argument is an integer or float value of the number of seconds to pause. For example, `pyautogui.typewrite('Hello world!', 0.25)` will wait a quarter-second after typing *H*, another quarter-second after *e*, and so on. This gradual typewriter effect may be useful for slower applications that can't process keystrokes fast enough to keep up with PyAutoGUI.

For characters such as *A* or *!*, PyAutoGUI will automatically simulate holding down the SHIFT key as well.

Key Names

Not all keys are easy to represent with single text characters. For example, how do you represent SHIFT or the left arrow key as a single character? In PyAutoGUI, these keyboard keys are represented by short string values instead: `'esc'` for the ESC key or `'enter'` for the ENTER key.

Instead of a single string argument, a list of these keyboard key strings can be passed to `typewrite()`. For example, the following call presses the A key, then the B key, then the left arrow key twice, and finally the X and Y keys:

```
>>> pyautogui.typewrite(['a', 'b', 'left', 'left', 'X', 'Y'])
```

Because pressing the left arrow key moves the keyboard cursor, this will output *XYab*. Table 18-1 lists the PyAutoGUI keyboard key strings that you can pass to `typewrite()` to simulate pressing any combination of keys.

You can also examine the `pyautogui.KEYBOARD_KEYS` list to see all possible keyboard key strings that PyAutoGUI will accept. The `'shift'` string refers to the left SHIFT key and is equivalent to `'shiftleft'`. The same applies for `'ctrl'`, `'alt'`, and `'win'` strings; they all refer to the left-side key.

Table 18-1: PyKeyboard Attributes

Keyboard key string	Meaning
'a', 'b', 'c', 'A', 'B', 'C', '1', '2', '3', '!', '@', '#', and so on	The keys for single characters
'enter' (or 'return' or '\n')	The ENTER key
'esc'	The ESC key
'shiftleft', 'shiftright'	The left and right SHIFT keys
'altleft', 'altright'	The left and right ALT keys
'ctrlleft', 'ctrlright'	The left and right CTRL keys
'tab' (or '\t')	The TAB key
'backspace', 'delete'	The BACKSPACE and DELETE keys
'pageup', 'pagedown'	The PAGE UP and PAGE DOWN keys
'home', 'end'	The HOME and END keys
'up', 'down', 'left', 'right'	The up, down, left, and right arrow keys
'f1', 'f2', 'f3', and so on	The F1 to F12 keys
'volumemute', 'volumedown', 'volumeup'	The mute, volume down, and volume up keys (some keyboards do not have these keys, but your operating system will still be able to understand these simulated keypresses)
'pause'	The PAUSE key
'capslock', 'numlock', 'scrolllock'	The CAPS LOCK, NUM LOCK, and SCROLL LOCK keys
'insert'	The INS or INSERT key
'printscreen'	The PRTSC or PRINT SCREEN key
'winleft', 'winright'	The left and right WIN keys (on Windows)
'command'	The Command (⌘) key (on OS X)
'option'	The OPTION key (on OS X)

Pressing and Releasing the Keyboard

Much like the mouseDown() and mouseUp() functions, pyautogui.keyDown() and pyautogui.keyUp() will send virtual keypresses and releases to the computer. They are passed a keyboard key string (see Table 18-1) for their argument. For convenience, PyAutoGUI provides the pyautogui.press() function, which calls both of these functions to simulate a complete keypress.

Run the following code, which will type a dollar sign character (obtained by holding the SHIFT key and pressing 4):

```
>>> pyautogui.keyDown('shift'); pyautogui.press('4'); pyautogui.keyUp('shift')
```

This line presses down SHIFT, presses (and releases) 4, and then releases SHIFT. If you need to type a string into a text field, the typewrite() function is more suitable. But for applications that take single-key commands, the press() function is the simpler approach.

Hotkey Combinations

A *hotkey* or *shortcut* is a combination of keypresses to invoke some application function. The common hotkey for copying a selection is CTRL-C (on Windows and Linux) or ⌘-C (on OS X). The user presses and holds the CTRL key, then presses the C key, and then releases the C and CTRL keys. To do this with PyAutoGUI's keyDown() and keyUp() functions, you would have to enter the following:

```
pyautogui.keyDown('ctrl')
pyautogui.keyDown('c')
pyautogui.keyUp('c')
pyautogui.keyUp('ctrl')
```

This is rather complicated. Instead, use the pyautogui.hotkey() function, which takes multiple keyboard key string arguments, presses them in order, and releases them in the reverse order. For the CTRL-C example, the code would simply be as follows:

```
pyautogui.hotkey('ctrl', 'c')
```

This function is especially useful for larger hotkey combinations. In Word, the CTRL-ALT-SHIFT-S hotkey combination displays the Style pane. Instead of making eight different function calls (four keyDown() calls and four keyUp() calls), you can just call hotkey('ctrl', 'alt', 'shift', 's').

With a new IDLE file editor window in the upper-left corner of your screen, enter the following into the interactive shell (in OS X, replace 'alt' with 'ctrl'):

```
>>> import pyautogui, time
>>> def commentAfterDelay():
❶      pyautogui.click(100, 100)
❷      pyautogui.typewrite('In IDLE, Alt-3 comments out a line.')
        time.sleep(2)
❸      pyautogui.hotkey('alt', '3')

>>> commentAfterDelay()
```

This defines a function commentAfterDelay() that, when called, will click the file editor window to bring it into focus ❶, type *In IDLE, Atl-3 comments out a line* ❷, pause for 2 seconds, and then simulate pressing the ALT-3 hotkey (or CTRL-3 on OS X) ❸. This keyboard shortcut adds two # characters to the current line, commenting it out. (This is a useful trick to know when writing your own code in IDLE.)

Review of the PyAutoGUI Functions

Since this chapter covered many different functions, here is a quick summary reference:

moveTo(*x, y*)   Moves the mouse cursor to the given *x* and *y* coordinates.

moveRel(*xOffset, yOffset*)   Moves the mouse cursor relative to its current position.

dragTo(*x, y*)   Moves the mouse cursor while the left button is held down.

dragRel(*xOffset, yOffset*)   Moves the mouse cursor relative to its current position while the left button is held down.

click(*x, y, button*)   Simulates a click (left button by default).

rightClick()   Simulates a right-button click.

middleClick()   Simulates a middle-button click.

doubleClick()   Simulates a double left-button click.

mouseDown(*x, y, button*)   Simulates pressing down the given button at the position *x, y*.

mouseUp(*x, y, button*)   Simulates releasing the given button at the position *x, y*.

scroll(*units*)   Simulates the scroll wheel. A positive argument scrolls up; a negative argument scrolls down.

typewrite(*message*)   Types the characters in the given message string.

typewrite([*key1, key2, key3*])   Types the given keyboard key strings.

press(*key*)   Presses the given keyboard key string.

keyDown(*key*)   Simulates pressing down the given keyboard key.

keyUp(*key*)   Simulates releasing the given keyboard key.

hotkey([*key1, key2, key3*])   Simulates pressing the given keyboard key strings down in order and then releasing them in reverse order.

screenshot()   Returns a screenshot as an Image object. (See Chapter 17 for information on Image objects.)

Project: Automatic Form Filler

Of all the boring tasks, filling out forms is the most dreaded of chores. It's only fitting that now, in the final chapter project, you will slay it. Say you have a huge amount of data in a spreadsheet, and you have to tediously retype it into some other application's form interface—with no intern to do it for you. Although some applications will have an Import feature that will allow you to upload a spreadsheet with the information, sometimes it seems that there is no other way than mindlessly clicking and typing for hours on end. You've come this far in this book; you know that *of course* there's another way.

The form for this project is a Google Docs form that you can find at *http://nostarch.com/automatestuff*. It looks like Figure 18-4.

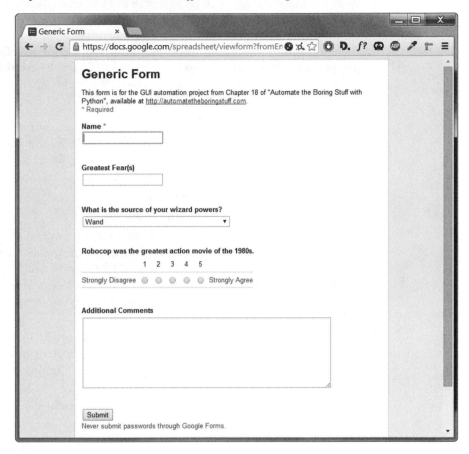

Figure 18-4: The form used for this project

At a high level, here's what your program should do:

- Click the first text field of the form.
- Move through the form, typing information into each field.
- Click the Submit button.
- Repeat the process with the next set of data.

This means your code will need to do the following:

- Call pyautogui.click() to click the form and Submit button.
- Call pyautogui.typewrite() to enter text into the fields.
- Handle the KeyboardInterrupt exception so the user can press CTRL-C to quit.

Open a new file editor window and save it as *formFiller.py*.

Step 1: Figure Out the Steps

Before writing code, you need to figure out the exact keystrokes and mouse clicks that will fill out the form once. The *mouseNow.py* script on page 417 can help you figure out specific mouse coordinates. You need to know only the coordinates of the first text field. After clicking the first field, you can just press TAB to move focus to the next field. This will save you from having to figure out the x- and y-coordinates to click for every field.

Here are the steps for entering data into the form:

1. Click the Name field. (Use *mouseNow.py* to determine the coordinates after maximizing the browser window. On OS X, you may need to click twice: once to put the browser in focus and again to click the Name field.)

2. Type a name and then press TAB.

3. Type a greatest fear and then press TAB.

4. Press the down arrow key the correct number of times to select the wizard power source: once for *wand*, twice for *amulet*, three times for *crystal ball*, and four times for *money*. Then press TAB. (Note that on OS X, you will have to press the down arrow key one more time for each option. For some browsers, you may need to press the ENTER key as well.)

5. Press the right arrow key to select the answer to the RoboCop question. Press it once for *2*, twice for *3*, three times for *4*, or four times for *5*; or just press the spacebar to select *1* (which is highlighted by default). Then press TAB.

6. Type an additional comment and then press TAB.

7. Press the ENTER key to "click" the Submit button.

8. After submitting the form, the browser will take you to a page where you will need to click a link to return to the form page.

Note that if you run this program again later, you may have to update the mouse click coordinates, since the browser window might have changed position. To work around this, always make sure the browser window is maximized before finding the coordinates of the first form field. Also, different browsers on different operating systems might work slightly differently from the steps given here, so check that these keystroke combinations work for your computer before running your program.

Step 2: Set Up Coordinates

Load the example form you downloaded (Figure 18-4) in a browser and maximize your browser window. Open a new Terminal or command line window to run the *mouseNow.py* script, and then mouse over the Name field to figure out its the x- and y-coordinates. These numbers will be assigned to the nameField variable in your program. Also, find out the x- and y-coordinates and RGB tuple value of the blue Submit button. These values will be assigned to the submitButton and submitButtonColor variables, respectively.

Next, fill in some dummy data for the form and click **Submit**. You need to see what the next page looks like so that you can use *mouseNow.py* to find the coordinates of the *Submit another response* link on this new page.

Make your source code look like the following, being sure to replace all the values in italics with the coordinates you determined from your own tests:

```python
#! python3
# formFiller.py - Automatically fills in the form.

import pyautogui, time

# Set these to the correct coordinates for your computer.
nameField = (648, 319)
submitButton = (651, 817)
submitButtonColor = (75, 141, 249)
submitAnotherLink = (760, 224)

# TODO: Give the user a chance to kill the script.

# TODO: Wait until the form page has loaded.

# TODO: Fill out the Name Field.

# TODO: Fill out the Greatest Fear(s) field.

# TODO: Fill out the Source of Wizard Powers field.

# TODO: Fill out the RoboCop field.

# TODO: Fill out the Additional Comments field.

# TODO: Click Submit.

# TODO: Wait until form page has loaded.

# TODO: Click the Submit another response link.
```

Now you need the data you actually want to enter into this form. In the real world, this data might come from a spreadsheet, a plaintext file, or a website, and it would require additional code to load into the program. But for this project, you'll just hardcode all this data in a variable. Add the following to your program:

```python
#! python3
# formFiller.py - Automatically fills in the form.

--snip--

formData = [{'name': 'Alice', 'fear': 'eavesdroppers', 'source': 'wand',
            'robocop': 4, 'comments': 'Tell Bob I said hi.'},
           {'name': 'Bob', 'fear': 'bees', 'source': 'amulet', 'robocop': 4,
            'comments': 'n/a'},
```

```
    {'name': 'Carol', 'fear': 'puppets', 'source': 'crystal ball',
    'robocop': 1, 'comments': 'Please take the puppets out of the
    break room.'},
    {'name': 'Alex Murphy', 'fear': 'ED-209', 'source': 'money',
    'robocop': 5, 'comments': 'Protect the innocent. Serve the public
    trust. Uphold the law.'},
    ]
```

--snip--

The formData list contains four dictionaries for four different names. Each dictionary has names of text fields as keys and responses as values. The last bit of setup is to set PyAutoGUI's PAUSE variable to wait half a second after each function call. Add the following to your program after the formData assignment statement:

```
pyautogui.PAUSE = 0.5
```

Step 3: Start Typing Data

A for loop will iterate over each of the dictionaries in the formData list, passing the values in the dictionary to the PyAutoGUI functions that will virtually type in the text fields.

Add the following code to your program:

```
#! python3
# formFiller.py - Automatically fills in the form.

--snip--

for person in formData:
    # Give the user a chance to kill the script.
    print('>>> 5 SECOND PAUSE TO LET USER PRESS CTRL-C <<<')
❶   time.sleep(5)

    # Wait until the form page has loaded.
❷   while not pyautogui.pixelMatchesColor(submitButton[0], submitButton[1],
    submitButtonColor):
        time.sleep(0.5)
```

--snip--

As a small safety feature, the script has a five-second pause ❶ that gives the user a chance to hit CTRL-C (or move the mouse cursor to the upper-left corner of the screen to raise the FailSafeException exception) to shut the program down in case it's doing something unexpected. Then the program waits until the Submit button's color is visible ❷, letting the program know that the form page has loaded. Remember that you figured out the coordinate and color information in step 2 and stored it in the `submitButton` and `submitButtonColor` variables. To use `pixelMatchesColor()`, you pass the coordinates `submitButton[0]` and `submitButton[1]`, and the color `submitButtonColor`.

After the code that waits until the Submit button's color is visible, add the following:

```python3
#! python3
# formFiller.py - Automatically fills in the form.

--snip--

❶    print('Entering %s info...' % (person['name']))
❷    pyautogui.click(nameField[0], nameField[1])

     # Fill out the Name field.
❸    pyautogui.typewrite(person['name'] + '\t')

     # Fill out the Greatest Fear(s) field.
❹    pyautogui.typewrite(person['fear'] + '\t')

--snip--
```

We add an occasional `print()` call to display the program's status in its Terminal window to let the user know what's going on ❶.

Since the program knows that the form is loaded, it's time to call `click()` to click the Name field ❷ and `typewrite()` to enter the string in `person['name']` ❸. The `'\t'` character is added to the end of the string passed to `typewrite()` to simulate pressing TAB, which moves the keyboard focus to the next field, Greatest Fear(s). Another call to `typewrite()` will type the string in `person['fear']` into this field and then tab to the next field in the form ❹.

Step 4: Handle Select Lists and Radio Buttons

The drop-down menu for the "wizard powers" question and the radio buttons for the RoboCop field are trickier to handle than the text fields. To click these options with the mouse, you would have to figure out the x- and y-coordinates of each possible option. It's easier to use the keyboard arrow keys to make a selection instead.

Add the following to your program:

```python3
#! python3
# formFiller.py - Automatically fills in the form.

--snip--

     # Fill out the Source of Wizard Powers field.
❶    if person['source'] == 'wand':
❷        pyautogui.typewrite(['down', '\t'])
```

```
        elif person['source'] == 'amulet':
            pyautogui.typewrite(['down', 'down', '\t'])
        elif person['source'] == 'crystal ball':
            pyautogui.typewrite(['down', 'down', 'down', '\t'])
        elif person['source'] == 'money':
            pyautogui.typewrite(['down', 'down', 'down', 'down', '\t'])

        # Fill out the RoboCop field.
❸      if person['robocop'] == 1:
❹          pyautogui.typewrite([' ', '\t'])
        elif person['robocop'] == 2:
            pyautogui.typewrite(['right', '\t'])
        elif person['robocop'] == 3:
            pyautogui.typewrite(['right', 'right', '\t'])
        elif person['robocop'] == 4:
            pyautogui.typewrite(['right', 'right', 'right', '\t'])
        elif person['robocop'] == 5:
            pyautogui.typewrite(['right', 'right', 'right', 'right', '\t'])
```

--snip--

Once the drop-down menu has focus (remember that you wrote code to simulate pressing TAB after filling out the Greatest Fear(s) field), pressing the down arrow key will move to the next item in the selection list. Depending on the value in person['source'], your program should send a number of down arrow keypresses before tabbing to the next field. If the value at the 'source' key in this user's dictionary is 'wand' ❶, we simulate pressing the down arrow key once (to select *Wand*) and pressing TAB ❷. If the value at the 'source' key is 'amulet', we simulate pressing the down arrow key twice and pressing TAB, and so on for the other possible answers.

The radio buttons for the RoboCop question can be selected with the right arrow keys—or, if you want to select the first choice ❸, by just pressing the spacebar ❹.

Step 5: Submit the Form and Wait

You can fill out the Additional Comments field with the typewrite() function by passing person['comments'] as an argument. You can type an additional '\t' to move the keyboard focus to the next field or the Submit button. Once the Submit button is in focus, calling pyautogui.press('enter') will simulate pressing the ENTER key and submit the form. After submitting the form, your program will wait five seconds for the next page to load.

Once the new page has loaded, it will have a *Submit another response* link that will direct the browser to a new, empty form page. You stored the coordinates of this link as a tuple in submitAnotherLink in step 2, so pass these coordinates to pyautogui.click() to click this link.

With the new form ready to go, the script's outer for loop can continue to the next iteration and enter the next person's information into the form.

Complete your program by adding the following code:

```python
#! python3
# formFiller.py - Automatically fills in the form.

--snip--

    # Fill out the Additional Comments field.
    pyautogui.typewrite(person['comments'] + '\t')

    # Click Submit.
    pyautogui.press('enter')

    # Wait until form page has loaded.
    print('Clicked Submit.')
    time.sleep(5)

    # Click the Submit another response link.
    pyautogui.click(submitAnotherLink[0], submitAnotherLink[1])
```

Once the main for loop has finished, the program will have plugged in the information for each person. In this example, there are only four people to enter. But if you had *4,000* people, then writing a program to do this would save you a lot of time and typing!

Summary

GUI automation with the pyautogui module allows you to interact with applications on your computer by controlling the mouse and keyboard. While this approach is flexible enough to do anything that a human user can do, the downside is that these programs are fairly blind to what they are clicking or typing. When writing GUI automation programs, try to ensure that they will crash quickly if they're given bad instructions. Crashing is annoying, but it's much better than the program continuing in error.

You can move the mouse cursor around the screen and simulate mouse clicks, keystrokes, and keyboard shortcuts with PyAutoGUI. The pyautogui module can also check the colors on the screen, which can provide your GUI automation program with enough of an idea of the screen contents to know whether it has gotten offtrack. You can even give PyAutoGUI a screenshot and let it figure out the coordinates of the area you want to click.

You can combine all of these PyAutoGUI features to automate any mindlessly repetitive task on your computer. In fact, it can be downright hypnotic to watch the mouse cursor move on its own and see text appear on the screen automatically. Why not spend the time you saved by sitting back and watching your program do all your work for you? There's a certain satisfaction that comes from seeing how your cleverness has saved you from the boring stuff.

Practice Questions

1. How can you trigger PyAutoGUI's fail safe to stop a program?
2. What function returns the current resolution()?
3. What function returns the coordinates for the mouse cursor's current position?
4. What is the difference between pyautogui.moveTo() and pyautogui.moveRel()?
5. What functions can be used to drag the mouse?
6. What function call will type out the characters of "Hello world!"?
7. How can you do keypresses for special keys such as the keyboard's left arrow key?
8. How can you save the current contents of the screen to an image file named *screenshot.png*?
9. What code would set a two second pause after every PyAutoGUI function call?

Practice Projects

For practice, write programs that do the following.

Looking Busy

Many instant messaging programs determine whether you are idle, or away from your computer, by detecting a lack of mouse movement over some period of time—say, ten minutes. Maybe you'd like to sneak away from your desk for a while but don't want others to see your instant messenger status go into idle mode. Write a script to nudge your mouse cursor slightly every ten seconds. The nudge should be small enough so that it won't get in the way if you do happen to need to use your computer while the script is running.

Instant Messenger Bot

Google Talk, Skype, Yahoo Messenger, AIM, and other instant messaging applications often use proprietary protocols that make it difficult for others to write Python modules that can interact with these programs. But even these proprietary protocols can't stop you from writing a GUI automation tool.

The Google Talk application has a search bar that lets you enter a username on your friend list and open a messaging window when you press ENTER. The keyboard focus automatically moves to the new window. Other instant messenger applications have similar ways to open new message windows. Write a program that will automatically send out a notification message to a select group of people on your friend list. Your program may have to deal with exceptional cases, such as friends being offline, the chat window appearing at different coordinates on the screen, or confirmation boxes that interrupt your messaging. Your program will have to take screen-shots to guide its GUI interaction and adopt ways of detecting when its virtual keystrokes aren't being sent.

NOTE   *You may want to set up some fake test accounts so that you don't accidentally spam your real friends while writing this program.*

Game-Playing Bot Tutorial

There is a great tutorial titled "How to Build a Python Bot That Can Play Web Games" that you can find at *http://nostarch.com/automatestuff/*. This tutorial explains how to create a GUI automation program in Python that plays a Flash game called Sushi Go Round. The game involves clicking the correct ingredient buttons to fill customers' sushi orders. The faster you fill orders without mistakes, the more points you get. This is a perfectly suited task for a GUI automation program—and a way to cheat to a high score! The tutorial covers many of the same topics that this chapter covers but also includes descriptions of PyAutoGUI's basic image recognition features.

A

INSTALLING
THIRD-PARTY MODULES

 Beyond the standard library of modules packaged with Python, other developers have written their own modules to extend Python's capabilities even further. The primary way to install third-party modules is to use Python's pip tool. This tool securely downloads and installs Python modules onto your computer from *https://pypi.python.org/*, the website of the Python Software Foundation. PyPI, or the Python Package Index, is a sort of free app store for Python modules.

The pip Tool

The executable file for the pip tool is called *pip* on Windows and *pip3* on OS X and Linux. On Windows, you can find pip at *C:\Python34\Scripts\pip.exe*. On OS X, it is in */Library/Frameworks/Python.framework/Versions/3.4/bin/pip3*. On Linux, it is in */usr/bin/pip3*.

While pip comes automatically installed with Python 3.4 on Windows and OS X, you must install it separately on Linux. To install pip3 on Ubuntu or Debian Linux, open a new Terminal window and enter **sudo apt-get install python3-pip**. To install pip3 on Fedora Linux, enter **sudo yum install python3 -pip** into a Terminal window. You will need to enter the administrator password for your computer in order to install this software.

Installing Third-Party Modules

The pip tool is meant to be run from the command line: You pass it the command `install` followed by the name of the module you want to install. For example, on Windows you would enter `pip install ModuleName`, where *ModuleName* is the name of the module. On OS X and Linux, you'll have to run pip3 with the `sudo` prefix to grant administrative privileges to install the module. You would need to type `sudo pip3 install ModuleName`.

If you already have the module installed but would like to upgrade it to the latest version available on PyPI, run `pip install –U ModuleName` (or `pip3 install –U ModuleName` on OS X and Linux).

After installing the module, you can test that it installed successfully by running `import ModuleName` in the interactive shell. If no error messages are displayed, you can assume the module was installed successfully.

You can install all of the modules covered in this book by running the commands listed next. (Remember to replace `pip` with `pip3` if you're on OS X or Linux.)

- `pip install send2trash`
- `pip install requests`
- `pip install beautifulsoup4`
- `pip install selenium`
- `pip install openpyxl`
- `pip install PyPDF2`
- `pip install python-docx` (install python-docx, not docx)
- `pip install imapclient`
- `pip install pyzmail`
- `pip install twilio`
- `pip install pillow`
- `pip install pyobjc-core` (on OS X only)
- `pip install pyobjc` (on OS X only)
- `pip install python3-xlib` (on Linux only)
- `pip install pyautogui`

NOTE *For OS X users: The pyobjc module can take 20 minutes or longer to install, so don't be alarmed if it takes a while. You should also install the pyobjc-core module first, which will reduce the overall installation time.*

B

RUNNING PROGRAMS

If you have a program open in IDLE's file editor, running it is a simple matter of pressing F5 or selecting the Run ▸ Run Module menu item. This is an easy way to run programs while writing them, but opening IDLE to run your finished programs can be a burden. There are more convenient ways to execute Python scripts.

Shebang Line

The first line of all your Python programs should be a *shebang* line, which tells your computer that you want Python to execute this program. The shebang line begins with #!, but the rest depends on your operating system.

- On Windows, the shebang line is #! python3.
- On OS X, the shebang line is #! /usr/bin/env python3.
- On Linux, the shebang line is #! /usr/bin/python3.

You will be able to run Python scripts from IDLE without the shebang line, but the line is needed to run them from the command line.

Running Python Programs on Windows

On Windows, the Python 3.4 interpreter is located at *C:\Python34\python.exe*. Alternatively, the convenient *py.exe* program will read the shebang line at the top of the *.py* file's source code and run the appropriate version of Python for that script. The *py.exe* program will make sure to run the Python program with the correct version of Python if multiple versions are installed on your computer.

To make it convenient to run your Python program, create a *.bat batch file* for running the Python program with *py.exe*. To make a batch file, make a new text file containing a single line like the following:

```
@py.exe C:\path\to\your\pythonScript.py %*
@pause
```

Replace this path with the absolute path to your own program, and save this file with a *.bat* file extension (for example, *pythonScript.bat*). This batch file will keep you from having to type the full absolute path for the Python program every time you want to run it. @pause will add "Press any key to continue..." after the end of the Python script to prevent the program's window from disappearing too quickly. I recommend you place all your batch and *.py* files in a single folder, such as *C:\MyPythonScripts* or *C:\Users\YourName\PythonScripts*.

The *C:\MyPythonScripts* folder should be added to the system path on Windows so that you can run the batch files in it from the Run dialog. To do this, modify the PATH environment variable. Click the **Start** button and type **Edit environment variables for your account**. This option should autocomplete after you've begun to type it. The Environment Variables window that appears will look like Figure B-1.

From System variables, select the Path variable and click **Edit**. In the Value text field, append a semicolon, type **C:\MyPythonScripts**, and then click **OK**. Now you can run any Python script

Figure B-1: The Environment Variables window on Windows

in the *C:\MyPythonScripts* folder by simply pressing WIN-R and entering the script's name. Running pythonScript, for instance, will run *pythonScript.bat*, which in turn will save you from having to run the whole command py.exe C:\MyPythonScripts\pythonScript.py from the Run dialog.

Running Python Programs on OS X and Linux

On OS X, selecting Applications ▶ Utilities ▶ Terminal will bring up a *Terminal* window. A Terminal window is a way to enter commands on your computer using only text, rather than clicking through a graphic interface. To bring up the Terminal window on Ubuntu Linux, press the WIN (or SUPER) key to bring up Dash and type in **Terminal**.

The Terminal window will begin in the home folder of your user account. If my username is *asweigart*, the home folder will be */Users/asweigart* on OS X and */home/asweigart* on Linux. The tilde (~) character is a shortcut for your home folder, so you can enter cd ~ to change to your home folder. You can also use the cd command to change the current working directory to any other directory. On both OS X and Linux, the pwd command will print the current working directory.

To run your Python programs, save your *.py* file to your home folder. Then, change the *.py* file's permissions to make it executable by running chmod +x pythonScript.py. File permissions are beyond the scope of this book, but you will need to run this command on your Python file if you want to run the program from the Terminal window. Once you do so, you will be able to run your script whenever you want by opening a Terminal window and entering ./pythonScript.py. The shebang line at the top of the script will tell the operating system where to locate the Python interpreter.

Running Python Programs with Assertions Disabled

You can disable the assert statements in your Python programs for a slight performance improvement. When running Python from the terminal, include the -O switch after python or python3 and before the name of the *.py* file. This will run an optimized version of your program that skips the assertion checks.

C

ANSWERS TO THE PRACTICE QUESTIONS

This appendix contains the answers to the practice problems at the end of each chapter. I highly recommend that you take the time to work through these problems. Programming is more than memorizing syntax and a list of function names. As when learning a foreign language, the more practice you put into it, the more you will get out of it. There are many websites with practice programming problems as well. You can find a list of these at *http://nostarch.com/automatestuff/*.

Chapter 1

1. The operators are +, -, *, and /. The values are 'hello', -88.8, and 5.

2. The string is 'spam'; the variable is spam. Strings always start and end with quotes.

3. The three data types introduced in this chapter are integers, floating-point numbers, and strings.

4. An expression is a combination of values and operators. All expressions evaluate (that is, reduce) to a single value.

5. An expression evaluates to a single value. A statement does not.

6. The bacon variable is set to 20. The bacon + 1 expression does not reassign the value in bacon (that would need an assignment statement: bacon = bacon + 1).

7. Both expressions evaluate to the string 'spamspamspam'.

8. Variable names cannot begin with a number.

9. The int(), float(), and str() functions will evaluate to the integer, floating-point number, and string versions of the value passed to them.

10. The expression causes an error because 99 is an integer, and only strings can be concatenated to other strings with the + operator. The correct way is I have eaten ' + str(99) + ' burritos.'.

Chapter 2

1. True and False, using capital *T* and *F*, with the rest of the word in lowercase

2. and, or, and not

3. True and True is True.
   True and False is False.
   False and True is False.
   False and False is False.
   True or True is True.
   True or False is True.
   False or True is True.
   False or False is False.
   not True is False.
   not False is True.

4. False
   False
   True
   False
   False
   True

5. `==`, `!=`, `<`, `>`, `<=`, and `>=`.

6. `==` is the equal to operator that compares two values and evaluates to a Boolean, while `=` is the assignment operator that stores a value in a variable.

7. A condition is an expression used in a flow control statement that evaluates to a Boolean value.

8. The three blocks are everything inside the `if` statement and the lines `print('bacon')` and `print('ham')`.

```
print('eggs')
if spam > 5:
    print('bacon')
else:
    print('ham')
print('spam')
```

9. The code:

```
if spam == 1:
    print('Hello')
elif spam == 2:
    print('Howdy')
else:
    print('Greetings!')
```

10. Press CTRL-C to stop a program stuck in an infinite loop.

11. The break statement will move the execution outside and just after a loop. The continue statement will move the execution to the start of the loop.

12. They all do the same thing. The range(10) call ranges from 0 up to (but not including) 10, range(0, 10) explicitly tells the loop to start at 0, and range(0, 10, 1) explicitly tells the loop to increase the variable by 1 on each iteration.

13. The code:

```
for i in range(1, 11):
    print(i)
```

and:

```
i = 1
while i <= 10:
    print(i)
    i = i + 1
```

14. This function can be called with `spam.bacon()`.

Chapter 3

1. Functions reduce the need for duplicate code. This makes programs shorter, easier to read, and easier to update.

2. The code in a function executes when the function is called, not when the function is defined.

3. The `def` statement defines (that is, creates) a function.

4. A function consists of the `def` statement and the code in its `def` clause. A function call is what moves the program execution into the function, and the function call evaluates to the function's return value.

5. There is one global scope, and a local scope is created whenever a function is called.

6. When a function returns, the local scope is destroyed, and all the variables in it are forgotten.

7. A return value is the value that a function call evaluates to. Like any value, a return value can be used as part of an expression.

8. If there is no return statement for a function, its return value is `None`.

9. A `global` statement will force a variable in a function to refer to the global variable.

10. The data type of `None` is `NoneType`.

11. That `import` statement imports a module named `areallyourpetsnamederic`. (This isn't a real Python module, by the way.)

12. This function can be called with `spam.bacon()`.

13. Place the line of code that might cause an error in a `try` clause.

14. The code that could potentially cause an error goes in the `try` clause. The code that executes if an error happens goes in the `except` clause.

Chapter 4

1. The empty list value, which is a list value that contains no items. This is similar to how `''` is the empty string value.

2. `spam[2] = 'hello'` (Notice that the third value in a list is at index 2 because the first index is 0.)

3. `'d'` (Note that `'3' * 2` is the string `'33'`, which is passed to `int()` before being divided by 11. This eventually evaluates to 3. Expressions can be used wherever values are used.)

4. `'d'` (Negative indexes count from the end.)

5. `['a', 'b']`

6. `1`

7. `[3.14, 'cat', 11, 'cat', True, 99]`

8. `[3.14, 11, 'cat', True]`

9. The operator for list concatenation is +, while the operator for replication is *. (This is the same as for strings.)

10. While append() will add values only to the end of a list, insert() can add them anywhere in the list.

11. The del statement and the remove() list method are two ways to remove values from a list.

12. Both lists and strings can be passed to len(), have indexes and slices, be used in for loops, be concatenated or replicated, and be used with the in and not in operators.

13. Lists are mutable; they can have values added, removed, or changed. Tuples are immutable; they cannot be changed at all. Also, tuples are written using parentheses, (and), while lists use the square brackets, [and].

14. (42,) (The trailing comma is mandatory.)

15. The tuple() and list() functions, respectively

16. They contain references to list values.

17. The copy.copy() function will do a shallow copy of a list, while the copy.deepcopy() function will do a deep copy of a list. That is, only copy.deepcopy() will duplicate any lists inside the list.

Chapter 5

1. Two curly brackets: {}

2. {'foo': 42}

3. The items stored in a dictionary are unordered, while the items in a list are ordered.

4. You get a KeyError error.

5. There is no difference. The in operator checks whether a value exists as a key in the dictionary.

6. 'cat' in spam checks whether there is a 'cat' key in the dictionary, while 'cat' in spam.values() checks whether there is a value 'cat' for one of the keys in spam.

7. spam.setdefault('color', 'black')

8. pprint.pprint()

Chapter 6

1. Escape characters represent characters in string values that would otherwise be difficult or impossible to type into code.

2. \n is a newline; \t is a tab.

3. The \\ escape character will represent a backslash character.

4.	The single quote in `Howl's` is fine because you've used double quotes to mark the beginning and end of the string.

5.	Multiline strings allow you to use newlines in strings without the `\n` escape character.

6.	The expressions evaluate to the following:

  * `'e'`
  * `'Hello'`
  * `'Hello'`
  * `'lo world!`

7.	The expressions evaluate to the following:

  * `'HELLO'`
  * `True`
  * `'hello'`

8.	The expressions evaluate to the following:

  * `['Remember,', 'remember,', 'the', 'fifth', 'of', 'November.']`
  * `'There-can-be-only-one.'`

9.	The `rjust()`, `ljust()`, and `center()` string methods, respectively

10.	The `lstrip()` and `rstrip()` methods remove whitespace from the left and right ends of a string, respectively.

Chapter 7

1.	The `re.compile()` function returns `Regex` objects.

2.	Raw strings are used so that backslashes do not have to be escaped.

3.	The `search()` method returns `Match` objects.

4.	The `group()` method returns strings of the matched text.

5.	Group `0` is the entire match, group `1` covers the first set of parentheses, and group `2` covers the second set of parentheses.

6.	Periods and parentheses can be escaped with a backslash: `\.`, `\(`, and `\)`.

7.	If the regex has no groups, a list of strings is returned. If the regex has groups, a list of tuples of strings is returned.

8.	The | character signifies matching "either, or" between two groups.

9.	The `?` character can either mean " match zero or one of the preceding group" or be used to signify nongreedy matching.

10.	The + matches one or more. The * matches zero or more.

11.	The `{3}` matches exactly three instances of the preceding group. The `{3,5}` matches between three and five instances.

12.	The `\d`, `\w`, and `\s` shorthand character classes match a single digit, word, or space character, respectively.

13.	The `\D`, `\W`, and `\S` shorthand character classes match a single character that is not a digit, word, or space character, respectively.

14. Passing re.I or re.IGNORECASE as the second argument to re.compile() will make the matching case insensitive.

15. The . character normally matches any character except the newline character. If re.DOTALL is passed as the second argument to re.compile(), then the dot will also match newline characters.

16. The .* performs a greedy match, and the .*? performs a nongreedy match.

17. Either [0-9a-z] or [a-z0-9]

18. 'X drummers, X pipers, five rings, X hens'

19. The re.VERBOSE argument allows you to add whitespace and comments to the string passed to re.compile().

20. re.compile(r'^\d{1,3}(,\d{3})*$') will create this regex, but other regex strings can produce a similar regular expression.

21. re.compile(r'[A-Z][a-z]*\sNakamoto')

22. re.compile(r'(Alice|Bob|Carol)\s(eats|pets|throws)\s(apples|cats|baseballs)\.', re.IGNORECASE)

Chapter 8

1. Relative paths are relative to the current working directory.

2. Absolute paths start with the root folder, such as / or *C:*.

3. The os.getcwd() function returns the current working directory. The os.chdir() function *changes* the current working directory.

4. The . folder is the current folder, and .. is the parent folder.

5. *C:\bacon\eggs* is the dir name, while *spam.txt* is the base name.

6. The string 'r' for read mode, 'w' for write mode, and 'a' for append mode

7. An existing file opened in write mode is erased and completely overwritten.

8. The read() method returns the file's entire contents as a single string value. The readlines() method returns a list of strings, where each string is a line from the file's contents.

9. A shelf value resembles a dictionary value; it has keys and values, along with keys() and values() methods that work similarly to the dictionary methods of the same names.

Chapter 9

1. The shutil.copy() function will copy a single file, while shutil.copytree() will copy an entire folder, along with all its contents.

2. The shutil.move() function is used for renaming files, as well as moving them.

3. The send2trash functions will move a file or folder to the recycle bin, while shutil functions will permanently delete files and folders.

4. The `zipfile.ZipFile()` function is equivalent to the `open()` function; the first argument is the filename, and the second argument is the mode to open the ZIP file in (read, write, or append).

Chapter 10

1. `assert spam >= 10, 'The spam variable is less than 10.'`

2. Either `assert eggs.lower() != bacon.lower(), 'The eggs and bacon variables are the same!'` or `assert eggs.upper() != bacon.upper(), 'The eggs and bacon variables are the same!'`

3. `assert False, 'This assertion always triggers.'`

4. To be able to call `logging.debug()`, you must have these two lines at the start of your program:

```
import logging
logging.basicConfig(level=logging.DEBUG, format=' %(asctime)s -
%(levelname)s -  %(message)s')
```

5. To be able to send logging messages to a file named *programLog.txt* with `logging.debug()`, you must have these two lines at the start of your program:

```
import logging
>>> logging.basicConfig(filename='programLog.txt', level=logging.DEBUG,
format=' %(asctime)s -  %(levelname)s -  %(message)s')
```

6. DEBUG, INFO, WARNING, ERROR, and CRITICAL

7. `logging.disable(logging.CRITICAL)`

8. You can disable logging messages without removing the logging function calls. You can selectively disable lower-level logging messages. You can create logging messages. Logging messages provides a timestamp.

9. The Step button will move the debugger into a function call. The Over button will quickly execute the function call without stepping into it. The Out button will quickly execute the rest of the code until it steps out of the function it currently is in.

10. After you click Go, the debugger will stop when it has reached the end of the program or a line with a breakpoint.

11. A breakpoint is a setting on a line of code that causes the debugger to pause when the program execution reaches the line.

12. To set a breakpoint in IDLE, right-click the line and select **Set Breakpoint** from the context menu.

Chapter 11

1. The `webbrowser` module has an `open()` method that will launch a web browser to a specific URL, and that's it. The `requests` module can download files and pages from the Web. The `BeautifulSoup` module parses HTML. Finally, the `selenium` module can launch and control a browser.

2. The `requests.get()` function returns a `Response` object, which has a `text` attribute that contains the downloaded content as a string.

3. The `raise_for_status()` method raises an exception if the download had problems and does nothing if the download succeeded.

4. The `status_code` attribute of the `Response` object contains the HTTP status code.

5. After opening the new file on your computer in `'wb'` "write binary" mode, use a `for` loop that iterates over the `Response` object's `iter_content()` method to write out chunks to the file. Here's an example:

```
saveFile = open('filename.html', 'wb')
for chunk in res.iter_content(100000):
    saveFile.write(chunk)
```

6. F12 brings up the developer tools in Chrome. Pressing CTRL-SHIFT-C (on Windows and Linux) or ⌘-OPTION-C (on OS X) brings up the developer tools in Firefox.

7. Right-click the element in the page, and select **Inspect Element** from the menu.

8. `'#main'`

9. `'.highlight'`

10. `'div div'`

11. `'button[value="favorite"]'`

12. `spam.getText()`

13. `linkElem.attrs`

14. The selenium module is imported with `from selenium import webdriver`.

15. The `find_element_*` methods return the first matching element as a `WebElement` object. The `find_elements_*` methods return a list of all matching elements as `WebElement` objects.

16. The `click()` and `send_keys()` methods simulate mouse clicks and keyboard keys, respectively.

17. Calling the `submit()` method on any element within a form submits the form.

18. The `forward()`, `back()`, and `refresh()` `WebDriver` object methods simulate these browser buttons.

Chapter 12

1. The openpyxl.load_workbook() function returns a Workbook object.

2. The get_sheet_names() method returns a Worksheet object.

3. Call wb.get_sheet_by_name('Sheet1').

4. Use wb.active.

5. sheet['C5'].value or sheet.cell(row=5, column=3).value

6. sheet['C5'] = 'Hello' or sheet.cell(row=5, column=3).value = 'Hello'

7. cell.row and cell.column

8. They hold the highest column and row with values in the sheet, respectively, as integer values.

9. openpyxl.cell.column_index_from_string('M')

10. openpyxl.cell.get_column_letter(14)

11. sheet['A1':'F1']

12. wb.save('example.xlsx')

13. A formula is set the same way as any value. Set the cell's value attribute to a string of the formula text. Remember that formulas begin with the = sign.

14. When calling load_workbook(), pass True for the data_only keyword argument.

15. sheet.row_dimensions[5].height = 100

16. sheet.column_dimensions['C'].hidden = True

17. OpenPyXL 2.3.3 does not load freeze panes, print titles, images, or charts.

18. Freeze panes are rows and columns that will always appear on the screen. They are useful for headers.

19. openpyxl.chart.Reference(), openpyxl.chart.Series(), openpyxl.chart .BarChart(), chartObj.append(seriesObj), and add_chart()

Chapter 13

1. A File object returned from open()

2. Read-binary ('rb') for PdfFileReader() and write-binary ('wb') for PdfFileWriter()

3. Calling getPage(4) will return a Page object for page 5, since page 0 is the first page.

4. The numPages variable stores an integer of the number of pages in the PdfFileReader object.

5. Call decrypt('swordfish').

6. The rotateClockwise() and rotateCounterClockwise() methods. The degrees to rotate is passed as an integer argument.

7. `docx.Document('demo.docx')`

8. A document contains multiple paragraphs. A paragraph begins on a new line and contains multiple runs. Runs are contiguous groups of characters within a paragraph.

9. Use `doc.paragraphs`.

10. A `Run` object has these variables (*not* a Paragraph).

11. `True` always makes the `Run` object bolded and `False` makes it always not bolded, no matter what the style's bold setting is. `None` will make the `Run` object just use the style's bold setting.

12. Call the `docx.Document()` function.

13. `doc.add_paragraph('Hello there!')`

14. The integers 0, 1, 2, 3, and 4

Chapter 14

1. In Excel, spreadsheets can have values of data types other than strings; cells can have different fonts, sizes, or color settings; cells can have varying widths and heights; adjacent cells can be merged; and you can embed images and charts.

2. You pass a `File` object, obtained from a call to `open()`.

3. `File` objects need to be opened in read-binary (`'rb'`) for `Reader` objects and write-binary (`'wb'`) for `Writer` objects.

4. The `writerow()` method

5. The `delimiter` argument changes the string used to separate cells in a row. The `lineterminator` argument changes the string used to separate rows.

6. `json.loads()`

7. `json.dumps()`

Chapter 15

1. A reference moment that many date and time programs use. The moment is January 1st, 1970, UTC.

2. `time.time()`

3. `time.sleep(5)`

4. It returns the closest integer to the argument passed. For example, `round(2.4)` returns 2.

5. A datetime object represents a specific moment in time. A `timedelta` object represents a duration of time.

6. `threadObj = threading.Thread(target=spam)`

7. `threadObj.start()`

8. Make sure that code running in one thread does not read or write the same variables as code running in another thread.

9. `subprocess.Popen('c:\\Windows\\System32\\calc.exe')`

Chapter 16

1. SMTP and IMAP, respectively

2. `smtplib.SMTP()`, `smtpObj.ehlo()`, `smptObj.starttls()`, and `smtpObj.login()`

3. `imapclient.IMAPClient()` and `imapObj.login()`

4. A list of strings of IMAP keywords, such as `'BEFORE <date>'`, `'FROM <string>'`, or `'SEEN'`

5. Assign the variable `imaplib._MAXLINE` a large integer value, such as `10000000`.

6. The `pyzmail` module reads downloaded emails.

7. You will need the Twilio account SID number, the authentication token number, and your Twilio phone number.

Chapter 17

1. An RGBA value is a tuple of 4 integers, each ranging from 0 to 255. The four integers correspond to the amount of red, green, blue, and alpha (transparency) in the color.

2. A function call to `ImageColor.getcolor('CornflowerBlue', 'RGBA')` will return `(100, 149, 237, 255)`, the RGBA value for that color.

3. A box tuple is a tuple value of four integers: the left edge x-coordinate, the top edge y-coordinate, the width, and the height, respectively.

4. `Image.open('zophie.png')`

5. `imageObj.size` is a tuple of two integers, the width and the height.

6. `imageObj.crop((0, 50, 50, 50))`. Notice that you are passing a box tuple to `crop()`, not four separate integer arguments.

7. Call the `imageObj.save('new_filename.png')` method of the `Image` object.

8. The `ImageDraw` module contains code to draw on images.

9. `ImageDraw` objects have shape-drawing methods such as `point()`, `line()`, or `rectangle()`. They are returned by passing the `Image` object to the `ImageDraw.Draw()` function.

Chapter 18

1. Move the mouse to the top-left corner of the screen, that is, the (0, 0) coordinates.

2. `pyautogui.size()` returns a tuple with two integers for the width and height of the screen.

3. `pyautogui.position()` returns a tuple with two integers for the x- and y-coordinates of the mouse cursor.

4. The `moveTo()` function moves the mouse to absolute coordinates on the screen, while the `moveRel()` function moves the mouse relative to the mouse's current position.

5. `pyautogui.dragTo()` and `pyautogui.dragRel()`

6. `pyautogui.typewrite('Hello world!')`

7. Either pass a list of keyboard key strings to `pyautogui.typewrite()` (such as `'left'`) or pass a single keyboard key string to `pyautogui.press()`.

8. `pyautogui.screenshot('screenshot.png')`

9. `pyautogui.PAUSE = 2`

INDEX

B

C

formulas, in Excel spreadsheets,
283–284
forward() method, 261
forward slash (/), 174–175
FROM search key, 370
fromtimestamp() function, 341, 346
functions. *See also names of individual*
functions
    arguments, 23, 63
    as "black box", 72
    built-in, 57
    def statements, 63
    exception handling, 72–74
    keyword arguments, 65–66
    None value and, 65
    overview, 61–62
    parameters, 63
    return values, 63–65

G

get_addresses() method, 374
get_attribute() method, 258
getcolor() function, 388–389, 393
get_column_letter() function, 270
getcwd() function, 175
get() function
    overview, 109
    requests module, 237
get_payload() method, 374–375
getpixel() function, 400, 423, 424
get_sheet_by_name() method, 268
get_sheet_names() method, 268
getsize() function, 179
get_subject() method, 374
getText() function, 308–309
GIF format, 392
global scope, 70–71
Gmail, 363, 365, 367
gmail_search() method, 372
Google Maps, 234–236
graphical user interface automation.
    See GUI (graphical user
    interface) automation
greater than (>) operator, 33
greater than or equal to (>=)
    operator, 33
greedy matching
    dot-star for, 161
    in regular expressions, 156–157
group() method, 151, 152–153
groups, regular expression

matching
    greedy, 156–157
    nongreedy, 157
    one or more, 155–156
    optional, 154–155
    specific reptitions, 156
    zero or more, 155
    using parentheses, 152–153
    using pipe character in, 153–154
Guess the Number program, 74–76
GUI (graphical user interface)
    automation. *See also*
    form filler project
    controlling keyboard, 426–429
        hotkey combinations, 429
        key names, 427–428
        pressing and releasing, 428–429
        sending string from keyboard,
        426–427
    controlling mouse, 415–417,
        419–423
        clicking mouse, 420
        dragging mouse, 420–422
        scrolling mouse, 422–423
    determining mouse position,
        417–419
    image recognition, 425–426
    installing pyautogui module, 414
    logging out of program, 414
    overview, 413–414
    screenshots, 423–424
    stopping program, 414–415

H

%H directive, 344
hash character (#), 126
headings, Word document, 314–315
help
    asking online, 9–10
    for error messages, 8–9
hotkey combinations, 429
hotkey() function, 429, 430
Hotmail.com, 363, 367
HTML (Hypertext Markup Language)
    browser developer tools and,
        242–243
    finding elements, 244
    learning resources, 240
    overview, 240–241
    viewing page source, 241–242

I

%I directive, 344
id attribute, 241
IDLE (interactive development environment)
    creating programs, 21–22
    debugging in
        overview, 225–227
        stepping through program, 227–229
        using breakpoints, 229–231
    expressions in, 14–16
    overview, 8
    running scripts outside of, 136
    starting, 7–8
if statements
    overview, 38–39
    using in while loop, 46–47
imageDraw module, 406
imageDraw objects, 406–408
ImageFont objects, 408–410
Image objects, 391–399
images
    adding logo to, 401–405
    attributes for, 392–393
    box tuples, 390
    color values in, 388–389
    coordinates in, 389–390
    copying and pasting in, 394–396
    cropping, 393–394
    drawing on
        example program, 407–408
        ellipses, 407
        ImageDraw module, 406
        lines, 406–407
        points, 406
        polygons, 407
        rectangles, 407
        text, 408–410
    flipping, 398–399
    opening with Pillow, 390–391
    pixel manipulation, 400
    recognition of, 425–426
    resizing, 397
    RGBA values, 388–389
    rotating, 398–399
    transparent pixels, 397
IMAP (Internet Message Access Protocol)
    defined, 366
    deleting messages, 375
    disconnecting from server, 375–376
    fetching messages, 372–375
    folders, 368–369
    logging into server, 368
    searching messages, 368–371
imapclient module, 366
IMAPClient objects, 367–368
immutable data types, 94–96
importing modules
    overview, 57–58
    pyautogui module, 417
imprint attribute, 311
im variable, 423
indentation, 93
indexes
    for dictionaries. *See* keys, dictionary
    for lists
        changing values using, 83
        getting value using, 80–81
        negative, 82
        removing values from list using, 84
    for strings, 126–127
IndexError, 106
index() method, 89
infinite loops, 49, 51, 418
INFO level, 223, 224
in operator
    using with dictionaries, 109
    using with lists, 87
    using with strings, 127
input() function
    overview, 23–24, 89–90
    using for sensitive information, 365
installing
    openpyxl module, 266
    pyautogui module, 414
    Python, 6–7
    selenium module, 256
    third-party modules, 441–442
int, 17. See also integers
integer division/floored quotient (//) operator, 15
integers
    floating-point equivalence, 27
    overview, 17
interactive development environment. *See* IDLE (interactive development environment)
interactive shell. *See* IDLE
Internet Explorer, developer tools in, 242–243

Internet Message Access Protocol. *See*
IMAP (Internet Message
Access Protocol)
interpreter, Python, 7
int() function, 25–28
isabs() function, 177
isalnum() method, 129–131
isalpha() method, 129–130
isdecimal() method, 129–131
isdir() function, 180
is_displayed() method, 258
is_enabled() method, 258
isfile() function, 180
islower() method, 128–129
is_selected() method, 258
isspace() method, 130
istitle() method, 130
isupper() method, 128–129
italic attribute, 311
items() method, 107–108
iter_content() method, 239–240

J

%j directive, 344
join() method, 131–132, 174–175,
177, 352
JPEG format, 392
JSON files
APIs for, 327–328
defined, 319–320
format overview, 327–328
reading, 328–329
and weather data project, 329–332
writing, 329
justifying text, 133–134

K

keyboard
controlling, with PyAutoGUI
hotkey combinations, 429
pressing and releasing keys,
428–429
sending string from keyboard,
426–427
key names, 427–428
KeyboardInterrupt exception, 340,
417, 418
keyDown() function, 428, 429, 430
keys, dictionary, 105

keys() method, 107–108
keyUp() function, 428, 429, 430
keyword arguments, 65–66

L

LARGER search key, 370
launchd, 354–355
launching programs
and countdown project, 357–358
opening files with default
applications, 355–356
opening websites, 355
overview, 352–354
passing command line arguments
to processes, 354
poll() method, 353
running Python scripts, 355
scheduling, 354–355
sleep() function, 355
wait() method, 354
len() function, 307–308
finding number of values in list, 83
overview, 24–25
less than (<) operator, 33
less than or equal to (<=) operator, 33
LibreOffice, 265, 306
line breaks, Word document, 315
LineChart() function, 289
line continuation character (\), 93
line() method, 406–407
linked styles, 310
Linux
backslash vs. forward slash, 174–175
cron, 354
installing Python, 7
installing third-party modules, 442
launching processes from
Python, 353
logging out of automation
program, 414
opening files with default
applications, 355
pip tool on, 441–442
Python support, 4
running Python programs on, 445
starting IDLE, 8
Unix philosophy, 356
listdir() function, 179
list_folders() method, 368–369
list() function, 321, 426

O

ON search key, 369
open() function, 181–182, 234,
        355–356, 391
opening files, 181–182
OpenOffice, 265, 306
open program, 355
openpyxl module, installing, 266
operators
    augmented assignment, 88–89
    binary, 35–36
    comparison, 33–35
    defined, 14
    math, 15
    using binary and comparison
        operators together, 36–37
order of operations, 15
or operator, 36
OR search key, 370
OS X
    backslash vs. forward slash, 174–175
    installing Python, 7
    installing third-party modules, 442
    launchd, 354
    launching processes from
        Python, 356
    logging out of automation
        program, 414
    opening files with default
        applications, 355–356
    pip tool on, 441–442
    Python support, 4
    running Python programs on, 445
    starting IDLE, 8
    Unix philosophy, 356
outline attribute, 311
Outlook.com, 363, 367

P

%p directive, 344
page breaks, Word document, 315
Page objects, 297
Paragraph objects, 307
paragraphs, Word document, 309–310
parameters, function, 63
parentheses (), 96–97, 152–153
parsing, defined, 245
passing arguments, 23
passing references, 100

passwords
    application-specific, 365
    managing project, 136–138
        command-line arguments, 137
        copying password, 137–138
        data structures, 136–137
        overview, 136
pastebin.com, 10
paste() method, 135, 394, 395
paths
    absolute vs. relative, 175–176
    backslash vs. forward slash, 174–175
    current working directory, 175
    overview, 173–174
    os.path module
        absolute paths in, 177–179
        file sizes, 179–180
        folder contents, 179–180
        overview, 177
        path validity, 180
        relative paths in, 177–179
PAUSE variable, 415, 434
PdfFileReader objects, 297–298
PDF files
    combining pages from multiple
        files, 303–306
        adding pages, 303
        finding PDF files, 304
        opening PDFs, 304–305
        overview, 303
        saving results, 305–306
    creating, 298–299
    decrypting, 297–298
    encrypting, 302–303
    extracting text from, 296–297
    format overview, 295–296
    pages in
        copying, 299–300
        overlaying, 301–302
        rotating, 300–301
PdfFileWriter objects, 298–299
pformat() function
    overview, 111–112
    saving variables in text files using,
        185–186
phone numbers, extracting, 165–169
    creating regex, 166
    finding matches on clipboard,
        167–168
    joining matches into a
        string, 168
    overview, 165–166

RESOURCES

Visit *https://nostarch.com/automatestuff/* for resources, errata, and more information.